THE 'INEVITABLE' UNION

Books by Maurice Lee, Jr.

JAMES STEWART, EARL OF MORAY (New York: Columbia University Press, 1953)

JOHN MAITLAND OF THIRLESTANE AND THE FOUNDATION OF THE STEWART DESPOTISM IN SCOTLAND (Princeton: Princeton University Press 1959)

THE CABAL (Urbana: University of Illinois Press 1965)

JAMES I AND HENRI IV: AN ESSAY IN ENGLISH FOREIGN POLICY (Urbana: University of Illinois Press 1970)

DUDLEY CARLETON TO JOHN CHAMBERLAIN: JACOBEAN LETTERS, 1603–1624 (New Brunswick, N.J.: Rutgers University Press 1972)

GOVERNMENT BY PEN: SCOTLAND UNDER JAMES VI AND I (Urbana: University of Illinois Press 1980)

THE ROAD TO REVOLUTION: SCOTLAND UNDER CHARLES I, 1625–1637 (Urbana: University of Illinois Press 1985)

GREAT BRITAIN'S SOLOMON: JAMES VI AND I IN HIS THREE KINGDOMS (Urbana: University of Illinois Press 1990)

THE HEIRESSES OF BUCCLEUCH: MARRIAGE, MONEY, AND POLITICS IN SEVENTEENTH-CENTURY BRITAIN (East Linton: Tuckwell Press 1996)

THE 'INEVITABLE' UNION

and Other Essays on
Early Modern Scotland

Maurice Lee, Jr.

TUCKWELL PRESS

First published in Great Britain in 2003 by
Tuckwell Press
The Mill House
Phantassie
East Linton
East Lothian EH40 3DG
Scotland

Copyright © Maurice Lee, Jr., 2003

ISBN 1 86232 107 8

British Library Cataloguing in Publication Data

A catalogue record for this book is available
on request from the British Library

The right of Maurice Lee, Jr. to be identified as the author
of this work has been asserted by him in accordance
with the Copyright, Design and Patent Act 1988

Typeset by Hewer Text Ltd, Edinburgh
Printed and bound by Biddles Ltd, King's Lynn

This book is dedicated to my professors at Princeton University, especially to E. Harris Harbison, Joseph R. Strayer, and Gordon A. Craig.
They taught me my trade. My scholarly virtues, such as they are, are largely owing to them.
My shortcomings are my own.

Contents

Preface

Over the years I have had a good many conversations that went something like this:

> Stranger at a party: What do you do, Mr. Lee?
> M.L.: I'm a professor of history.
> S.a.a.p.: What sort of history?
> M.L.: Early modern British. Scottish history, mostly.
> S.a.a.p.: *Scottish* history! Why on earth do you want to do that? Small, unimportant place like that—nothing but golf courses and whisky. Are you a Scot, or something?

As it happens, my mother was of Scottish descent, and my father had a Scottish grandmother, so I suppose I'm more Scots than anything else. But I've never thought of myself as a hyphenated American; the Lees have been over here far too long for that. I came to Scottish history, not through inherited urge, but by accident.

In the winter of 1947–8, as a second-year graduate student at Princeton, I was casting about for a dissertation topic. Qualifying exams were scheduled for May, and I had to have something to tell my committee. I wanted a sixteenth-century subject because I planned to work on the interaction of politics and religion, an interest that came naturally to those who grew up in the 1930s and served (in my case very briefly and tamely) in World War II. Furthermore, my professor, E. Harris Harbison, liked to point out the similarities between the ideological conflicts of our own time and those of the century after 1560: confessional loyalties that transcended state boundaries, plots, counterplots, assassinations, fifth columns, spies in embassies, witch hunts of all kinds. Because I'm not very good at languages, I thought it best to find a topic within what John Pocock calls the Atlantic archipelago. And I wanted something I could handle fairly quickly, and on this side of the Atlantic—the Princeton history department was not enthusiastic about students who dawdled, and money for travel was hard to come by. In the course of my searches I came across the Regent Moray, Mary Queen of Scots' half-brother. He met all my requirements. He was the leader of the Protestant party in Scotland in the 1560s, arguably its most important figure, not excluding John Knox; he as much as anyone was responsible for the success of the religious revolution there. Because of his involvement in his sister's sad and spectacular career the sources were in print: I could do the research in America. His career was (for my purposes) blessedly short: he was assassinated at the age of 39. And, astonishingly, he had never had a biographer.

Professor Harbison, rather bemusedly, gave me his blessing; off I went to the library. Moray was researched and written up in two years and, after considerable rewriting and (especially) cutting, in print in five.[1] It was a brash, young man's book; I would write it differently if I were doing it now, though I believe that its major conclusions have held up pretty well – at least, no one has seen fit to publish another study of Moray's career. Gordon Donaldson, whom I did not then know but who became a close friend, scolded me in the course of his review in the *Scottish Historical Review* for not having consulted any manuscript material, especially that in the Scottish Record Office. He was quite right; all my subsequent books have been products of research in the archives.

My work on the Moray book was enlightening in an altogether unexpected way. I discovered that there was a vast amount of work to do in every field of Scottish history, and, as far as I could see, very few people doing it. There was, of course, the constant stream of books on Mary Queen of Scots and Bonnie Prince Charlie; both industries continue to flourish to this day, with no end in sight. But there wasn't much else. The standard scholarly survey, that of P. Hume Brown, was published in the first decade of the century. The *Scottish Historical Review* had gone out of business in 1928, and had revived, very recently, in 1947. Significantly, the Scottish History Society continued to publish its annual volume of sources without pause. The scholars working in Scottish history when I began – and many of them were very fine scholars indeed – were editors, publishing sources, often with long, learned, brilliant introductions; they wrote articles, but they did not write books. The archetype was the then holder of the chair of Scottish history at the University of Edinburgh, W. Croft Dickinson. He was a great editor and a splendid scholar, but apart from a highly compressed textbook, he never wrote a book.[2] I pointed out the dearth of recent books in Scottish history in a bibliographical survey of 'Scottish History since 1940' published in 1959, the year my second monograph appeared, and quoted A.A.M. Duncan's lament that 'Scholars have become the victims of cranks – who misspell their names and misrepresent their words – because scholars see the gaps in our knowledge, and only cranks dare to essay comprehensive studies in Scottish history'.[3] I'm inclined to think that a good part of my reputation as an historian of Scotland

1 *James Stewart, Earl of Moray: A Political Study of the Reformation in Scotland* (New York, 1953).
2 Interestingly, all the holders of this chair have made substantial contributions as editors, perhaps because of the proximity of the Record Office. The current professor, Michael Lynch, is, admittedly, a different sort of editor, of the *Innes Review*.
3 'Scottish History since 1940' appeared in the *Canadian Historical Review* xl (1959), 319-32. It was one of a series commissioned by the North American Conference on British Studies, and, with the others, was reprinted, with some additions, in *Changing Views on British History*, ed E. C. Furber (Cambridge, Mass., 1966). The monograph is *John Maitland of Thirlestane* (Princeton, 1959). Professor Duncan's remark is in *SHR* xxxv (Oct. 1956), 150.

rests on the fact that I began to publish books in the 1950s, before most others did.

The drought of books on Scottish history ended in the 1960s, first with the publication of Donaldson's remarkable and controversial account of the Scottish Reformation,[4] and then with the *Edinburgh History of Scotland*, the greatly needed replacement for Hume Brown, in four volumes; Donaldson was the general editor, and author of one of the four. In his admiring and most interesting biography James Kirk, Donaldson's student and occasional scholarly antagonist, called him the most prolific and influential Scottish historian of the twentieth century, and rightly so.[5] In the past thirty years there has been a steady stream of books and articles of all kinds, so much so that it is virtually impossible to keep up with all the necessary reading, especially now that historians of England have awakened to the 'British' dimension of their own history. I was once, most embarrassingly, the victim of this flood of publication. In the late 1970s the Conference on British Studies decided to publish a second volume of bibliographical articles, on the work that had appeared in the last twenty years. *Faute de mieux* I was once again asked to write on Scotland. I was diligent, and got my contribution to the editor at the end of 1979. For various reasons beyond the editor's control the volume did not appear until 1984. Never was an historiographical survey so out of date! It's my one published work on Scottish history that I hoped nobody in the field would read. Scottish history flourishes now as never before; we are, truly, living in a golden age.

To get back to the stranger-at-a-party's question: Scottish history is catnip to those of us who are suspicious of sweeping historical generalizations, who are, to employ the terms J. H. Hexter used in his memorable assault on the methodology of Christopher Hill, splitters rather than lumpers. Sidney Burrell long ago demonstrated how the Scottish evidence wreaked havoc with the Weber thesis;[6] my own assessment of the damage it did to another grandiose construct, the 'General Crisis of the Seventeenth Century', may be found in chap. 8 below. Scotland is also ideally suited for investigation of the interaction of politics and ideology. The religious revolution there was unique. Scotland was one of the two places in Europe – the Dutch Netherlands was the other – where Protestantism was established in defiance of the wishes of the government. The Protestant rebels in both places benefited from nationalist resentment of foreign rule, and both had the help, reluctantly given, of Queen Elizabeth, who wisely refused to try to assert any sort of political control in return for her aid. It was far more difficult for the Dutch to extrude the king of Spain, the heir of a long line of dukes of Burgundy, than it was for the Scots to free themselves from their recently and insecurely

4 *The Reformation in Scotland* (Cambridge, 1960).
5 J. Kirk, *Her Majesty's Historiographer: Gordon Donaldson, 1913-1993* (Edinburgh, 1996), vii.
6 S. A. Burrell, 'Calvinism, Capitalism, and the Middle Classes: Some Afterthoughts on an Old Problem', *Journal of Modern History* xxxii (1960), 129-41.

established French overlords. The Dutch sometimes call their war of independence the Eighty Years War; the Scots' armed struggle lasted far less than
eighty weeks. In the end the Dutch rid themselves not only of their Spanish
rulers but also of monarchy itself. The Scots did not; Scottish Protestants
captured the monarchy with the overthrow of their native-born Frenchified
queen in 1567. The fifty-eight-year reign of James VI, the most significant in
modern Scottish history, saw the establishment, not only of the new religious
dispensation, but also of a new sort of kingship, what might be called, *pace* G.
R. Elton, the Stewart revolution in government. Scotland is an even better
place than England to study the process of state-building, because in James's
time, thanks to the Anglo-Scottish alliance of 1586, outside pressure on the
king and his collaborators was at a minimum. James did for Scotland what
Henry VIII did for England, but far less brutally and far more successfully.[7] It
is gratifying that the man so wrongly described by Anglocentric historians as
the wisest fool in Christendom is at last receiving his due.

I have devoted most of my scholarly career to Scotland in James's time, and
in that of his successor down to the famous riot in St. Giles in July 1637 that
inaugurated Scotland's time of troubles.[8] My two book-length ventures into
English history[9] have had their Scottish elements and have dealt with politics
and ideology; only my most recent book[10] has eschewed ideology altogether.
I have been a writer of books rather than articles; the contents of this volume
are the product of research on a book either recently published or in prospect,
except for the pieces – both new – on Mary Queen of Scots and the Gowrie
Conspiracy. Now that I have reached my Biblical allotment of years I don't
know how much more work I'll be able to do, although I do hope to finish the
book on Restoration politics (and, of course, ideology) which prompted me to
write the other three hitherto unpublished pieces in this volume. As I sit here
at my desk in the autumn of 1999 and reflect on my fifty years as a working
scholar, my chief reflection is that I've had an absolutely wonderful time. If I
had it all to do over again, I would – only I'd try to do it better.

It is customary to end a foreward with acknowledgements. But how can I
do that, for help extended over fifty years? Some individual obligations are
noted in the dedication. Beyond that, all I can do is thank my family, my dear,
dead parents and my wife and children; my colleagues at Princeton University, the University of Illinois, and Rutgers University, and many students

7 In small things as in large: it is James's descendants, not Henry's, who occupy the
throne of the United Kingdom. One hesitates to speculate on what James might
have thought of his twentieth-century successors.
8 The recent books are *Government by Pen: Scotland under King James VI and I*
(Urbana, Ill, 1980), *The Road to Revolution: Scotland under Charles I, 1625-1637*
(Urbana, 1985), and *Great Britain's Solomon: James VI and I in his Three Kingdoms*
(Urbana, 1990).
9 *The Cabal* (Urbana, 1965), and *James I and Henri IV* (Urbana, 1970).
10 *The Heiresses of Buccleuch: Marriage, Money, and Politics in Seventeenth-century Britain*
(East Linton, 1996).

too; my fellow historians of Scotland, here and abroad, living and dead; librarians and publishers, typists and editors. And special thanks to two people: to John Tuckwell, who, somewhat to my surprise, agreed to publish this collection, and to Michelle Witte Patient, once my student, now my good friend and indispensable collaborator, because she understands computers and how to put things on disks. Bless you both!

Cranbury, New Jersey

Acknowledgements

My thanks are owing to the following for permission to reprint previously published material:

To the Princeton University Press, for 'Sir Richard Maitland of Lethington', which appeared in T. K. Rabb & J. Siegel, eds., *Action and Conviction in Early Modern Europe* (1969).

To the *Scottish Historical Review* for 'John Knox and his *History*' (1966), 'James VI's Government of Scotland after 1603' (1976), and 'Scotland and the "General Crisis" of the Seventeenth Century' (1984).

To the *Journal of Modern History* for 'The Fall of the Regent Morton' (1956).

To *Church History* for 'James VI and the Revival of Episcopacy in Scotland' (1974).

To the Scottish Academic Press for 'King James's Popish Chancellor', which appeared in I. B. Cowan and D. Shaw, eds., *The Renaissance and Reformation in Scotland* (1982).

To the *Journal of British Studies* for 'Archbishop Spottiswoode as Historian' (1973).

To *Albion* for ' Charles I and the End of Conciliar Government in Scotland' (1980) and 'The Buccleuch Marriage Contract' (1993).

To the Cambridge University Press for 'Scotland, the Union, and the Idea of a "General Crisis"', which appeared in R. A. Mason, ed., *Scots and Britons* (1994).

These articles appear in this book as they were originally written. The texts have not been updated, or altered save occasionally for the sake of some consistency in the spelling, punctuation, and footnoting, and to correct factual errors.

Abbreviations frequently used in the notes

APS	*The Acts of the Parliament of Scotland*, 12 vols., ed. T. Thomson and C. Innes (Edinburgh, 1814–1875)
BL	British Library, London
CSPS	*Calendar of State Papers Relating to Scotland and Mary Queen of Scots 1547–1603*, 13 vols., ed. J. Bain *et al* (Edinburgh, 1898–1969)
EHR	*English Historical Review*
HMC	Historical Manuscripts Commission, London
NLS	National Library of Scotland, Edinburgh
PRO	Public Record Office, London
RMS	*Registrum Magni Sigilli Regum Scotorum*, 11 vols., ed. J. M. Thomson *et al* (Edinburgh, 1814–1914)
RPCS	*The Register of the Privy Council of Scotland*, 1st, 2nd, and 3rd series, ed. J. H. Burton *et al* (Edinburgh 1877–1970)
RSCHS	*Records of the Scottish Church History Society*
Salisbury Mss.	HMC, *Calendar of the Manuscripts of the Marquis of Salisbury*, 23 vols., ed. M. S. Giuseppi *et al* (London, 1883–1973)
SHR	*Scottish Historical Review*
SHS	Scottish History Society, Edinburgh
SRO	Scottish Record Office, Edinburgh (now the National Archives of Scotland)
STS	Scottish Text Society, Edinburgh

1

The 'Inevitable' Union: Absentee Government in Scotland, 1603–1707

In 1994 a reviewer commented in the *Times Literary Supplement* that 'No one need expect the centenary of the 300-year United Kingdom *Reich*, when it arrives in a decade's time, to be a riot of street parties and commercial sponsorship . . . On neither side of the Border has it ever been a cause for rejoicing, and on the Scots side, in the course of the present century, it has been deplored'.[1] The Scots have done more than deplore the *Reich*; they have begun to dismantle it. The Scottish parliament lives again. Whether the current arrangement will be permanent, or merely a prelude to the complete undoing of what King James VI and I called the bigamous marriage of 1603 is very much an open question.

In 1707 Scottish hostility to parliamentary union was, if anything, even more vehement than it has recently been. Opposition was noisy and widespread, and supporters were far from enthusiastic. Many in the Scottish parliament voted for union for mercenary reasons – hope of future gain or gain already realized – others, because every conceivable alternative seemed worse. Lord Chancellor Seafield genuinely believed in it, and worked very hard to bring it about. Yet he could muster no more than the wryly resigned, 'Now there's an end of an old song', when he applied his signature to the act. There was no enthusiasm in London either. The English political establishment was grimly determined to force union on the Scots in order to solve an intolerable and dangerous political problem. To gain Scottish consent English politicians were prepared to make concessions, but everyone on both sides of the Tweed understood that if there was no consent there would be force. Union was going to happen whether the Scots wanted it or not. It was inevitable because the political and strategic interests of England demanded it, not because of the actions of those non-existent disinterested and self-sacrificing statesmen so admired by the Whiggish-minded historians of the first third of the twentieth century.[2] The men of

---

1 K. Miller, *Times Literary Supplement*, 17 June 1994, p. 5
2 The best recent account of the union of 1707, with an excellent bibliography, is B.P. Levack, *The Formation of the British State* (Oxford, 1987). See also P.W.J. Riley, *The Union of England and Scotland* (Manchester, 1978), a detailed, Namier-like study of the Scottish picture from the accession of Anne, and W. Ferguson, *Scotland's Relations with England: A Survey to 1707* (Edinburgh, 1977), the definitive scuttling of the old Whig view that disinterested and self-sacrificing statesmen made the union, though Ferguson in his enthusiasm for demolition pushes his arguments too hard. For commentary see M. Lee, Jr., 'The Anglo-Scottish Union of 1707: The Debate Reopened', *British Studies Monitor* ix (1979), 23–34.

the time understood the situation. 'The true state of the matter', commented James Johnston, who had been secretary of state under William II and III, 'was whether Scotland would be subject to an English Ministry without trade, or be subject to an English Parliament with trade'.[3] Scots politicians gave their consent; the armies of Marlborough did not cross the Tweed. But no one rejoiced at the end of the old song.

The inevitable union was, in fact, a confession of failure: the century-long experiment in absentee government had collapsed. In theory Scotland was England's equal. The king of Scots had inherited the English crown, and might have governed his new realms from Edinburgh. No such thought ever crossed the mind of King James VI and I, or if it did, he instantly rejected it. So his ancient kingdom, like his newly acquired Irish realm, would be governed from a distance. But they were alike in no other way. Ireland was a dependency, recently conquered, where executive authority was delegated to a crown-appointed English governor with a military title, lord lieutenant (or, less exaltedly, lord deputy) and an armed force at his disposal. In spite of its status as a 'kingdom', Ireland was in fact an English province. Scotland after 1603 was not like that – or was it? A recent survey of Scotland in the seventeenth century is entitled *Kingdom or Province?* and the question mark is apt.[4] Which was Scotland to be? In the end, in 1707, the answer was definitively rendered. Scotland was a province.

But in the beginning it was not so. Since Scotland was separate but equal, the king had to govern this anomaly, this independent country with all its institutions intact and unchanged, from 300 miles away. The obvious solution presented itself: the king would govern through a Scottish official who, it was understood, spoke for him. This agent might be based in London or Edinburgh, and might be any member of the administration: sometimes treasurer, sometimes chancellor, sometimes secretary, sometimes commissioner, once merely president of the privy council. His authority did not depend upon his office, but upon the fact that he had the king's confidence. The system worked as long as the agent himself had the confidence of the people who counted in Scotland, the landed classes, and the policy he implemented was acceptable to them. If one or the other of these elements was missing, breakdown occurred, most notably in the later 1630s and after 1689. In both cases the result was the reduction of Scotland to the status of a province, temporarily under Cromwell, permanently under the last of the Stewarts. As James V had mournfully predicted on his deathbed, it would pass with a lass.

The historians of seventeenth-century Scotland have been aware of the problem of absentee government there, of course, and the full-scale accounts

3 Quoted in G.M. Trevelyan, *England Under Queen Anne*, 3 vols. (London, 1930–4), ii, 272.
4 Keith Brown, *Kingdom or Province? Scotland and the Regal Union 1603–1715* (New York, 1992).

of most sections of the period deal with it.[5] The one major lacuna is for the years 1660–1688, a gap which I hope to fill, partially at least, with my current work on Restoration politics noted in the final essay in this volume. What follows here does not pretend to be an analysis of the checkered course of government-by-agent during the century of absentee rule of an 'independent' Scotland. It is no more than a sketch outlining the dimensions of the problem, based to a considerable extent on my previous work, and written in the hope that it might induce some brave scholar to tackle the matter in depth, and perhaps compare it with the absentee government of Ireland – a large but worthwhile undertaking.

*   *   *

In the beginning the first king of England, Scotland, and Ireland did not imagine that there was any problem. Devising machinery to govern Scotland *in absentia* was the last thing on James's mind as he journeyed south in the euphoric springtime of 1603. Prior to his departure he made a few temporary arrangements,[6] but nothing more was necessary, since that closer union of the kingdoms of England and Scotland which was so dear to his heart and, to his mind, so obviously logical and beneficial, would soon become a reality. In the meantime he would make all the necessary decisions for Scotland, as he had been doing since the death of Lord Chancellor Maitland in 1595. Virtually every official in his inner circle of advisers accompanied him to London. Some were promptly appointed to the English privy council, and two were given positions in the English government. These anticipations of union, and the Scottish monopoly of positions in the king's bedchamber, did not sit well with the people who counted in England, as is well known. The government in Edinburgh was so short-handed that by July 1603 the one member of the inner circle who did not travel south with James, Alexander Seton, president of the court of session and soon to become earl of Dunfermline and lord chancellor, wrote to Robert Cecil warning him that the Scottish government's ability to act was being seriously affected.[7] James saw the point, and a number of officials began to return home. By February 1604 it became the rule that members of the Scottish government could not go to court without a royal

---

5 M. Lee, Jr., *Government by Pen: Scotland Under James VI and I* (Urbana, 1980) and
   The Road to Revolution: Scotland Under Charles I (Urbana, 1985), A. Macinnes,
   Charles I and the Making of the Covenanting Movement 1625–1641 (Edinburgh, 1991),
   P. Donald, *An Uncounselled King: Charles I and the Scottish Troubles 1637–1641*
   (Cambridge, 1990), D. Stevenson, *The Scottish Revolution 1637–44* (Newton Abbot,
   1973) and *Revolution and Counter-revolution in Scotland, 1644–1651* (London, 1977),
   F. Dow, *Cromwellian Scotland 1651–1660* (Edinburgh, 1979), and P.W.J. Riley, *King
   William and the Scottish Politicians* (Edinburgh, 1979).
6 *RPCS* vi, 556–61.
7 PRO, SP 14/2, no. 37.

license, on the ground that their absence impaired the efficiency of the Edinburgh administration.[8]

One official who did not return home was the lord treasurer, George Home of Spott, earl of Dunbar and now chancellor of the exchequer in England. Dunbar began as a courtier, became treasurer in 1601, and in 1603 was arguably the king's closest political confidant. Robert Cecil read the signs accurately and quickly established an excellent and mutually beneficial working relationship with him. The fading of James's hopes for a unified kingdom of Great Britain meant that for the foreseeable future there would be no change in Scotland's current political structure. Dunbar, politically ambitious but with no agenda of his own save to get rich, was determined to retain his pre-eminence in Scottish affairs. This entailed implementing the king's agenda there, the most important item of which was the restoration of the authority of the bishops in the Scottish church. Thanks to a misstep by his only real rival, Lord Chancellor Dunfermline, Dunbar secured his pre-eminence. But there was a dilemma. His influence with James depended on personal contact, even to the point of accompanying the king in the hunting field, which he detested.[9] But carrying out James's agenda could not be done at long distance. What to do?

Dunbar did the obvious thing: he travelled, and thus established a pattern followed by many other principal royal agents in the future. Some, like Dunbar, and Lauderdale in the reign of Charles II, had their base at Whitehall and travelled to Scotland when necessary; others, like Menteith and Traquair in the reign of Charles I, were based in Edinburgh and came to court when necessary. The location of the royal agent depended on the nature of his relationship with the king. James was a gregarious man with all sorts of friends – male friends: women bored him. Dunbar was a man whom James liked to have around – not a favourite like Buckingham or an intellectual like Bishop Andrewes, but simply a man who was good company. He was also a competent, ruthless, and dependable political operator, and was extremely successful in carrying out the king's wishes. His dominance in Scottish affairs remained unchallenged until his death in 1611.[10]

Dunbar's successor as James's agent was Lord Chancellor Dunfermline, whose regime was entirely different. Dunfermline remained in Edinburgh and travelled as little as possible. He was a fastidious lawyerly intellectual who was uncomfortable at James's raffish court; he was more effective with James at a distance, employing his witty, learned pen. Where Dunbar prevailed through intimidation of colleague and foe alike, Dunfermline built consensus, a consensus facilitated by the network of family alliances he created through his three marriages and those of his and his eldest brother's

---

8 *RPCS* vi, 602.

9 'We are all become wild men wandering in a forest from the morning till the evening', he complained to Salisbury in 1607. *Salisbury Mss.* xix, 209–10. For Dunfermline's misstep see 'King James's Popish Chancellor', below.

10 For Dunbar's accomplishments see Lee, *Government by Pen*, chap. 3.

children. Gradually and subtly the initiative shifted. In Dunbar's time policy was made in Whitehall and transmitted to Edinburgh, often by Dunbar in person, though on some issues the privy councillors' recommendations prevailed, when they were able to convince James that what he wanted would not work. For example, James at the council's urging abandoned the policy of colonization of the Highlands by Lowland 'adventurers' in the wake of its failure in Lewis in favour of working through the clan chiefs themselves to 'civilize' what James regarded as a barbarous area. In the Dunfermline era the normal pattern was that the council made policy and then persuaded the king to agree.[11] It was a council that carried a great deal of weight – the most influential privy council in the hundred-plus years of absentee government. Every important Scottish official was now in Edinburgh rather than at court,[12] and the council also contained bishops and every member of the court of session. The king knew these men and trusted them. The key figures in the administration, Dunfermline, Sir Thomas Hamilton, 'Tam o' the Cowgate', now earl of Melrose and both secretary of state and president of the court of session, a most unusual combination of offices, and the earl of Mar, 'Jock o' the Slates', lord treasurer after 1616, were James's old friends; Mar had shared his schoolroom when they were boys. Their channels to the king were also old friends: Mar's cousin Thomas Erskine, earl of Kellie, captain of the guard, whose son married one of Dunfermline's daughters, and John Murray of Lochmaben, keeper of the privy purse and, in 1624, earl of Annandale. It was a comfortable, conservative system that worked well in most respects.[13] The friends and their master grew old together. Dunfermline's death in 1622 made no difference; the *troika* of Melrose, Mar, and the new chancellor, Sir George Hay of Nethercliff, carried on as before.

James's knowledge of Scotland and the people who counted there made his years of absentee government unique. None of his successors, from Charles I to Anne, knew anything much about Scotland or showed much interest in finding out. The first casualty of Charles's regime was the Dunfermline system he inherited. It could have survived only if Charles had been as

11 For the post-Dunbar years in Jacobean Scotland see *ibid.*, chaps. 4–6. Jenny Wormald, 'James VI, James I and the Identity of Britain', *The British Problem c. 1534–1707*, ed. B. Bradshaw and J. Morrill (Basingstoke, 1996), 158, suggests that James now wanted his agent located in Edinburgh because of anti-Scottish feeling in England. This argument is not convincing: what irritated Englishmen was not how James governed Scotland, but rather the Scottish monopoly of bedchamber posts and their disproportionate share of royal largesse. These did not change with Dunbar's death.

12 James's favourite Robert Ker (or Carr), earl of Somerset, was indeed lord treasurer from 1613 to 1616, but his deputy, Sir Gideon Murray of Elibank, did the work, and there is no evidence that Somerset concerned himself with policy questions.

13 Dunfermline, whom everyone knew to be a Catholic, though he publicly conformed, stayed out of religious issues. James's lack of accurate information on religious opinion in Scotland was in large measure responsible for the blunder of the Five Articles of Perth. See Lee, *Government by Pen*, chap. 5.

indifferent to Scotland as he was ignorant of it. He was anything but indifferent. He meant to rule there as well as reign, and there was to be a change of both men and measures. He did not care for either his father's old confidants at court, Kellie and Annandale, or the leaders of the government in Edinburgh. Instead he listened to two courtiers, deracinated Scots who were out of touch with the Scottish scene. One was Sir William Alexander of Menstrie, a gentleman of Charles' bedchamber, a poet who had collaborated with James on a metrical version of the Psalms and who was the chief promoter of the plan to colonize Nova Scotia, a project which much interested Charles. In 1626 he became secretary of state resident at court. From this time forward it was normal for the secretary (or one of the two secretaries: the office was frequently divided) to be in attendance on the king and handle his correspondence with Edinburgh officialdom.[14] Charles's other Scottish adviser was Robert Maxwell, earl of Nithsdale, an arrogant, quarrelsome, stupid man and a Catholic who owed his position to the favour of the great Buckingham: he had married one of Buckingham's cousins. There was much amiss in Scotland, in Charles's view; both church and crown were underfunded, and the great men too powerful. Before he could set about making any changes, however, he had to eliminate, or at least seriously reduce, the ability of those who ran the Scottish establishment to oppose him.

So Charles proceeded to destroy the Dunfermline system by reducing the powerful privy council he had inherited to a docile and subservient body, as it had been in the days of Dunbar. His first step was to separate the privy council from the judicial bench: henceforth no councillor could be a member of the court of session. He further weakened the influence and prestige of the court by prohibiting nobility from sitting as ordinary judges and by declaring that judges would sit during pleasure rather than good behaviour. He also insisted that judges' commissions expired on the demise of the crown, a dubious claim for which there was no precedent. The upshot was the replacement of seven of the fifteen judges, and a much less independent-minded court. The council was much weakened by the loss of its judicial members; Charles simply ignored it when he chose to do so. Melrose, who had to resign as president of the session in 1626, was forced out of the secretaryship in the following year. Mar was eventually driven to resign as treasurer; his replacement, the earl of Morton, had thoughtfully betrothed his son and heir to Buckingham's niece. The lord chancellor was bribed with a peerage and did as he was told.[15]

Charles had thus alienated his officials in Scotland without replacing them, and he had no one to implement his extremely controversial policy. Nithsdale

14 Between 1608 and 1612 Sir Alexander Hay of Whitburgh was secretary of state residing at James's court, and for three years, 1609–12, was sole secretary. His political influence was minimal; in 1612 he was forced out in favour of Melrose. After 1612 there was no resident secretary at James's court.
15 For all this see 'Charles I and the End of Conciliar Government in Scotland', below.

was held in scorn and contempt, and Alexander had neither the standing nor the personality to emulate Dunbar. Fortunately Charles stumbled upon a man who could help him and whom he came to like and trust, William Graham, earl of Menteith. Menteith was an ancient aristocrat; the people who counted in Scotland would listen to him. He persuaded Charles to explain his policies more fully and clearly; it developed that they were not as threatening to the establishment as had first been thought, when, as Archbishop Spottiswoode put it, people feared that Charles would 'call in question all men's rights since King Fergus'.[16] Menteith also persuaded the king to move more slowly, to consult the various interest groups, and to accept the principle of compensation for loss of property rights. Like Dunbar, Menteith travelled; by contrast, his base was in Edinburgh, where he was president of the council. And, unlike Dunbar, he travelled, not to intimidate, but to explain. Gradually the panic subsided.

Thus the system of government by agent revived after the five-year hiatus following Dunfermline's death. Menteith's tenure was very brief, however. Like Charles, he did not make friends easily and was something of a loner. He did make enemies, among them Sir John Scott of Scotstarvit, the director of the chancery, a close associate of Secretary Alexander in the Nova Scotia venture and a man who had the king's ear. Scotstarvit, a greedy and malicious troublemaker, 'a busy man in foul weather, and one whose covetousness far exceeded his honesty',[17] engineered Menteith's fall in 1633 by undermining the king's confidence in him. The timing was an unhappy coincidence for Charles. In that same year he made his long-delayed visit to Scotland for his coronation and made a disastrous impression on the Scottish aristocracy, who simultaneously lost their spokesman.

Among those who had helped to ruin Menteith was the treasurer-depute, Sir John Stewart of Traquair, who became earl in 1633 and lord treasurer three years later. He aspired to replace Menteith and in some ways did so; by 1634 he was travelling back and forth between Edinburgh and London on an average of twice a year. Traquair was able and efficient, but his position was significantly weaker than Menteith's. He was not an aristocrat, and did not have the material, in the form of marriageable siblings and children, to create an aristocratic affinity in the manner of Lord Chancellor Dunfermline, the last man to have become the king's principal agent owing to his talents as a bureaucrat. Charles found Traquair useful but did not like him. Since he was a jumped-up laird, the aristocracy regarded him with suspicion. Worst of all, the king was making more and more use of bishops in government and giving them more and more of his time as his and Archbishop Laud's plans for alterations in the Scottish church unfolded. Traquair could not oppose

16 16 July 1627, Spottiswoode to Annandale, J.F.S. Gordon, *Ecclesiastical Chronicle for Scotland*, 4 vols. (London, 1875), i, 487–8.
17 These are the words of Sir James Balfour, the Lyon King of Arms; *The Historical Works of Sir James Balfour*, J. Haig, ed. (Edinburgh, 1824–5), ii, 147.

these plans because he was dependent on Laud's goodwill to retain that of the king. The appointment of Archbishop Spottiswoode as chancellor in 1634, the first clerical lord chancellor since the Reformation, was an alarming portent, and not only to Traquair, but he could neither prevent nor oppose it. As Traquair saw it, the bishops were the chief threat to his ambition to become another Dunbar. So, as the plans to impose the new prayer book went forward, Traquair did nothing to warn the king of what was likely to happen. He expected a backlash, and hoped that the bishops would be politically ruined. He did not anticipate that he, too, would be engulfed.[18]

The carefully orchestrated riot against the new prayer book in St. Giles took place on 23 July 1637. On 28 November 1638, the General Assembly of the church of Scotland, which had not been allowed to meet for twenty years, defied the king's commissioner, the marquis of Hamilton, and refused to disperse at his order: the first act of the Scottish revolution. During those sixteen months Charles's ability to govern Scotland gradually collapsed. He had no shortage of information. Messengers and messages came regularly from the north; at one point, in the spring of 1638, spokesmen for the bishops, the government, and the king's opponents, the Covenanters, were simultaneously at court. Charles, as always, heard what he wished to hear, and for too long he believed that the problem was not serious and that a show of firmness would cause the protesters to give way. Traquair by the end of 1637 was urging compromise and conciliation; Charles paid no attention and ordered him to implement the uncompromising policy he had advised the king to abandon. Of the two Scots at court who had been at Charles's side from the beginning one, Secretary Alexander, was now a cipher to whom no one listened. He was reduced to asking the papal agent George Con, of all people, to persuade the king that the protesters were serious. Nithsdale, unfortunately, still had the king's ear. He was very critical of both bishops and privy councillors, urged the king never to withdraw the service book, and by early 1638 was advocating the use of force, apparently with Henrietta Maria's blessing.[19]

Charles's system of absentee government – issuing written orders through Secretary Alexander and consulting personally with a principal agent based in Edinburgh – was evidently bankrupt. His orders were not obeyed, and his officials had no credibility. Nithsdale even advised the king in November 1637 not to permit any bishop or privy councillor to come to court.[20] Many of them were being labelled 'incendiaries', men who deliberately aroused the king's anger against his own subjects. So in April 1638 Charles changed course. He appointed a new agent, his close friend the marquis of Hamilton, with the title of commissioner, a royal representative empowered to act in the

---

18   For Charles's reign to 1637 see Lee, *Road to Revolution*, and Macinnes, *Charles I.*

19   The most detailed account of these months is Donald, *Uncounselled King*, chaps. 1–3. See also Stevenson, *Scottish Revolution*, chaps. 2–3.

20   Donald, *Uncounselled King*, 55.

king's name. This was unusual. Charles had never appointed a commissioner before, and James had done so only to conduct sessions of parliament in his absence. But no meeting of parliament was now in the offing; the grant of the title was to emphasize the fact that Hamilton alone now spoke for the king. At the same time Charles began to contemplate the use of force. He instructed Hamilton not only to work to bring the discontented back to their obedience voluntarily, but also to advise as to the most efficient ways to compel them if they would not yield.[21]

The fact that Charles had to entrust this difficult and delicate task to a courtier like Hamilton is an indication of the bankruptcy of his policy. Hamilton was a great landowner and the king's friend, to be sure, but he was also a soldier with no experience in government who before 1638 had been minimally involved in Scottish affairs except when there was financial advantage for him.[22] Still, he was the best choice available to Charles. He worked hard, and he gave Charles sensible advice, both by letter and in person: he made the journey between London and Edinburgh five times between May and September. He was not the best of negotiators, but his failure was hardly his fault.[23]

In the summer of 1638 Charles took a step that he might usefully have taken when he became king: he appointed a committee to advise him on Scottish affairs. Such a committee had not existed before. James had no need of one, and prior to the troubles Charles had not felt the need either. At this point, unfortunately, the composition and purpose of the committee was not helpful to the peace process. It was a subcommittee of the English privy council, and its purpose was to prepare for war. So the crisis produced two new instruments of absentee government: an advisory committee in London and a royal commissioner who was far more visibly an official agent than Dunbar and the others had been. Hamilton urged that the office be continued, on the ground that someone must be responsible for carrying out the king's orders.[24] Both committee and commissioner would be used again in the future.

Charles's system in Scotland collapsed in part because he did not understand that he could not govern there in the same way as his father. He did not have James's intimate knowledge of the place and the people, and he could never have attained it even if he had been willing to try. James had employed two methods: an effective aristocratic spokesman and then a powerful privy council. Charles destroyed the powerful council and abandoned his only effective spokesman. Worse still, he then staged an unfair show trial of a dissident member of the aristocracy, Lord Balmerino, for purposes of in-

---

21 *Ibid.*, 75.
22 On this point see Gilbert Burnet, *The Memoires of the Lives and Actions of James and William, Dukes of Hamilton* (London, 1673), 26.
23 For Hamilton's mission see Donald, *Uncounselled King*, chap. 3; Stevenson, *Scottish Revolution*, chap. 3.
24 Stevenson, *Scottish Revolution*, 122.

timidation; the result was disastrous.[25] His activist policy in Scotland could have succeeded only if he had built some consensus for it. Such a result, given what he wished to do, might have been beyond him. But he did not even try.

*   *   *

Once the General Assembly of the church defied Commissioner Hamilton's orders by refusing to dissolve, his master the king no longer governed Scotland. After November 1638 Charles was reduced to negotiating with those in power in Edinburgh or trying, unsuccessfully, to subdue them by force. Nor did Charles II rule in his ancient kingdom after 1649, either *in absentia* or in person during the awful year he spent there. From 1638 to 1651, for the only time in the seventeenth century, there was no absentee government in Scotland. Interestingly enough, the men in control in Edinburgh showed no interest in separating Scotland from England; it was the most radical of the regimes that came to power during these years that in 1649 proclaimed Charles II king of England and Ireland as well as Scotland. The most vehement critics of the regime of Charles I did not want to undo what had been done in 1603. All parties wanted the union to continue – on their terms.

*   *   *

Governing Scotland from London began again in 1651, after the battle of Worcester, in entirely different circumstances. Scotland was now a conquered country, saddled with an English army of occupation commanded by an English general who received his instructions from the council of state or, after 1653, from the Lord Protector and his advisers. This unprecedented situation gave rise to unprecedented questions. Would any of the institutions of the monarchy survive? Would there be a civilian government in Edinburgh at all, and if so would it contain any Scots? Would any Scots be in a position to influence the authorities in London? The republican government could do as it pleased: what would it choose to do?[26]

Throughout the republican period the various governments employed the system Charles had adopted in 1638. Policy questions went first to a committee of the council of state. This committee was in existence by the beginning of 1651. At that time it dealt with both Scottish and Irish affairs; during the Protectorate there was a separate committee for each area. The Rump's first impulse was simply to treat Scotland as an English conquest, but by October 1651 it had adopted the policy which was to endure all through the republican era. Scotland – and Ireland too – were to be incorporated into a single government for the whole of the British Isles. Necessarily there would

25 For this episode see Lee, *Road to Revolution*, 157–62.
26 The following paragraphs are based mostly on Dow, *Cromwellian Scotland*.

be some delay in implementing this: the Scots were instructed to elect commissioners to discuss with an English commission, not the principle of incorporation – they had to accept that in advance – but only its terms. Incorporation was not popular in Scotland, largely on account of distaste for the Commonwealth's religious policy. Areas and communities unwilling to endorse the principle invited reprisals: Glasgow, for example, had to play host to nine companies of soldiers until it changed its mind.

Pending the outcome of the discussions on incorporation the Rump sent an eight-man commission which included five army officers north to reconstitute a government for Scotland. It did its job rapidly and efficiently in the first months of 1652. Local government continued much as before, except that courts of regality and barony were abolished: the Commonwealth regarded the great landowners as enemies and wished to depress their influence. Seven commissioners for the administration of justice, four of them English, replaced both the court of session and the justice-general, but at the beginning only the English commissioners heard criminal cases. A commission for sequestrations was set up, and another for the visitation of universities. The parliamentary commissioners also set the amount of the assessment Scots had to pay each month to support their real masters, the occupying army.[27]

Discussions on the terms of union began in 1652, but the only thing that had been settled by the time Cromwell put an end to the Rump in April 1653 was that the English commissioners would make all the decisions. The Scots could make suggestions – they proposed sixty Scottish MPs for the projected parliament – but the English decided: there would be thirty. In 1653 the council of the army authorized five Scottish (and six Irish) members for Barebones Parliament, which in its turn discussed the projected union but decided nothing. So the final decision was formally made in the Instrument of Government, the constitution of the Protectorate. Not surprisingly, Scotland was allotted thirty MPs.[28]

Until 1655 decisions on civil government in Scotland were made by the council of state in London and implemented by the commander-in-chief: Richard Deane, then Robert Lilburne, and finally, beginning in April 1654, George Monck. In May 1655 Cromwell, on the council's advice, appointed a nine-man council of state for Scotland which would sit in Edinburgh. It included only two Scots; its first president was an Irish peer, Lord Broghill. In one sense the change was largely cosmetic, in that Scots were scarcely more influential in their government than before, but it was an indication that the English government had concluded that the best way to reconcile the Scots to English rule was to create governmental machinery that more closely resembled that of the past. It also decided, perhaps because of the difficulty it

27 For the work of this commission see *Scotland and the Commonwealth*, ed. C.H. Firth, SHS (Edinburgh, 1895), intro., pp. xxvii–xli.
28 For these negotiations see *The Cromwellian Union*, ed. C.S. Terry, SHS (Edinburgh, 1902), intro., pp. xvi–lix, and Dow, *Cromwellian Scotland*, chap. 2.

had in subduing the royalist rebellion known as Glencairn's rising, to conciliate the aristocracy and the lairds: the policy of attempting to undermine their influence with other sections of Scottish society had not worked.[29] So it re-established barony courts and commissions of the peace, which included many soldiers. It reduced the fines levied on various aristocratic royalists, often by as much as two-thirds, and relaxed the rules on the collection of debt – by this time most aristocrats were heavily in debt. It dropped a plan to authorize the commissioners for the administration of justice to appoint burgh officials, which would have suspended self-government in the burghs. It abandoned an effort to bring the Scottish legal system more into line with that of England. By 1658 there was a Scottish majority on the commission for the administration of justice, and the office of lord advocate was filled after a six-year hiatus.

What these policy changes demonstrated was that the Protector's government listened to its agents in Edinburgh, especially Monck, and acted accordingly. Monck, in turn, was careful to keep his own agent, his wife's brother Thomas Clarges, in London, to be sure that his own views reached the Protector. The new council of state in Edinburgh took few initiatives save in religion, where Broghill successfully cultivated the moderate majority among the clergy, the so-called Resolutioners, and persuaded them to stop praying publicly for Charles II. For the most part the council served as a transmission belt for orders from Whitehall. There was a good deal of micromanagement. In November 1654, for example, the Lord Protector interested himself in the affairs of the very wealthy countess of Buccleuch and her sister, who were still children; he wrote to the council of tutors established by their deceased father that the little girls should remain in their mother's care until they were eleven or twelve years old.[30] In 1657 the son of the earl of Eglinton had the fine he was assessed to avoid the sequestration of his estate reduced by over 75%, but only after the council at Whitehall had considered his appeal.[31]

The Anglo-Scottish union of the 1650s foreshadowed what was to happen after 1707, in the way in which the machinery of government operated as well as in substantive areas such as economic union and the telescoping of parliamentary constituencies. In both cases the political institutions and functionaries of the Scottish central government disappeared altogether or were rendered meaningless, though the law courts (and the law) survived. Decisions were made in Whitehall. Of course there was one glaring difference, which has tended to overshadow the similarities: the presence of an English military force. By the end of the Protectorate the Scottish government was far more 'civilian' in form than at the beginning, and far more Scots had places in it – in the 1940s they would have been called collaborationists. But

---

29 On this point see Dow, *Cromwellian Scotland*, 53, 61, 77, 159, 179.
30 SRO, GD 157, no. 3092. The girls' mother had remarried, and was now countess of Wemyss.
31 Dow, *Cromwellian Scotland*, 220.

behind the façade General Monck always had the last word. Indeed, after Broghill's departure in August 1656 because he had been elected to parliament for Edinburgh – such was the nature of 'Scottish' representation in the parliaments of the Protectorate – Monck ran the civilian machinery as well. His were the standard methods of the military occupier, the carrot and the stick, and his priorities were clear. In arguing that the marquis of Argyll should not be allowed to sit in Richard Cromwell's parliament in 1659 he wrote, 'Truly I thinke . . . there is noe Man in the three Nations does more disaffect the English Interest than hee'.[32]

General Monck, who believed in civilian government, would probably have approved of the kind of army that governed Scotland after 1707: an army of Scottish placemen, marshalled by Scottish politicians who had something to offer to their English masters: votes. Scotland therefore occasionally required thought and attention on the part of English officialdom. After the union the surface forms were different, but the nature of the relationship between Walpole and Islay, or Pitt and Dundas, was very similar to that between Cromwell and Monck. What mattered was the English interest, and Scots had only marginally more input into the decision-making process than they had in the days of the republic. What the English politicians of the later seventeenth century stored in their memory of that decade was that a widely unpopular union could be made to work. When Monck led his army south in 1660 Scotland remained quiet.

* * *

Edward, earl of Clarendon, who had never been to Scotland, did not care for either Scotland or Scots; the pages of his great historical and autobiographical works breathe suspicion, contempt, and dislike.[33] King Charles II, now happily restored to his three kingdoms, had been to Scotland, and vowed that he would be hanged before he ever returned.[34] He too disliked Scots, though he made some exceptions, mostly for those who had accompanied him on his foredoomed invasion of England that ended at Worcester. He wanted to have as little to do with that ghastly place as possible. Clarendon would have preferred to retain the Cromwellian system there, since it did solve the problem of absentee government. The Scots themselves, he mendaciously commented, would have preferred it, 'But the king would not build

32 24 Mar. 1659, Monck to Samuel Disbrowe, *Scotland and the Protectorate*, ed. C.H. Firth, SHS (Edinburgh, 1899) 411–2.
33 There is no satisfactory account of Scottish politics in the reign of Charles II. Two helpful recent books are R. Hutton, *Charles II, King of England, Scotland, and Ireland* (Oxford, 1989), and Julia Buckroyd, *Church and State in Scotland 1660–1681* (Edinburgh, 1980).
34 See his comment to the duc d'Orléans after his escape from the disaster at Worcester, quoted in S.R. Gardiner, *History of the Commonwealth and Protectorate*, new ed., 4 vols. (London, 1903) ii, 57.

according to Cromwell's models'.[35] So there was to be a separate government in Edinburgh again. Clarendon sought to retain as much of the Cromwellian structure as he could. The government was to be in the hands of a royal commissioner whose tenure, like that of Hamilton in 1638, was to be independent of sessions of parliament. The English garrisons, left behind by Monck, would remain. The man picked to be commissioner, the earl of Middleton, was a professional soldier who had done good service for both Charles and his father and whom both he and Clarendon liked and trusted. The insignificance in their scheme of things of that former engine of government, the privy council, is indicated by the fact that it was not even reconstituted until July 1661, fourteen months after the king's return. When it was finally appointed it contained five English officials, including Clarendon himself. These would be the men who, meeting in Whitehall with the king (and, often, with his brother, a diligent administrator), would, like the republican conciliar committees of the 1650s, determine Scottish policy. It was, in fact, the structure employed under the Protectorate without the formal union. Unlike Monck, however, Commissioner Middleton was to be an errand boy, carrying out orders. He was not expected to exercise any independent judgement or authority.

The system did not last because on one crucial matter Clarendon did not get his way. One aspect of Charles I's system that was restored was the permanent residence in Whitehall of the Scottish secretary of state (an office that did not exist in the 1650s) to handle the correspondence with Edinburgh. Clarendon wanted Charles to appoint Middleton's friend the earl of Newburgh, another soldier and a man Clarendon could control, to this office. Charles instead opted for John Maitland, earl of Lauderdale, an experienced politician whom Charles had known and liked since 1648. Lauderdale was, like Middleton, a Worcestor Scot; he had spent the 1650s in various English prisons after his capture there. He was also an ex-Covenanter and a presbyterian. Clarendon disliked and distrusted him but could not prevent his appointment as secretary. This made Lauderdale potentially very influential because, as he quickly came to appreciate if he did not already know it, Charles hated paperwork and preferred to receive his information orally. Access to the king was everything. Lauderdale had access, and he was ambitious. The stage was set for a struggle for power.

It took Lauderdale seven years to ensure that henceforth, as his kinsman and political ally the earl of Tweeddale put it, 'the keys shall hing [sic] at the right belt'.[36] His ambition was to become another Dunbar, but with the difference that at Charles's court there would be no Thomas Erskines or John Murrays as alternate channels to the king: he would have a monopoly of news from Scotland. The first task was to destroy Clarendon's system, and, step by

35 Edward, Earl of Clarendon, *A Continuation of His History of the Great Rebellion*, 2 vols. (Oxford, 1857), i, 362.
36 28 May 1667, Tweeddale to Lauderdale, BL Add. Ms. 23126, f. 232.

step, Lauderdale did so. First the English garrisons went, a very popular move in Scotland, though the republican practice of quartering soldiers – Scottish soldiers now – on fractious communities continued. Middleton destroyed himself because he did not play the part Clarendon had assigned to him. He behaved independently in ways that did not commend themselves to Charles. He paid insufficient attention to orders, and finally came to ruin by making a clumsy attempt to drive Lauderdale from office. He was gone by 1663. Lauderdale's one serious setback was his failure to prevent the restoration of diocesan episcopacy, which the Act Rescissory of 1661 did not automatically bring about. Ronald Hutton argues that this act went beyond the intentions of the king and Clarendon, that Middleton and his allies 'had effectively snatched the making of religious policy from his [Charles's] hands'.[37] This is an exaggeration; the final decision remained with Charles, who at Clarendon's urging brought back the bishops. From Lauderdale's point of view this was a managerial complication as well as a political error. The episcopal party in Scotland distrusted him, and its leaders could communicate with their English counterparts. Lauderdale could not keep the archbishop of Canterbury away from the king; what would be necessary was that the archbishop heard from Scotland only what Lauderdale wanted him to hear.

Middleton's departure did not turn Lauderdale into the king's chief Scottish agent. He had to share power with the earl of Rothes, another Worcester Scot, a plausible and insinuating man with a penchant for the bottle, who became royal commissioner and lord treasurer, and the ambitious and untrustworthy Archbishop Sharp of St. Andrews, whom Lauderdale kept an eye on by employing his brother, William Sharp, as his personal man of business in Edinburgh. Rothes and Sharp were not apt to offend by behaving independently, as Middleton had done. They were politically insensitive, however, and did not see that following Clarendon's (and Middleton's) hard line in religious policy might cause backlash. Lauderdale did see this, but did nothing: he was giving his rivals enough rope.[38] He was, in fact, emulating the tactics of Traquair. Unlike Traquair he succeeded, because the backlash came in the form of a minor rebellion late in 1666. Religious rebellions in Scotland made the king understandably nervous; he remembered 1637. Lauderdale persuaded him that Rothes's and Sharp's policy had been the cause. At the same time Clarendon was tottering to his fall for reasons quite unconnected with events in Scotland. By mid-1667 Clarendon was gone, and his Whitehall council with him. Charles transferred Rothes from the treasury to the chancellorship and removed him as commissioner, to his great distress. Lauderdale saw to it that he was not allowed to come to court to plead his case in person with Charles: Lauderdale feared his

37 Hutton, *Charles II*, 161–2.
38 On this point see 20 Sept. 1667, Sir Robert Moray to Lauderdale, BL Add. Ms. 23128, fos. 54–5.

charm and glib tongue.[39] Sharp was converted into a bootlicker: there would be no more dangerous letters to Archbishop Sheldon, who had supported Sharp's bid for the chancellorship in 1665. The subservience of the episcopal bench was heavily underscored when Sharp's fellow archbishop, Burnet of Glasgow, was forced to resign because he complained of Lauderdale's new religious policy. Lauderdale, now royal commissioner, had created his monopoly and reigned supreme. Dunbar's system had been revived.

The keys hung at Lauderdale's belt for twelve years. Like Dunbar he travelled. Beginning in 1663, before he became commissioner, he was present at every session of parliament, and after 1667 often spent many weeks in Scotland, either before or after the session. Unlike Middleton he reported fully to Charles and when necessary referred matters back to him: Charles did not like *faits accomplis* and surprises. Lauderdale could not afford to risk the breakdown of his monopoly during his absences; he also needed absolutely reliable men in the Edinburgh administration to carry out his (and Charles's) orders when he was at Whitehall. His system thus required two or three close collaborators. There had to be a substitute secretary at Whitehall when he was in the north; when he was at court the treasury commission, now the most important administrative body in Edinburgh, had to be in dependable hands – after Rothes's removal there was no thought of appointing another lord treasurer who would be a potential rival. The key was the office of treasurer depute. Lauderdale had it earmarked for his brother Charles when its elderly incumbent retired. Charles Maitland's appointment in 1671 precipitated the breakup of Lauderdale's first set of collaborators, consisting of the earl of Tweeddale, who wanted the office, and Sir Robert Moray.[40] Over the next eight years the roster of Lauderdale's political partners changed frequently, as the secretary sought for men who were both competent and obedient, *apparatchiks* without ambitions or ideas of their own who could at the same time deal with the Scottish aristocracy. His brother Charles, both venal and incompetent, turned into a liability but could not be jettisoned. In the later 1670s Lauderdale turned to the ancient aristocracy itself: Atholl for a time, Argyll, the earl of Moray. His difficulties steadily increased as his methods alienated more and more people and he could find no solution to the religious unrest which, if he had had his way at the beginning of Charles's reign, might never have developed. By 1673 the opposition had surfaced in parliament and made that normally manageable body temporarily uncontrollable.[41] Yet through it all Lauderdale retained the king's favour. To the repeated calls for his dismissal from both Scots and English politicians Charles invariably replied that Lauderdale's every action was for the good of the king's service. Lauderdale's monopoly of the information Charles received, and his ability to

39 25 June 1667, Lauderdale to Moray, NLS, Ms. 7023, f. 52.
40 There were policy differences between Tweeddale and Lauderdale, and also the savage family quarrel described in 'The Troubles of a Family Man', below.
41 For the session of 1673 see J. Patrick, 'The Origins of the Opposition to Lauderdale in the Scottish Parliament of 1673,' *SHR* liii (1974), 1–21.

anticipate complaints and blame them on dissident English politicians like Shaftesbury, stood him in very good stead.[42]

It was Lauderdale himself who unwittingly paved the way for his successor. In 1679, sensing that his power was slipping, he suggested that the duke of York be sent to Scotland. There had been another religious rebellion which Lauderdale's policies, including a particularly egregious example of the quartering of soldiers on recalcitrant people, had helped to provoke. It was put down by the duke of Monmouth (and Buccleuch: his wife was a great Scottish heiress), the king's dangerously popular illegitimate son. The king did not wish to leave Monmouth in Scotland, and agreed to send his brother instead. James stayed three months, went to England, then, in the autumn of 1680, returned and spent over a year and a half in Scotland. In the spring of 1680 Lauderdale suffered a stroke and at last resigned. He was let down gently; his current political ally the earl of Moray took his place as secretary. The great duke's day was done and so, Scottish politicians hoped, was his tight-fisted monopoly.[43]

Lauderdale's departure and James's presence in Edinburgh created an entirely new political situation. James was the king's commissioner, as Lauderdale had been, a royal agent indeed, but also royalty in person. He came with his family; once again there was a court in Holyrood, which pleased the Scots enormously. James played on their pride by reviving the knightly Order of the Thistle and commissioning the portraits of all the Scottish kings, going back to Fergus, which still hang on the walls of Holyrood Palace. He reached out to the various aristrocratic factions, bringing disgruntled opponents of the Lauderdale regime such as Tweeddale back into political life. The only jarring note was the trial, on a grotesque treason charge, of the earl of Argyll, Lauderdale's kinsman and supporter and a man very unpopular in the highlands for his rapacity and abuse of office. The purpose was to deprive Argyll of offices and power rather than life, but the outcome made the aristocracy nervous: the methods were reminiscent of those of Charles I.

When James left Scotland for the last time in May 1682 he left behind him an administration without an agent. Instead there was an inner ring of some six or seven men who promptly began to intrigue against each other. There were no more permanently appointed royal commissioners. The Scottish council in London, which Lauderdale had reduced to impotence, revived and occasionally met. But in one respect there was no change from Lauderdale's time. Access was still everything – access, now, to James, who took the initiative in determining Scottish policy, though he was not always able to carry his brother with him. The Scottish secretary in Whitehall after 1682, the second earl of Middleton, helped to ruin the chancellor James had left behind

---

42 On this point see the useful discussion in Hutton, *Charles II*, 314–5.
43 Lauderdale died in August 1682; his brother Charles was immediately fired as treasurer depute and fined for malversation in office.

him, the earl of Aberdeen; by June 1684 Aberdeen was gone, replaced by James Drummond, earl of Perth. The decision was James's. In August of that year Charles made a decision that determined the future in Scotland: he transferred Middleton to an English secretaryship – the first Scot he ever appointed to an English political office, though Middleton was in fact more English than Scots by upbringing. The new Scottish secretary in London was John Drummond of Lundin, Perth's younger brother and close ally. Gradually the Drummonds squeezed out all their rivals. The last to go, in 1686, was the lord treasurer, the duke of Queensberry, because he would not support repeal of the Test Act and toleration for Catholics, amongst whom, now, were the Drummond brothers. Perth trumpeted the fact that what finally persuaded him – along with a reading of Bishop Bossuet – was the deathbed conversion of Charles II![44]

Thus the Catholic duumvirate of James's agents – James became James VII and II in 1685 – Perth in Edinburgh and, in London, the younger Drummond, earl of Melfort in 1686, governed Scotland. There was no need to travel; the brothers worked as one. They provided James with his intelligence, and told him what he wanted to hear: that his policy was working. Kathleen Colquhoun argues that there was more ambivalence about James's Catholicizing policy in Scotland than in England, 'not because popery was not despised there, but because the attachment to the national church was not as strong in Scotland'.[45] The administration became increasingly Catholic. Secretary Moray converted in 1686, and the Catholic earl of Dumbarton was commander of the Scottish army, such as it was. Nevertheless the Drummonds, out of either caution or jealousy of possible rivals, made no effort to build a Catholic party; even great Catholic aristocrats such as the duke of Gordon, a former political ally, were kept at arm's length. The policy of toleration of Catholics which they and their master so vigorously advocated did alarm the landed classes, who saw in it a potential threat to their property. Yet Scotland remained quiet: the threat to Protestantism and property, and the political monopoly of the Drummonds, produced no explosion. The conditions were not unlike those of 1637; the result was not. Revolution in 1688–89 spread from south to north, not, as in 1637–42, from north to south. The fragmented condition of the nobility, divided and suspicious of each other, helps to account for this. So, too, did their memory of the awful consequences for them as a class of the overturning of Charles I. There may have been some residual reassurance in the fact that, by contrast with England, James's Catholic officials were members of great aristocratic families: Drummonds, Gordons, Douglases, Stewarts. Once they were rid of the unpopular Drummond monopoly – Perth fled from Edinburgh owing to the anti-Catholic riots organized by Queens-

44 The political manoeuvring of the decade after 1679 is carefully spelled out in K. Colquhoun, 'Issue of the Late Civill Wars': James, Duke of York, and the Government of Scotland 1679–1689 (Ph.D. dissertation, University of Illinois, Urbana, 1993.)

45 Ibid., 433.

berry and Atholl in December 1688 – the magnates were far less concerned to rid themselves of the king. The duke of Hamilton urged James to take refuge in Scotland, where, said Hamilton, he would be welcome provided he left his Catholic advisers behind him. James, however, chose to follow the advice of Melfort and the extreme Catholics and fled to France.[46] His government of Scotland was over. So, too, as it turned out, was government by agent.

*   *   *

The accession of King William II and III completely changed the parameters of absentee government in Scotland. Henceforth the most important political problem was the successful management of parliament, which had never been the case in the past. Historians have recently come to believe, thanks largely to the work of Jenny Wormald,[47] that the Scottish parliament was never as easy to control as had previously been thought – Lauderdale discovered this in 1673 and never met another – but thanks to the committee of the articles the crown could expect to get what it wanted most of the time. The revolution settlement saw the abolition of that committee. The need for taxes to fight the war against France meant that parliament had to meet regularly; between 1689 and 1707 there were only five years without a session. Successful management of parliament now meant creating some kind of coalition, i.e., bringing enough of the great magnates on board to produce a stable majority. The impossibility of doing this was what, in the end, forced the parliamentary union.[48]

There was one possible solution to William's governmental problem that might have worked, though the odds were against it. He could have tried to maintain the system of government by agent by choosing one of the great aristocrats at the outset and making him his Lauderdale, with control of Scottish patronage, a position to which they all aspired. Only one, the duke of Queensberry, had the requisite talent, but neither he nor any of the other three with enough influence to hope for or expect the position, Hamilton, Atholl, or Argyll, commended themselves to William and those who advised him on Scottish affairs. William knew nothing about Scotland and cared nothing for it. All he wanted from Scotland were soldiers for his army and that there should be no trouble there that might create difficulties for him in managing either the English parliament or the war. Before 1688 there had been a number of Scottish political refugees in the Netherlands whom he had come to know and trust. The most important of these for Scotland was William Carstares, an old friend, a presbyterian minister who had suffered imprisonment and

46 F.C. Turner, *James II* (New York, 1948), 435–6.
47 See, e.g., *Court, Kirk, and Community: Scotland 1470–1625* (London, 1981).
48 By far the most useful study of the politics of the 1690s is Riley, *King William*. The following paragraphs rely heavily on it, though I do not accept all of Riley's interpretations. A. Ian Dunlop, *William Carstares and the Kirk by Law Established* (Edinburgh, 1964), is also helpful.

torture under Charles II. He became William's chaplain. William turned over Scottish policy to him and to his Dutch favourite William Bentinck, earl of Portland, who knew no more about Scotland than William. The king trusted them to keep his interests uppermost in their minds, and they did not betray that trust. They were frequently inept but never disloyal.

Carstares thus became William's principal adviser on Scottish matters. John Macky, a contemporary observer, commented that 'Few Scotsmen had access to the King but by him, so that he was properly Viceroy of that Kingdom and was called at Court, "Cardinal Carstares"'.[49] He was not the king's agent in the usual sense, however. He was not a politician, was out of touch with Scottish politics, and never went there, since he travelled only with the king: William was the first king of Scots never to set foot in his kingdom. Carstares was not an aristocrat. Worse still, he was a clergyman, and the aristocracy had made it clear that they would not tolerate clergymen in political office. Macky exaggerated: Carstares could not wall off access to William on the part of Scottish politicians who came to London, and the evidence suggests that he did not try to do so. There were, therefore, in both this reign and the next, occasional gatherings like the one that analyzed what had happened at the parliament of 1695[50] – meetings of the 'Scots council', so to speak.

Carstares had an agenda, however, which determined the nature of the new Scottish administration. He wanted to establish a presbyterian church. William would have preferred for many reasons to preserve an episcopal system, but the bishops would not violate their oath to King James. So presbytery it was to be, a solution which, Carstares and his master believed, would not sit well with the Scottish nobility. They accepted the view of clerk register, Viscount Tarbat, the only important officer of James's government who held onto his office under William. 'The present Parliament', Tarbat wrote in 1689, 'is more numerous of Presbyterians . . . but the major part of the nobility and barons are not for Presbytery'.[51] The nobility was further irritated by the abolition of lay patronage. So Carstares, Portland, and William entrusted the government in Edinburgh to two returned exiles in whom they had confidence because they knew them. George, Lord Melville, raised to an earldom in 1690, became secretary of state, and the great lawyer Sir James Dalrymple of Stair, Viscount Stair in 1690, resumed the presidency of the court of session which he had held for ten years in the reign of Charles II. In 1691 his son would become Melville's colleague as secretary and be deeply involved in the massacre of Glencoe. They were reliable men and, in the case of the Dalrymples, very able. But they were not great lords, and they were jealous of each other. The intrigue and the sniping began almost at once.

William and his advisers had thus quite inadvertently ended the system of government by agent. They also shut out all four of the great magnates, who

49 John Macky, *Characters of the Nobility of Scotland*, quoted in Dunlop, *Carstares*, 92.
50 Riley, *King William*, 98–9.
51 Quoted in Dunlop, *Carstares*, 69.

each reacted by making difficulties for the government in order to undermine it and get power for himself. Their obvious forum was parliament, that now necessary institution, where they all were very influential. They proceeded to make it unmanageable. The dreary story of the complex political infighting of William's reign can be followed in the pages of Riley's study of *King William and the Scottish Politicians*; it need not be recapitulated here. By the end of 1695 Portland and Carstares concluded that their original plan was unworkable. They had tried various combinations of men of lesser influence; none had produced any stability. So at the beginning of 1696 the king reconstituted the ministry to bring the magnates on board. Queensberry and Argyll went to the treasury commission, Atholl's eldest son became secretary, and the second son of the recently deceased duke of Hamilton clerk register.[52] They promptly began to intrigue against each other. Queensberry and Argyll combined to drive out the other two, and then, predictably, fell out with each other. By the end of the reign Queensberry, whom Portland and Carstares reluctantly decided to support, had the upper hand. The situation could not last. Queensberry was determined to become the king's agent and create a monopoly of influence, which might be achieved for a moment but could not endure. Each of the magnates wanted a monopoly, none would willingly share power, none was strong enough to withstand an attack from the other three combined. There were many serious issues in the 1690s: relations between the now dominant presbyterians and the episcopalians, which was the question that most concerned Carstares, the implications and re-percussions of Glencoe, the impact of the war and of the four years of bad harvests that led to famine by 1697, the Darien fiasco – it was William's dissatisfaction at the passage of the act authorizing the Darien company that helped precipitate the decision to reconstitute the ministry in 1696. Scottish politicians apparently viewed these questions only in the light of how best to use them to further their own personal ambitions – though in fairness to the magnates, they had their own kinsmen and political followers to think of. They were expected to deliver places of one kind or another at the public trough. The result was an ungovernable kingdom with an unmanageable parliament and a paralyzed and useless privy council.[53]

By 1700 King William had concluded that the situation was impossible, and that the only solution was an incorporating union. In 1689 he had made such a proposal to the convention at the suggestion of the earl of Tweeddale, Lauderdale's old collaborator, who had been much involved in the abortive union negotiations of 1669–70[54] and who genuinely believed in union on

52 Both Atholl and the late duke's eldest son, still earl of Arran – his mother was duchess in her own right and did not resign the title to him until 1698 – were too tarred with Jacobitism to be given office.

53 See Riley's summary, *King William*, 157. I owe this assessment of the privy council at the end of William's reign to Professor Rosalind Mitchison, who has studied the manuscript record.

54 For this episode see M. Lee, Jr., *The Cabal* (Urbana, 1965), 43–68.

principle. The convention voted to name commissioners to negotiate a union, but the English parliament showed no interest. Nor, indeed, did William: such a negotiation would be a distraction, however advantageous union might be in theory.[55] But the current situation was intolerable. Furthermore, by 1700 a new complication had arisen. The death of Princess Anne's last child made the succession question urgent. The English parliament responded with the passage of the Act of Settlement in 1701, but it could not legislate for Scotland. It is no coincidence that in that same year English politicians showed their first signs of willingness to discuss the terms on which union might be negotiated.

Among the handful of Scottish politicians who shared William's views the most important was the newly created earl of Seafield, who had held one of the two secretaryships since 1696. Seafield understood magnate politics very well and saw how destructive they were. He also knew that his own political career could not flourish under such conditions. He could never be a Dunbar or a Lauderdale – no one could, now: the system of government by agent was dead. Seafield's best hope for a great career was to serve the crown, which union would strengthen in Scotland because it would eliminate the magnates' new power base in parliament. Prior to William's death Seafield had been a useful but not influential man, but with the accession of Anne in 1702 his position markedly improved. The influence of Portland and Carstares ended immediately. Anne knew as little about Scotland as William, although she had spent some time there when her father was in residence in Holyrood in the early 1680s, and she cared as little. Unlike her Stewart predecessors she had no Scot in her small inner circle. She depended for advice on Scotland on Marlborough and Godolphin and, to a lesser extent, Robert Harley; they occasionally staged discussions of Scottish affairs with assorted Scottish politicians for her benefit. Unlike William she could be pushed into endorsing decisions that distressed her. Of Queensberry she wrote in 1705, 'It grates my soul to take a man into my service that had not only betrayed me but tricked me several times', but at Godolphin's insistence she employed him.[56]

Anne's advisers felt about Scotland as William's did: it must not be a distraction in their conduct of the war. It was this circumstance that gave Seafield his chance. His impeccable reputation as a servant of the crown led Godolphin and Harley, who had to deal with the Scottish situation – Marlborough was busy elsewhere – to trust him. His growing importance led to his promotion to the chancellorship in 1702. This created a minor complication, since official correspondence went through the secretary, one of whom was at court – under Anne the two occupants of the office served in alternate months. Seafield and Godolphin solved the problem of confidenti-

---

55 See his remark to the earl of Jersey, quoted in Riley, *King William*, 160.
56 Quoted in Riley, *Union*, 127. This is the most detailed account of the political manoeuvring that led to the passage of the union treaty.

ality by setting up a separate channel of correspondence through the post-
master at Berwick.[57]

The story of the making of the union treaty need not be told again. It is
melancholy and sordid in most respects. Few would now subscribe unreservedly to the view that it was carried 'because a majority of Scotland's
spokesmen honestly believed that it was the course that promised best for the
nation', or because it was 'a very great feat of constructive statesmanship . . .
no more good or bad than the law of gravitation', though it may not have
been 'the greatest "political job" of the eighteenth century' either.[58] Money
changed hands; the extent to which it changed votes is still debated and not
altogether clear. Whether the payoffs were unusual or merely normal eight-
eenth-century practice is another debatable issue. Did Scotland benefit from
the union? The answer depends upon whom you ask. Riley, the closest
student of the politics of the period after the revolution of 1688–89, does not
regret the result. 'The parliament was no more than an instrument of magnate
rivalries and the kingdom was well rid of it'.[59] What is not debatable is that by
1707 the Scots had few options. Independence was impossible. England,
faced with the serious problem of her own security in a war against the
greatest power in Europe, a power which had recognized 'James III' as king,
would not permit the Scots to go their own way. Government by agent was
impossible under the present circumstances. This left only union by negotiation or union by force.

Government by an agent of the crown was a ramshackle system at best, but
it could be made to work, provided that the crown was content to follow
policies that did not provoke over-much controversy or seriously unsettle the
landed classes. The situation that had existed under James VI and I could
never be replicated. Under Charles I royal absolutism with an activist agenda
implemented by an agent in Edinburgh had collapsed after thirteen years
because of the nature of that agent and that agenda, and after thirteen more
years of self-government by shifting oligarchies, had led to English domination. After 1660 governing should have been easier. The landed classes,
appalled by the consequences of their defiance of the crown in 1637 and
thereafter, were not disposed to repeat that defiance. The crown, in its turn,
had no plans for changes in Scotland. All that these monarchs wanted was
that Scotland should be quiet. Government by agent was logical and necessary, because without one there was endless intrigue, as the people who
counted struggled for royal favour and a place at the public trough. So after
the Restoration royal authority, implemented by an agent in Whitehall, then
by the heir apparent, and finally by the latter's agents, lasted rather longer,

57 *Ibid.*, 82.
58 The opinions are respectively those of G.S. Pryde, *The Treaty of Union of Scotland
    and England 1707* (Edinburgh, 1950), intro., 34, G.N. Clark, *The Later Stuarts 1660–
    1714*, 2nd edn. (Oxford, 1955), 288, 292, and William Ferguson, 'The Making of the
    Treaty of Union of 1707', SHR xliii (1964), 110.
59 Riley, *King William*, 162.

although the crown's policies and methods often provoked dissent. What ended it were events in England.

After 1689 the crown found no way to adapt the system of government by agent to the changed circumstances of parliamentary management. So it collapsed, as it had in 1638, and the eventual result was the same: union and English domination. This time that domination proved permanent because of the change in the nature of the monarchy. A king with independent power can govern through independent agents. But in the parliamentary monarchy of William II and III and his successors there could be only one independent parliament. George III was to rediscover this truth, in Ireland, where the parliament ceased to exist, and in America, where crown-in-parliament ceased to rule. So the political polygamy which King James VI and I had deplored in appealing to his recalcitrant English parliament to support his proposals for union came to an end at last, ironically because the 'free monarchy' by which he set so much store had been shattered beyond repair.

2

Sir Richard Maitland of Lethington: A Christian Laird in the Age of Reformation (1969)

The name of Sir Richard Maitland of Lethington has echoed very faintly down the corridors of time for two reasons. He is remembered as a poet and, more importantly, as a collector and preserver of the poetry of others. Sir Richard was one of the first of Scotland's antiquaries, and as such he rendered a priceless service to the literary historians. Secondly, he is known as the father of two famous sons. The elder, William Maitland of Lethington, 'Secretary Maitland,' is familiar to all those who have even a passing acquaintance with the melancholy story of Mary Queen of Scots. The achievements and talents of the younger brother John, Lord Thirlestane, chancellor and political mentor to the young James VI, were less spectacular, if more lasting.[1] Richard Maitland ought also to be remembered in another capacity, as a Christian gentleman who lived in the age of Reformation and whose reactions to that age are extremely interesting because they shed a good deal of light, at least indirectly, on the nature of that Reformation in Scotland.

The traditional view of the Scottish Reformation – a view which can be largely attributed to the florid eloquence of John Knox – is that in the 1550's and 1560's Scotland was the scene of a vigorous clash of ideologies and personalities, which led to almost continuous violence: the Wars of the Congregation in 1559–1560, which resulted in the overturn of the old Church; the upheavals and spectacular murders of Mary's reign; and, finally, another civil war after the assassination of the Regent Moray, a war which at last came to an end in 1573 with the triumph of the Protestant faction. No one can deny the existence of these wars and murders, and of ideological conflict too. But the amount of violence has been exaggerated – far fewer people were killed in Scotland in the sixteenth century for either religious or political reasons than in 'stable' and 'civilized' England – and so, too, has the catastrophic nature of the events of 1560. Professor Gordon Donaldson, the author of the most recent full-scale study of the Scottish Reformation, puts the point this way: 'The Scottish reformation . . . was at once less precipitate and less radical than is often believed. From many points of view the year 1560, the conventional date of the Scottish reformation, is not very significant, and must have been

---

1 The standard biography of William Maitland is E. Russell, *Maitland of Lethington* (London, 1912). For John Maitland, see M. Lee, Jr., *John Maitland of Thirlestane and the Foundation of the Stewart Despotism in Scotland* (Princeton, 1959).

much less definitive in the eyes of contemporaries than it has come to be in the text books. Many changes had already taken place before 1560; contemporaries might have been hard put to it to define exactly what changes, if any, had been legally and constitutionally made in 1560; and after 1560 offices and emoluments remained substantially in the hands of those who had enjoyed them before.'[2]

The poetry of Richard Maitland stands as a remarkable commentary on the general accuracy of Professor Donaldson's opinion. But it does more than that; it also suggests an explanation of why the Scottish Reformation assumed the character and took the course it did, and is therefore of considerable significance as a source. That his poetry has been overlooked is attributable in part to its lack of literary value. None of it is great, and a good deal of it is not particularly original: Maitland wrote on a number of the same subjects as William Dunbar, whose poetry he had collected and whom he obviously greatly admired. But his verse, though ordinary as poetry, has the supreme advantage of being both topical and strictly contemporary; it was written from the late 1550's to the early 1570's, the crucial years in which the Reformation – whatever it was – took place.

Maitland was born in 1496, of an Anglo-Norman family of lairds who dwelt in the Lowlands south and east of Edinburgh. The Maitlands were a rising family: Sir Richard's mother was the daughter of Lord Seton, and his only sister married Lord Somerville. His father was killed at Flodden. After taking formal possession of his inheritance young Richard seems to have gone to France to complete his education by being trained in the law. In due course he returned, but his career was anything but spectacular; he was evidently not interested in becoming an active politician. In fact, we hear very little of him until he was well over fifty and his son William was beginning his rapid rise to power. In the 1550's Sir Richard was frequently employed as a commissioner in negotiations with England over border matters. He took no active part in the Wars of the Congregation, but, unlike William, now Secretary, he remained loyal to the Queen Regent – or so it is reasonable to conclude from the lines in his poem of welcome to Mary Queen of Scots on her return to her native land: 'Madame, I was true servant to thy mother, / And in her favour stood aye thankfully.'[3] The Queen rewarded him by making him a member of the College of Justice, the highest Scottish court, and in December 1562 she appointed him Keeper of the Privy Seal, in spite of the fact that he was now totally blind. These favors, of course, were attributable

---

2 Gordon Donaldson, *The Scottish Reformation* (Cambridge, 1960), p. 74.

3 'Of the Quenis arryvale in Scotland,' *The Maitland Folio Manuscript*, ed. W. A. Craigie, Scottish Text Society publication (Edinburgh, 1919), i, 35. The poetry quoted in this essay has been 'translated' into modern English in the interest of intelligibility. Spellings have been modernized, punctuation supplied, and Scots words anglicized. The rendering has been kept as literal as possible. An occasional Scots word has been retained for the sake of the meter or the rhyme; in these cases the English equivalent is supplied in parentheses.

less to the deeds of the father than to the merits of the son, who now shared
with the earl of Moray the position of chief advisor to Mary. And as the
fortunes of the Secretary rose and fell, so did those of Sir Richard. Favors
rained upon the family in the 1560's, but disaster issued from the Secretary's
losing choice in the confused struggles that followed the assassination of
Moray in 1570. One blow after another fell on the old man. His sons were
forfeited; the youngest, Thomas, died in Italy in 1572 at the early age of
twenty-seven; a year later, with the fall of Edinburgh castle, the spectacular
career of the Secretary came to its unhappy end. No legal action was taken
against Sir Richard, but his property was seized, on the pretext that it had
really belonged to the Secretary. All this was the doing of the Regent Morton;
it was not until Morton's loss of power in the late 1570's that the Maitland
family fortunes were restored, thanks to the abilities of Sir Richard's one
remaining son, John. The family property was returned, and in 1581 John
joined his father on the bench. Three years later advancing age prompted Sir
Richard to resign from the College of Justice. As a mark of favor, he was
allowed to nominate his successor; his choice, not surprisingly, fell on his
son's closest political associate at the moment, Sir Lewis Bellenden, the
Justice-clerk. In 1586 Sir Richard died, aged ninety.

Maitland's career thus spanned the most crucial years of the Scottish
Reformation. He was fully grown when Lutheran ideas first came to Scotland;
he played host to George Wishart just before the martyr's capture;[4] he died
two years before the Armada, just as his son John, now Secretary to the young
James VI, was hammering out that compromise between crown and kirk
which was to enable James to get control of kirk and aristocracy alike in the
1590's.

Yet the Reformation receives surprisingly little mention in Maitland's
poetry. It was not that he lacked concern for religious matters; on the
contrary, Maitland was a good Christian, in the sense that he accepted the
Christian ethic and lived by it as best he could. The evidence indicates that he
became a Protestant out of disgust at the worldliness and corruption of the
ancient Church, and not because he held any strong opinions on the questions
of justification by faith and predestination. His was the piety of the simple
man, for whom Christianity was a way of living rather than a matter of
intellectual commitment to a theological doctrine. The guidance provided by
Scripture was, for him, all that was necessary:

> To read or hear the holy writ,
> True knowledge shall I get in it:
> How I shall have me at all hours
> Both to my God and my neighbors,

4 *John Knox's History of the Reformation in Scotland*, ed. W. C. Dickinson (New York,
1950), i, 67. Knox describes Maitland as 'ever civil, albeit not persuaded in
religion.'

Instructing me to patiently
My trouble bear,
Sin to repent with true intent
While I am here.

Since in this earth I find no rest,
Rejoice in God I think it best,
Who, in this life, give me his grace,
Then bring me to that resting place
Where joy and gloir [glory] are evermore,
Peace and concord.
To that same joy do me convey,
Jesus our Lord.[5]

Maitland was not an indifferent man, then, yet he never became an enthusiast for either side. From the beginning he was critical of corruption in the clergy. In a poem written before the Wars of the Congregation he prays that God will

. . . take away the ignorance
Of churchmen that vices haunt,
And lead us a-rear,
That both good life and cunning want[lack],
Now in to this new year.[6]

During the war he prayed for religious concord; he wanted to see an end to heresy, but he was not prepared to commit himself by declaring who the heretics were:

God make us quit of all heresy
And put us once into the right way,
And in thy law we so instructed be
That we be not beguiled every day.
One sayeth this, another sayeth nay:
That we know not to whom we should adhere.
Christ send to us one rule to keep for aye
Without discord now in to this new year.[7]

Only once did Maitland devote an entire poem to the disputes between Protestants and Catholics, a poem written in 1570 and called, appropriately enough, 'On the Miseries of the Tyme.' The miseries were 'Pest, poverty, and most unkindly war.' Both sides, in Maitland's view, were

5 'Pleasouris of Aige,' *Folio*, i, 336–337.
6 'On the New Yeir,' *ibid.*, p. 25.
7 'Of the Assemblie of the Congregatioun,' *ibid.*, p. 33.

equally responsible for this unhappy situation. As for the Catholics, he chided,

> Some time the priests thought that they did well
> When that they made their beards and shaved their crown,
> Used round caps and gowns to their health
> And mass and matins said in their fashion,
> Though that all vices reigned in their person:
> Lechery, gluttony, vain glory, and avarice,
> With sword and fire for zeal of Religion
> Of Christian people oft made sacrifice.

The Protestants were no better:

> Now are Protestants risen among us
> Saying they will make Reformation.
> But yet as now more vices never reigned,
> As pride, envy, false dissimulation,
> Deceit, adultery, and fornication,
> Theft, robbery, slaughter, oppression of the poor,
> Of policy plain alteration.
> Of wrongful gear now no man taketh care.
> They think it well that they the Pope do call
> The Antichrist, and Mass idolatry,
> And then eat flesh upon the Fridays all:
> That they serve God right then accordingly,
> Though in all things they live most wickedly.
> But God commanded us his law to keep,
> First honor him, and then have charity
> With our neighbor, and for our sins to weep.

Both sides, Maitland concluded, had transgressed God's laws and should be held equally accountable for Scotland's troubles.[8]

What emerges most clearly from this poetic assessment is that Maitland was not interested in religious controversy as such. What did concern him, and very deeply, were the moral, political, and social consequences of the religious strife which the Reformation had brought to Scotland. Although he apparently had no driving urge for an active public career for himself and occasionally seemed a bit baffled by the political ambitions of his sons, there can be no doubt about the depth of his interest in the public weal. This patriotism, in the best sense of that much misused word, runs through most of his verse and shows itself in a good many different ways. The less elevated forms were there; for example, Maitland obviously disliked foreign influence in Scotland. The Wars of the Congregation

8 *Ibid.*, pp. 40–42.

were deplorable in themselves, he felt, but worse still was the foreign intervention which would inevitably result:

> I cannot sing for the vexation
> Of Frenchmen and the Congregation
> That has made trouble in this nation
> And many bare biging [building].
>> In this new year I see but war,
>> No cause to sing.
>> In this new year I see but war,
>> No cause there is to sing.
> I have no will to sing or dance
> For fear of England and of France.
> God send them sorrow and mischance
> Because of their coming.[9]

His opinions on this score did not change over the years. During the civil wars
of the 1570's, in a moving plea to both sides to settle their differences, he
urged the King's faction to

> Think on the words King Edward spoke to Bruce:
>> Have we naught else to do
>> But win a realm for you?

And to the Queen's partisans, who thought of asking France to send troops,
Maitland warned,

> Remember how they pleased you before.
> . . . .
>> Ere you were of them quit
>> You had enough ado.[10]

What he wanted was that Scotland be let alone – that she be allowed to go her
way in isolation without interference from any quarter:

> I pray God I hear tell
> We agree among ourselves,
> And then that all this whole country
> Of France and England both were free,
>> With them no more to mell [meddle].[11]

9 'On the New Yeir,' *The Maitland Quarto Manuscript*, ed. W. A. Craigie, Scottish
   Text Society publication (Edinburgh, 1920), p. 13b.
10 'Of Unione amangis the Lordis,' *Folio*, i, 310.
11 'Aganis the Weiris,' *ibid.*, p. 307.

What gave France and England their opportunity to intervene, of course, was the political confusion and strife which accompanied the religious revolution. Maitland never ceased to inveigh against this aspect of the Reformation. It was in fact this, and not the question of the idolatry of the Mass, which concerned him. The burden of a great deal of his poetry is contained in the first two lines of 'Aganis the Divisioun of the Lordis': 'O living lord, that made both heaven and hell,/From us expel this cruel civil war.'[12]

The title of this poem is significant. Maitland held both Catholics and Protestants responsible for Scotland's troubles. But within each faction the real culprits were the aristocratic leaders, who ought to have had the weal of the country at heart but who had completely lost sight of the common good. In fact, in Maitland's view, the blame for Scotland's unhappy state rested almost exclusively with the aristocracy. As the poem just cited says,

> What is the cause of all this great confusion,
> But the division of lords most potent
> In land and rent . . .[13]

Worse still, for many of these men, religious zeal or political principles were mere pretexts for the pursuit of ancient feuds or for simple greed. During the struggles of the 1570's between the partisans of the infant James VI and the deposed Queen Mary, Maitland put the point this way:

> Some have dissembled, yet proud in their conceit,
> But others spy out well enough their gait [way].
> Neither for king's nor queen's authority
> They strive, but for particularity,
> That cannot be content
> With their own land and rent
> As their fathers were before,
> Unless they fill their hands
> With other men's lands,
> Gear, victual, and store.[14]

The ravages of the civil war descended on Maitland himself, but he made very little of his own losses in his verse. In fact, one is inclined to wonder whether he would have mentioned them at all if it had not been for the fact that one of his properties was the barony of Blyth, which gave him a chance for an obvious play on words:

---

12 *Ibid.*, p. 303.
13 *Ibid.*, p. 304.
14 'Of Unione amangis the Lordis,' *ibid.*, p. 311.

Blind man, be blithe, though you be wronged,
Though Blyth be plundered, take no melancholy.
Thou shalt be blithe when they shall be hanged
That have despoiled Blyth so maliciously.[15]

Again and again he returned to the theme of the ruin the war was causing and the responsibility of the nobility for its continuance. All of these poems ended with a plea for peace and concord. The following is typical:

I pray to him that is lord of lords:
Bring all our lords to one perfect concord,
And with thy grace their spirits all inspire,
Among them kindle of charity the fire,
All rumor and envy
And faults passed by,
To be forgotten clean,
That justice' execution
For wickedness' punition
May on this land be seen.[16]

Maitland came gradually to realize that the chief sufferers from the civil war were the common people. During the Wars of the Congregation he evidently did not consider their plight very serious; his remarks were conventional and not very deeply felt.

God grant His grace to the inferiors
Of this poor realm, their quarrel to consider,
And to obey their superiors,
So that our head and lieges do confidder [confederate]
In peace and love for to remain together.
Then were we quit of all the men of war,
That all true folk from Berwick to Baquhidder
May live in rest unrobbed in this new year.[17]

Ten years later it was a different story. Maitland then showed far more concern about the disasters which had overtaken his social inferiors:

It is a pity to hear tell
How the poor commons of this land
From wrong cannot defend themselves
From reif [robbery] and spulze [despoiling] by some band

---

15 'The blind Baronis comfort,' *ibid.*, p. 43.
16 'Of Unione amangis the Lordis,' *ibid.*, p. 312.
17 'Of the Assemblie of the Congregatioun,' *ibid.*, p. 33.

Of soldiers of some side,
That none dare walk nor ride
For troubling of some wicked hand.
I know not how this realm shall stand
And scoundrels walk so wide.[18]

Maitland even devoted a whole poem to the subject: 'Aganis Oppressioun of the Commounis.'[19] The ordinary man was in a very bad way, Maitland said, but the civil war was not altogether to blame. Landlords had become much more oppressive. Rents had risen, and evictions for non-payment had naturally increased. 'Teinds' (tithes) that formerly were enjoyed by tenants had been appropriated by the landlords, especially those on the lands of the Catholic Church which had 'come in great temporal men's hands' – one of the undesirable features of the Reformation. But nowhere did Maitland suggest that the remedy for this situation lay in the hands of the oppressed. The lords, he said, must open their eyes to the situation and, for their own good, improve the lot of the ordinary man: 'Rich commons are right profitable /When they to serve their lord are able.'

Maitland was not an advocate of social reform; it never occurred to him to question the existing social structure. In fact, if anything, he attributed to that structure a fixity and permanence which it no longer possessed by the later sixteenth century. Henry Killigrew was overstating the case in his oft-quoted remark that the great nobles' power was in decay.[20] But it is certainly true that, relatively, their power was very much less than it had been a hundred years earlier. Maitland was not aware of this decline; he repeatedly blamed the aristocracy for all of Scotland's troubles, which he felt would be ended if only the lords would agree among themselves.

The reforms that Maitland did favor, therefore, were primarily administrative, and to achieve them he called upon the powers that be. As might be expected from one of his profession, improvement in the administration of justice was dear to him. In a singularly graceless poem he made several concrete proposals for reform.[21] The chief problem, as he saw it, was the excessive amount of time it took to get a case tried. This delay was extremely expensive for the rich; and, as for the rest,

The poor folk say that they for lack of spending
Must leave the law, it is so long in ending.
Long process them to poverty hath brought.

18 'Aganis the Weiris,' *ibid.*, p. 305.
19 *Ibid.*, pp. 331–332.
20 Nov. 11, 1572, Killigrew to Burghley, *CSPS* iv, 432..
21 'Complaint aganis the lang Law-sutes,' *Folio*, i, 429–431.

To remedy this situation Maitland proposed an increase in both the number and the quality of the senators of the College of Justice and – what was perhaps a reflection on the honesty of some of his colleagues – an increase in their stipends. The present fees, he said, were not paid regularly and fully. Even if they were, they would not be adequate, since 'What cost one pound before now costs three.' Maitland suggested that the money for the increased stipends could be obtained from the property of the old Church. Unfortunately such a solution was not politically feasible; the aristocrats who had laid hands on so much of that property were too powerful to be compelled to loosen their grasp.

Nowhere else in his poetry did Maitland attempt to deal with any comparable administrative problem; nowhere else did he make any precise proposals for reform. For, in fact, Richard Maitland was not fundamentally a reformer. He was, after all, already an old man before he began to write: he seems not to have started writing poetry before he reached sixty, although he doubtless began his activities as a collector of other people's verse much earlier.

Through his poetry there runs a very strong streak of nostalgia. It is backward-looking verse, the product of a man who had seen happier days in his youth, when he could stand apart from the political strife in which his aspiring sons were now involving him.

> Where is the blitheness that hath been
> Both in town and country seen
> Among lords and ladies schein [fair],
> Dancing, singing, game and play.
> But now I know not what they mean.
> All merriness is worn away.[22]

In every respect things had been better in our fathers' day, Maitland reminisced, both in trivial things, such as ladies' dress and behavior:

> Some will spend more, as I hear say,
> On drugs and spices in one day
> Than would their mothers in a year.[23]

and in serious matters:

> Treason is the most shameful thing
> That may in any country reign,
>   And should be hated most:
> But now in this unhappy time,

22 'Satire on the Age,' *ibid.*, p. 37.
23 'Satire on the Toun Ladyes,' *ibid.*, p. 299.

So many smitten with that crime
  That few dare others trust.[24]

Men's characters had decayed. There was 'Na Kyndnes at Court without Siller': the cash nexus had replaced the old ties of kinship.[25] Men were false, greedy, and ungrateful:

This world so false is, and unstable,
Of greediness insatiable,
In all estates such doubleness,
To find true friends few are able,
For kept is no old kindness.[26]

The prevailing vice was greed:

For greediness now guideth all estates,
Instructing them with covetous conceits,
Saying to some, why do you lack this land,
This tack, this farm, that lies so near at hand?
It for to get I can find twenty gaits [ways].[27]

Sometimes Maitland's sense of the times being out of joint led him to despair:

There was one Judas in that time
For silver did his master sell.
But now are smitten with that crime
A thousand more than I can tell
That do within this country dwell,
Would sell their souls, as I ween,
For gear unto the devil of hell,
In this worst world that e'er was seen.[28]

Usually, however, his mood was much more calm and resigned. Being gloomy, he judged, did no good:

Let us be blithe and glad,
My friends all, I pray:
To be pensive and sad,
Nothing it help us may.[29]

24 'Aganis Tressoun,' *ibid.*, p. 333.
25 *Ibid.*, pp. 335–336.
26 'On the Warldis Ingratitude,' *Quarto*, p. 82b.
27 'Advyce to Kyndnes,' *Folio*, i, 315.
28 'On gude Friday,' *Quarto*, p. 22b.
29 'Advyce to lesom Mirriness,' *Folio*, i, 320.

He was even able to joke, albeit a bit wryly, about his losses in the wars; recompense, he felt, would be granted him in heaven. He wrote charmingly of old age, warning old men against playing the gallant. As for himself, he said, he was no longer up to engaging in amorous pursuits:

> The fairest wench in all this town,
> Though I had her in her best gown,
>   Right bravely braild [arrayed],
> With her I might not play the loon,
>   I am so old.[30]

It was only natural, in view of this conservative, backward-looking attitude, that Maitland should have put very little stock in the possibilities of useful political action in the direction of reform, especially on the part of people such as himself, who were not members of the aristocracy. He had no objection to his sons' making careers for themselves at court, and he wrote a Polonius-like poem about how they should behave there: 'The Laird of Lethingtounis Counsale to his Sone Beand in the Court.'[31] It is full of the usual platitudes: keep good company, watch your tongue, tell the truth, avoid flattery and gambling and pride, be loyal to the prince. No one could take exception to this guidance. But there follows one piece of advice which well summarizes Maitland's attitude toward political activity, advice which none of his sons would heed:

> Beware in giving of a high counsel
> In matters great and doubtful specially,
> Which by the working of the world may fail,
> Though it seem never so apparently.
> Behold the world's instability
> That never still within one state doth bide,
> But changeth aye, as do the moon and sea.
> He ruleth well, that well in court can guide.

Here speaks the cautious man, the man afraid to take chances, to accept responsibility. The 'world's instability' was so great that positive action or advice would inevitably lead to trouble. Much better would it be for one to do nothing, to say nothing, to let others take responsibility; then, if things went badly, one could not be held accountable. Perhaps, under certain circumstances, this could be considered sound advice. His sons, however, refused to accept it, fundamentally because they did not agree with their father that 'To govern all and rule be not our bent.' They firmly believed that it was.

30 'Solace in Age,' *ibid.*, p. 330.
31 *Ibid.*, pp. 21–24.

The image that emerges from Maitland's self-portrait is that of the conservative *politique* – if one may use that word to describe such a reluctant politician. His principal concerns in public life were with social peace, the preservation of the traditional ordering of society, and the popular welfare. His views were conventional – commonplace, if you will – and, as often as not, were expressed in a commonplace way. The essential point to make about them, however, is that they were not the views of a man passionately concerned about religion. Maitland was pious enough, but he did not believe that religious controversy should be allowed to disrupt the public peace. He, like Erasmus, deplored the fact that the apple of discord had been thrown into the world, although, unlike Erasmus, he placed most of the responsibility on the old Church for its failure to reform itself, rather than on the Protestants.

Maitland's views are significant in two respects. First, they influenced – they could not help but influence – the political attitudes of his sons. Both William and John Maitland rose to the highest offices in the state. Both were extremely able men. Burghley, no mean judge, called William 'the flower of the wits of Scotland' and John 'the wisest man in Scotland.' Both were *politiques* through and through, William so much so that he took too lightly the influence which religious considerations might have on the ordinary man and made several serious political miscalculations as a result. John was equally a *politique*, although, warned by his brother's mistakes, he took much more account of the kirk and did his best to win its support for his efforts to strengthen the authority of the crown. The careers of both men demonstrate over and over again that in their general political outlook they were true sons of their father.

The similarity of Richard Maitland's views to those of his sons is obvious and easy to measure. It is much more difficult to be precise about what his opinions show about the nature of the Scottish Reformation, because the evidence is so largely negative. What Maitland did not say is more significant than what he did say. His belief that Christianity is primarily a matter of ethics and his lack of concern with religious issues as such confirm the views of Professor Donaldson which were quoted at the beginning of this essay. They also suggest that, in common with most revolutions, the religious upheaval in Scotland was brought about by a minority and opposed by a minority, that the majority of people were not concerned with the issues which were dear to the hearts of John Knox and Ninian Winzet. The era of the Reformation, in Scotland as in England, was not a religious-minded age. The succeeding age, the era of the Counter-reformation, of Puritan and Jesuit, certainly was. But in the Scotland of John Knox the Covenanting mentality simply did not exist, save in Knox himself and some few who thought like him – and that is one reason why Knox, in his *History*, saved some of his most deeply felt criticism for those whom he regarded as backsliding Protestants, like the earl of Moray.

It is this widespread apathy respecting matters of theological difference and church organization which gives the Scottish Reformation its peculiar character. It helps to explain many things: the continuity which Professor Donaldson stresses; the relatively small numbers of people engaged on each side in the Wars of the Congregation;[32] the tergiversations of people like Châtelherault, who was far more concerned with the welfare of the house of Hamilton than with the welfare of whatever religion he was professing at any given time; the willingness of a patently sincere Protestant like Moray to allow the Queen to have her Mass. It also helps to explain a good deal of Mary's outlook and policy, including her belief that she could get away with marrying Bothwell by Protestant rites. The existence of this apathy has been overlooked in the past by most scholars, because the history of this period was written in the first instance by religious partisans like Knox and David Calderwood and because we, as historians, have fallen victim to our own clichés, to those sweeping generalizations which we like to use in the opening paragraphs of chapters of text-books or in the first (or last) five minutes of an undergraduate lecture. Thus we tell our classes – and, indeed, we believe – that medieval Europe was 'primarily a religious community' and that the transition to modern times was marked by a 'process of secularization,' to quote a well-known textbook.[33] This assertion is no doubt true – up to a point. Insofar as it suggests, however, that the process of secularization was a steady and irreversible affair, it is misleading. It has made us assume that, because the men of the Counter-reformation were preoccupied with religious questions, the men of the Reformation must have been so too. But this conclusion does not necessarily follow. Charles V, Thomas Cromwell, Paul III, for example – how closely do they resemble Philip II, Francis Walsingham, Pius V? So it was in Scotland: the age of Mary and Moray and Knox was not the age of Alexander Henderson and Johnston of Wariston.

Now it may well be objected that this essay has done precisely what its author has just been complaining of, that it has constructed a sweeping generalization about the religious apathy of the period of the 1550's and 1560's in Scotland on the flimsiest scaffolding, the writings of one man, who may not even have been typical of his class. Certainly Maitland's avocation of writing and collecting poetry was atypical, nor is there any way of showing how many lairds shared his views. Nevertheless, an examination of the poetical satires that were turned out on broadsheets during this period suggests that Maitland's habit of viewing the Reformation in non-religious terms was widely shared by ethically minded men like himself, as well as by those who, like the Regent Morton, were a good deal less concerned with living a Christian life. In the outburst of poetical indignation which followed upon the murder of Moray, for example, the political motivations and consequences of the deed were the aspects of the affair that received the

---

32 This point is stressed by W. L. Mathieson, *Politics and Religion: A Study in Scottish History from the Reformation to the Revolution* (Glasgow, 1902), i, 67–70; he, too, suggests widespread apathy as the explanation.

33 R. R. Palmer, *A History of the Modern World*, 2nd edn. (New York, 1956), p. 44.

most stress.[34] What is put forward in this essay is nothing more than the most tentative kind of hypothesis, which has been brought to mind by a reading of Sir Richard Maitland's poetry. Far more work needs to be done before this hypothesis can be either substantiated or disproved. But it does not appear to do violence to the facts, which point, the more the Age of Reformation is studied, to the conclusion that everywhere, not just in England, politics was the decisive force. Henry VIII and his entourage were not unique in their time.

34 *Satrical Poems of the Time of the Reformation*, ed. J. Cranstoun, Scottish Text Society publication (Edinburgh, 1891), i, nos. 12–23.

3

Mary Queen of Scots:
The Next Assignment

What is there to say about Mary Queen of Scots that has not been said in the past four hundred years? A spate of publications appeared a decade ago to commemorate the dolorous stroke of 1587; with one exception the truly original work that appeared dealt with Mary's times rather than with Mary herself – for example, Margaret Sanderson's splendid series of sketches of *Mary Stewart's People*,[1] and some of the essays that appeared in the *Innes Review*.[2] The one exception is Jenny Wormald's prosecutorial *Mary Queen of Scots: A Study in Failure*,[3] a book which is not really a biography but a study of kingship in Scotland, Mary's place in the long line of Stewart rulers, and her inability to measure up to the requirements of the job. This is a very controversial book, which has been both lavishly praised and severely criticized.[4] It is also a brief book, hastily written in order to meet the deadline of the quartercentenery. But it, along with Gordon Donaldson's remarkable prosopographical analysis of Mary's supporters (and opponents), *All the Queen's Men*,[5] points the way to the next assignment in Marian scholarship. We have had enough of Mary's personal tragedy. What is needed is an in-depth study of Mary's household and court in Scotland, the influence of the court in politics, and the workings of her government. Whoever undertakes this analysis should emphasize one aspect of Mary's career which previous scholars – Wormald, Donaldson, Antonia Fraser, Michael Lynch[6] – have suggested but not made explicit. It is a central fact of her reign, and a major key to her failure. In Scotland Mary Queen of Scots was a foreigner.

A foreigner. All the evidence makes this abundantly clear. She was French. Her mother, Mary of Guise, was a Frenchwoman; she never knew her father, King James V. At the age of five she was taken to France, to be raised as the future queen of France. The oneness of French and Scots, of king-dauphin and

1 Edinburgh, 1987.
2 These have been published separately: *Mary Stewart, Queen in Three Kingdoms*, ed. Michael Lynch (Oxford, 1988).
3 London, 1988.
4 See, e.g., John Guy's laudatory review, *Times Literary Supplement*, 29 July – 4 Aug. 1988, 835, and Michael Lynch's strictures, *Journal of Ecclesiastical History* xli (1990), 69–73. For my views see *Catholic Historical Review* lxxiv (1988), 618.
5 London, 1983.
6 Antonia Fraser, *Mary Queen of Scots* (New York, 1971). M. Lynch, 'Queen Mary's Triumph: the Baptismal Celebrations at Stirling in December 1566', *SHR* lxix (1990), 1–21.

queen-dauphine, was a *Leitmotiv* of the court of Henri II.[7] The Guises were her family, much more so than the Stewarts, as the bequests she made in 1566 if she should die in childbirth clearly show.[8] She spoke French, she wrote in French, her library was mostly French, she surrounded herself with French servants to whom she was always very close, and with Scots who had French connections. Fraser, in her chapters on Mary's upbringing in her fine biography, points out that the Scots who accompanied the little girl to France in 1548, save for the four Maries, were carefully got rid of, including, eventually, her governess, the attractive Lady Fleming (an aunt: a bastard of James IV, and the mother of one of the Maries), who proved too attractive to Henri II, and too indiscreet about it, to please Henri's mistress, Diane de Poitiers.[9] When Mary returned to Scotland she brought her French servants with her, and paid some 250 of them out of her income as queen dowager of France.[10] Among them was her secretary, Pierre Raulet, who spent much time journeying to and from France with the queen's letters. When he fell from favour in December 1564 Mary – fatally – replaced him with David Riccio.[11] Mary longed for news from France, and followed events there as closely as possible. There was the terrible day when she learned of the murder of her uncle the duke of Guise. She wept for weeks; Queen Elizabeth's comforting letter, which the English agent Thomas Randolph had solicited, did not stem the flow of tears. Randolph described how he, the earl of Argyll, and Mary's austere brother the earl of Moray, worked on her and finally 'wrung out a laughter or two', which, Randolph said, caused her ladies to look more kindly on him.[12] Mary's heart was still in her *chère France*.

As with her servants, so with her court: it was French, as French as Mary could make it without peopling it with French nobles and courtiers.[13] Her three Guise uncles, who accompanied her to Scotland in 1561, all went home within six months, though not before the marquis d'Elboeuf made himself notorious by venturing out one night during the Christmas season with Mary's brother Lord John Stewart and the earl of Bothwell to force their attentions on a woman who was reportedly the earl of Arran's mistress. The queen was not amused.[14] The key to understanding Mary's court lies with the

7 On this point see M.H. Merriman, 'Mary Queen of France', in Lynch, *Mary Stewart*. 30–52.
8 See *Inventaires de la Royne Descosse*, ed. Joseph Robertson, Bannatyne Club (Edinburgh, 1833).
9 Fraser, *Mary*, 44, 61–2.
10 Donaldson, *Queen's Men*, 66–7, provides a list of the most important of these servants. Fraser stresses Mary's closeness to them; *Mary*, 206. See also M. Greengrass, 'Mary, Dowager Queen of France', in Lynch, *Mary Stewart*, 173–7.
11 15 Dec. 1564, Thomas Randolph to William Cecil, *CSPS*, ii, 101.
12 18 Mar., 1 Apr. 1563, Randolph to Cecil, *CSPS*, i, 689, ii, 1–4.
13 Fraser, *Mary*, 203.
14 See *ibid.*, 196–97. Bothwell disliked Arran, and undoubtedly instigated the prank; the others went along for fun. Lord John was about to marry Bothwell's sister, which helps to explain his presence.

four Maries, who were as French by upbringing as Mary herself, and their connections.[15] Mary Beaton and Mary Seton had French mothers, Mary Livingston a French stepmother, while Mary Fleming, as explained, was a cousin whose mother, if not French, had been the French king's mistress. Her brother, Lord Fleming, was the queen's chamberlain, her sister the wife of Lord Livingston, Mary Livingston's brother. Lord Seton was the master of the queen's household. Mary Beaton's father was in the queen's household in France; her aunt, one of James V's mistresses, was the mother of the queen's half-sister Jean, countess of Argyll, who, after the Maries, was probably the queen's closest female confidante. Mary frequently visited the Livingstons and the Setons, who lived near Edinburgh. It was an extremely closely-knit group. The only others who were close to the queen were her half-siblings: Lady Argyll and two of her brothers, Lord Robert and her favorite, Lord John. Both the brothers had spent a good deal of time in France. Randolph notes as early as October 1561 that Lord John, with his 'leaping and dancing', was in high favour. He was to marry Bothwell's sister – 'some say', added Randolph, 'that he [Bothwell] is near sib unto her grace', a reference to the scandalous story, which Knox hints at, that his father was sexually involved with Mary of Guise.[16] Lord John named his son Francis, after Mary's first husband, and to her great sorrow died young. Lord Robert, the future earl of Orkney, was almost as close to the queen, and was the only man of rank present at the supper party in Holyrood that was fatal to David Riccio.

This was the core of the court. There were others, of course. Donaldson points to a number of men of lesser rank who had places there and whom the queen favoured, like Sir Simon Preston of Cragmillar, at whose castle the famous conference took place in the autumn of 1566, and Sir James Melvill of Halhill, that most ingratiating of men. And, in the later years, two much more important figures, the earls of Bothwell and Huntly. Neither appeared on the scene until 1565, after Mary forgave Huntly for the sins of his father (who had died in arms against the queen in 1562 and had been posthumously forfeited), and Bothwell for his own; he promptly married Huntly's sister. But the heart of Mary's circle was always the Maries and their kin until Riccio, disastrously, was added to it.

There are two aspects of this French-connected royal circle that are worth underlining. First, it was quite separate from the political establishment, the privy council and the queen's senior officials, whose principal figures were her brother Moray and the secretary of state, Maitland of Lethingon. These two men were often at court, of course – Maitland eventually married Mary Fleming – but they were not the queen's intimates. And those intimates were not much involved in politics. True, Lord Seton and, later, Preston of

---

15　Donaldson develops this point; see *Queen's Men*, 58–60. Much of what follows is based on chap. 4 of this remarkable book.

16　John Knox, *History of the Reformation in Scotland*, ed. W. C. Dickinson, 2 vols. (New York, 1950), i, 71, 322. *CSPS* i, 561–4.

Craigmillar, became provosts of Edinburgh thanks to the queen's influence, and Melvill of Halhill went on diplomatic missions. But only once did one of Mary's inner circle become a major political player: David Riccio, and the result was disaster. Significantly Randolph, writing a week before Riccio's murder (to which he was hopefully looking forward) wrote that the earl of Morton, the lord chancellor, was to be deprived of the great seal, which, so the rumour went, 'shall be given to keep to David, as Rubie (*sic*: Rubay) had it', a reference to Mary of Guise's use of French administrators during her regency, which had so heavily contributed to her ruin.[17]

Secondly, Mary made no effort to expand her inner circle to include the great aristocrats whose attitude toward her would ultimately determine her success or failure as queen. As Wormald's numerous studies of Scottish kingship have made clear, the great Scottish landowners were willing to follow a ruler who was prepared to lead. And these men's support was more necessary now than ever before, because the alternative of relying, as James V had, upon the leaders of a wealthy and well-endowed church, was no longer available. And Mary did not lead. She was charming and affable to everyone, and men responded – the holy water of the court worked wonders, as John Knox irritably remarked. But being affable is not the same thing as having a policy, and Mary had no domestic agenda. She did not identify with her kingdom and its people in any way. All her energy, all her initiatives, were concentrated on finding the (from her point of view) best possible foreign husband and being recognized as Elizabeth's successor. Her hard work on this entirely personal set of priorities has obscured the fact that she had no domestic policy, nowhere to lead her great men. Her only domestic initiative, the lurch toward a re-Catholicizing policy in the latter part of 1565, was badly prepared, insufficiently supported, and dropped after the murder of Riccio, her principal agent. Since she had no direction in which to lead her great nobles, it is not surprising that she was content with her little circle of intimates at court.

Life at Mary's court was as much like that of the French court in which she grew up as she could make it. Masques abounded, on feast days and at wedding parties, even at the austere Moray's marriage to the Earl Marischal's daughter in 1562, and of course at her own wedding in 1565. Mary loved weddings and took a hand at arranging many at court – that of Lord Fleming, for instance[18] – an enthusiasm shared by her son King James. The celebrations at James's baptism in December 1566, the last great public Catholic ceremony in Mary's Scotland, imitated various French festivals, especially those at Bayonne in June 1565, which were staged to celebrate the meeting of the kings of France and Spain there.[19] On the night that was fatal to her husband Mary

17 6 Mar. 1566, Randolph to Cecil, *CSPS* ii, 264.
18 3 May 1562, Randolph to Cecil, *CSPS* i, 622.
19 Lynch, 'Queen Mary's Triumph', 5–15. Lynch, p. 14, points to the likely presence of a French court painter.

hurried back to Holyrood from Kirk O'Field because she had promised to attend he wedding masque of one of her French servants. The queen and her friends were young and full of fun – 'brought up in joyousity', in Knox's sour phrase[20] – and her court was a lively place. Some of the games even involved cross-dressing: one Sunday a team dressed as women, led by Lord Robert Stewart, defeated a team dressed in weird foreign costumes led by the marquis d'Elboeuf, at running the ring.[21] Above all there was the dancing. Mary loved to dance; she was good at it; she danced whenever possible, with her 'French fillocks, fiddlers, and others of that band'.[22] Knox thundered from the pulpit against this vile and immoral pastime. He was 'so hard on us that we have laid aside much of our dancing', wrote Randolph in the Christmas season of 1562, but it was probably the bad news from France that prompted Mary's decision, rather 'than for fear of him'.[23]

Not only did Mary imitate the lifestyle of the French court as best as she could with the resources available to her, she also patterned her governing style on that of France. Her model was the only one she knew, that of Henri II, who had been something of an adoptive father to her. Henri was very good with children, and Mary was evidently fond of him as well as of Henri's children, her playmates as she grew up. Henri was not the best of role models as a king, however. A handsome, phlegmatic, indecisive man, he was influenced by those close to him, Mary's kinfolk the Guises on the one hand, and the Montmorency faction on the other, not to mention his mistress Diane de Poitiers, and, surprisingly, in his later years, his wife, Catherine de Medici. Henri had a passion for hunting, which Catherine enjoyed and Diane did not. So Catherine talked to Henri on the hunt.[24]

Henri's court was decorous and elegant and, like all royal courts, peripatetic. So was Mary's – she was frequently on progress. Henri was more interested in outdoor than indoor activities, but he was a patron of the arts and, according to his biographer, the royal *joyeuse entrée* into his kingdom's great cities reached the peak of its splendor during his reign.[25] Mary could hardly imitate him here, though her official entry into Edinburgh was quite grand: 'fain would fools have counterfeited France', grumbled Knox.[26] Mary

20 Knox, *History* ii, 25.
21 7 Dec. 1561, Randolph to Cecil, *CSPS* i, 576.
22 Knox, *History*, i, 25.
23 *CSPS*, i, 674.
24 F.J. Baumgartner, *Henry II* (Durham, N.C., 1988), 65, 99.
25 *Ibid.*, 92. Merriman, 'Mary Queen of France', 37–40, contains an excellent account of his *entrée* into Rouen in 1550, one purpose of which was to welcome Mary of Guise on her visit to France to see her daughter.
26 Knox, *History* ii, 21. Edinburgh's Protestant authorities did what they could: they arranged for a Bible and psalm book to be presented to Mary, and according to Randolph, only the Catholic earl of Huntly's intervention prevented the burning of a priest in effigy. It would appear that Knox had little to grumble about. See A. A. Macdonald, 'Mary Stewart's Entry into Edinburgh: an Ambiguous Triumph', *Innes Review* xlii (1991), 101–10.

copied Henri's governing style in another important respect: she did not attend the meetings of the privy council. The French system was, of course, far more bureaucratic that that of Scotland. Real decisions got made early in the morning, right after the royal levée, by the king and a hand-picked group of his closest confidants, plus the four secretaries of state, a body regularized as the *conseil des affaires*. That was business for the day, as far as Henri was concerned. The formal *conseil privé*, a much larger group which included all the members of the *conseil des affaires* and a lot of other people, met in the afternoon – twice a week for judicial business. The king did not attend. Its decisions could be referred to him for approval, but that was not always necessary, especially where routine administration was concerned.[27] The Scottish privy council was very like the *conseil privé*, especially with respect to administrative and judicial business. It is not surprising that Mary did not attend. There was no Scottish equivalent of the *conseil des affaires*; Mary might have created one, but saw no reason to do so. The council even drew up a rota so that there would always be a group of councillors at her disposal for consultation, an action normally taken only during minorities. Mary paid it no heed. Wormald's picture of Mary sitting upstairs with her friends in Holyroodhouse while her councillors toiled on the nation's business down below is overdrawn, but only slightly.[28] Mary behaved as she did, not because she was innately lazy, but because the domestic problems that constituted the council's business did not interest her.

So French Mary lived and governed in the French fashion as queen of Scotland. She made no effort to conceal the fact that she was *Marie, reine d'Écosse*. Why have historians not understood this? The answer can be encapsulated in two words: John Knox. Knox did understand that Mary was French, which meant that she was rotten to the core. Over and over in the pages of his *History* he hammered at this point. Would that all the French had gone home after the disturbance at Mary's first Mass: 'for so had Scotland been rid of an unprofitable burden of devouring strangers, and of the malediction of God that has stricken and will yet strike for idolatry'.[29] When Mary went on progress, towns made gifts to her, 'and thereof were the French enriched'.[30] One of Mary's French servants was made pregnant by an apothecary, who attempted to abort the unwanted child by medical means, and succeeded in killing it 'in the mother's bellie'. They were found out, and hanged for infanticide.[31] Knox regarded this as one more of 'the fruits that she [Mary] brought forth of France'.[32] But Knox pushed his denunciations much too far. Mary, he wrote, encouraged the lovesick poet Châtelard (French, of

27 For the French governmental structure under Henri II see N. M. Sutherland, *The French Secretaries of State in the Age of Catherine de Medici* (London, 1962), chap. 4.
28 Wormald, *Mary*, 118–9.
29 Knox, *History* ii, 9.
30 *Ibid.*, 20.
31 21, 31 Dec. 1563, Randolph to Cecil, *CSPS* ii, 29–30, 33.
32 Knox, *History* ii, 102–3.

course), and, when he was discovered in her bedroom, wanted Moray to stab him to keep him from talking.[33] Knox told the scurrilous tale of the ball after Henri II's official entry into Orléans, with Mary's uncle the cardinal telling the king that he was, of course, entitled to first choice among all the wives and maidens present, and the cardinal would pick second. 'Such pastime to them is but joyousity, wherein our Queen was brought up', wrote Knox. 'We call her not a whore . . . but she was brought up in the company of the wildest whoremongers . . . What she was, and is, herself best knows, and God (we doubt not) will further declare'.[34]

This was simply unbelievable. The Châtelard incident horrified and frightened Mary, who afterwards insisted on Mary Fleming sharing her bed.[35] Whatever the king and the cardinal did or did not do in Orléans many years ago said nothing about Mary's morals. Historians simply did not, and do not, believe Knox's innuendos about Mary's sexual proclivities and behaviour. Knox declared that she was immoral because she was French: if he was wrong about the one, he was wrong about the other.

Knox was not the only observer of Mary's six years of active rule who saw that she was French. Thomas Randolph did – but the holy water of the court, which Knox so greatly feared, had its effect on him. Commenting in January 1562 on the financial settlement that required holders of church benefices to pay one third of their income to the government, Randolph remarked that the queen needed money. Prices were high, expenses were heavy, and she had been 'brought up in that licentious country where charges are measureless, and we [she] so accustomed unto those matters, that nothing liketh us, that is not as that is.'[36] A month later, when Mary's uncle d'Elboeuf cut short his stay is Scotland because his wife was ill, Randolph declared that everyone was glad to see him go – everyone, presumably, but Mary. He was unnecessary and expensive, said Randolph: his food allowance was £3 sterling a day.[37] But gradually Randolph softened. He got on well with Lord Livingston, who of all the Maries' male kin was closest to the queen.[38] Commenting on the affair of the apothecary and the servant girl, which followed the Châtelard incident by some months, he wrote, 'We have had many evil fortunes by our French

33   *Ibid.*, 68–9.
34   *Ibid.*, 35–6.
35   10 Mar. 1563, Randolph to Cecil, *CSPS* i, 688. Fraser's account of this business is a good one: *Mary*, 233–7. No one has ever suggested that there was a sexual relationship between the two women. Imagine what the historians would have said if, after the Gowrie conspiracy, King James had summoned Thomas Erskine or John Ramsay, the heroes of that mysterious day, into his bed!
36   *CSPS* i, 591–2. One use to which Mary put the money was to pay a pension to (in Knox's phrase) 'that poltroon and vile knave' David Riccio. In December 1565, at a time when she had cut off payments to the Protestant ministers, she used £50 to play cards. *Accounts of the Collectors of Thirds of Benefices*, ed. G. Donaldson, SHS (Edinburgh, 1949), 155, 180, 187.
37   28 Feb. 1562, Randolph to Cecil, *CSPS* i, 607.
38   19 Feb. 1566, Randolph to Cecil, *CSPS* ii, 256–7.

folk, and yet I fear we love them over well'.[39] It was the Maries who seduced Randolph, who mentioned them more and more frequently in his letters. He had an eye for Mary Beaton in particular. The queen noticed. She gave Randolph special treatment at court festivities,[40] seated him next to Mary Beaton at dinner, and arranged for him to partner her in a game of billiards against Mary and Darnley when that disastrous young man first appeared at court. 'My mistress Beaton and I' won, he reported, and Darnley paid up.[41] When Mary defied Elizabeth in order to marry Darnley, Randolph deplored the ruin that she had brought on herself, but he did not lash out at her for being French. Her failings were personal. He wrote in May 1565 of 'the pitiful and lamentable estate of this poor Queen . . . so altered in affection towards the Lord Darnley that she hath brought her honour in question, her estate in hazard, her country to be torn in pieces'.[42] The queen's Svengali was 'David', who 'works all' and is 'only governor to her good man', he wrote a month later. 'David', of course, was not French. Randolph sympathized with the sufferings of his friends the Maries, who 'are like to break their hearts to see their whole credit lost in court', he lamented in October.[43]

The terrible drama of Mary's last two years on her throne has helped to obscure the fact of her foreignness. Historians have correctly described what happened in personal terms: her fatal infatuation with a handsome fool to whom she was predisposed by the accident of his birth, and its ruinous consequences. She was predisposed to him because he could strengthen her claim to a better crown. A better crown, be it in London, Paris, or Madrid: that was her goal. She was rootless in Scotland, and by her own choice, an exotic bird whose hope, whether consciously formulated or not, was to stay in this unsophisticated place no longer than necessary. She cared nothing for Scotland as such: when she married the dauphin she consigned her country to the crown of France if she should die without children. She was never at home in Holyroodhouse; her heart was in Fontainebleau and Amboise. Counterfactual history is always problematical, but it seems likely that if her personal disaster had never happened, her Frenchness would have made trouble for Mary sooner or later. The Scots' escape from annexation to France had been too narrow and too recent for them to accept a French ruler without challenge.

The name we all use for her, Mary Queen of Scots (she always signed herself *Marie*) has helped to conceal her foreignness.[44] So, too, has the fact that

39 31 Dec. 1563, Randolph to Cecil, *ibid.*, 33.
40 See the description of the Twelfth Night festivities in 1564, when 'Mary Fleming was Queen', *ibid.*, 34.
41 7 Apr. 1565, Randolph to the earl of Bedford, *ibid.*, 142.
42 21 May 1565, Randolph to the earl of Leicester, *ibid.*, 166.
43 *Ibid.*, 171, 232.
44 Mary is the only ruler habitually identified with her country in this way. Her nearest competitor is Ferdinand of Aragon, who is just as often identified as half of Ferdinand-and-Isabella. 'Mary Queen of Scots' has been called that since, at latest, the eighteenth century and David Hume's history, and perhaps earlier.

during her personal rule in Scotland she was queen of only one country. It is a commonplace amongst the historians of early modern Europe that a foreign ruler is going to have difficulties – Philip II is an obvious case in point. Both Mary's son and grandson governed realms that perceived them as foreign. King James was able to cope well enough in England, while King Charles failed miserably in Scotland. In all these cases, however, the ruler had a native land where he was not a stranger. Mary, uniquely, did not: she was a foreigner in the land of her birth, in the only land that acknowledged her as sovereign.

Here, then, is the challenge for the next student of Mary's years in Scotland: treat her, not as Mary Queen of Scots, but as Marie de France, come, *faute de mieux*, to spend some time in the land where she was born. The result should be enlightening.

4
John Knox and his *History* (1966)

At the beginning of Professor W. C. Dickinson's foreword to his splendid edition of John Knox's *History of the Reformation of Religion within the Realm of Scotland* stands the following quotation from Thomas Carlyle: 'It is really a loss to English and even to universal literature that Knox's hasty and strangely interesting, impressive and peculiar Book, called the *History of the Reformation in Scotland*, has not been rendered far more extensively legible to serious mankind at large'.[1] Carlyle was quite right. Knox's work is, of course, known to students of the Reformation, and of Scottish history, and, presumably, to most of those who work in the Tudor period generally; but it deserves a much wider audience. It is an extraordinarily vigorous piece of writing, and it tells virtually all that is known about Knox. Were it not for this book, the great reformer would be a much paler and less regarded figure to the historians of the period than he now is. Of all the great leaders of the Reformation, only Martin Luther has left behind a comparable self-portrait.

The quality of Knox's *History* as history has caused considerable divergence of view. The reformer's admirers, M'Crie and Hume Brown, for example, have praised it almost without qualification.[2] At the other extreme stands Andrew Lang, who found Knox as intolerable as Queen Mary must have, and who devoted a book, *John Knox and the Reformation*, to the proposition that the *History* was slippery and untruthful. In these varying discussions of the *History* one problem has been almost entirely ignored: why Knox wrote the book at all. This is a question which historians usually do not ask of other historians, for obvious reasons. But Knox was not a historian by profession, and so in his case the question is worth asking. When the *History* and Knox's career as preacher and writer are considered with this in mind, the inescapable conclusion is that Knox wrote the *History* from compulsion, either interior or exterior, and that he was not really a historian at all.

This is not simply because Knox was biased. Of course he was biased, and cheerfully admitted it – in which he more nearly resembles the historians of this century than those of some intervening ages. In this post-Freudian era we all confess to bias, and no longer believe that exactly what happened can be found out and set down in such a way that historical work can stand for ages without rewriting. The crux of the matter is the author's state of mind. Thomas Macaulay and Karl Marx were equally convinced that they saw into

---

1 *John Knox's History of the Reformation in Scotland*, ed. W.C. Dickinson, 2 vols. (Edinburgh, 1949), i, p. xi.
2 The Rev. Thomas M'Crie (1811) and P. Hume Brown (1895) were biographers of Knox.

the true nature of mid-nineteenth-century industrial society; they were equally prejudiced; they each had a historical explanation of the evolution of that society. Yet Macaulay was a true historian and Marx was not: and why? Because Macaulay was genuinely concerned to determine the causes which brought about the society he so much admired, whereas Marx already knew the causes – or perhaps more properly the 'cause' – and used history merely to demonstrate the accuracy of his philosophical theory and, more importantly, to justify the course of action which he advocated for his own time and for the future.

Knox, like Marx, had a single-track philosophy of history. The hearts of men, their thoughts, and their actions, are in the hands of God. 'Worldly men may think that all this came but by misorder and fortune (as they term it)', wrote Knox of the disaster at Solway Moss in 1542, 'but whosoever has the least spunk of the knowledge of God may as evidently see the work of his hand in this discomfiture, as ever was seen in any of the battles left to us in register by the Holy Ghost'.[3] Oliver Sinclair, the defeated Scottish commander, was an enemy to God, to be sure; but the defeats suffered by the soldiers of the Lord in the Wars of the Congregation were equally His handiwork: 'God would not give the victory so suddenly lest that man should glory in his own strength'.[4] Similar references to particular providence can be found throughout the *History* and in the reformer's other writings. Knox was not a fool, and he knew the importance of worldly considerations to the weak instruments of the Lord. In writing to England in September 1559 to ask for money for the Congregation, he put it this way: 'If I did not perfectly understand their necessity, I would not write so precisely, for I nothing doubt to obtain of them, *by the authority of God's word*, what lieth in their power . . . but the knowledge of their poverty, and the desire which I have that the cause prosper, maketh me bold to speak my judgement'.[5] Yet the victory of the Congregation was God's. 'For what was our force? What was our number? Yea, what wisdom or worldly policy was into us, to have brought to a good end so great an enterprise? Our very enemies can bear witness. And yet in how great purity God did establish amongst us his true religion, as well in doctrine as in ceremonies!'[6]

Marx wrote history to demonstrate to a skeptical and hostile world the truth of his theories; Knox did not. There was no need to prove anything so evident as God's all-pervading providence. Furthermore Knox's mind was not primarily either expository or analytical; temperamentally he was an exhorter, a preacher of deeds and action, whose natural milieu was the pulpit. It is a pity that his sermons have not survived; they would give us more of the

3 *Knox's History*, i, 37.
4 *Ibid.*, i, 312.
5 *The Works of John Knox*, ed. D. Laing, 6 vols., Bannatyne Club and Wodrow Society (Edinburgh, 1846–64), vi, 80. I have modernised the spelling in the quotations from the *Works*, and have supplied the italics in this case.
6 *Knox's History*, ii, 3.

flavour of the man than the formal writing which he published. Beyond doubt the dullest of all his works is the dreary tract on predestination;[7] all his best work has the touch of the mob orator about it – the *Monstrous Regiment of Women*, for example.[8] He was an extemporaneous speaker, not given to committing his sermons to writing, as is known from the preface to the only sermon he ever published.[9] Knox himself realized where his talents lay, and this helps to explain why he steadily refused to publish the *History* during his own lifetime. After Mary's downfall the triumphant protestants, including the Regent Moray, were anxious that he publish. Knox wrote to Moray's secretary, John Wood, asking pardon of his friends that 'in that one head I play the churl, retaining to myself that which will rather hurt me, than profit them, during my days . . . and then it shall be in the opinion of others, whether it shall be suppressed, or comes to light'.[10]

Why then did this man, whose talents were essentially oral, write the *History* at all? Here the question of dating the time of writing of the various books of the *History* becomes crucial.[11] The first mention of the *History* comes in a letter of Knox to a friend in England, written on 23 October 1559,[12] just after the Congregation had 'deposed' the Catholic regent, Mary of Guise; the book's purpose, clearly, was propagandistic, to justify the action of the protestant party. The result of Knox's labours was the present Book II, which gives an account of events from the beginning of 1558 to November 1559. As the preface makes clear, the book was designed for two sets of readers: 'our brethren in all realms' – that is, England – so that they 'may understand how falsely we are accused of tumult and rebellion', and also 'our brethren, natural Scotsmen, of what religion soever they may be'. For those Scots who did not sympathise with Knox's religious goals, the appeal was a patriotic one: the Congregation sought 'the liberty of this our native country to remain free from the bondage and tyranny of strangers'.[13] And, indeed, throughout the first three books, especially in Book II, Knox harps upon this string: the protestant party is the patriotic party; the rule of Mary of Guise means subjugation by France.

The book was hastily and sloppily written; it was almost certainly completed in rough draft before the appearance of the English fleet in the Forth in January 1560, which signalised the open intervention of the English government and made the book in large part unnecessary. Until that open intervention, it was incumbent on Knox both to conceal the fact that he and his fellow-rebels were negotiating with England, and to pave the way for English

7 *Works*, v, 7–468.
8 *Works*, iv, 349–422.
9 It is reprinted in *Works*, vi, 229–73.
10 *Ibid.*, vi, 558. The letter is dated 14 Feb. 1567/8.
11 Dickinson discusses the problem with lucidity and acumen in his introduction; *Knox's History*, i, pp. lxxxviii–xcv.
12 *Works*, vi, 86–8.
13 *Knox's History*, i, 146.

intervention by making the Congregation's behaviour appear in the most favourable possible light. Hence the many omissions and misleading statements, some of which are perilously close to outright lies, which have been so severely criticized by Andrew Lang.[14] Hence too the steady insistence on the duplicity and injustice of Mary of Guise, insistence which was designed to justify the political (as opposed to the religious) logic behind the Congregation's renunciation of her authority: 'the Queen Regent denied her chief duty to the subjects of this realm, which was to minister justice unto them indifferently, to preserve their liberties from invasion of strangers'.[15] The book is to a considerable extent a scissors-and-paste job, rather like the later volumes of Sir Winston Churchill's war memoirs, consisting of documents held together by narrative passages. This is a boon to historians, but it is not very effective propaganda, and it was probably as well for the fortunes of the Congregation that they did not depend upon Knox's pen for success. When the need for publication passed, Knox put the book aside. In September 1560, two months after the final victory of the protestants and their English allies, the English agent Thomas Randolph raised the question of publication with Knox, who was politely evasive. He would send what he had written to Cecil. If the secretary liked it, he would continue, but 'he must have further help than is to be had in this country, for more assured knowledge of things passed than he hath himself, or can come by here'.[16] There is no evidence that he ever sent Cecil the manuscript.

Book II, then, was undertaken out of urgent necessity, and was written at a time when the fortunes of the Congregation were at a low ebb; it closes with the gloomy prayer; 'Look upon us, O Lord, in the multitude of thy mercies; for we are brought even to the deep of the dungeon'.[17] So it was with the rest of the *History*. Book III, which carried the story from November 1559 to the arrival of Mary in August 1561, was certainly written next. Just when Knox began it, and finished the first draft of it, is not entirely clear. The occasional dates inserted in the manuscript and marginalia of Book III (and of Books I and IV) are not conclusive, since Knox kept the manuscript by him and revised it from time to time. The revisions were extremely haphazard; they were mostly in the form of casual and venomous *obiter dicta*. For example, he concluded an account of a French success during the siege of Leith in 1560, which Mary of Guise went off to Mass to celebrate, as follows: 'But whoredom and idolatry agree well together, and that our Court can witness this day, 16 May 1566'.[18] Knox made no attempt to iron out the inconsistencies

---

14 See, for example, Lang's account of the truce of July 1559, A. Lang, *John Knox and the Reformation* (London, 1905), 140–50. For Knox's purposes in writing Book II, and for a scathing attack on its veracity, see Lang's article, 'Knox as historian', *SHR*, ii (1905), 113–30.
15 *Knox's History*, i, 250.
16 23 Sept. 1560, Randolph to Cecil, *Works*, vi, 121.
17 *Knox's History*, i, 271.
18 *Ibid.*, i, 319.

between Books II and III; he admitted in Book III what he had denied in Book II, that the Congregation was seeking help in England in July 1559. There was, in fact, almost no detectable revision of Book II at all, save for a few references – that to Queen Mary as a habitual liar, for instance, presumably added after her return in August 1561.[19]

The tone of Book III suggests that it was begun no earlier than the second half of 1563, that it was a product of Knox's steadily mounting dismay at the turn events had taken since Mary's return. From the beginning he was convinced of the queen's iniquity and of the hopelessness of any attempt to wean her away from her 'devilish opinion'. 'In her appeareth no amendment, but an obstinate proceeding from evil to worse', he wrote to his friend Mrs. Lock in October 1561.[20] What upset Knox was not the queen's idolatry, but the fact that so many of his erstwhile allies in the Congregation were prepared to countenance it for worldly reasons. Now for the first time Knox allowed his hatred of Mary of Guise to appear. He must have hated her when he wrote Book II, but in that book he carefully refrained from charging her with anything more than political immorality. Now her private character was slanderously and quite unjustly attacked.[21] These venomous assaults on Mary of Guise and her daughter, which run throughout Books I, III, and IV, are the worst blots on these books as history. There is nowhere near as much deliberately misleading writing as in Book II, although the account is always one-sided, papists are always described in extremely pejorative language, and Knox's memory occasionally plays him tricks, notably in the relation (in Book I) of the siege of St. Andrews after the murder of Cardinal Beaton in 1546.[22]

More significant, perhaps, than the slanders of Mary of Guise are the criticisms in Book III of the leaders of the protestant party: of the secretary, Maitland of Lethington, who mocked at Knox's preaching in August 1560, of Lord Erskine, who refused to sign the Book of Discipline on account of his Jezebel wife and his private greed, of the future earl of Moray because he would not agree to tell Queen Mary, when he, as the representative of the Congregation, went to her in France in the spring of 1561, that she could not hear Mass privately.[23] 'God, for his great mercy's sake, preserve us yet from further bondage, in the which we are like to fall if he provide not remedy, for our Nobility will yet remain blind still, and will follow her affections, come after what so may', Knox wrote in concluding his account of the band drawn up by the protestant party in April 1560; he was clearly referring to the state of affairs which obtained after Mary's return.[24] It is possible that Book III was

19 *Ibid.*, i, 192.
20 *Works*, vi, 130.
21 Instances are numerous and well known; perhaps the worst was the suggestion that James V was not Mary's father, *Knox's History*, i, 322.
22 On this point see Lang, *John Knox*, 23–7.
23 *Knox's History*, i, 335, 344, 354–5.
24 *Ibid.*, i, 317.

begun much later, that it, like Books I and IV, was a product of Knox's enforced retirement in the west during the months that followed the murder of Riccio in March 1566. But the restrained tone of the book – restrained at least, by comparison with the later two – suggests a somewhat earlier dating.

The problem of dating the writing of Books I and IV is somewhat simpler, save in one respect. They were both written between the spring of 1566 and the summer of 1567, probably at the beginning of this fifteenth-month period. The preface to Book I suggests that it was written before Book IV, since Knox speaks of having written of the events of 1558–61,

> with which the Collector and Writer for that time was content, and never minded further to have travailed in that kind of writing. But, after invocation of the name of God, and after consultation with some faithful [brethren concerning that which] was thought by them expedient to advance God's glory, and to edify this present generation and the posterity to come, it was concluded that faithful rehearsal should be made of such personages as God had made instruments of his glory, by opposing of themselves to manifest abuses, superstition, and idolatry; and, albeit there be no great number, yet are they more than the Collector would have looked for at the beginning, and therefore is the volume somewhat enlarged above his expectation.[25]

This passage has been quoted at length because it seems to cast some doubt upon the generally accepted view that Book I was written before Book IV. The preface to Book IV was written in May 1566[26]; if the task of writing Book I was as considerable as Knox implies, it is very doubtful that he could have completed it, even in draft, in two months. Furthermore Book I is almost all Knox's own narrative, save for a long passage from Foxe on the martyrdom of Wishart; there is a minimum of scissors-and-paste work. The preface to Book I suggests that Knox regarded Books I–III as a unit: the story of the first triumph of the saints of the God over 'these bloody wolves who claim to themselves the title of clergy'[27] – which may account for the language quoted above. There is also internal evidence that parts of Book I were either written or revised after the completion of Book IV. For example, there are two references to the death of Darnley in Book I,[28] and none in Book IV. Perhaps the best guess is that the two books were written simultaneously.

The two books may have been written very close together in point of time, but their purposes were entirely dissimilar. Book I is, as Knox says, an account of the coming of protestantism to Scotland, but it is much more than that. One of Knox's intentions, certainly, was to praise 'that blessed martyr of

25 *Ibid.*, i, 5–6.
26 *Ibid.*, ii, 4.
27 *Ibid.*, i, 6.
28 *Ibid.*, i, 44, 59.

God, Master George Wishart . . . a man of such graces as before him were never within this realm',[29] who in Knox's account becomes a sort of Christ-figure. Another of his purposes was to continue his attack on Mary of Guise, on her daughter – sometimes by implication, sometimes directly – and, of course, on the Roman Antichrist. Even here, in this account of things gone by, Knox gives vent to his wrath at the way in which the protestant leaders had allowed their victory in 1560 to slip from their hands. After describing his release from the French galleys in 1550, he points the moral: God looks after His own. 'This same blind generation, whether it will or not, shall be compelled to see that He will have respect to them that are unjustly pursued; that He will pardon their former offences; that He will restore them to the liberty of their country and commonwealth again'. And who are those who are unjustly pursued? Why, the murderers of 'that great abuser of this commonwealth, that poltroon and vile knave Davie . . . who all, for this just act, and most worthy of all praise, *are now unworthily left of their brethren* and suffer the bitterness of banishment and exile'.[30]

The italicised phrase above contains the key to Book IV, which carries the story from Mary's return down to the middle of 1564. There are numerous references, of course, to the personal, political, and religious iniquities of the queen, and to the devilish Roman harlot. But the real object of Knox's criticism is not Mary, not even worldly and sycophantic mockers like Lethington, but rather those earnest protestants, particularly the earl of Moray, who allowed themselves to be taken in by Mary. The estrangement between Moray and Knox began shortly after the queen's return, when Moray prevented a mob of protestant zealots from breaking up her private Mass; the two broke openly in May 1563, when the earl declined to allow the raising of any question of the legal establishment of protestantism in the parliament, and, according to Knox, from the worst of motives.

> The Earldom of Moray needed confirmation, and many things were to
> be ratified that concerned the help of friends and servants; and
> therefore they might not urge the Queen, for if they so did, she would
> hold no Parliament; and what then should become of them that had
> melled with the slaughter of the Earl of Huntly? . . . The matter fell so
> hot betwixt the Earl of Moray . . . and John Knox, that familiarly after
> that time they spoke not together more than a year and half.[31]

And Book IV ends with the sentence; 'In all the time the Earl of Moray was so formed to John Knox that neither by word nor write was there any communication betwixt them'.[32]

29 *Ibid.*, i, 60.
30 *Ibid.*, i, 112; italics mine.
31 *Ibid.*, ii, 78. The reference to Huntly is to the series of events that culminated in the battle of Corrichie in October 1562.
32 *Ibid.*, ii, 134.

The whole of Book IV is directed at Moray, and Knox wrote in dis-illusionment and bitterness of heart at the backsliding of the man on whom he had counted, above all others, to fight singlemindedly for the victory of Christ's evangel. Knox made his purpose clear in the preface. The godly had won a great triumph, which Knox had described in Books I–III, but now they were miserably dispersed; and why? 'Because . . . suddenly the most part of us declined from the purity of God's word, and began to follow the world; and so again to shake hands with the devil, and with idolatry'.[33] When Knox protested against Moray's stand on the queen's Mass, he was judged to be an unquiet spirit. 'My Lord, my Master, may not be thus used; he has that honour to be the Queen's brother; and therefore we will that all men shall understand that he must tender her as his sister; and whosoever will counsel him to displease her . . . shall not find him their friend; yea, they are worthy to be hanged that would so counsel him, etc.'[34] Moray had not even learned his lesson from the events of 1565; the Darnley marriage, the Chase-about Raid, and his own period of exile. He had been rescued from imminent forfeiture by the murder of Riccio, and yet now, in the middle of 1566, he unworthily allowed the murderers to remain in exile. Knox's attack was bitter, and at the same time reproachful – it was the criticism of a man who did not understand. 'God be merciful to some of our own', he wrote, 'for they were not all blameless that her wicked will was so far obeyed'.[35] There were no shades of grey in Knox's world; a man was either in the army of the Lord or in that of the Devil. He could not see the complexities and difficulties in Moray's position, and he could not fathom the intricacies of Moray's mental processes. He was, indeed, right on one point: Moray did not trust in the arm of the Lord alone to achieve the victory of Christ's evangel.

Book IV is incomplete. It ends abruptly with the sentence quoted above on the estrangement of Moray and Knox, which follows a long account of a debate between Knox and Lethington at the General Assembly of June 1564 on the right of the godly to revolt against an idolatrous magistrate. Knox planned to carry the story at least as far as the murder of Riccio;[36] he seems to have gathered some notes to that end; but he stopped, and wrote no more. He did not say why he stopped, but it is logical to suppose that it was for the same reason that obtained in 1560: the *History* was no longer necessary. The events of the first half of 1567 brought about a second triumph of the godly, and Moray, once again in the reformer's good graces, was regent for the infant James VI. Some gloating references to Mary's overthrow were added to the text here and there after June 1567, and there is further evidence of tinkering in 1571, when, with Moray dead at the hands of an assassin, and

33 *Ibid.*, ii, 4.
34 *Ibid.*, ii, 5.
35 *Ibid.*, ii, 22.
36 *Ibid.*, ii, 106.

Lethington, the 'father of all mischief',[37] at the head of a strong party of supporters of the deposed queen, it looked as if the *History* might be necessary after all. Whether these additions in 1571 indicated that Knox was seriously considering publication will never be known; his health was failing, and he died in the following year.

The conclusion is inescapable that Knox wrote these three books, not for the purpose of telling the story for the sake of posterity, not even for putting on record the justification of the behavior of the godly, as he had had in Book II, but rather that he wrote them as a sort of sermon, a sermon without an audience. Knox was a preaching man; to spread the word of God, to tell the truth as he saw it, was a compulsion with him, and he went on preaching to the end.[38] When he could preach to a live audience, he did not write; he only took to his pen when his voice was silent. As he himself said in the preface to his only published sermon, he considered himself 'rather called of my God to instruct the ignorant, comfort the sorrowful, confirm the weak, and rebuke the proud, by tongue and lively voice in these most corrupt days, than to compose books for the age to come'.[39] The whole of what might be called his publication record bears this out. After his return to Scotland in 1559, the only works he published, other than writings for a public purpose like the *Book of Common Order*, were the account of his disputation with the abbot of Crossraguel in 1562[40] and this one sermon, allegedly seditious, which he had delivered before Darnley in 1565; and in both cases he published in order to stop the circulation of what he regarded as lying rumours. Almost all of the work he published was turned out in the years 1553–9, the years of exile when he had no congregation in England or Scotland to preach to.

In like manner the *History* was written in those times when Knox could not preach. It is a preacher's book, a preaching book, one long inflammatory speech in behalf of God's truth as Knox saw it, interspersed with documents which, by breaking the flow of the narrative, tend to conceal that fact that it is a sermon. Because the documents are there, because of the vigour and force and humour of Knox's style, because of the bad taste, even, which is evidence of the quality of sixteenth-century polemic, the *History* is worth reading. But Knox was not a historian, and not merely because, unlike other historians, he did not thirst to see himself in print. Past events to him were worth transcribing only to glorify God, and to show His handiwork and the futility of opposing Him. Was not this one of the purposes of Scripture? Knox was the creature and agent of God, and must always be about his Master's business, preaching with his mouth when it was possible, with his

37 *Ibid.*, ii, 65. The phrase occurs in a marginal note dated 1571.
38 See, for instance, James Melville's well-known account of Knox in his last years at St. Andrews in *Autobiography and Diary of Mr James Melvill*, ed. R. Pitcairn, Wodrow Society (Edinburgh, 1842), 26, 33.
39 *Works*, vi, 229.
40 *Ibid.*, 149–220.

pen when it was not. His *History* is his literary monument, but he would not have thought it of very much worth. He would have preferred his countrymen to say of him what was said of Christopher Wren: *Si monumentum requiris, circumspice.*

5

The Fall of the Regent Morton:
A Problem in Satellite Diplomacy (1956)

ONE of the terms most frequently used in any present-day discussion of international relations is 'satellite'. A satellite is generally defined as a small or weak state dependent on some great power; and, in these days of ideological conflict, the implication is that the satellite shares the ideology of the great power. It is an axiom of power politics that a great power will acquire as many satellites as possible and never let any of them go, lest they gravitate toward some other unfriendly power. In the last few years we have seen how the Soviet Union has clung to East Germany and how the United States has applauded, if not actually fostered, a change of regime in Guatemala.

Ours is not the only age marked by ideological conflict between important powers and by satellite diplomacy. The later sixteenth century was a period of bitter ideological struggle between Catholic and Protestant throughout western Europe, a struggle whose climax was reached in the destruction of the Spanish Armada. The two antagonists in that conflict, England and Spain, each had problems in connection with their satellites. Spanish diplomacy in Italy in this period, for example, was that of a great power endeavouring – for the most part successfully – to keep its satellites in line.

For England the problem was not that of many satellites but of one – Scotland. Thanks to the Reformation, the age-old enmity between the two countries had been transformed into an uneasy alliance by the 1570's, after the deposition and imprisonment of Mary Queen of Scots. Mary had been replaced on the Scottish throne by her infant son, James VI, and the country was ruled by a series of pro-English regents, of whom the last was the earl of Morton. At the beginning of Morton's regency Elizabeth had sent an army into Scotland to help him capture Edinburgh castle, held by the supporters of Mary. Morton was a Protestant and a firm believer in the English alliance. He was particularly obnoxious to the deposed queen and her friends: among other things, he had discovered the famous Casket Letters. Yet, when Morton ran into political difficulties in the later 1570's, Elizabeth intervened on his behalf only with words, and she allowed her only satellite to fall into the hands of a party which, whatever its ultimate goals, was not favourably disposed toward England.

Two major explanations have been advanced for Elizabeth's behavior in this crisis. Froude attributes it to the queen's parsimony, treacherousness, and general stupidity. 'Every one but Elizabeth saw through the situation', he writes, '. . . all the Protestants in Scotland, peers and commons, were ready to take arms when the first English soldier had stepped . . . on Scottish soil.' Abandoning Morton to his fate 'made shipwreck of Elizabeth's honour.'[1] Conyers Read, in his study of Walsingham, rightly points out that Froude's assessment of the strength of the pro-English party at this juncture is not supported by the evidence, but he then proceeds to go to the opposite extreme. Elizabeth, he says, might have been willing to send an army into Scotland to save Morton if the latter had had enough supporters to serve as a suitable front. 'Elizabeth might have consented to join forces with any respectable number of his adherents. She was not prepared to fight *the whole Scottish nation* on his behalf.'[2] Now it is simply not true to say that an English army would have been opposed by 'the whole Scottish nation' in this situation. Two of the greatest earls in Scotland, Angus and Mar, were open supporters of Morton, and there is evidence that there were others who were prepared to support the fallen regent, had England openly committed herself to his cause. The answer, then, must lie elsewhere.

A large part of that answer can be found in the situation on the continent of Europe in the later 1570's. It was from this direction, not from Scotland, that Elizabeth believed England to be threatened now. The danger lay in the possibility of a Catholic crusade led by France and Spain against England, the leading Protestant state in Europe. Elizabeth's task, therefore, was to prevent an alliance between France and Spain and also, if possible, to keep them busy elsewhere so that they could not attack England. The religious civil wars in France, which reduced that country to a condition of distracted near-impotence for thirty years, was a great help to the queen. Spain was the real threat. In fact, the French considered themselves to be menaced by Spain too, and the Anglo-French alliance of 1572 was the result. In view of French weakness, however, this alliance afforded but little protection to England.

Elizabeth's chief weapon in dealing with Spain was the revolt in the Netherlands. The queen's policy towards the Netherlands was extremely complex and constantly shifting and is not easy to summarize briefly. Three things the queen wished to avoid. Worst of all would be a complete Spanish victory, which would free Philip of Spain for an attack on England. Almost as bad would be successful French intervention, turning the Netherlands into a satellite of France. On the other hand, a certain amount of French intervention would be useful: it would embroil France with Spain and keep Philip from getting the upper hand. It would also make it unnecessary for England herself to intervene – the third eventuality Elizabeth wished to avoid.

1 J.A. Froude, *History of England from the Fall of Wolsey to the Defeat of the Spanish Armada*, 12 vols. (New York, 1870), xi, 302, 310, 326.
2 C. Read, *Mr. Secretary Walsingham and the Policy of Queen Elizabeth*, 3 vols. (Cambridge, Mass., 1925), ii, 172. Italics mine.

Matters in the Netherlands reached a crisis in 1578. The pacification of 1577 had broken down, and Don John of Austria, Philip's governor, was making military headway against the rebels. A strong faction in France, headed by the duc d'Alençon, younger brother of Henri III, wanted to intervene. In the summer of 1578 Elizabeth decided to encourage French intervention under Alençon's leadership and simultaneously renew the old negotiations for Alençon's marriage to herself. In this way she could avoid direct English involvement, which some of her advisers were urging on her, and at the same time she could control Alençon, who would certainly do nothing to damage English interests if he were the prospective husband of the queen of England.[3]

This English preoccupation with the Netherlands must be borne in mind in any consideration of Elizabeth's Scottish policy. Scotland must be kept as a satellite if possible, and that meant supporting Morton. Spain must be kept out at all costs. But what if France, England's ally – and, of course, in bygone days the 'auld ally' of the Scots against England – took to dabbling in Scottish politics again? Could England openly oppose France in Scotland and retain her indispensable alliance on the continent, particularly in the Netherlands? These are the crucial points upon which English policy toward Morton was to turn.

The chief responsibility for Morton's fall from power rests, in the first instance, on his own head. It must be confessed that no one was willing to fight for Morton for the sake of his *beaux yeux*; he was personally very unpopular. Here is the testimony of one of his political enemies, James Melville: Morton was 'proud and disdainful . . . he despised the rest of the nobility . . . under pretext of justice, used to commit divers wrongs and extortions . . . He was loved by none and envied and hated by many, so that they all looked through their fingers to see his fall.'[4] On the other hand, David Calderwood, a Presbyterian divine, writes that on the occasion of Morton's imprisonment, 'it was a pitiful sight to many, to see him who had done so much for establishing religion, and had hazarded his life, land, and goods in setting up and maintaining the king's authority, to be overthrown by such as had never given a sincere proof of their profession, yea, labored to advance Popery.'[5] This, however, was an *ex post facto* judgement; the kirk had not been happy with Morton's religious policy while he was regent, and it was not until after his death that the ministers came to regard him as a true defender of the faith.[6]

---

3 For a good account of the situation in the Netherlands at this time see J.B. Black, *The Reign of Elizabeth* (Oxford, 1936), 287–303.
4 Sir James Melville of Halhill, *Memoirs of his own Life*, ed. T. Thomson, Bannatyne Club (Edinburgh, 1827), 260, 266.
5 D. Calderwood, *The History of the Kirk of Scotland*, 8 vols., ed. T. Thomson, Wodrow Society (Edinburgh, 1842–49). iii, 483. Yet Calderwood regarded Morton's earlier removal from the regency as an act of God. *Ibid.*, 394, 396.
6 See, for instance, Andrew Melville's letter in 1583 to the pastors of Geneva, given in *The Autobiography and Diary of Mr. James Melvill*, ed. R. Pitcairn, Wodrow Society (Edinburgh, 1842), 161.

The fact was that Morton had made a great many enemies during his regency, in spite of the orderly government he gave to a country where political and personal violence were everyday affairs. He had alienated the kirk by his episcopal policy and by his contemptuous attitude toward the General Assembly. When Andrew Melville attempted to read him a lecture on the error of his ways, he replied, 'There wil never be quietness in this country till half a dozen of you be hanged or banished the country.'[7] This sort of thing did not sit well with men who believed that Calvin's polity in Geneva was the last word in political wisdom, and Morton's attempt to keep them in hand, after the English fashion, by a state-controlled episcopate angered them even further. Their attacks on episcopacy mounted steadily and climaxed in a violent denunciation in the General Assembly of July 1580, six months before Morton's arrest.[8]

A great many of the nobility, too, disliked Morton. Those who were Catholics and sympathetic to Mary, such as the earl of Atholl, were hostile as a matter of course. But many Protestants, too, began to turn against him. Morton was determined to keep the country quiet, and he punished noble offenders by heavy fines and occasionally by imprisonment. Furthermore, he wanted to regain for the crown property which it rightfully owned, and those who were forced to disgorge were, naturally, resentful.[9] Morton, not surprisingly, got a reputation for rapacity which was not entirely deserved.[10] He did not even get on very well with his own family.[11] Furthermore, he annoyed the mercantile class by his debasement of the coinage, which even the historian of the house of Douglas, generally friendly to him, condemns.[12] In short, Morton had

---

7 *Ibid.*, 67–8.

8 Calderwood, *History* iii, 469–70.

9 For example, the earl of Argyll. See *ibid.*, 394.

10 When Morton was deprived of his regency in 1578 he insisted on an inventory of the contents of Edinburgh Castle before he would surrender it. The inventory was made by three lords – Rothes, Ruthven, and Herries – who were more or less neutral in this crisis, and Morton was given a discharge signed by the council, including his enemies Argyll and Atholl. The relevant correspondence and documents are in *Registrum Honoris de Morton*, 2 vols., ed. C. Innes (Edinburgh, 1853), i, 101–15. On the other side, see HMC, 12th report, App., Pt. viii, 81, 100, 102–3, for the documents dealing with Morton's extortionate treatment of Lord Hume, and the account of Morton's financial practices in *The Historie and Life of King James the Sext*, ed. T. Thomson, Bannatyne Club (Edinburgh, 1825), 147–52, 157–8, 160–2. There is a very able defense of Morton's policy while regent in his article in the *Dictionary of National Biography*, written by T.F. Henderson.

11 See the accounts of his quarrels with the earl of Angus and Douglas of Lochleven in David Hume of Godscroft, *The History of the House and Race of Douglas and Angus*, 2 vols., (Edinburgh, 1743), ii, 239–40, 246–51.

12 *Ibid.*, 243–4. Calderwood, *History* iii, 302, says that this action 'procured great envy and hatred of the commons'.

alienated a great many of the important people in Scotland. This might not have mattered so much if there had been a real danger to protestantism, as in the 1560's, which would have held the Protestant party together under his leadership. But in the late 1570's no threat to the religion was apparent; so, many of the Protestants were willing to see their erstwhile leader go under.[13]

The blow fell in March 1578. The earls of Atholl and Argyll seized Stirling, where the king, a boy of almost twelve,[14] was residing, with the connivance of the Master of Erskine, who was in charge of the royal household. An impromptu council was organized, and the king was declared of age, which of course meant the end of Morton's regency. The latter, rather surprisingly, decided not to fight back; he even proclaimed his own deposition at the Market Cross in Edinburgh on 12 March.[15] Why he followed this course is not entirely clear. It may be, as Lang suggests, that 'he had his plan in reserve', but the evidence would seem to contradict this.[16] It is possible that he was weary of the burden; he had so hinted before, and he repeated the sentiment at this juncture.[17] He certainly was not caught completely by surprise, as his letters to his cousin Douglas of Lochleven show.[18] But for whatever reason, Morton made no resistance – except to insist on the inventory of Edinburgh castle – and he retired to Lochleven to do some gardening.[19]

The fall of the regent caused a considerable stir abroad. On the continent the Catholic governments rejoiced, and the imprisoned queen began to build air castles again.[20] Elizabeth was annoyed. In January she had sent Thomas Randolph, a man with much experience in Scottish affairs, into Scotland to try to patch up the differences between Morton and his enemies.[21] Now she wrote that she was astonished by Morton's fall, and she instructed Randolph

---

13 Morton's lack of popularity at the end of his regency is indicated by Randolph's letter of 28 Feb. 1578, *CSPS* v, 274.

14 James evidently had no personal liking for Morton, a sentiment which may have been encouraged by his tutor, George Buchanan, who, according to Melville, *Memoirs*, 262–3, had quarreled with the regent over a horse.

15 David Moysie, *Memoirs of the Affairs of Scotland*, ed. J. Dennistoun, Bannatyne Club (Edinburgh, 1830), 2.

16 A. Lang, *A History of Scotland from the Roman Occupation*, 4 vols. (Edinburgh, 1907), ii, 261. Morton's plan, as it worked out, depended on the earl of Mar, yet two days before the coup he was complaining about his desertion by the house of Mar. 2 Mar. 1578, Morton to Lochleven, Innes, *Registrum* i, 87–9.

17 4 Mar. 1578, Morton to Lochleven, *ibid.*, 90–1. 29 Oct. 1577, Castelnau de la Mauvissière to Henri III, *Papiers d'état relatifs à l'histoire de l'Ecosse au XVIe siècle*, 4 vols., ed. A. Teulet, Bannatyne Club (Paris, 1852–60), ii, 362–4.

18 See especially the letter of 2 Mar., Innes, *Registrum*, i, 87–9.

19 Melville, *Memoirs*, 264.

20 16 Mar. 1578, Don Juan de Vargas to Philip II, *Papiers d'état* iii, 171–2. 30 Apr., Mary to Bishop Leslie, *CSPS* v, 288–9.

21 30 Jan., 7 Feb. 1578, instructions to Randolph, *CSPS* v, 268–70, 271.

and Robert Bowes to tell Morton that she would support him and to be severe with Argyll and Atholl – but not too severe, lest they try to make an agreement with France.[22] The English government, however, was not particularly worried by Morton's fall. Even the alarmist Walsingham, although not pleased by the turn of events, wrote that Morton had been deposed on account of personal rivalries and that the situation was not immediately critical.[23]

As it turned out, Walsingham was right. Morton had been preparing a counterstroke, and on 26 April he brought it off. His instrument was the young earl of Mar; Morton persuaded Mar that he should assert his rights as governor of the king and keeper of Stirling castle, offices which were virtually hereditary in the head of the house of Erskine and which had been filled by the earl's uncle, the Master of Erskine, on account of Mar's youth. On 26 April Mar seized Stirling castle with the help of two of his cousins, the lay abbots of Dryburgh and Cambuskenneth. As soon as Morton heard of the success of the coup, he sent a message to Angus to be ready to march with all the Douglas strength at an hour's warning.[24] But Morton wanted to avoid a fight if he could. The Master of Erskine was solaced by being permitted to retain the governorship of Edinburgh castle, which he had been promised. The earl of Montrose, one of the anti-Morton faction, who turned up at Stirling on the twenty-seventh, was put off with fair words. Morton himself had a friendly supper with Argyll and Atholl in May, at which some sort of agreement was reached, but he promptly broke it by going to Stirling in person to control the young king. Atholl and Argyll protested loudly against this and also against Morton's transfer of an impending parliament from Edinburgh to Stirling. Morton disregarded their protests, and, when Montrose and Lindsay appeared at the parliament to challenge the legality of its proceedings, they were ordered to 'remain within their lodgings'.[25] At this new display of Morton's intransigence, Atholl and Argyll resolved to fight.[26] Both sides collected the forces. But, as the strength of the parties was very nearly even, neither side was willing to push matters to a conclusion, and they were willing enough to accept a compromise arranged by Bowes. Argyll and Atholl accepted Morton as

22 *Ibid.*, 279–80.
23 16 Mar. 1578, Walsingham to Randolph and Bowes, *Queen Elizabeth and Her Times*, 2 vols., ed. T. Wright (London, 1838), ii, 79–80. The Spanish ambassador did report that England was planning to send troops to help Morton, but that the plans had been cancelled on the return of Randolph. 12, 22 Apr. 1578, Mendoza to Philip II, *Calendar of State Papers, Spanish*, 4 vols., ed. M. A. S. Hume (London, 1892–9), ii, 575–8. Possibly Randolph knew of Morton's plans.
24 28 Apr. 1578, Bowes to Burghley, P. F. Tytler, *History of Scotland*, 9 vols. (Edinburgh, 1841–3), viii, 363–5.
25 17 July 1578, *RPCS*, iii, 8.
26 See their proclamation against Morton in Calderwood, *History* iii, 419–22.

the leading personality in the government, but Atholl retained the chancellorship, and two of his allies, Montrose and Lindsay, were added to the council.[27]

Elizabeth had been watching all these goings-on with half an eye while she debated the situation in the Netherlands and finally resolved on the renewal of the Alençon marriage plan. On 20 May she sent letters to various people in Scotland, letters which were friendly to Morton.[28] When she heard that fighting might break out, she sent orders to Hunsdon and Huntingdon, her commanders on the border, to be prepared to intervene by force.[29] This order was actually sent after Bowes had arranged his pacification, but Hunsdon, as soon as he learned of the possibility of trouble, anticipated his government's instructions. He sent messages to those borderers who were hostile to Morton warning them to remain quiet or he 'would presently set fire in their houses behind their backs'.[30] This doubtless had its effect.

Elizabeth was pleased that Morton was back in power, but she would do very little to help him consolidate his position. In July Morton sent the Scottish secretary, the commandator of Dunfermline, to England. He hoped to negotiate a close alliance with England, to get some financial aid, and also to obtain the Lennox estates in England for the king.[31] In return the Scots were prepared to ratify the eighteen-year-old treaty of Edinburgh. The leading English councillors, including Burghley and Walsingham, were hopeful that Elizabeth would seize the opportunity to strengthen Morton and make safe the 'postern gate'.[32] To their dismay, Elizabeth refused. She was willing enough to talk about a league and about the Lennox estates, but she would not part with any money, and this was the crux of the matter. Elizabeth was feeling financially pressed. She had recently agreed to spend £100,000 in the Netherlands, and she had nothing to spare for Scotland.[33]

One reason for Elizabeth's reluctance to commit herself to Morton was the fact that Morton's opponents were making a great show of their friendship for England.[34] Elizabeth, as usual, was trying to get something for nothing. If

27 13–14 Aug. 1578, Articles between James VI and the lords, *CSPS* v, 316.
28 *Ibid.*, 292–4.
29 29 Aug. 1578, Wilson to Walsingham, *Calendar of State Papers, Foreign, Elizabeth*, ed. J. Stevenson *et al*, 23 vols. (London, 1863–1950), xiii, 138–9. See also Read, *Walsingham* ii, 151.
30 19 Aug. 1578, Hunsdon to Leicester, *CSPS* v, 317.
31 Lady Lennox, James's grandmother, had recently died. Morton in this matter was undoubtedly trying to please James and thus to regain some measure of personal ascendancy over the king, who was, theoretically, running his own government.
32 The phrase is Walsingham's: 2 Sept. 1578, Walsingham to Burghley, *CSP For. Eliz.* xiii, 171–3.
33 The details of the negotiations are to be found in *CSPS* v, 297–300, 306–13. See also Read, *Walsingham* ii, 148–51. Burghley attributed the failure partly to a recurrence of Elizabeth's scruples over her treatment of Mary. The treasurer found this attitude deplorable. 29 July 1578, Burghley to Cobham and Walsingham, *CSP For. Eliz.* xiii, 101–2.
34 19 Aug. 1578, Hunsdon to Burghley, *CSPS* v, 317–18. See also *ibid.*, 318–20.

both sides in Scotland were dependent on her for support, she need not support either one. Their strength was about equal; all Elizabeth had to do was to see that it remained equal and no harm could come to her from Scotland.[35] This policy had its dangers, but it was inexpensive, and, as always, this was a very important consideration with Elizabeth.

So Morton had to fend for himself. He did not care for the balancing policy of England, as Bowes warned in November; 'he still thinks his long service is overlooked'. Bowes himself was worried by Elizabeth's parsimony: another power might build up a considerable party by a little judicious spending.[36] But nothing was done. So Morton was compelled to get along as best he could with his recent enemies. Argyll was persuaded to co-operate; he resumed his place on the council on 28 October.[37] But Atholl, who hated Morton, held aloof; he was, in fact, negotiating for Spanish support against Morton. But Philip, as usual, was unwilling to commit himself.[38] So Atholl eventually accepted the bait which Morton held out to him: he would co-operate with Morton in return for the destruction of the Hamiltons.[39] The Hamiltons, as next heirs to the throne, were disliked by all the Stewarts (Atholl was a Stewart) and the Douglases, Morton's family, were bent on avenging the regent Moray, who had been murdered by a Hamilton. The charge against the Hamiltons was their part in this murder and also in that of the regent Lennox, the king's grandfather and a Stewart.[40]

The actual physical assault on the Hamiltons' castles did not get under way until May 1579. Before it started, Atholl suddenly died, on 25 April, after a reconciliation banquet sponsored by Morton and presided over by Mar. It was immediately assumed that he had been poisoned, and by Morton.[41] The story went around that the only doctor among those consulted who ventured to dispute the verdict of poison tasted a little of the contents of the stomach and almost died himself.[42] While it never was proved, then or since, that

---

35   This view was not shared by the queen's councillors. Burghley was very unhappy about it, and Secretary Wilson scornfully wrote that the pro-English sentiments of Morton's enemies were no more to be credited than that the Catholic Atholl 'is suddenly become a most earnest Protestant'. 31 Aug. 1578, Burghley to Walsingham, *CSP For. Eliz.* xiii, 163–4. 9 Sept., Wilson to Walsingham, *ibid.*, 189–91.

36   24 Nov. 1578, Bowes to Walsingham, *CSPS*, 326–7.

37   *RPCS* iii, 41.

38   For these negotiations see Vargas's letters to Philip II, *Papiers d'état* iii, 192–5, 197–9, 206–8, 220–4, 226–9 – these letters runs from Aug. 1578 to Mar. 1579 – and 15, 22 Oct. 1578, Philip II to Vargas, *ibid.*, 202–4.

39   Atholl's first appearance in the *sederunt* of the privy council, on 17 Mar. 1579, coincided with the opening of the attack on the Hamiltons. *RPCS* iii, 115. See also HMC, *Salisbury Mss.* ii, 256–7.

40   *RPCS* iii, 146–7.

41   E.g., 14 May 1579, Castelnau to Henri III, *Papiers d'état* ii, 394–6; *James the Sext*, 174.

42   Calderwood, *History* iii, 442–3. Calderwood, who was not unfriendly to Morton, says 'Morton was slandered as guilty of the poisoning, but he cleared himself at his execution', meaning that he denied it at that time.

Atholl was poisoned or that, if he was, Morton was responsible, it has generally been assumed that there might be some truth in the tale, since Atholl's death was 'so extremely opportune for Morton'. This phrase is Andrew Lang's; yet Lang was not at all convinced that the earl was poisoned. Digestive difficulties, he pointed out, were common after Scottish political banquets: 'Atholl may have died of haggis, friar's partens, sheep-head, and cockie-leekie'.[43]

But, whatever the cause, Atholl's death was really not at all opportune for Morton. The latter had just managed to complete the task of reconciliation with his foes; the circumstances surrounding the sudden removal of one of the greatest of them made all the others suspicious and hostile again. Only a very foolish man would not have foreseen that this would be the result, and Morton was no fool. Furthermore – although this neither Morton nor anyone else could know at the time – it left the way open for the appearance of the far more dangerous d'Aubigny as leader of the opposition to Morton.

The persecution of the Hamiltons had been undertaken by Morton as a means of reconciliation with Atholl; once Atholl was dead, Morton would have been wise to put a stop to it. The main beneficiaries of the ruin of the Hamiltons were the Stewarts, who, since Atholl's death, could be counted on to oppose Morton at every opportunity. Furthermore, Elizabeth was annoyed. She felt that, under the terms of the pacification of Perth of 1573, by which the Hamiltons had made their peace with Morton, then regent, she should have been consulted before any action was taken against them, and she took up their case in September 1579, after the damage was done, when she sent Captain Errington to Scotland.[44] The wrangle over this matter carried on into the next year and certainly did not make for increased friendliness between Elizabeth and Morton, whom she and Errington held responsible for King James's refusal to make any concessions to the fallen family.[45] She was further annoyed by Morton's dispatch of an agent to England to work against the Alençon marriage.[46] Apart from the religious aspects of the proposal, it was obviously in the Scottish interest that Elizabeth die childless. The ruin of the Hamiltons, then, helped to ruin Morton in the long run, for it deprived him of potential allies against d'Aubigny, and it irritated Elizabeth at a time when it was essential for Morton to remain on good terms with her at all costs. Coupled with the circumstances of Atholl's death, the whole business was little short of disastrous.

In September 1579 Morton's nemesis appeared in Scotland in the person of Esmé Stuart, sieur d'Aubigny, a frenchified Scot who was a close cousin of the

43 Lang, *History* ii, 263.
44 *CSPS* v, 349–50.
45 24 May 1579, advertisements from Edinburgh, *Salisbury Mss.* ii, 257–9. See also Errington's dispatch of 31 Dec. 1579, *CSPS* v, 368–70.
46 29 July 1579, Castelnau to Henri III, *Papiers d'état* ii, 405–6.

king. He was a smooth and artful man whose ultimate purposes have always remained somewhat obscure; but it is certain that he wanted power for himself and that he was closely connected with the Guises – but not, be it noted, with Mary.[47] If the confused plotting of 1582 may be taken as an indication of d'Aubigny's purpose, he evidently planned to recatholicize England and Scotland by force, with the aid of Spain, the Guises, and the Jesuits.[48] But for the time being all this was concealed. On the surface he was simply James's cousin, come to congratulate him on his assumption of the government.

D'Aubigny was the first of a series of handsome, polished men – of whom Buckingham was the last and most famous – who succeeded in winning an absolute ascendancy over James VI. In d'Aubigny's case there is little to wonder at. He was friendly, amusing, and deferential, which Morton and the rest of the Scottish aristocracy decidedly were not. In a brief time he had so captivated the king that James could not do without him. As early as 10 October Errington wrote, 'Touching M. d'Aubigny, it appears that the king is much delighted with his company; and he is like to win into special favour, and not only to be earl of Lennox . . . but also to have some part of the Hamiltons' lands, if he may be drawn to religion'. Errington also noted that he was living very lavishly and suspected that he was being financed by 'some greater than himself'.[49] In his next report Errington indicated the way the wind was beginning to blow. D'Aubigny was striking up an alliance with Morton's enemies, notably Argyll.[50] Morton became increasingly unhappy about this state of affairs.[51] Clearly, trouble was brewing in Scotland – certainly for Morton, possibly for England.

From the beginning Elizabeth and her ministers took a great interest in d'Aubigny's doings in Scotland. Errington's reports, and the letters of Bowes from Berwick, indicated the steadily growing influence of the newcomer, who was playing his cards with great skill. He professed himself in favour of the English alliance and declared that he had an open mind in the question of

47 15 May 1579, Bishop Leslie to the Cardinal of Como, *Narratives of Scottish Catholics under Mary Stuart and James VI*, ed. W. Forbes-Leith (Edinburgh, 1885), 134–7. 29 Aug. 1579, Paulet to Walsingham and Wilson, *CSP For. Eliz.* xiv, 50–1. D'Aubigny's connection with the Guises was known in England at least a year before he landed in Scotland. 2 Aug. 1578, Shrewsbury to Leicester, *CSPS* v, 314. Even after Morton's death Mary remained suspicious of d'Aubigny; see her letter of 18 Sept. 1581 to the archbishop of Glasgow, *Receuil des lettres de Marie Stuart*, ed. A. Labanoff, 7 vols. (London, 1852), v, 253–63.
48 Lang, *History* ii, 279–82.
49 *CSPS* v, 354–5.
50 *Ibid.*, 355–7.
51 31 Dec. 1579, 'State of Scotland', *ibid.*, 370–2. The author of this memorial, doubtless Errington, exaggerated when he implied that Morton had withdrawn from governmental affairs. The *sederunts* of the privy council for these months show fairly regular attendance on his part.

religion. Errington evidently took most of this at face value; Bowes was not so sure.[52] Walsingham and the other councillors were suspicious; they urged the queen to send 'some persons of good quality' to Scotland 'to procure that the earl of Morton may be called again to the administration of public affairs'.[53] Elizabeth, however, was not to be stampeded; she was still bothered about the Hamilton business, and a speech by Morton which alluded unflatteringly to the Alençon marriage project doubtless nettled her.[54] She did, however, send Errington back to Scotland with instructions to stir up the ministers secretly against d'Aubigny on the religious question.[55] Beyond this, for the moment, she would not go.

Morton's position continued to decay throughout the spring and summer of 1580. In March d'Aubigny was created earl of Lennox.[56] Each party accused the other – with no apparent truth – of wanting to seize the king and carry him off: Morton, to England, Lennox, to France. In April Bowes reported a rumour which eventually would be proved true: that Lennox and his friends were planning to bring back to Scotland the egregious Sir James Balfour to accuse Morton of participation in the murder of Darnley.[57] It was reported that Lennox planned to get the king to dismiss certain officials who were friendly to Morton.[58] As these dismissals were not carried out, it may be assumed that the threat was sufficient. Murray of Tullibardine, the comptroller, who had worked closely with Morton, faded discreetly into the background. Dunfermline, the secretary, went over to Lennox; so, too, did Ruthven, the treasurer.[59] This was a serious matter, since Ruthven was a man of considerable importance, and Bowes worked hard to win him back. An incident in October 1580 made this impossible. Ruthven was at odds with Lord Oliphant; a scuffle took place between the followers of the two, and Alexander Stewart of Traquair, a friend of Ruthven's, was killed. After a futile effort to reconcile the parties, Morton sided with Oliphant, who was closely related to Douglas of Lochleven. Ruthven was, naturally, enraged, and so were the Stewarts; this ended whatever feeble hopes Morton may have had of building a party among the Stewarts.[60] This was not the first time that Morton allowed family loyalty to cloud his political judgment; this was one of his blind spots.

52 31 Dec. 1579, 'State of Scotland', *ibid.*, 370–2. 20 Feb. 1580, Bowes to Leicester, *ibid.*, 378–9. But even Bowes was occasionally complacent about a state of affairs, which saw both sides full of professions of goodwill to England. See his letter of 16 Apr. 1580, *ibid.*, 396–7.
53 2 Feb. 1580, Walsingham to Cobham, *CSP For. Eliz.* xiv, 146.
54 30 Jan. 1580, Bowes to Leicester, *CSPS* v, 377–8.
55 22 Feb. 1580, instructions to Captain Errington, *ibid.*, 381–3.
56 19 Mar. 1580, Bowes to Leicester, *ibid.*, 384–5.
57 *Ibid.*, 386–8.
58 16 Apr. 1580, Errington to Burghley and Walsingham, *ibid.*, 394–6.
59 See Bowes's letter of 18 Oct. 1580, *ibid.*, 525–9.
60 Calderwood, *History* iii, 479–80. For Morton's overtures to the Stewarts see Bowes's letter of 25 Sept. 1580, *CSPS* v, 510–13.

Meanwhile Lennox, with great skill, was turning his greatest political liability, his Catholicism, into an asset by his deft method of renouncing it. On his arrival the kirk had been intensely suspicious: 'the ministers are daily forewarning the king for dealing with Papists and tyrants,' wrote Errington in October 1579.[61] Two months later, things had changed considerably: 'the ministers . . . are resolved of M. d'Aubigny's good inclination to religion.'[62] The English observers were not at all convinced of Lennox's sincerity, which, indeed, was very questionable.[63] Lennox moved steadily onward, however, and in May 1580 announced his conversion to the true faith.[64] The king, who had been earnestly labouring with his papistical cousin to show him the error of his ways, was doubtless delighted.[65] At the same time, Lennox was deferential to the General Assembly, assuring them of his sincerity and asking them to supply him with a pastor who knew French.[66] He even appeared to be in sympathy with their position on episcopacy.[67] Small wonder that the majority of the ministers could see no threat to the religion in the struggle between him and Morton. Those few who ventured to attack the favourite were summarily silenced.[68] Morton was reaping the consequences of his cavalier attitude to the kirk in the days of his greatness.

Morton, in fact, was becoming thoroughly alarmed. His support within Scotland was steadily diminishing. Elizabeth's attitude was so ambivalent that as late as April 1580 many people in Scotland did not know whether she preferred Morton or Argyll.[69] 'He [Morton] hath found,' wrote Bowes, 'great inconstancy in sundry of this counsel [sic] . . . in whom he trusted'.[70] His efforts to mend his political fences did not work out very well.[71] There seemed to be only two courses open to Morton: he must 'provide his own safety', as Bowes put it in a letter to Walsingham on 23 May and that meant reconciliation with Lennox on whatever terms he could get; or he must get

---

61 *CSPS* v, 355–7.
62 31 Dec. 1579, 'State of Scotland', *ibid.*, 370–2.
63 See, for instance, Bowes's letter of 2 Apr. 1580, *ibid.*, 386–8. It is worth noting that the duke of Guise was reported to have 'only smiled' when he heard of Lennox's conversion. 7 June 1580, Cobham to Walsingham, *CSP For. Eliz.* xiv, 293–5.
64 16 May 1580, Bowes to Burghley and Walsingham, *CSPS* v, 427–9.
65 4 Apr. 1580, Errington to Burghley, *ibid.* 388–9.
66 Calderwood, *History* iii, 468–9. 477.
67 See the pronouncement of the council on this point on 9 May 1581, *RPCS* iii, 383–4. T. McCrie, *Life of Andrew Melville*, 2nd edn., 2 vols. (Edinburgh, 1824), i, 175, regards this as the virtual abolition of episcopacy.
68 See, in *RPCS* iii, 335, the treatment meted out to John Durie in Dec. 1580. See also *Melvill Autobiography*, 80.
69 4 Apr. 1580, Errington to Burghley, *CSPS* v, 388–9.
70 10 May 1580, Bowes to Burghley and Walsingham, *The Correspondence of Robert Bowes*, ed. J. Stevenson (London, 1842), 50–9.
71 See, for instance, 3 June 1580, Bowes to Burghley and Walsingham, *CSPS* v, 441–4, for the result of Morton's attempted reconciliation with the Kerrs and Humes.

firm and open English support. He kept pressing Bowes, and through him the English government, to let him know definitely what support he could expect.[72]

To ask Elizabeth to commit herself definitely to anything was to ask a great deal, as Morton well knew; yet he may be excused for expecting something more of the queen than he had yet received. In mid-April Elizabeth at the urging of her council sent Bowes back to Scotland, but his instructions amounted to a policy of half-measures. He was to try to undermine Lennox's credit with everyone concerned and to strengthen that of Morton, and Morton's advice was to be asked as to the best way of accomplishing this. But he was not to antagonize Lennox; he was merely to give him a friendly warning to behave himself – although, as Walsingham put it, 'she can hardly be persuaded that he can be drawn to run any other than the French course'. James was to be cajoled and urged to help work out a common policy against Spain. But the really effective argument – money – was not to be employed, with one exception: £500 was doled out to bribe the laird of Drumquhassel and the Master of Erskine, the captains of Dumbarton and Edinburgh castles respectively, to remain loyal to English interests.[73]

Bowes was in Scotland about a month on this mission and accomplished very little. He did succeed in bribing Drumquhassel, but he could not weaken the influence of Lennox. Lennox was so powerful, Bowes reported, that no one dared openly to oppose him. Morton was not in a good frame of mind. He and his friends realized the necessity of remaining at court to influence James, but they could not afford it: perhaps Elizabeth would finance them? Morton also advised a direct pension to James as the best means of influencing his policy. But, in an unguarded moment, Morton evidently indicated that he felt that there was no need for haste in the matter of the pension; this, Walsingham rather dolefully wrote to Bowes, was the most pleasing news of all to the queen.[74] All in all, Morton left the impression that he and his friends were anxious to be of service to Elizabeth, but only if she would support them openly.[75]

But support Morton openly was just what Elizabeth would not do. On 22 June she did rouse herself to the point of writing a friendly letter to the earl asking for advice,[76] spurred on, doubtless, by Bowes's continued warnings and by a letter from Cobham in France retailing rumours of a plot against Morton's life.[77] But Morton had already given his advice; his reply, while humble in tone, amounted to a flat refusal to act unless 'it shall please your

---

72 *Bowes Corr.*, 68–9.
73 *Ibid.*, 31–7.
74 1 June 1580, Walsingham to Bowes, *CSPS* v, 440–1.
75 For Bowes's mission see *ibid.*, 403–37.
76 *Ibid.*, 455–6.
77 For Bowes's letters see *ibid.*, 436–7, 440–5, 449–50. Cobham's letter is in *CSP For. Eliz.* xiv, 308–9.

majesty to travail in that matter wherein your highness perceives such peril'.[78] In fact, Morton was preparing to make his peace with Lennox. Elizabeth, he felt, was up to her old stalling tactics. 'As for this letter received from her majesty', wrote Archibald Douglas to Bowes, 'he takes that in so evil part that he thinks it . . . devised by some that love him not.' He was willing, however, to wait another two weeks before committing himself to Lennox.[79] The only result of this was Elizabeth's indignant denial that she was plotting against Morton and a renewed request for advice.[80] Morton refused even to answer this in writing. He was still willing to follow the queen if she would act, he told Bowes via messenger; he denied that he had reconciled himself with Lennox. 'Yet many think', wrote Bowes, 'that they be entered into friendly terms'.[81]

Morton's difficulties did not move Elizabeth; but the news, relayed by Bowes on 27 August that Lennox had made himself master of Dumbarton castle, did.[82] The favourite had been made captain of Dumbarton in July, but as long as the castle remained in the hands of Drumquhassel, Elizabeth was unconcerned. But on 25 August Lennox had trapped Drumquhassel in Edinburgh and forced him to give up the keys. Elizabeth was now really alarmed: Dumbarton was the gateway to Scotland by sea, and this looked like a step in a plot by Lennox to introduce foreign troops into Scotland. On 31 August the queen ordered Bowes back into Scotland. He was to insist on an interview with the king and the council with Lennox excluded and to declare that Lennox was a papist and a French agent. No documentary proof was to be offered, simply Elizabeth's assurance that this was so. Bowes was also to hint that unless James proved conciliatory, steps might be taken in parliament against his claim to the English succession. If this failed to work, Bowes was to plot violence with Morton; Hunsdon, the governor of Berwick, was to be instructed to 'yield any assistance that shall be by them required'.[83] In other words, Elizabeth was at last willing to use force.

But not for long. On the very next day Walsingham was compelled to inform Bowes that the authorization to use force was rescinded. Peaceful methods must be used first; only if they failed would Elizabeth take up again the question of sending troops. Walsingham was convinced that this meant ruin, but there was nothing he could do about it.[84]

Once again Bowes could accomplish nothing. James refused to listen to any accusations against Lennox unless the latter were present. Portentous declarations, furthermore, would not be enough: 'they cannot

78 16 July 1580, Morton to Elizabeth, CSPS v, 463.
79 31 July 1580, Archibald Douglas to Bowes, ibid., 470–1.
80 10 Aug. 1580, Walsingham to Bowes, ibid., 481–3.
81 22 Aug. 1580, Bowes to Burghley and Walsingham, ibid., 487–8.
82 Ibid., 490.
83 Ibid., 492–4, 497.
84 1 Sept. 1580, Walsingham to Bowes, ibid., 495.

give credit to matters of suspicion or jealousy, but look for evident actions directly to be proved and made known to them'.[85] Under these circumstances Bowes was convinced 'that words are of no value in this realm at this time'.[86] Walsingham was of the same opinion. He wrote Bowes on 10 September that Hunsdon had informed the queen that Morton was so weak that there was no way of strengthening him. This was just the sort of thing Walsingham did not want the queen to hear; Bowes was urged 'if he can, to remove the doubt, with some good probable reasons'.[87] Bowes did what he could, but on 25 September he was forced to report that Lennox had been created lord chamberlain, with control over the king's household.[88] Morton obviously was becoming no stronger, and with Bowes's failure and recall, on 7 October his doom was sealed. On 31 December the great earl was accused of participation in the murder of Darnley by Captain James Stewart of Ochiltree, soon to be earl of Arran, and, curiously enough, a brother-in-law of John Knox. Shortly thereafter Morton was taken off to Dumbarton castle to await his fate.

Thus did Elizabeth abandon her most reliable supporter in her only satellite, and in so doing she ran the very considerable risk of allowing power there to fall into the hands of a group whose policy would not be dictated by considerations of friendship for England or of the maintenance of protestantism. She permitted this to happen, not because she was infinitely fickle and treacherous, not because Morton was indeed abandoned of all, but because of the menacing state of affairs on the European continent.

The international horizon looked very black indeed to the queen in the latter half of 1580. First and most important were the events in Portugal. On 25 August 1580, the duke of Alva entered Lisbon,[89] thus making good the claim of Philip of Spain to the vacant Portuguese throne. The annexation of Portugal, with all that it implied in terms of colonial resources, upset what passed for the European balance of power in the sixteenth century decisively in favour of Spain. Nor was this all. Philip had at last hit on the right man for the governorship of the Netherlands – Alexander of Parma. By 1580 it looked as if Parma might yet subdue all of Philip's rebellious subjects there – a grim thought for the English. In some ways even more alarming was the fact that the Catholic Church and Spain began to launch a two-pronged attack on England itself. In 1580 the Jesuit mission, headed by Persons and Campion, landed in England. In 1579 and 1580 two small forces, made up mostly of Spaniards and Italians, landed in Ireland to help a rebellion there. They were

85 20 Sept. 1580, Bowes to Burghley and Walsingham, *ibid.*, 506–9.
86 20 Sept. 1580, Bowes to Walsingham, *ibid.*, 510.
87 *Ibid.*, 499. I have accepted Read's attribution of this letter to Walsingham rather than to the council as a whole. Read, *Walsingham* ii, 164.
88 *CSPS* v, 510–3.
89 13 Sept. 1580, Cobham to Walsingham, *CSP For. Eliz.* xiv, 416.

easily defeated – but might not the attempt be repeated, with greater forces than before?

Given all these facts, it is not surprising that Elizabeth should have thrown herself almost unreservedly into the arms of France. The Alençon marriage project, which had faded out to some extent late in 1579, was revived. More significant still, Elizabeth positively urged Alençon to go to the defense of the Netherlands, and she helped mediate between the Huguenots and the Catholics in the current installment of the French civil war – ended by the treaty of Fleix in November 1580 – in order that the French government might support Alençon against Spain. For the moment, at least, Elizabeth had almost forgotten her dread of French domination of the Netherlands. Not entirely, of course: she hoped to keep control of Alençon via the renewal of the marriage project. But Elizabeth planned on even more extensive co-operation with France than this. Throughout the autumn of 1580 she had been urging an alliance on the French in behalf of the Portuguese pretender; in December the French agreed to negotiate.[90]

Viewed from the vantage point of Elizabeth's French policy, her attitude toward events in Scotland becomes clear. Lennox, in her view, was a French agent, an ally of the Guises certainly, and, given the recent ascendancy of the Guises at the French court,[91] probably of the government as well.[92] She did not like Lennox; she fervently hoped that, somehow or other, the Scots themselves would pull him down. But she dared not act against him herself lest she destroy her chance of obtaining the French alliance, in which Scotland was to be 'comprehended' in any case.[93] The French ambassador in London, the wily and experienced Castelnau de la Mauvissière, was aware of Elizabeth's dilemma. He kept reminding her that she would be violating her treaties with France if she intervened in Scotland. He hinted that Lennox, with whom he had been in communication, had the backing of the French government.[94] It was reported that Lennox was about to send commissioners to France to renew the Franco-Scottish alliance.[95] Elizabeth was caught. She felt compelled to sacrifice Morton, despite her promises to him,[96] in order to achieve the French alliance. She doubtless consoled herself with the thought

---

90 For Elizabeth's policy toward France at this time see Read, *Walsingham* ii, 41–4; Black, *Reign of Elizabeth*, 304–6.

91 Read, *Walsingham* ii, 41.

92 The Spanish ambassador in London evidently thought so too. 31 Nov. 1580, 9 Jan. 1581, Mendoza to Philip II, *CSP Spanish* iii, 63–5, 76–8.

93 *CSP For. Eliz.* xv, 105–6.

94 G. Hubault, *Michel de Castelnau* (Paris, 1856), 32–41. See also 27 May 1580, Castelnau to Henri III, *Papiers d'état* ii, 424–8. The French had been applying pressure of this kind ever since 1578. See 5 Sept. 1578, the council to Paulet, *CSP For. Eliz.* xiii, 179–81.

95 4 Oct. 1580, Cobham to the secretaries, *CSP For. Eliz.* xiv, 440–1.

96 In the order of recall to Bowes of 7 Oct. the envoy was instructed to tell Morton that 'she will never see him abandoned'. *CSPS* v, 522–4.

that, with the expected treaty, Lennox's French principals would prevent him from doing England any harm.[97]

The arrest of Morton, however, seems to have come as a shock to Elizabeth, in spite of reports that something like this would happen.[98] Morton out of power was an unpleasant but bearable contingency; he could always be supported at some later time, if circumstances warranted. But Morton dead and his party destroyed, and Lennox permanently entrenched in power, was much less palatable. Elizabeth reacted swiftly. On 6 January 1581, Randolph was sent to Scotland with instructions to save Morton's life, to emphasize heavily the threat to religion represented by Lennox, to build a party out of Morton's friends, and – most important of all – to use force if necessary. Hunsdon and Huntingdon were ordered to prepare an army of 2,500 men.[99]

Randolph could accomplish nothing during his two months' stay in Scotland. Various attempts to discredit Lennox, threats on the succession question, a two-hour harangue delivered to the convention of estates – all were useless; the estates' reply was to vote £40,000 Scots to raise troops to resist a possible English invasion. The envoy, very reluctantly, had to fall back on the plan of building up a party in Scotland to act by force, presumably in co-operation with the army Hunsdon and Huntingdon were collecting on the border.[100]

Randolph from the beginning was doubtful of the success of this approach. He thought that much more was likely to come of bargaining with Lennox, who, he thought, might possibly be won over to a pro-English position. Lennox had, after all, signed a very Protestant confession of faith on 20 January.[101] Walsingham on 3 February reproved Randolph sharply for such an idea and ordered him not to 'harp any more upon that string', since no good could come of it.[102] Randolph nevertheless continued to take a very gloomy view of Morton's prospects: the earl had very few supporters, and the success of an English invasion was improbable. He once more urged negotiation, not directly with Lennox, but indirectly, through a meeting of

97 The overriding importance of France in Elizabeth's policy in 1580 can be seen in Walsingham's correspondence. E.g., on 1 June he wrote Bowes that he was trying to persuade the queen to take a firm stand in Scotland, 'but they are now so entangled with the handling of this French matter that all other causes, be they of never so great importance, must for the time give place'. *Ibid.*, 440–1; see also his letters of 22 June and 10 Sept. 1580, *ibid.*, 455, 499.

98 See, for instance, Cobham's letter of 4 Oct. 1580 reporting that Lennox had been in touch with Sir James Balfour with respect to evidence against Morton, *CSP For. Eliz.* xiv, 439–40.

99 *CSPS* v, 572–5, 579–80, 585–6, 700.

100 Randolph's negotiations may be followed in *ibid.*, 572 ff. See especially Randolph's summary of his activities, written after he left Scotland, *ibid.*, 689–97. One of the interesting sidelights of these negotiations is the question of the authenticity of the documents produced by Randolph to discredit Lennox. On this point see *ibid.*, 615–8, 675–8.

101 *Papiers d'état* ii, 436–40.

102 *CSPS* v, 606. See also Read, *Walsingham* ii, 165–66.

commissioners which was ostensibly to be summoned to deal with border matters.[103]

The English officials on the border, however, and especially Bowes and Hunsdon, viewed the situation differently. They were convinced, evidently by Archibald Douglas, who had taken refuge in England, that Morton had far more friends than Randolph thought he did, and they were anxious to fight. They did not like Randolph's plan for a meeting of commissioners: it would alienate Morton's friends. There was evidently also some personal animus between Hunsdon and Randolph.[104] The result of this conflicting advice was that the English government was 'very doubtful and irresolute' – meaning, of course, that the queen was irresolute.[105] The council inclined to the view of Hunsdon and Bowes,[106] but the queen, as always, preferred the cheaper and easier alternative, especially since Randolph's and Bowes's letters indicated that a plot was in the offing.[107] A new Riccio affair would solve the queen's problem.

It might be well now to consider the problem of the amount of strength Morton in fact had in Scotland. At the very minimum he had the support of two of Scotland's greatest houses, those of Douglas and Erskine, and also of the earl of Glencairn. This much is stated by Randolph.[108] In addition, Bowes claimed that Morton could count on the earls of Rothes and Montrose and on Lords Ruthven, Lindsay, Boyd, and Cathcart.[109] This information was doubtless obtained from Archibald Douglas and was exaggerated. Ruthven was hostile to Morton, as we have seen. Montrose was one of Morton's original opponents but was currently engaged in an intrigue with Angus' wife, who was Rothes' daughter. Angus discovered what was going on and almost caught the pair *in flagrante delicto*; he believed that a plot was intended against him. Rothes was annoyed with Montrose but soon became even angrier at Angus, who sent the errant lady back to her father and thus made a public scandal of the business.[110] There was no hope that these two would support Morton. Lindsay and Cathcart, on the other hand, could be counted on and possibly Herries as well; Boyd, though, may well have been double-dealing.[111]

103 8 Feb., 11, 13 Mar. 1581, Randolph to Walsingham, *CSPS* v, 623–4, 651–2, 653–4.
104 18 Feb. 1581, earl of Bedford to Randolph, *ibid.*, 639–40. For the attitude of Bowes, Hunsdon, and Huntingdon see *ibid.*, 624–5, 629–30, 631, 641–4.
105 7 Mar. 1581, Walsingham to Randolph, *ibid.*, 650–1. Even the cautious Burghley was convinced that only violence would serve. See his minute of 7 Mar. to Bowes, *Collection of State Papers . . . left by William Cecil, Lord Burghley*, 2 vols., ed. W. Murdin (London, 1740–59), ii, 343.
106 18 Mar. 1581, Walsingham to Randolph, Read, *Walsingham* ii, 168–70.
107 7 Feb. 1581, Bowes to Walsingham, *CSPS* v, 619–20.
108 Mar., Randolph's report of his negotiations, *ibid.*, 689–97.
109 24 Feb. 1581, Bowes to Walsingham, *ibid.*, 641–4.
110 28 Feb. 1581, Randolph to Hunsdon, *ibid.*, 645–6. See also Sir H. Maxwell, *A History of the House of Douglas*, 2 vols. (London, 1902), ii, 137–8.
111 Mar., Randolph's report of his negotiations, *CSPS* v, 689–97. See also Bowes's letters of 11 and 16 Jan. 1581, *ibid.*, 580, 586–7.

There were others, too – the Oliphants, on whose behalf Morton had alienated Ruthven, and the earl of Eglinton, who was openly hostile to Lennox and was excluded from the parliament of 1581 in consequence.[112] Furthermore, determined action on the part of England might well produce additional support; as Randolph put it, several of the nobility were 'well affected to see many things here reformed; but no man so hardy as, either in private to the king or in public to the council, dare say what he thinks'.[113]

There were also the ministers, some of whom were becoming suspicious of Lennox. John Durie, who in October had accused Morton and Lennox alike of factionalism, was punished in December for attacking Lennox alone.[114] John Craig, on the Sunday following Morton's arrest, preached against false accusations and was threatened by Lennox's henchman, Captain Stewart, Morton's accuser.[115] Some members of the middle class, too, were restless; they feared that their trade might suffer if Lennox's course led to a rupture with England. Edinburgh had 'offered liberally for his delivery' on the news of Morton's arrest, according to Bowes, and, when the earl was brought back to the capital for trial, over one hundred and fifty burgesses were ordered to quit the town temporarily, leaving their wives and property behind, as a precautionary measure.[116]

All this clearly shows that there was a fair amount of support for an English invasion on Morton's behalf. Elizabeth would not have been fighting the whole Scottish nation had she ordered Hundson and Huntingdon to march. The explanation for her failure to intervene lies elsewhere. One cause, certainly, was the deplorable condition of the border levies. It had been almost ten years since the last English expedition, and the men on the muster rolls were sadly lacking in equipment.[117] Hunsdon and Huntingdon were very unhappy about this state of affairs and kept asking for help from London[118] – a circumstance that undoubtedly helped dampen whatever enthusiasm Elizabeth may have had for an adventurous policy.

112 Sir W. Fraser, *Memorials of the Montgomeries, Earls of Eglinton*, 2 vols. (Edinburgh, 1859), i, 44. Also excluded were Mar, Glencairn, Lindsay, Boyd, Ochiltree (the father of Captain Stewart), and Lord Herries, the border rival of Lord Maxwell. Tytler, *History*, viii, 87. Maxwell had obtained Morton's title. Angus was in exile at this time.
113 23 Feb. 1581, Randolph to Walsingham, *CSPS*. v, 640–1.
114 6 Oct. 1580, Bowes to Burghley and Walsingham, *ibid.*, 519–21. *RPCS* iii, 335.
115 7 Jan. 1581, Bowes to Burghley and Walsingham, *CSPS*. v, 575–8.
116 7 Jan. 1581, Bowes to Burghley and Walsingham, *ibid.*, 575–8. Calderwood, *History* iii, 486. 2 June 1581, Mendoza to Philip II, *CSP Spanish* iii, 121–5. Lennox had been wooing the merchants; he obtained 'great favour among the boroughs, by the commendation of their suits to the king'. 9 July 1580, Bowes to Burghley and Walsingham, *CSPS*. v, 461–2.
117 For example, in the muster of Allerdale, in Cumberland, of the 1,040 able-bodied men only 244 were completely equipped. *Calendar of Letters and Papers relating to the Affairs of the Borders of England and Scotland*, 2 vols., ed. J. Bain (Edinburgh, 1894–6), i, 42–3. For other musters see *ibid.*, 14–24, 43–66, 118.
118 See, for instance, Hunsdon's letters of 3 and 6 Feb. 1581, *CSPS* v, 605, 614–5.

The queen's delaying tactics also proved costly. In the middle of March the plot of Angus and his friends against Lennox was discovered. Douglas of Whittingham, who knew everything about it, was arrested and, upon being threatened with torture, confessed everything. Morton's servants were arrested and tortured, and Angus was ordered to put himself in ward beyond the Spey. Randolph himself was implicated. The result was the collapse of Angus' party; its members hastened to make their peace with the king.[119] An anonymous accusation was posted on Randolph's door in Edinburgh, and a shot was fired through his window. He deemed it prudent to retire to Berwick.[120]

Hunsdon, in sending on one of Randolph's letters about the discovery of the plot to Walsingham, confessed to being in despair;[121] and Huntingdon, who had fluctuated between optimism and gloom, was firmly convinced that an invasion would be useless.[122] He was resigned to salvaging as much as possible out of Randolph's plan of a meeting of commissioners – a plan that Randolph himself now felt could not save Morton.[123] Hope flared briefly when Hunsdon, who was still bellicose, reported a meeting he, Randolph, and Bowes had with an agent of Angus and Mar, who were still prepared to fight.[124] The English government, which had ordered the discharge of the army on 26 March, reversed itself temporarily on the thirty-first, when it received Hunsdon's dispatch.[125] But a few days later the final decision came; the army was to be disbanded. The council explained to Hunsdon that they had proposed to the queen that a force of nine to ten thousand men be raised and sent to Scotland. She would not hear of it; so the order to disband was being sent.[126] Morton was left to his fate.

It is possible that Elizabeth might have sent troops into Scotland, on the pretext of restoring order, if Angus's plot had succeeded. It was her one real hope of getting rid of Lennox, for once again, as in 1580, she was prevented from open action against him by her desire for an alliance with France. A memorandum drawn up by Burghley on 25 April makes this clear. Burghley

119   RPCS iii, 368.
120   The discovery of the conspiracy and its consequences can be traced in CSPS v, for the second half of Mar. 1581, especially in Randolph's letters of 16, 18, 20, 23, and 25 Mar., pp. 661–3, 665–7, 670–1, 675–6, 679. The libel posted on Randolph's door is given in Calderwood, History iii, 507–10.
121   21 Mar. 1581, Hunsdon to Walsingham, CSPS v, 671.
122   8 Jan., 9 Feb. 1581, Huntingdon to Walsingham, 21 Mar., Huntingdon to Randolph, 22 Mar., Huntingdon to Walsingham, ibid., 579–80, 624–5, 672–3, 674.
123   30 Mar. 1581, Randolph to Walsingham, ibid., 686–7.
124   29 Mar. 1581, Hunsdon to Walsingham, ibid., 684–5.
125   Ibid., 681–3, 689.
126   8 Apr. 1581, the council to Hunsdon, ibid., vi, 3–4. Walsingham had felt all along that a force of this size would probably be needed; see his letters to Randolph on 25 Jan. and 18 Mar. 1581, ibid. v, 591–2, 664–5. In Sir James Melville's opinion the English policy of military threats was hurtful to Morton: it simply angered his enemies without deterring them. Memoirs, 266.

had no illusions about Lennox; he regarded James's favourite as a papist and as pro-French, but he would be harmless if the Alençon marriage took place. If the queen decided not to marry, on the other hand, steps must be taken against Lennox, or he must be neutralized by seeing to it that the failure of the marriage did not entail a breach with France.[127] This sort of thinking was encouraged by Castelnau, who continued to exert pressure against intervention. Elizabeth did not want to fight. On 27 February, the Spanish ambassador reported that she had exploded at Walsingham, supposedly for countenancing a plot to invade Scotland without her leave, by way of 'reprisal' for a staged border raid. 'You Puritan', she reportedly exclaimed, 'you will never be content until you drive me into war on all sides and bring the king of Spain on to me'.[128] The story may not be true, but it does indicate Elizabeth's state of mind at this juncture. She and Burghley rather halfheartedly tried to persuade Castelnau that Lennox was a Spanish agent, but the ambassador was not to be taken in by such a transparent device.[129] By 9 April he was able to write to his king that Elizabeth would not intervene in Scotland, 'de peur de vous déplaire'.[130]

The irony of this situation lay in the fact that the French government felt just as much need of the projected alliance as did the English. They were not prepared to support Lennox openly for fear of a breach with England. Cobham, the English ambassador in France, so reported on 20 April,[131] but by that time it was too late. In mid-May a splendid embassy from France landed in England; it was in the midst of its deliberations with the English government over the marriage treaty and the alliance when the end came for Morton.[132]

On 1 June Morton was tried and convicted in Edinburgh for being 'art and part' of the murder of Darnley. The conviction was technically unjust – he had not contrived the murder – but in substance fair enough, since by his own confession he had foreknowledge of Bothwell's plans. He was executed on the following day and made an edifying end.[133] His enemies rejoiced. A typical comment was that of the Spanish ambassador in London, who was

127 *Salisbury Mss.* ii, 387–8.
128 *CSP Spanish* iii, 84–6.
129 Elizabeth and Burghley did not invent this story; they had been receiving reports to that effect from Cobham in France. *CSP For. Eliz.* xv, 18–23, 65–9. The Spanish were, in fact, interested in Scotland at this time – see De Tassis's letter of 10 Apr. 1581 to Philip II, *Papiers d'état* iii, 262–8 – and Mary was anxious for Spanish intervention and also for the removal of James to Spain. See her letters of 24 July 1580 and 4 Mar. 1581 to the archbishop of Glasgow, Labanoff, *Receuil* v, 171–7, 211–7.
130 *Papiers d'état* ii, 456–8. See also his letters of 10 and 28 Feb. 1581, *ibid.*, 441–453, 453–5.
131 *CSP For. Eliz.* xv, 121–5. See also Hubault, *Castelnau*, 40.
132 Read, *Walsnhgham* ii, 47–8.
133 The eyewitness account of Morton's confession and execution is in Calderwood, *History* iii, 557–75.

delighted that 'God should have decreed that this pernicious heretic should be removed with so exemplary a punishment'.[134]

Thus died the last of the important leaders of that aristocratic coalition which, in alliance with England, had made and kept Scotland Protestant. His downfall was due, in the first instance, to his policy while he was regent: he alienated too many people. But in a very real sense he was also a sacrifice to the exigencies of English foreign policy. By 1580 he was incapable of maintaining himself in Scotland by his own strength, and, unfortunately for him, in that year Elizabeth believed that she could not afford to support him and run the risk of alienating France. England's only satellite had to be sacrificed, if by such a sacrifice the great danger represented by Spain could be turned aside. Elizabeth may have misread the situation – it might have been possible to save both Morton and the French alliance. But to this extent, at least, she was right: it was on the continent and, more specifically, in the Netherlands, and not in Scotland, that England's destiny was now to be decided.

134 15 June 1581, Mendoza to Philip II, *CSP Spanish* iii, 130–2.

6

James VI and the Revival of
Episcopacy in Scotland, 1596-1600
(1974)

King James VI and I had a taste for aphorisms, a circumstance which has occasionally misled the historians of his reign. James's deeply held and lifelong attachment to the doctrine of the divine right of kings is well known and unquestionable; so when, at the Hampton Court Conference, he said 'No bishop, no king', it has perhaps been too readily assumed that his devotion to episcopacy as a system of church government was as unswerving and permanent as his belief in divine right. The king's admiration for the Church of England and its prelates, his threat at Hampton Court to harry the Puritans out of the land, his savage attack in *Basilikon Doron* on those 'fiery spirited men in the ministry' who 'fed themselves with the hope to become *Tribuni plebis*' but who were really 'very pests in Church and Commonweal . . . breathing nothing but sedition and calumnies'[1] – all this is so familiar as scarcely to require repeating. It is also well known that when he began to govern for himself in Scotland in the 1580s the position of the Scottish bishops was feeble. It continued to worsen for about a decade, as the king and his advisers found it desirable for political reasons to make concessions to the dominant presbyterian wing of the kirk, until the presbyterian historian David Calderwood could write of the year 1596, 'The Kirk of Scotland was now come to her perfection'.[2] Then, beginning in 1596, the tide began to run in the opposite direction. The king turned against the presbyterians and began to harass them in various ways, as a prelude to accomplishing what lay nearest his heart: the restoration of a genuine, functioning diocesan episcopacy on the English pattern. This took some time; the first bishops were not appointed till 1600, and their powers were not fully restored till 1610. Their restoration was, nevertheless, what the king had in mind from the beginning. Friend and foe alike agreed on this, both David Calderwood, who bitterly opposed the king's policy, and John Spottiswoode, whom James made archbishop of St. Andrews and commissioned to write the history of the church in his reign. Later historians have followed where these two have led. Gordon Donaldson, the author of the most authoritative recent account of Scotland during James's reign, says that to the king 'bishops were the obvious agents . . . for bringing about the subordination of the ministers', while for D. H. Willson, who wrote the best modern biography of James, his employment of his power after 1596 to impose

---

1 *The Political Works of James I*, ed. C. H. McIlwain (Cambridge, Mass., 1918), 23-4.
2 Calderwood, *History* v, 387.

bishops on the kirk was 'all but inevitable'. Willson finds it 'surprising' that the king should even consider any other alternative.[3]

This reading of the evidence is open to serious question. For one thing, it rests upon a doubtful interpretation of James's character and policy. It makes him out to be much too cleverly Machiavellian: a man who knew where he was going from the beginning, who was bent on having bishops at whatever cost and who engaged in a long series of far-sighted, devious and ultimately successful maneuvers to achieve his end – 'a witty, politic Prince, whose far-fetched drifts and politic plots the more simple did not espy', in the words of the hostile John Row.[4] This seems to be a case of reading history backwards, which is what both Spottiswoode and Calderwood did. In the first place, James was no Laudian believer in the divine right of bishops. To him episcopacy was simply a means to an end: the exaltation of the power of the king, who was indeed God's vice-gerent, in church and state alike. As far as the Scottish church was concerned, what this meant in practical terms was that the clergy both collectively and individually must be made to recognize the king's authority, stop meddling in politics, stop criticizing the king politically and personally from the pulpit and in their frequent conclaves. Far too many ministers, wrote James, took the line 'that all Kings and Princes were naturally enemies to the liberty of the Church, and could never patiently bear the yoke of Christ: with such sound doctrine fed they their flocks'. And when more moderate churchmen remonstrated with them, they raised the cry of equality: 'parity in the Church . . . parity the mother of confusion, and enemy to Unity, which is the mother of order'.[5] It was these turbulent spirits, these would-be *Tribuni plebis*, who had to be brought under control if James was ever to be master in his own house. Episcopacy was one way of doing this, in James's opinion (on the evidence of *Basilikon Doron*) ideally the most attractive way, but not the only way and furthermore, one which involved such serious practical difficulties as to give the king pause for a long time. Between the quashing of the Edinburgh riot of 17 December 1596 and 14 October 1600, when James' appointment of clerical moderates to three vacant sees signalized his final decision in favor of episcopacy, the king experimented with several methods of controlling the church; it was not until the summer of 1600 that he definitively made up his mind.

Before the start of his campaign the king had no real control over the government of the church and precious little influence in it. The presbyterian structure had been recognized by law in 1592. There were still people around called 'bishops' in 1596, but half the sees were vacant, and those who filled the others took very little part in the affairs of the kirk, though they had the right

3 G. Donaldson, *Scotland: James V – James VII* (Edinburgh, 1965), 198. D. H. Willson, *King James VI and I* (London, 1956), 125. For Calderwood see, for example, his *History*, v, 587. For Spottiswoode see his *History*, ii, 340-2.
4 John Row, *The History of the Kirk of Scotland*, ed. D. H. Laing, Wodrow Society (Edinburgh, 1842), 165.
5 McIlwain, *Political Works*, 23.

to vote in parliament. The feebleness of the king's position was made painfully apparent to him and everyone else at the General Assembly of the kirk held in March 1596. James came personally to this Assembly to ask support for a tax; the Assembly refused. He asked it to instruct ministers to stop public criticism of himself without previous notification, so that he would have a chance to correct the fault complained of; it not only refused to do this, but also adopted a series of resolutions pillorying the king, his court, and his administration. 'His majesty is blotted with banning and swearing . . . The queen's majesty . . . not repairing to the Word and Sacraments, night-walking, balling, etc. . . . Universal neglect of justice . . .buying of pleas, delaying of justice, and bribery' as well as such more widespread failings as sacrilege, profanation of the Sabbath, bloodshed, deadly feuds, adultery, fornication, incest, excessive drinking and gluttony, 'which is no doubt the cause of the dearth and famine'; in short, 'an universal coldness and decay of zeal in all estates, joined with ignorance and contempt of the Word, ministry, and sacraments'.[6] Small wonder that, later in the year, Andrew Melville, the leader of the dominant faction in the church, could make his famous speech to James, calling the king of Scots a mere member of the kingdom of Christ, with the conviction that he was accurately describing existing conditions in the two kingdoms.

The chain of events which led to the establishment of the crown's power over the church began, really, in October 1595, with the death of Lord Chancellor John Maitland of Thirlestane. Maitland had been the principal advocate of the policy of alliance and cooperation with the kirk against the fractious Scottish aristocracy; he had supported the legislation of 1592; he had died in partial eclipse, but having lived long enough to see his policy vindicated by the involuntary departure from Scotland of both the principal exponent of aristocratic gangsterism, the earl of Bothwell, and the leader of the Catholic party, the earl of Huntly.[7] The vacant chancellorship was not filled; instead, the king at the beginning of 1596 appointed an eight-man commission with virtually unlimited control over the financial affairs of the kingdom, and furthermore, appointed the members for life. From the kirk's point of view this was a change decidedly for the worse. The leading figure on the commission (which came to be known as the Octavians), Alexander Seton, the president of the Court of Session, came from a Catholic family and was suspected of being a Papist, and most of the other members of the commission were believed to be either Catholic or lukewarm in religion; 'the one half whereof were suspected Papists and the rest little better', according to Andrew Melville's nephew.[8] Seton was aiming at the vacant chancellorship, a prospect which both the kirk and Queen Elizabeth's agent in Scotland

---

6 Calderwood, *History* v, 408-11.
7 For Maitland see M. Lee, Jr., *John Maitland of Thirlestane* (Princeton, 1959).
8 *The Autobiography and Diary of Mr. James Melvill*, ed. R. Pitcairn, Wodrow Society (Edinburgh, 1842), 330.

viewed with dismay.[9] There were other indications of a pro-Catholic drift, the most alarming of which was the prospect of the return of the earl of Huntly. The king had always liked Huntly and been lenient with him, in spite of Huntly's chronic disloyalty and frequent rebellions, his dealings with Spain and his murder of his enemy the earl of Moray, a crime which he had never expiated. Huntly's wife, a cousin of the king's, was still in possession of her husband's property and was much at court. To the kirk Huntly was a figure of loathing and terror; he stood for what it most detested in Scottish life, popery and aristocratic lawlessness. Now, in September 1596, at a Convention of Estates filled with friends of Huntly and of the other exiled Catholic earls, Errol and Angus, the suspect Seton, 'a Papist, made a prepared harangue, whereby to persuade the king and estates to call home these earls, lest, like Coriolanus the Roman, or Themistocles the Athenian, they should join with the enemies, and create an unresistable danger to the estate of the country.'[10] The kirk decided to strike back.

It was the practice of each General Assembly to appoint a group of commissioners to act as watchdogs over the church's interests until the next Assembly should meet. These commissioners now met, protested to the king – this was the occasion of Andrew Melville's 'two kingdoms' speech; he also called James 'God's sillie vassal', a phrase not calculated to please[11] – and, getting no satisfaction, came together again with representatives of various synods on October 20 and adopted policies which led directly to a confrontation with the king. They set up a permanent watchdog committee in Edinburgh which was to meet every day, and, if in its judgment the situation warranted it, summon a General Assembly – a direct attack upon the king's right to participate in the summoning of such meetings. They ordered the renewal of the excommunication of the Catholic earls. They ordered Seton to appear before the synod of Lothian to answer 'for dealing in favours of the earl of Huntly'. And they ordered a public fast for the first Sunday in December, a decision which, as everyone knew, would produce an outburst of clerical rhetoric which was apt to be both insulting and seditious.[12]

In the face of this provocation the government acted with considerable restraint. Seton agreed to appear voluntarily before the synod of Lothian if the summons was withdrawn. Four privy councillors, speaking in the king's name, promised that no favor would be shown to the Catholic earls until they satisfied the kirk. James insisted, however, that the General Assembly, like parliament, could not meet without his consent or take any action without his approval, and he would not tolerate seditious sermons. It was one of the latter which provoked the crisis: in mid-October David Black, minister of St. Andrews, had allegedly called all kings children of the devil and accused Queen Elizabeth

9　See, for example, 16 Nov. 1595, Roger Aston to Robert Bowes, *CSPS* xii, 60-1.
10　*Melvill Autobiography*, 368-9.
11　See Calderwood, *History* v, 439-41.
12　*Ibid.*, 443-8.

of atheism. Black, upon being summoned to answer for his language, revived Andrew Melville's position of 1584 and refused to admit the jurisdiction of the Privy Council; he could be judged in the first instance, he said, only 'by the prophets, whose lips he [God] has appointed to be the keepers of his heavenly wisdom'.[13] The watchdog committee of the kirk supported him to a man, and distributed copies of Black's statement to the presbyteries.

James could not tolerate this renascence of clerical intransigence. On account of Black's attack on Elizabeth he could proceed against Black secure in the knowledge that the English government would support him rather than the Protestant radicals with whom it had so frequently collaborated in the past. The watchdog committee, on learning of the king's anger at their behavior, summoned a General Assembly for early January. James issued a proclamation prohibiting any such meeting and ordering the committee of ministers to disband and return to their flocks, which they refused to do until the order was repeated two weeks later.[14] The king was careful to point out that he was not prohibiting regular clerical meetings, such as presbyteries and synods, and he gave indications that he was prepared to be lenient with Black, once the latter had acknowledged his jurisdiction.[15] Black remained contumacious and was ordered into ward; the king ordered the sheriffs to silence any seditious preachers who came to their attention, and at the same time proposed to make use of one of the few means he had to influence the clergy: he threatened to cut off the income of any minister who refused to acknowledge his jurisdiction in writing.[16] This decision was taken on 13 December; four days later came the famous riot in Edinburgh, with its demands for the recall of the clerical commissioners, the removal of the requirement that ministers acknowledge the king's jurisdiction in writing in order to receive their stipends, the expulsion of the Catholic earls and the dismissal from office of three of the Octavians, including Seton, who, indeed, went in some peril of his life – the crowd had been excited by hearing the story of Haman and Mordecai. The speedy collapse of resistance in Edinburgh in the face of the king's threat to withdraw the agencies of government, particularly the law courts, from the city, and the discrediting of the ministers of Edinburgh owing to their ill-advised attempt to appeal for help to Protestant aristocrats such as Lord John Hamilton and the earl of Mar in language which suggested that what they really wanted was armed intervention,[17] gave the king his opportunity. The objective was clear enough: to gain control of the church so that the intolerable recent behavior of those who now controlled the church and spoke in its name could not recur. The difficult

13 Black's declinature, dated 18 Nov. 1596, is in Calderwood, *History* v, 457-9. For the crisis of 1584 see Lee, *Maitland*, 54-9.
14 Calderwood, *History* v, 456-68, 501-2. *RPCS* v, 332-3.
15 *RPCS* v, 343-4. Calderwood, *History* v, 482.
16 *RPCS* v, 444-9.
17 Calderwood, *History* v, 515. HMC, *Report on the Manuscripts of the Earl of Mar and Kellie*, ed. H. Paton (London, 1904). 46.

question concerned the choice of means. And in the beginning there was no suggestion that the answer lay in the revival of episcopacy.[18]

One means which the king had at his disposal to influence the clergy was financial. It was generally agreed that most clerical incomes were inadequate, and for some time there had been considerable pressure on the government to act. One consequence was the so-called 'Constant Platt' worked out by the secretary of state, John Lindsay of Balcarres, one of the Octavians, and made public early in 1596. This plan would have provided every parish minister in Scotland with an adequate income, and as such it was welcomed by clergy of all shades of opinion – Calderwood, who was very hostile to the Octavians, called it 'the best and most exact that was ever devised'.[19] There were too many vested interests which would have suffered if Lindsay's plan had been adopted, however, and it was never put into effect. The problem of clerical salaries remained; James was concerned to do something about it, and in the long run he did.[20] The king was well aware, however, of the political uses to which he could put the prospect of increased stipends; this was the carrot which he held out time and again to the clergy to persuade them to acquiesce in the aggrandizement of his power over the church. James's position was not an easy one; he had to make good at least partially on his promises in spite of the government's chronic financial embarrassment, and to do so in a way which would not provoke a backlash from those nobles and lairds who by one means or another had gotten possession of various sorts of church property and whose financial interests would therefore be threatened if diocesan episcopacy were restored. Such a restoration would meet a good deal of opposition; it might even revive that coalition of aristocrats and preachers which had been fatal to the king's mother and which Maitland's efforts had so recently broken up.

The king therefore tried first to establish his authority in the church by gaining control of the General Assembly. The first step was to reassert the royal rights in the matter of the time and place of meetings. At the last General Assembly the next one had been scheduled for late April 1597 in St. Andrews; James now called it for late February at Perth. Moving the time ahead forestalled any possible complaints of delay. As for the place: previous General Assemblies had almost always met either in Edinburgh or St. Andrews, where they were dominated by Andrew Melville and his supporters. The idea now was to encourage the attendance of more moderate ministers, particularly from the north and northeast. The king's agent, Sir

18 The fullest account of the events of the last part of 1596 is in Calderwood, *History* v, 443-535. The riot is, of course, mentioned in all contemporary accounts. It seems likely that the December troubles were exacerbated by a group of courtiers who had no love for the Octavians and wished to pull them down.

19 *Ibid.*, 433. The text of the Constant Platt is on pp. 421-33.

20 On this point see W. R. Foster, 'A Constant Platt achieved: Provision for the Ministry, 1600-38', in *Reformation and Revolution*, ed. D. Shaw (Edinburgh, 1967), 124-40.

Patrick Murray, was sent on a tour of the northern presbyteries to this end in January, and was very successful. A far larger number than usual of ministers from the north attended: 'every one of them great courtiers' who 'found fault with . . . the Popes of Edinburgh, that they had not handled matters well, and almost lost the king.'[21] The radical ministers, led by James Melville, fought back by claiming that the meeting was not a proper General Assembly at all and that, at most, it could discuss only those matters stipulated in the king's letter of summons. James replied by forcing a vote on the issue; according to the English agent, Robert Bowes, he threatened never to hold another Assembly if the vote went against him.[22] It did not: the Assembly voted that it was, indeed, a legal and proper General Assembly, though it added the word 'extraordinary', perhaps to save face and gain a few waverers' votes. The king had made good his powers of summons, and was to make skillful and frequent use of them in the following years.

The experiment of holding the meeting in Perth was also a success. There were to be five more meetings of the General Assembly before 1603, two in Dundee, one in Montrose, one in Burntisland, and one in Edinburgh, but at Holyroodhouse where James could keep an eye on it rather than in one of the town churches. Another experiment of 1597 was less successful: both at Perth and at the May meeting in Dundee James arranged for simultaneous meetings of the Convention of Estates. As a device for overawing the assembled ministers this turned out to be clumsy; the ministers protested that a joint meeting between themselves and the Convention was not to be construed as a session of the Assembly or as an acknowledgement on their part of any jurisdiction by the Convention in ecclesiastical questions.[23] The sources do not indicate what percentage of the Assembly took this stand; it must have been sufficiently large to persuade the king that such simultaneous meetings would serve no useful purpose. It also seems likely that the large numbers of people who must have descended on Perth and, three months later, on Dundee caused an intolerable strain on the towns' resources. So the king fell back on what was a much more effective means of influencing people, namely, personal lobbying. James attended all the General Assemblies, conducting interviews with ministers, both individually and in groups, and winning a good deal of support by this means, as James Melville ruefully admitted.[24] The difficulty with this method was that it was time-consuming – at one meeting James spent so much time with the clergy that the courtiers complained that they were unable to see him[25] – and it had to be repeated at

[handwritten marginal note: this could not be done if the king is in England]

21 Calderwood, *History* v, 606.
22 9 Mar. 1597, Bowes to Burghley, *CSPS* xii, 482-5. Andrew Melville was not there, owing to the simultaneous election of the rector of the University of St. Andrews; his supporters held that the king's timing was deliberate, to insure Melville's absence. Calderwood, *History* v, 606-7.
23 Calderwood, *History* v, 608.
24 *Melvill Autobiography*, 403-4.
25 *Ibid.*, 542-3.

each Assembly with each separate issue. It was not something which God's vice-gerent ought to have to do.

The principal reason for the summoning of the Perth Assembly was to get the kirk's opinion with respect to a list of fifty-five questions. These had been drawn up, probably by Secretary Lindsay, in the autumn of 1596 while the Black affair was coming to a head, and were circulated in advance to the various presbyteries and synods, in most cases by royal agents like Sir Patrick Murray, whose job it was to try to assure favorable answers.[26] The king's preamble stated that their purpose was to settle controverted and obscure questions in order that 'a pleasant harmony and mutual concurrence between us may be established'; Calderwood's view was that they were designed 'to brangle the discipline'.[27] Calderwood was nearer the truth; the questions were designed to drive a wedge between the moderate and radical wings of the ministry, as had been done during the previous dispute over declinature of jurisdiction in the 1580s. They were not very successful. There were far too many of them, and the king had allowed too little time for his agents successfully to influence the presbyteries. At the Perth Assembly, therefore, James in effect shelved the questions and replaced them with an interim list of eleven articles which had to do with criticism from the pulpit of the government and of private individuals, restraint in the use of excommunication, extraordinary meetings of ministers without the king's consent and the question of 'any points of the external policy and government or discipline of the kirk that are not especially concerning salvation'. This last item, which summarized the first two questions on the original list of fifty-five, was as close as the king came to raising the question of church government. He got some satisfaction on the other points, but not on this. The reply was that the king, his agents or 'the pastors' could raise questions respecting the external government of the kirk '*in a General Assembly*' (italics mine); there, and there alone, the decision would lie. A commission of fourteen ministers was appointed to discuss the unanswered questions with the king and report to the next General Assembly.[28]

James professed satisfaction with the accomplishments of this assembly,[29] but it was clear that he was not going to gain very much by pursuing the device of the list of questions, either eleven or fifty-five. He nevertheless went ahead with the Assembly planned for Dundee in May. For one thing, he wanted the Assembly to recommend the restoration of the Catholic earls. The Perth Assembly appointed commissions to interrogate the earls and see if they were willing to accept the stringent conditions under which they might be released from excommunication. The earls agreed, and so in May the

26 See, for instance, the instructions for the presbytery of Aberdeen, dated 15 Jan. 1597, in *The Warrender Papers*, ed. A. I. Cameron, SHS (Edinburgh, 1932), ii, 302-7.
27 Calderwood, *History*, v, 577, 584.
28 The fullest account of this Assembly is in Calderwood, *History* v, 606-22, from which the quotations are taken.
29 9 Mar. 1597, Bowes to Burghley, *CSPS* xii, 482-5.

Assembly very suspiciously absolved the repentant sinners. James's second principal objective at the Dundee Assembly was procedural, and represented a new device for gaining control of the church: through the church's own commissioners. If the king could get a group of commissioners appointed with a majority sympathetic to his point of view and with a commission general enough to allow them to act on church questions in accordance with his wishes, then he might be able not only to dominate the church while the General Assembly was not in session, but also to emasculate the General Assembly itself and turn it into a rubber stamp for the actions of its commissioners. If James accomplished this, there would be no need to alter the forms of government within the church.

The way was carefully prepared. Conciliatory gestures were made toward the ministers of Edinburgh. The king's nominee, Robert Rollock, principal of the University of Edinburgh, was chosen as moderator: a very shrewd choice, since Rollock was a man of unimpeachable credentials and moderate temper whose sympathies were now with the king rather than the extremists. Sir Patrick Murray even tried to induce James Melville to persuade his uncle Andrew to go home; predictably, he failed.[30] The king was present, used his powers of persuasion and effectively dangled the bait of the Constant Platt. And so he got what he wanted: a commission to consult with him on specific questions such as the provision of stipends and the planting of kirks and also 'generally to give their advice to his Majesty in all affairs concerning the weal of the kirk, and entertainment of peace and obedience to his Majesty within this realm'.[31] Of the fourteen ministers named to this commission only four could be considered hostile to James; the quorum was seven, so that some opponents of the king could be 'put in the roll for the fashion', as one presbyterian contemporary put it.[32]

Looking back many years later on the appointment of this commission, David Calderwood put it this way:

> They were the king's led horse, and usurped boldly the power of the General Assembly and government of the whole kirk. All ecclesiastical matters which were to be treated in General Assemblies from henceforth, was [sic] first prepared and dressed at court, and then in the full Assemblies concluded by plurality of purchased votes . . . So the commissioners were as a wedge taken out of the kirk, to rend her with her own forces, and the very needle which drew in the thread of the bishops.[33]

30 *Melvill Autobiography*, 414-6.
31 Calderwood, *History* v, 646.
32 William Scot, *An Apologetical Narration of the State and Government of the Kirk of Scotland since the Reformation*, ed. D. Laing, Wodrow Society (Edinburgh, 1846), 94-5. Scot was minister of Kennoway in Fife in 1597.
33 Calderwood, *History* v, 644.

This verdict is somewhat misleading. If the commissioners had worked as efficiently as Calderwood said, there would have been no need for bishops at all.

James put his new weapon to work at once. Robert Wallace, a minister at St. Andrews, had attacked Secretary Lindsay from the pulpit. The commissioners summoned him; he denied that they had jurisdiction, and they promptly deprived him. At the same time they deprived David Black and replaced him with one of themselves, George Gledstanes, the future archbishop of St. Andrews. They also overturned a sentence by the St. Andrews presbytery against a minister accused of non-residence. They then proceeded to conduct a visitation of the university there, of which Andrew Melville was rector. Melville was deprived of the rectorship, but no charges against him could be made to stick, and he was given a new title, dean of the faculty of theology. The most important action of the commissioners was their declaration that henceforth no university faculty member could have a parish, or sit in presbyteries or synods. The university had the right to elect a representative to the General Assembly, but the man chosen was not eligible for reelection for three years.[34] These enactments were aimed at Andrew Melville, to confine him to teaching and thus reduce his influence.

The commissioners had made a good beginning; but James was a man who liked to be prepared against all eventualities, and in the course of the second half of 1597 he began to consider using parliament as an alternative to the plan of controlling the kirk by controlling the General Assembly. Admittedly this was a lot less satisfactory, since there were a number of church questions on which parliament could not legislate, but it could be used in some ways, as had been done in England. The question of the clerical vote in parliament had caused concern to the kirk for years; the radical-dominated General Assembly of March 1596 complained that there were 'in parliaments sacrilegious persons, as abbots, priors, dumb bishops voting in the name of the kirk'.[35] Secretary Lindsay, in the Constant Platt, had proposed a solution. Each presbytery was to choose a parliamentary commissioner; out of this group the rest of the estates would pick a number which, when added to the present possessors of benefices (whose right to sit would not be disturbed) would provide the church with a bloc of representatives as large as that of any other estate. After the present holders of prelacies died off, all the church's representatives would be chosen from the commissioners of presbyteries.[36] This plan may well have been the starting point of the deliberations of the Assembly's commissioners; one of their principal responsibilities was to settle the ministers' stipends, and Lindsay's scheme must have been before them.

It is not clear whether the initiative in opening the question of parlia-

---

34 Spottiswoode, *History* iii, 62-6. *Melvill Autobiography*, 417-9.
35 Calderwood, *History* v, 411. The abbots and priors referred to were lay commendators, like the lawyer Edward Bruce, 'abbot' of Kinloss.
36 *Ibid.*, 430-1.

mentary representation came from the king or the commissioners; it did not come from the General Assembly.[37] When the issue came before the committee of the articles at the parliament of December 1597, it created a serious dilemma. The commissioners asked for the vote in parliament, to be wielded by those commissioned by the General Assembly, the dissolution of the great benefices for the benefit of ordinary ministers, and the establishment of a commission to provide those ministers with competent livings out of the teinds (tithes). The king later claimed that he was willing to support these requests, but that the privy council would not. This was disingenuous. The king was prepared to swallow the commissioners' plan only if he had a hand in the selection of the clerical representatives; otherwise the delegation might be full of troublemakers like the Melvilles.[38] The council and the committee of the articles,[39] however, would have nothing to do with any plan that posed any threat to the *status quo* with respect to possession of church lands – either Lindsay's proposal, or the commissioners' or any scheme which contemplated the genuine revival of diocesan episcopacy, which would be equally threatening in a different way. It seems likely that the committee of the articles would have preferred to do nothing at all, 'the abbots, priors, Lords of Session, and such of the nobility as they drew to assist them, were against [it]', wrote Calderwood.[40] The king insisted, however, and so they had to respond; no one could pretend that the church was properly represented at present.

The committee of the articles therefore devised a scheme which, they hoped, would settle the question of representation and at the same time safeguard the interests of the landholding class. They could not, they said, abolish episcopacy; this would be tantamount to destroying one of the estates of parliament, which the other estates could not do. So parliament enacted that any clergyman whom the king wished to appoint to a prelacy would have the right to vote in parliament, just as in the past. What place such a minister would have in the kirk parliament left to the king and the General Assembly to decide. The present act was not to be construed as repealing any of the legislation now in force respecting the jurisdiction and discipline of the kirk.[41] The purpose here was plain. The General Assembly would not consent to the revival of prelacy in any real sense, especially in any sense which entailed the revival of a group of clerical landholders like the bishops of the

37 *Melvill Autobiography*, 530.
38 16, 23 Dec. 1597, George Nicolson to Robert Cecil, *CSPS* xiii, 132-4, 142-3.
39 We do not know the membership of the committee of the articles for this parliament. The lists we do have, for other parliaments of this period, indicate that privy councillors dominated the committee; there is no reason to believe that this parliament was different. The committee was all-powerful in that it alone proposed legislation to the full parliament.
40 Calderwood, *History* v, 668.
41 The text of the act is given in Calderwood, *History* v, 669-70. See also 17 Dec. 1597, John Macartney to Cecil, *CSPS* xiii, 134-7.

old church.[42] The aristocracy and the lairds would not have to disgorge their church property.

The king in his discussions with the Assembly's commissioners showed no great enthusiasm for parliament's action, but he promptly summoned a General Assembly to discuss it, once more altering the time and place previously stipulated. The letter of summons laid considerable stress on James's opinion that parliament's action 'shall be a mean, in short time, to vindicate the ministry from their present contempt and poverty'.[43] It was clear that there would be considerable opposition. Not even the king's most talented troubleshooter, Sir Patrick Murray, could keep the synod of Fife, dominated as usual by the Melvilles, from taking the line that it would be preferable to forego the vote in parliament than to obtain it if it could be had only by reviving episcopacy.[44] It therefore behooved the king to maneuver very carefully at the Assembly, which he did. The crucial issue was put off until the end of the session, to give the king time to lobby, to make concessions on minor matters and, perhaps, to weary some opponents of the measure and get them to go home. Andrew Melville, who was not a member of this Assembly thanks to the recent visitation of St. Andrews, turned up; the king ordered him away. On a whole series of grievances ranging from adulterous marriages to abuse of lay patronage James suggested referral to the next meeting of parliament, in order to emphasize the importance of representation there for the kirk. Once again there was heavy stress on the matter of clerical stipends, both to underline the argument that the most effective way to ameliorate the economic condition of the church was through parliament and to renew the powers of the commissioners of the Assembly. This last was done; the commission was somewhat more circumscribed than that of 1597, but it was still broad enough to allow the commissioners a fairly free hand. The commission was enlarged from fourteen to twenty-one, with nine as a quorum; two-thirds of the membership was favorable to the king.[45]

At last, on the seventh day of the meeting, the main question was broached. James began with a careful speech in which he declared that the kirk needed parliamentary representation to avoid poverty and contempt: 'I mind not . . . to bring in Papistical or Anglican bishopping; but only to have the best and wisest of the ministry appointed by the General Assembly, to have place in council and Parliament, to sit upon their own matters, and see them done, and not to stand always at the door, like poor supplicants, despised, and

42 James Melville went so far as to express the opinion that parliament intended to sabotage the plan by tying it to prelacy, on the ground that no honest minister would accept the title of bishop. See *Melvill Autobiography*, 530.
43 23 Dec. 1597, Nicolson to Cecil, *CSPS* xiii, 139-42. The meeting was moved from Stirling in May to Dundee in March. See Spottiswoode, *History* iii, 68-9. The letter of summons is in Calderwood, *History* v, 671-3.
44 Calderwood, *History* v, 680-1.
45 See the commission in *ibid.*, 691-3.

nothing regarded'.[46] There is no reason to question the king's sincerity here; there would be great difficulties in the way of the bringing in of 'Anglican bishopping' and nothing much to be gained by it, particularly if future clerical assemblies went as well as this one. When the roll was called the first vote in favor was cast by Gilbert Body, 'a drunken Orkney ass'; the northern clergy voted solidly for the king, and by a majority of ten the Assembly approved the principle that ministers should have the vote in parliament as representatives of the kirk.[47]

The narrowness of the victory may have persuaded the king that it would be unwise to take up the question of implementation in detail at this Assembly. So, on the last day the meeting only two additional matters were decided: that the kirk should have as many representatives as it had had in pre-Reformation days, that is, fifty-one, and that both the king and the kirk should have a hand in the selection. Other questions were to be discussed by the presbyteries in the next few weeks; on the first Tuesday in June all the provincial synods were to meet and pick three delegates to meet with the king and seven university members (including Andrew Melville) at his summons. This meeting could either settle the remaining questions or, in the case of disagreement, leave the matter to the next General Assembly.[48]

Reporting on this meeting to Burghley, the English agent in Edinburgh, George Nicolson, commented, 'But I cannot believe but that the bishops shall be yet established.[49] He still thought so in late July, on the eve of the meeting of the delegates at Falkland which James had called in accordance with the resolution of the Dundee assembly: 'the king will have it that the bishops must be, which in end will be his trouble, when it comes to their establishment and restoring to the living by Parliament, which the nobility will resist for their own particulars'.[50] Nicolson's informants may have exaggerated James's eagerness to follow English models: developments at the synod of Fife on the first Tuesday in June do not suggest that creating bishops was James's policy. As usual Sir Patrick Murray was James's agent at this most difficult of all synods; his chief purpose was to get three acceptable delegates chosen to the Falkland convention, which he did by arranging to put a large number of radicals in nomination, thus causing the radical majority to split its vote. The significant aspect of this synod was the line taken by the presbytery of Cupar, whose leading figure was Thomas Buchanan, one of the king's supporters and one of the three delegates elected owing to Murray's maneuvers. On the matter of method of election, the Cupar presbytery held that

46 *Ibid.*, 694.
47 *Ibid.*, 695. Calderwood alleges that some of the affirmative votes were cast by 'laics wanting commission'.
48 The fullest account of this Assembly is in Calderwood, *History* v, 682-702. Scot, *Apologetical Narration*, 106, claims that the synods were all scheduled for the same day to make it impossible to concert opposition to the king's plans.
49 *CSPS* xiii, 174.
50 25 July 1598, Nicolson to Cecil, *ibid.*, 241-3.

the kirk should make up a slate of five or six names for each vacancy, of which the king would pick one; the others wanted to eliminate the king's role in the electoral process. The Cupar presbytery was willing that the minister so chosen be called either *bishop* or *commissioner* and keep his place for life, unless removed for cause; the others insisted on the word *commissioner*, and that his term last only from one General Assembly to the next.[51] It is reasonable to assume that the stance of the Cupar presbytery represented the king's views in June 1598; the essence of what the king wanted was not the title of bishop but that he have a hand in picking the clerical representatives, and that they be permanent. Permanence was the key; the office of parliamentary representative could be combined with that of commissioner of the General Assembly, whose power to discipline refractory clergy had been demonstrated at St. Andrews in 1597, and the king would have a hand-picked body of clergy to work with, which would make it unnecessary to call the General Assembly very often, and to dominate it when it did meet. They would be to the Assembly what the committee of the articles was to parliament.

We unfortunately know very little about the Falkland convention; what we do know is that the king did not get what he wanted, save in the matter of picking the representatives. The convention agreed that the General Assembly would name a slate of six for each vacancy, and the king would pick one. If none of the six was acceptable to him, a second slate would be given him, from which he had to choose. The convention stipulated, however, that the nominee could act in parliament only on instructions, that he must give an account of his doings annually to the General Assembly, that he might enjoy the income of a prelacy (after provision for all ministers within the prelacy), but that, whatever his title, he was in no sense a prelate but merely a minister like any other. On the vexed question of his title, and the more serious one of the permanency of his appointment, no decision was reached, though the convention indicated that it preferred the title of *commissioner*, if parliament would accept the word; these accordingly were left to the next meeting of the General Assembly.[52]

It is difficult to account for this setback. One factor certainly was clerical reaction to changes at court: the decline in the influence of the staunchly Protestant treasurer, Walter Stewart, prior of Blantyre, and the replacement of Lindsay, who died later in the year, as secretary by James Elphinstone, who was widely believed to be a Catholic. Since Maitland's death James had relied to a considerable extent on Lindsay's advice in dealing with the church. Lindsay was a moderate and a compromiser who never showed any enthusiasm for episcopacy; his removal from the scene made the king's eventual adoption of an episcopal polity more likely than before. Another cause for clerical alarm was James's bad timing in restoring to his benefice the aged

51 *Melvill Autobiography*, 441-2.
52 The fullest account is in Spottiswoode, *History* iii, 73-5.

Catholic archbishop of Glasgow, who had been living in France for almost forty years as ambassador, sometimes official sometimes not, to the French court; it reminded people too sharply of Popish episcopacy.[53] Critical sermons were preached, notably by Robert Bruce, the recently restored minister of Edinburgh; James said that 'he took it in worse part than the 17 of December and that Mr. Robert seeks nothing but to discredit him with his subjects'.[54] James insisted that Bruce and the others be punished; but after the Falkland meeting he agreed to leave their punishment to their respective presbyteries, and that the archbishop must conform if he ever returned to Scotland.[55] If the king was to persuade the General Assembly to accept his scheme, he would have to walk warily on such matters as favors to a Catholic archbishop. On the other hand, if it proved impossible to persuade the Assembly to consent to a plan which potentially weakened its powers, it was always possible for the king simply to appoint bishops. He had never lost the power to do so; the question was one of feasibility. That his mind was running along these lines is suggested by the passage on bishops in *Basilikon Doron*, which was written about this time, while the king was feeling his disappointment at the result of the Falkland convention. The reestablishment of bishops – though not, of course, 'proud Papal bishops' – might now be the only alternative, and it had positive advantages, since it would not only put an end to the anarchic doctrine of parity but also 'reestablish the old institution of three estates in Parliament which can no otherwise be done'.[56] Of course there were obstacles, including what James called 'that vile act of Annexation' (of 1587, annexing church property to the crown), which he now regretted, not because it kept him from appointing bishops – it did not – but rather because it had created such a large lay vested interest which would oppose his doing so.

The king was not yet ready to take the radical stop of reviving episcopacy on his own authority, however; it might still be possible to get a General Assembly to do what the Falkland convention would not do. An Assembly was scheduled for July 1599. James postponed it first till the autumn, then to the following spring, to give himself time to create a majority for his point of view and partly to counter a potentially embarrassing leak: the contents of *Basilikon Doron* became known. In May William Bowes reported that James had 'defamed' the ministers. Andrew Melville circulated a list of eighteen propositions drawn from the book which he called 'Anglo-pisco-papistical', which was shown to the synod of Fife in September.[57] The embarrassment

---

53 The restoration was accomplished at a Convention of Estates on 29 June 1598, *RPCS* v, 464.

54 25 July 1598, Nicolson to Cecil, *CSPS* xiii, 241-3.

55 2 Aug. 1598, Nicolson to Cecil, *ibid.*, 249-51.

56 McIlwain, *Political Works*, 24. Willson, *James VI and I*, 126, puts the writing of *Basilikon Doron* in the summer or autumn of 1598, as does James Craigie, ed., *The Basilikon Doron of King James VI*, STS (Edinburgh, 1950), ii, 4. See also *CSPS* xiii, 347.

57 Calderwood, *History* v, 726; *Melvill Autobiography*, 444-6; 12 May 1599, Bowes to Cecil, *CSPS* xiii, 466-7.

On kirk voting in Parliament

was temporary, but may have contributed to the unsatisfactory outcome of
the ministerial conference James held at Holyroodhouse in November, to 'lay
the ground of his purpose for erecting bishops the next General Assembly',
now scheduled for March.[58] The king's opponents argued strongly that the
clergy should not vote in parliament, which, they held, represented land
rather than classes of people. When the government's supporters objected
that many previous General Assemblies had asked for the vote, the reply was
that they had asked only that no one vote in the name of the kirk who was not
commissioned to do so, and that no Assembly prior to that of 1598 had
approved the notion of ministers voting in parliament. The involvement of
clerics in secular government was contrary to scripture; at best, laymen such
as elders or deacons might represent the kirk. There were also lengthy and
inconclusive debates as to whether or not the representative should be
permanent and on the title of bishop. After two days of this James put an
end to the conference, angrily declaring that he had called the meeting to
resolve differences, but apparently the only result was to confirm people in
their previously held opinions. He ended with a threat: if the General
Assembly refused to accept his views, the clergy would have only themselves
to blame for their poverty. As for him, he could not afford to lack one of his
estates in parliament, and he would find ways to remedy the defect.[59]

So in a very real sense the Montrose General Assembly of March 1600 was
decisive for the future of episcopacy; it made certain that the king would
adopt this policy by eliminating any possible alternative means of controlling
the church. By this time episcopacy was looking more attractive in itself, as a
means of producing uniformity with England in anticipation of the great day
for which the king was so impatiently waiting; so wrote George Nicolson
shortly before the Assembly met.[60] The Assembly, in spite of the king's
lobbying, rebuffed him decisively. It accepted the decisions of the Falkland
convention, including the title of commissioner, and all the restrictions on the
parliamentary representatives, with the additional proviso that no commissioner was *ex officio* a member of the General Assembly; he would have a vote
there only if he were elected in the usual way. On the vital points of how the
commissioners were to be chosen and their permanence, the Assembly was
even less tractable than the convention. At one stage it voted by 51-48 that the
commissioners should be elected annually by each presbytery, which would
have eliminated the king's role entirely; all James could do was to persuade
them to adopt the Falkland method of election and to have the General
Assembly annually renew the representatives' commissions; presumably if

58 *RPCS* vi, 28-9. The quoted comment, by the English agent Nicolson, was made in
   May, when it was expected that the preliminary meeting would be held in July
   and the Assembly in September. *CSPS* xiii, 464-5.
59 Calderwood, *History* v, 746-61. *Melvill Autobiography*, 447-62.
60 9 Mar. 1600, Nicolson to Cecil, HMC, *Salisbury Mss.* x, 59-62. James's government
   was imitating England in other respects as well; see the orders of the privy council
   regarding poor relief, 1 Apr. 1600, *RPCS* vi, 98-9.

the Assembly disapproved of their doings, new commissioners would be chosen.[61]

This was defeat, and James knew it. The king, wrote Nicolson on March 25, asked the Assembly to consent to bishops; it refused. He asked that the commissioners be appointed *ad vitam aut culpam*; it refused that too. Yet the obstacle to the outright appointment of bishops remained; 'the nobility having their livings will never be brought to return them, as I can no way see how the King will effect his aimed at intent'. When the king was warned to move cautiously, 'he said, what help, if he fell to be a miserable King, his subjects must be as miserable subjects'.[62] It was only much later that the doings of the Montrose Assembly came to be regarded as part of the king's master plan and Calderwood could write, 'Thus the Trojan horse, the Episcopacy, was brought in, busked and covered with caveats, that the danger and deformity might not be seen.'; or Spottiswoode could say, smugly and inaccurately, 'And now there rested no more but to nominate persons to the bishoprics that were void.'[63] These accounts, written in the knowledge of what the following decade would bring, have seriously misled historians; if both sides agree, it must be so.

The truth is that the Montrose Assembly and what followed stripped James of his options. He had found no sure way to control a General Assembly, or to destroy parity in the kirk with its own consent and create a body of churchmen through whom he could control the rest. The restrictions with which the Assembly surrounded its parliamentary representatives, whatever they were called, required, if they were observed, that the Assembly meet every year. True, the group of commissioners appointed at the General Assembly was useful to work with, and the king continued to have a large majority on this commission; but even they regarded the decision made at Montrose as binding on them.[64] The king had not succeeded in turning the commissioners into another committee of the articles and the Assembly into a rubber stamp. The desirable but difficult course of reviving episcopacy was all that remained. For a time James hesitated, but the aftermath of the Gowrie conspiracy persuaded him to act. Some of the Edinburgh ministers, notably Robert Bruce, were skeptical of the king's version of the events at Gowrie House. The king ordered them to stop preaching and instructed the Edinburgh presbytery to replace them, but the presbytery refused to do so unless and until they were properly deprived.[65] It was necessary to call parliament to take the essential legal steps against the dead earl and his family; the question of representation therefore had to be resolved. So, by October 1600 James had made up his mind: he would appoint bishops himself. On 14 October 1600, the king held a meeting of the Assembly commissioners and

---

61 Calderwood, *History* vi, 1-26, has a full account of this Assembly.
62 *CSPS* xiii, 629-30.
63 Calderwood, *History* vi, 20. Spottiswoode, *History* iii, 82.
64 15 Nov. 1600, Nicolson to Cecil, *CSPS* xiii, 733-4.
65 21 Aug. 1600, Nicolson to Cecil, *ibid.*, 690-1.

representatives of the synods, ostensibly to deal with the question of the Edinburgh ministers. The meeting agreed that they could not be replaced without due process; James replied that he would not have them preaching in Edinburgh; so a three-man delegation, made up of the representatives of the synod of Fife, was sent to ask the ministers if they would consent to a voluntary transfer. While the three radicals were gone the king and the rest of the meeting 'nominated and choosed three bishops'.[66] The die was cast. The rumours at once began that the king would press for the repeal of the act of annexation; but James knew better. The most that he did was to tell parliament that he thought repeal was a good idea, but he would not urge it, and it was not done.[67] James in fact moved very slowly indeed; he made only two other episcopal appointments before his accession to the English throne, and at that time the General Assembly was still maintaining that the Montrose Assembly's restrictions on the clerical representatives in parliament were in force.[68]

The king's control over the kirk was still extremely weak at the time of Queen Elizabeth's death. Since the riot of December 1596 he had provided himself with General Assemblies which were more amenable than before but not certainly controllable; he had arranged on each occasion for the choice of a group of commissioners of Assembly with whom he could work; he had pretty well gotten control of the time and place of the Assembly's meeting; and he had appointed five bishops. But they were bishops in name only, and the sequence of events suggests that, however much James may have preferred episcopacy as a solution, he adopted it chiefly because none of the other devices for control of the church which he had tried turned out to be workable. There was no guarantee in 1603 that James VI would be able to make the episcopal device work either. It was the fact that he became James I, with all the vast accretion of power which that implied, that made the revival of prelacy in Scotland a success.

66 Calderwood, *History* vi, 95-6.
67 19 Oct., 12 Nov. 1600, Nicolson to Cecil, *CSPS* xiii, 713-5, 729-31.
68 See Calderwood, *History* vi, 173-6, for the complaints of the synod of Fife, and the Assembly's responses, at the Assembly of Nov. 1602.

7

The Gowrie Conspiracy Revisited*

The Gowrie Conspiracy used to invite speculation. Like the murder of Lord Darnley, it is one of the celebrated mysteries of the sixteenth century. It is highly unlikely that any more evidence as to what actually occurred in the turret and gallery chamber of Gowrie House on 5 August 1600 will ever turn up, and so the truth will never be certainly known – the participants themselves did not know exactly what happened. In one major way, however, this tragedy is very different from that of Kirk O'Field. In Darnley's case there are a number of explanations that pretty well fit the known facts; in this case there are none that do. A century ago that wonderfully versatile man of letters and connoisseur of historical mysteries Andrew Lang devoted a whole book – still the clearest and most detailed account – to the question, and concluded that Gowrie had indeed conspired against James. Shortly thereafter another such connoisseur, William Roughead, made the affair the first of a book of essays on Scottish puzzles, and came to precisely the opposite conclusion: James had conspired against Gowrie. In the 1950s W.F. Arbuckle wrote a two-part article in the *Scottish Historical Review*. In 1970 G.M. Thomson gave the affair half a book, combining it, rather oddly, with the Appin murder, a very different sort of business.[1] Since that time it has received little attention, save from King James's biographers, all of whom mention it, either in passing or at some length. The two principal multi-volume histories of Scotland of recent years barely glance at it.[2] It was over in a day, after all, and resulted in nothing more than the ruin of one aristocratic family. Those who have paid heed have been so bemused by trying to sort out what actually happened that they have neglected to set the affair in its proper context, the political situation that existed in the summer of 1600. By contrast, historians of England have treated the almost simultaneous, and equally rapid, self-destruction of the earl of Essex as a matter of considerable significance. So Gowrie's fate is worth another look, not as mystery, but as political event.

There are three, and only three, possible explanations of the deaths of John

* I wish to thank Dr. Julian Goodare for his most helpful comments on an earlier version of this paper.

1 A. Lang, *James VI and the Gowrie Mystery* (London, 1902). W. Roughead, *The Riddle of the Ruthvens and Other Studies* (Edinburgh, 1919). W.F. Arbuckle, 'The Gowrie Conspiracy', *SHR* xxxvi (1957), 1–24, 89–110. G.M. Thomson, *A Kind of Justice: Two Studies in Treason* (London, 1970).

2 G. Donaldson, *Scotland: James V–James VII* (Edinburgh, 1965), gives it one page, J. Wormald, *Court, Kirk, and Community: Scotland 1470–1625* (London, 1981), two incidental mentions.

Ruthven, third earl of Gowrie, and his younger brother Alexander on that August afternoon. Either they were the victims of a successful murder plot on the part of King James, or their own plot against the king, to murder him, as James said, or to kidnap him, backfired, or an unpremeditated quarrel broke out, which escalated into deadly violence. None of these explanations can be made to fit with all the facts as given by those present, including the king himself, whose story, bolstered by the depositions of his entourage and of those members of Gowrie's household whose testimony was helpful, con-stituted the official account.[3] Even at the time, and in the king's own capital city, there were sceptics, notably Robert Bruce, the principal preacher in Edinburgh, and the doubters were certainly right to question some of the details of James's version of events.[4] As Roughead has observed, 'We cannot tell what *are* facts in this strange case, abounding as it does in suppressions, falsehoods, and inconsistencies'.[5]

There is little point in trying to piece together a consistent account of what happened on 5 August. What can be done is to explain why anything happened at all, and what it all meant. In their absorption in trying to sort out the sequence of events, those who have written about the affair have not come to grips with the most crucial of all questions: why did King James go to Gowrie House in the first place? He was not paying a friendly social call. He did not like Gowrie, and with good reason. From the beginning – nay, even before the beginning – the Ruthvens had been his enemies. Gowrie's grand-father, Lord Ruthven, was the principal figure in the murder of David Riccio; if fear caused women to miscarry, James might never have been born, as he sourly reminded Gowrie six weeks or so before that fatal 5 August.[6] Gowrie's father, the first earl, and his associates forcibly detained the sixteen-year-old king in Ruthven Castle, outside Perth, in the summer of 1582 and forced James's much-loved cousin Esmé Stuart, duke of Lennox, to leave Scotland forever. James contrived to escape from the so-called Ruthven Raiders; Gowrie plotted to seize the king again, failed, and was beheaded for treason in 1584, after having, perhaps, been entrapped into a confession in return for a promise that his life would be spared.[7] As a young teen-ager the third earl had followed his vengeful mother and his much older brother-in-law John Stewart, earl of Atholl, in their alliance with James's frightening cousin Francis Stewart, earl of Bothwell, in his running feud with James. The two

3 The basic documents can be found in R. Pitcairn, *Ancient Criminal Trials in Scotland*, 7 vols., Bannatyne Club, (Edinburgh, 1833), pt. ii, 146–322. The king's narrative is on pp. 210–8.
4 The fullest account of the sceptical reaction is in Calderwood, *History*, vi, 27–99; see especially pp. 67–75. Calderwood, a presbyterian who thoroughly disapproved of James's episcopal policies, clearly sympathized with Bruce. In fairness, he printed James's account, pp. 28–45.
5 Roughead, *Riddle*, 30.
6 Calderwood, *History* vi, 71.
7 See *CSPS* vii, 103–7.

countesses of Gowrie and Atholl had made it possible for Bothwell, in July 1593, to trap James, most embarrassingly, in his own palace when he had just arisen from the privy.[8]

In 1594 young Gowrie went abroad to study at Padua, perhaps the only Italian university where a Protestant would be unmolested. Five years later he set out for home. He travelled in leisurely fashion, spending three months in Geneva, where he impressed Theodore Béza with his zeal for the true faith.[9] The English ambassador in Paris, Sir Henry Neville, praised him to Robert Cecil, the English secretary of state, as a potentially useful man, since he was both sound in religion and an admirer of Queen Elizabeth.[10] In London, which Gowrie reached in early April 1600, he had a private interview with the queen and excellent treatment from Cecil. James's own agent in London, James Hudson, described him to Cecil as 'one of the best accomplished of his age of that nation . . . for learning, travel, and good qualities'.[11] In late May he arrived in Edinburgh. The rumour had preceded him that he had returned at the urging of the leaders of the kirk, or of the court faction led by Lord Chancellor Montrose and the bedchamber group headed by Sir George Home of Spott, or both. Gowrie's reappearance attracted a crowd; James allegedly remarked, rather irritably, 'There were more with his father when he was conveyed to the scaffold'.[12] Gowrie's interview with the king was difficult. James 'marveled the ministers met him not! with many other speeches', reported Sir John Carey, the deputy governor of Berwick. The king sardonically commented that Queen Elizabeth had cosseted Gowrie and sent him home with pockets full of gold; the earl replied that the queen had indeed received him well but offered him no gold, and besides, 'he had gold enough for himself'.[13]

Another queen also received him well. Anna of Denmark had two of his sisters, Beatrix and Barbara, in her household, and she was partial to anyone who, like Gowrie, was potentially a political foe of the earl of Mar, the head of the house of Erskine, whose guardianship of her eldest son Prince Henry Anna bitterly resented. As Henry's guardian Mar, the king's boyhood friend, was doing the same job that his father had done for King James when James was a child. Try as Anna might, she could never shake James's trust in Mar or

---

8 For the complicated politics behind the hostility between Bothwell and King James see M. Lee, Jr., *John Maitland of Thirlestane* (Princeton, 1959), 229–64. By 1593 this hostility had some of the aspects of a family feud. Bothwell was a Stewart; many of the Stewarts were outraged at James's failure to pursue the earl of Huntly for his murder of the 'bonny earl of Moray', another Stewart. Atholl was the leader of the Stewart faction; Gowrie's mother was a Stewart.

9 Calderwood, *History*, vi, 67.

10 Pitcairn, *Trials* ii, 315.

11 3 Apr. 1600, Hudson to Cecil, *CSPS* xiii, 630.

12 Calderwood, *History* vi, 70–1.

13 29 May 1600, Sir John Carey to Cecil, *Calendar of Letters and Papers relating to the Affairs of the Borders of England and Scotland*, ed. J. Bain, 2 vols. (Edinburgh, 1894–6), ii, 659.

pry her son loose from his guardianship. What commended Gowrie to Anna was that he was apparently returning as the ally of Lord Chancellor Montrose, the leader of the anti-Mar faction at court. Gowrie knew Montrose well; they had been associates in Gowrie's days as a follower of Bothwell. Gowrie had no personal hostility to Mar, who had been a friend of his father's. But he may well have heard harsh things about Mar from Cecil, who undoubtedly knew that Mar was in friendly correspondence with the earl of Essex, Cecil's great rival at Elizabeth's court.[14]

Gowrie's return came at a very awkward juncture in James's affairs. The king's finances were in messier condition than usual. After the unfortunate but politically necessary dissolution in 1597 of the Octavians, an efficient but much too Catholic exchequer commission, there had been a series of three lord treasurers, none of whom had performed well, and one of whom made the king look foolish. The earl of Cassillis, so the story went, owed his appointment to the fact that his wife was rich. When she refused to open her purse, Cassillis abandoned his post. The incumbent in 1600, the master of Elphinstone, the elder brother of the secretary of state, was clearly not the answer. All these treasurers were constantly bad-mouthed by James's favourite courtier, Sir George Home of Spott, who wanted the job, and, in 1601, would get it.

James was, therefore, living from hand to mouth. Furthermore, his three-year campaign to get control of the kirk had recently run into serious difficulties. He wanted the General Assembly to consent to the creation of a group of permanent commissioners whom he would appoint and who would serve as the church's representatives in parliament. In March 1600 the Assembly decisively rebuffed him. He might be able to pick his commissioners from a slate proffered by the Assembly, but the Assembly would instruct them on their conduct in parliament and review that conduct annually. James faced the stark choice of having to accept this defeat or adopt the politically much more delicate course of appointing bishops, which would not only enrage the dangerous number of hard-line presbyterians among the clergy but also alarm all those landholders who had gotten control of church lands.[15] James's opponents in the kirk feared the worst. The king believed that they had prompted the return of their supporter Gowrie at this juncture; hence his comment, quoted above, at his interview with the earl.

As if all this were not enough, James regarded the situation in England with growing alarm. The old lady in Whitehall was an unconscionable time a-dying, and the great prize might yet slip through his fingers. Ever since the publication in 1594 of the Jesuit Robert Persons's book denying the right of any heretic to succeed to the English throne James's greatest fear had been the

14 For Mar and Essex see H.G. Stafford, *James VI of Scotland and the Throne of England* (New York, 1940), 203.
15 On this question see M. Lee, Jr., 'James VI and the Revival of Episcopacy in Scotland: 1596–1600', above.

candidacy of Philip II's daughter the Infanta Isabella. In 1599 Isabella moved closer to Elizabeth's throne, geographically at least, having come to Flanders as co-ruler there with her new husband, the Archduke Albert; she now had an army at her disposal. In December of that year there were reports that a potential rival already on the scene, James's cousin Arbella Stewart, was to make a great marriage, with the Archduke Matthias, which, wrote Cecil's informant Roger Aston, 'he [James] was no ways content of but would hinder it if he could'.[16] James was fearful. Under pressure from his crypto-Catholic secretary of state, James Elphinstone, he began to follow a double line in his pursuit of the succession. He undertook a series of unofficial negotiations with continental Catholic powers, including even the Pope, in order to disarm their potential opposition to his claim, and, more officially and openly, he asked friendly Protestant governments to apply diplomatic pressure in London on his behalf. In 1597 parliament voted a tax to fund the latter missions, but only one was sent, to Denmark and Germany; most of the money was frittered away entertaining Queen Anna's alcoholic brother the duke of Holstein when he came to visit in 1598. James's tactics angered Elizabeth and produced very meager results.

The second line James followed was to interfere in English court politics to build a party for himself. Of the factions at the English court James greatly preferred that of the queen's favourite, the earl of Essex, with whom he was in touch, to that of Secretary Cecil. Essex favoured continued war with Spain; Cecil hankered after peace – and peace would be dangerous for James. Peace would make the Infanta a much less implausible candidate for the succession and allow her party to grow. Unhappily for James, Essex blundered in Ireland, returned home without permission in September 1599 to face a wrathful monarch, and apparently ruined himself forever – he was languishing under house arrest in the spring of 1600, when Gowrie returned to Britain. James believed that Essex's ruin spelt disaster for him; he was convinced, wrote George Nicolson, the English agent in Edinburgh, in April 1600, that Cecil held the Infanta 'pro sole oriente'.[17] With Essex's fall from favour James began to think about the need to use force, or the threat of force, to make good his claim to succeed Elizabeth when she should die. In December 1599 the Convention of Estates agreed that arms might be imported, but refused to raise a tax to pay for them. The tax was much 'gragged' at, wrote Aston, because of the size of the amount James wanted, the novelty of the proposed method of assessment, and the suspicion that the money might be squandered as the last tax had been: there was no confidence in James's financial officers.[18]

This was a serious rebuff, but in the spring of 1600 James resolved to try

16 *CSPS* xiii, 585.
17 20 Apr. 1600, Nicolson to Cecil, *ibid.*, 631–4.
18 27 Nov., 15 Dec. 1599, Nicolson to Cecil, 16 Dec., Aston to Cecil, *ibid.*, 579–80, 582–5.

again. He saw a gleam of hope in the appointment of Lord Mountjoy as Essex's successor in Ireland. Mountjoy, an Essex partisan, sent James a message in February 1600 proposing what amounted to a joint military démarche to restore Essex and secure the succession for James. The king did not and could not commit himself: without money he could do nothing. So in April, and again in June, he called a Convention of Estates to ask for a tax. He had prepared the way as carefully as he could, but in vain. In April he got the Estates to accept the new method of assessment, but only through a piece of parliamentary chicanery, and in June he met with a flat refusal. He asked for an enormous amount of money: 100,000 crowns, or £333,333 Scots. The lairds and the burghs would not hear of raising a tax of such size. The lord president of the court of session and former Octavian, Alexander Seton, a Catholic, declared that even the huge amount James requested could not fund an army large enough to conquer England, and the newly returned Gowrie, taking advantage of the first public forum afforded to him, declared that it would be dishonourable for James to ask for more money than the country could give. James, who had spread the rumour that Elizabeth was ailing in order to make his need for money for an army appear more urgent, was furious, especially at the lairds and burghs, and at Gowrie.[19] He had gone out of his way to conciliate the earl: on 20 June, just before the meeting of the Estates, the court of session had given Gowrie a year's respite from pursuit by his creditors, citing the fact that the crown owed his father over £48,000 for expenses incurred during his long tenure as lord treasurer from 1571 to 1584. James himself had been present at the meeting of the court.[20] Gowrie's ostentatious leadership in opposition to the tax was rank ingratitude, and foolish to boot: how could he expect to be paid back if the crown had no money? The king was also angry at Seton, but not for long: the lord president had merely told the truth, after all, and as provost of Edinburgh he had an obligation to support the capital in opposition to the tax.[21] The Convention had been a fiasco. James could not have been in a happy frame of mind when he rode off to Falkland for the summer in early July, a week or so after the end

---

19   29 June, 9 July 1600, Nicolson to Cecil, *ibid.*, 661–4, 667–71. Among others who made known their opposition to James's proposal were Lord Seton, the president's brother, and ex-treasurer Cassillis. Gowrie's potential political allies, Montrose and the courtiers, maintained low profiles. Mar and the Erskines supported the king's request, perhaps, Nicolson opined, because they knew it would fail, and were in high favour. For a careful account of James's manoeuvres on taxation see J. Goodare, 'Parliamentary Taxation in Scotland, 1560–1603', *SHR* lxviii (1989), 23–52, esp. pp. 42–5.

20   H. Arnot, *A Collection and Abridgement of Celebrated Criminal Trials in Scotland* (Glasgow, 1812), 417–8.

21   James did not make a similar allowance for Gowrie as provost of Perth, perhaps because he was responsible for Seton's appointment but not for Gowrie's. The reaction in Perth to the events of 5 August shows that Gowrie was popular there. Given his six-year absence and his youth – he was 22 – his stand on the taxation is the best explanation of that popularity.

of the Convention. His attempt to a adopt hard line toward England had failed. His ambitious plan to reform the tax structure had collapsed, his finances were in chaos, and his financial offers both incompetent and unpopular. His campaign to recover control of the kirk had stalled. The immediate future looked bleak. James could hardly know that a turning point lay just ahead.

*   *   *

One undisputed fact about James's decision to go to Gowrie House on 5 August was that he made it on the spur of the moment. On the Monday of the previous week, 28 July, he went from Falkland to Linlithgow to meet with his privy council on border matters – a warden of the west march had recently been killed – and he expected to return in a fortnight, on 11 August, to resume the discussion. On 29 July he rode back to Falkland in order to begin hunting the buck on the first of August.[22] On 5 August he was on the point of setting out on the morning's hunt when he had the conversation with Alexander Ruthven that led to the day's tragedy. Alexander, said the official account, had been instructed by his brother the earl to ride to Falkland early that morning and bring the king back to Perth with him.[23] The king hesitated; it was not until after the hunt was under way that he summoned Alexander and told him that he would go with him to Perth, but not until after the kill.

What could Alexander have said to James, to persuade him – almost – to forego the sport he loved above anything in the world, in favour of a visit to the house of a man he cordially disliked? The story given out, that Alexander had happened upon a mysterious stranger with a pot of gold the day before, is incredible. Nobody believed it. Nobody believed it at the time. Even the king's own account makes it plain that the one man with whom James said he shared it before he got to Gowrie House, the duke of Lennox, did not believe it. There is a second version, far more plausible, which Nicolson reported in his first letter after the event, written on 6 August: that Gowrie had found treasure in his house, in an old tower.[24] The difficulty with this scenario was that if Gowrie already knew of the treasure, there was no need for haste: Alexander's line, said James, was that the king had to come right away, before his brother discovered the man with the pot of gold, or the king would lose most of his potential profit. All this was utterly absurd, and was concocted, either just before or just after the event, in order to explain why the king was in such a hurry to get to Gowrie House. Even Lennox, who had been Gowrie's (and Alexander's) brother-in-

---

22 All this is contained in Nicolson's letter of 30 July to Cecil, *CSPS* xiii, 674.
23 This detail comes from the deposition of Andrew Henderson, Gowrie's chamberlain for the lands of Scone, the self-confessed 'man in the tower'; Gowrie had ordered him to accompany Alexander. The king's narrative simply says that Alexander appeared on the morning of the 5th.
24 *CSPS* xiii, 678–80.

law, and was, therefore, perhaps more apt to believe Alexander than anyone else in James's entourage, scoffed at it.[25] It was a balloon that would not fly. But once James used it, he was stuck with it.

To return, then, to the original question: why did James go to Gowrie House? Nicolson's second dispatch on the affair, written on 11 August, provides a clue. It is rumoured in Edinburgh, wrote Nicolson, that Gowrie had been much favoured in England, especially by Elizabeth, with whom he had had a long, secret meeting. And there, Nicolson went on, he was 'drawn to this intended purpose against the king'.[26] Was Gowrie, then, acting in the English interest? If so, what was it the English wanted him to do?

In the spring of 1600, when Gowrie was in London, the English political situation looked difficult and dangerous to Robert Cecil. True, his rival Essex had stumbled, and stumbled badly, but there was no assurance that the queen would not forgive him. He had been placed in the custody of Lord Keeper Egerton at York House upon his return from Ireland the previous September, but in March 1600 he was allowed to return to his own residence, Essex House, and it was decided that he would not face a trial in Star Chamber. Instead, there would be a hearing before the council (duly held on 5 June, after Gowrie's departure), which would mean no more than a slap on the wrist. Cecil could not be sure that Essex would not rise again. And how reliable was his successor in Ireland? Mountjoy had been raised a Catholic; Essex's sister was his lover. His first skirmishes with the arch-rebel Tyrone took place in April and May; Mountjoy had some slight advantage, but the military results were inconclusive. The war, in Ireland and elsewhere, was hideously expensive. In addition to the naval campaigns it was a two-front war, not, as in the past, in France and Scotland, but in the Netherlands and Ireland. Costs had averaged some £350,000 annually since the Armada year, but for the year ending at Michaelmas 1599 they had risen to £570,688.[27] In the exchequer, wrote Cecil, 'the receipts are so short of the issue as my hair stands upright to think of it'.[28] War-weariness was evident in England. The glory days of 1588 were long gone, and now there was profitless stalemate. The escalating costs could be met only by selling land and borrowing. France had made peace with Spain in 1598, thus reducing Spain's burdens; Elizabeth called on Henri IV to pay his debt to her, but in vain. The situation in the Netherlands was tricky. The new rulers of the Spanish Netherlands, 'the Archdukes', they were called – Archduke Albert and the Infanta Isabella – were being conciliatory. Elizabeth and Cecil could not count on the fighting

---

25 In 1591 Lennox had married Gowrie's sister Sophia, who died within the year. Calderwood, *History* v, 128, says that James was 'highly offended' at the marriage.
26 *CSPS* xiii, 681–2.
27 R.B. Wernham, *The Return of the Armadas* (Oxford, 1994), 319. Much of what follows on the English situation is based on this excellent book, especially chap. 20.
28 Quoted in A.L. Rowse, *The Expansion of Elizabethan England* (London, 1955), 429.

there continuing indefinitely. An end to hostilities between Spain and her rebels would leave the English standing alone against the Spanish colossus. And they had their own Achilles' heel, in Ireland. In the spring of 1600 the report came that the long-anticipated and much feared Spanish expeditionary force would land there in August. Small wonder that the English government leapt at the chance to discuss peace with the agents of the Archdukes and Spain; the conference opened at Boulogne in mid-May, at the end of Gowrie's stay in London.

The Scottish situation made Cecil very uncomfortable. He knew that King James had been in touch with Essex, who had persuaded the king that Cecil was his enemy and favoured the Infanta's succession. He knew that James was in touch with Tyrone; in May Nicolson sent him a copy of a letter from Tyrone to James boasting of how well he was doing against the English forces.[29] Tyrone's agents bought military supplies in Glasgow, and James either could not or would not stop them. James's attitude toward the Catholics bothered Cecil. The Scottish administration was full of Catholics, including Secretary Elphinstone, who was encouraging James's hard line toward England. There were rumours, which proved to be only too well founded, that Queen Anna had converted to Catholicism. The drift of James's policy had worried Cecil for some time. In the spring of 1599 he wrote of 'the present state of Scotland, how it grows every day with more affection to Popery'. He had heard all sorts of stories about Catholic offers of support for James if he would go to war with England and promise freedom of conscience.[30] Cecil may not have put much stock in this, but he knew that James was trying to find the money to raise an army, and that his failure at the Convention of Estates in 1599 had not put an end to the plan. It was clear to Cecil that everybody in Scotland wanted James to succeed to the English throne; the arguments were about the best way of achieving that goal. Cecil regarded the king's attitude as dangerous. If he were to make some gesture of open hostility to England, Spain might decide to jettison the peace negotiations and send that expedition to Ireland. What to do? Cecil could not outbid Essex with James by, for example, raising his pension (if Elizabeth approved), a gesture which ultimately turned out to be effective with the impecunious king, but only after Essex was not only disgraced but dead, and James had to deal with Cecil or nobody. The one action that would completely alter James's attitude, Elizabeth's open acknowledgement of him as her successor, was out of the question.

Gowrie's appearance in London at this juncture offered possibilities. Ambassador Neville in Paris, in recommending Gowrie, put it this way: 'If your honour please to confer with him about these alterations feared in Scotland, I believe he will give you good satisfaction, and that you will find him a man of whom there may be exceeding good use made'. The language

29 *CSPS* xiii, 643–5.
30 *Ibid.*, xiii, 436, 531–3.

suggests that Neville had sounded him out – to do what? We do not know.[31] Nor do we know what Cecil, or Elizabeth, said to him in London, whether they urged a course of action on him, or merely allowed him to draw his own conclusions from their discussion of the political situation – and it is impossible to believe that they did not discuss the political situation. Cecil was much too cautious to commit anything to paper. In the following October he carefully wrote Nicolson, in a passage no doubt meant to be repeated, that he believed 'on my conscience there was some purpose in Gowrie to make a welter in that kingdom', a remark either altogether innocent or beautifully crafted to deny foreknowledge.[32] What Cecil and Elizabeth wanted is clear from England's situation in May. The negotiations with Spain were beginning. James, who clearly disliked them, must be kept from making mischief while they went on. That meant, first, preventing him from raising an army, which Gowrie helped to accomplish at the Convention of Estates in June. If the king could be prevented from doing anything at all until the outcome of the negotiations was clear, a matter of a few months, so much the better. Gowrie, the friend of the kirk, was to be used as Bothwell, that 'sanctified plague', had once been used, to preoccupy James and turn him from a policy that was not in keeping with English interests – to turn him, but not to overturn him. The English government had no interest in a reversion to the faction-ridden Scotland of James's minority.

Why should Gowrie listen to Cecil, and decide to stage what amounted to a second Raid of Ruthven? English gold is an unlikely explanation; he did say, after all, that he had money enough. Hereditary hostility to the king certainly played a part: James's account said that Alexander threatened to kill him to avenge his wrongfully executed father. Political ambition and religious enthusiasm were factors also. Gowrie was the ally of the king's opponents in the kirk: it was not too late to prevent the appointment of bishops, which those kirkmen greatly feared. It is noteworthy that some of the disappointed ministers, especially in Edinburgh, were the most public sceptics regarding the king's version of events. Though Gowrie acted alone, in the belief that the execution of 'a high and dangerous purpose' depended on involving as few people as possible,[33] he was confident of internal support if he succeeded, not only from the kirk but also from all those who did not want a confrontation with England.

31 27 Feb. 1600, Neville to Cecil, Pitcairn, *Trials* ii, 315. On 5 Dec. 1600 Nicolson reported that Robert Oliphant, one of Gowrie's servants, who was not in Perth on 5 August, had said that Gowrie 'had moved that matter to him in Paris and here', and that he had declined to help and tried vainly to dissuade Gowrie from proceeding. When the man to whom Oliphant made this comment repeated it, Oliphant fled. *CSPS* xiii, 748–9. This is the only indication we have that Gowrie was contemplating some action against the king before he arrived in England. See Lang's account, *Gowrie Mystery*, 71–9.

32 *Salisbury Mss.* x, 365.

33 So said his tutor, William Rynd, in his testimony after the event; Calderwood, *History* vi, 59–62.

What was Gowrie's plan? The best guess is that he proposed to get James to come to Gowrie House in haste, without his usual entourage, to receive a messenger from Elizabeth on the succession: nothing else could draw him so rapidly. There he could be seized and taken somewhere for temporary safekeeping, perhaps to Dirleton, where Gowrie's mother was in residence, or perhaps to Ruthven Castle, which was much nearer at hand; the Perth townhouse was not adequate as a place of detention. There was a report, which Nicolson discounted, of an English ship lurking off the coast 'about the time of the conspiracy', which might have brought a messenger, and which might be used, as Nicolson said, 'for transporting Gowrie' – and his in-voluntary guest – to Dirleton.[34] Once word of Gowrie's success spread, there would be support, perhaps in very high places. Three months after the event Roger Aston wrote that there was a report that Queen Anna knew of Gowrie's plans, and that Home of Spott had so informed the king. 'What the Queen's part was in the matter, God knows. The presumptions were great, both by letters and tokens, as also by her own behaviour after the deed was done'. The king, Aston went on, was doing his best to conceal her folly from the world.[35]

Two very young and inexperienced men were taking a ridiculously dangerous gamble. Gowrie's optimistic expectation that he could pull it off may have been owing to his long absence from Scotland. He had left an unsettled kingdom in 1594, with Bothwell still at large and the Catholic earls still unpunished; the Scotland of 1600 was a very different place. Gowrie's was an all-or-nothing shot: either James would take the bait and hurry to Gowrie House while his entourage pursued the stag, or he would not come at all. James's hesitation ruined the scheme. The first word Gowrie received was that the king had not made up his mind to come; the earl did not know that James would arrive, heavily accompanied, until he was almost at the gates. The rest of the events of that day suggest desperate improvisation on the part of the earl. There was a long wait for dinner; the best Gowrie could do was feed the king first, and provide nothing for his followers until James had almost finished. This would give the brothers the chance to lure the king upstairs to receive Elizabeth's messenger, into what would be his temporary prison in the turret, until Gowrie could somehow get those followers out of the house and, indeed, out of Perth. His spur-of-the-moment ploy failed, thanks to his gatekeeper, Robert Christie, whom he had not tipped off. When Gowrie's servant Thomas Cranston came to the earl, who was entertaining

34 3 Sept. 1600, Nicolson to Cecil, *CSPS* xiii, 703–5.
35 1 Nov. 1600, Aston to Cecil, *ibid.*, 792–4. These stories apparently circulated in England too. In February 1603 Aston, who had just returned from England, reported to Cecil that Anna had asked him how the English regarded her. He replied that the English believed that she was friendly to Gowrie's brothers and sisters and that they suspected her involvement in 'some late practice' against the king. She admitted the first and said that she knew nothing of the second. *Ibid.*, 1109–10.

James's followers in the garden, and cried that James had left the house and Gowrie shouted for horses for everyone, Christie, when asked, said that the king had not left. He used the back gate, said Gowrie. No, said Christie, the back gate is locked and I have the key.[36] Gowrie accused him of lying, vanished into the house, returned promptly, and said that James had indeed left. It was while Lennox, Mar, and the others were standing around at the gate, wondering what to do, that they heard James's cry of 'Treason!' Alexander, in despair at the failure and burning to avenge his father, had decided to kill the king, which was no part of Gowrie's plan. Within an hour both the brothers would be dead, taking their secret with them to the next world.

There is, and can be, no proof of the conjecture that it was a message about the succession that brought James to Gowrie House, because, of course, there was no such message. But why else would he go? His initial hesitation is understandable: he did not trust Gowrie and his brother. But the temptation was too great: the story might be true. Gowrie had just come from England; he had been closeted with Elizabeth; she might well decide to bypass official channels, knowing that James disliked Cecil, and deal directly, as monarch to monarch. So James decided to go and find out, once the buck was killed. Secrecy was essential: the pot of gold was the cover story. Did Cecil encourage Gowrie to repeat the Raid of Ruthven? We cannot know whether or not the plan was concocted in England. It is certainly not implausible to suppose that, at the very least, Cecil encouraged Gowrie to do what he could to keep James from active hostility to England; hence the earl's speech at the Convention of Estates. It is likely that the kidnapping was purely Gowrie's idea, but he was sure that he would have English support if he succeeded. After all, Elizabeth's government had applauded the original Ruthven Raid, in a much less dangerous time.

On Christmas Day 1600 the earl of Essex, now busy planning his own conspiracy, which led him to share, in more formal fashion, the fate of Gowrie, wrote to King James seeking support. Among the iniquities of Cecil and his allies, wrote Essex, were 'their juggling with our enemies, their practice for the Infanta of Spain, and their devilish plots with your Majesty's own subjects against your person and life', so that they might 'have the same pleasure in rocking a cradle which some in this state enjoyed when your Majesty first came to that crown'.[37] By this time parliament had formally condemned the Gowries for attempted murder, and, if the above conjectures are correct, James had every reason to think that they intended his death. The family was incorrigible; it was to be uprooted, and no one was to bear the name of Ruthven any more. He forced Queen Anna to dismiss Beatrix and Barbara from her household, to her great anger. He sent to arrest Gowrie's two younger brothers, who were at Dirleton with their mother; they escaped

36 Christie's testimony is in Pitcairn, *Trials* ii, 187–8.
37 *CSPS* xiii, 755–7.

in the nick of time and fled to Berwick, where a sympathetic Sir John Carey hid them for a few weeks before sending them south for their own safety.[38] James sent Sir George Home to Nicolson to say that James regarded receiving them as an unfriendly act; in February 1601 he wanted 'them delivered up in suspicion they are kept for their king's prejudice'.[39]

Rumours of English involvement with Gowrie were rife in Scotland. In his very first report, on 6 August, Nicolson wrote, 'Some false, lying villains gave it out I should have been this day morn at Leith by 3 of the clock and should say, being asked, . . . that I was there attending strange news from beyond the water'.[40] It was in his next letter that he reported that Gowrie while in England 'had been drawn to this intended purpose against the king'.[41] Did James think so? He was much too politic to say. On 14 August Nicolson wrote that 'a great Councillor' had assured him that 'the King believes none of these rumours that the matters should be bred in England but knows the truth and conceals it wisely' – a Delphic remark indeed, but which might refer to Gowrie's use of his perceived favour with Elizabeth to lure James into his trap. In fact, Nicolson wrote, James reportedly said that Gowrie had urged him to deal with the Pope.[42] But the rumours persisted. Gowrie got a cupboard of plate in England, where the plot was hatched (21 August); a 'knight of England' warned James to beware Gowrie (5 September); James was still calling Cecil 'a practicer for the Infanta' (19 October); there was great suspicion and dislike of the Master of Gray because he was in England (also 19 October) – though in fact James, after having ordered Gray to leave England and settle in France at some point distant from the coast, in December gave him permission to return to Scotland to perform some unnamed service.[43] Gray was believed to be an English agent.[44]

Even after the elimination of Essex allowed Cecil to clear the air, and convince James that he was not now, and never had been, a practicer for the Infanta, James's suspicions did not die; they simply focused on Queen Elizabeth. In the autumn of 1602 Beatrix Ruthven turned up in London, seeking help for herself and her brothers. All she wanted, Cecil opined, was to stay quietly there without being harassed, but the English government dared do nothing for her. As Cecil rather wearily informed Gray, Elizabeth believed that, in spite of the secrecy involved, James knew that she was being asked to show favour to the Ruthvens; if she did, she would reinforce his suspicion of her complicity in Gowrie's conspiracy. The thought even crossed Elizabeth's mind, apparently, that James was using Beatrix as a catspaw. The queen had 'a mind resolved to suspect all things that come *ab Aquilone*', and there was a

38 See his letters of 11 Aug., 24 Aug., and 4 Sept. 1600, *Border Papers* ii, 677, 682, 684.
39 *CSPS* xiii, 704, 733.
40 *Ibid.*, 679.
41 *Ibid.*, 681–2.
42 *Ibid.*, 684–6.
43 *Ibid.*, 690–1, 706–7, 711–3, 713–5, 726–7, 751–2.
44 17 Dec. 1600, Cecil to Gray, *ibid.*, 753–4.

report that Beatrix had recently crept into Scotland and seen Queen Anna. Beatrix got nothing from Elizabeth save pity; James apparently was satisfied.[45]

Whatever Cecil and his mistress may or may not have known of Gowrie's plans, there were those in England, especially border officials, who did not believe that Gowrie had any plans at all. Sir John Carey, who described Gowrie as 'the good earl', hinted at the king's responsibility. Alexander came to Falkland because James sent for him; Gowrie 'did not send for the King . . . neither knew of his coming till he was alighted at the door', he wrote Cecil on 11 August. Three weeks later, sending on two versions of events, 'on the King's part and on the earl's part', he supplied the motive. 'It is generally spoken in Scotland that England was the cause of his death, for that he was so well entertained there'.[46] The treasurer of Berwick, Sir William Bowes, who described Alexander as 'a learned, sweet and hurtless young man', thought it was an accident. James began the confrontation by calling Alexander's father a traitor, the youth took umbrage, the unarmed king shouted 'Treason!', and the rest followed.[47]

Neither of these explanations holds much water. The more credible of the two, that of the accidental quarrel, cannot provide an explanation of James's decision to go to Gowrie House in such haste. It also cannot explain either the need for a cover story or Gowrie's repeated insistence that James had left the house, in the face of the gatekeeper's denials. G. M. Thomson, who believes in this theory, can only say that 'on an impulse, during the hunt, James decided to invite himself and his retinue to dinner with Gowrie' in order to find out if Gowrie was some sort of English agent.[48] This is not very plausible. James was not given to acting on impulse, and he would hardly leave, as he did, on a winded horse, ahead of his retinue, and without waiting for the ritual disembowelling of the deer, without some better reason than a wish to see Gowrie. A more intriguing suggestion is that Gowrie asked James to come to Perth because he had a money-raising scheme to propose to the king, which might help fill James's pockets and get Gowrie his £48,000 back. Such a hypothesis is consistent with the theory of either a plot (if false) or an accidental quarrel (if true), and certainly has more to recommend it than Thomson's. But it is open to many of the same objections.

James's journey to Gowrie House was according to a plan – Gowrie's plan, not the king's. Not only was James not impulsive, he was not rash. As he himself put it to the sceptical Robert Bruce, 'If I would have taken their lives, I

45 N.D., but 1602, Cecil to Gray, *Letters and Papers relating to Patrick Master of Gray*, ed. T. Thomson, Bannatyne Club (Edinburgh, 1835), 188–90. See also Cecil's letters to Nicolson in October, and the latter's of 22 Sept. and 13 Nov. 1602, *CSPS* xiii, 1049, 1058–9, 1066, 1074.

46 *Border Papers* ii, 677, 678, 684.

47 2 Sept. 1600, Sir William Bowes to Sir John Stanhope, *CSPS* xiii, 702–3.

48 Thomson, *A Kind of Justice*, 80–1.

had causes enough', a Delphic comment. 'I needed not to hazard myself so'.[49] Murder in the form of accidental death was not James's style. He believed in the law. In spite of its difficulties the only explanation that holds water is that Gowrie had a plan, to seize the king, not kill him. The witnesses agree that he was genuinely surprised when John Ramsay shouted at him that the king was dead; he dropped his guard, and Ramsay ran him through. A dead king was no use to Gowrie – or to Robert Cecil, who did not support the Infanta. What Cecil wanted was to do a deal with James as soon as James could be persuaded to listen, as his subsequent behaviour made abundantly clear. Elizabeth would die soon; far better that her successor be a mature and experienced man with a family, not a boy or another woman, in the person of the Infanta or James's English-born cousin Arbella Stewart.

It is not likely that Gowrie could have succeeded in controlling the king for very long, even if his plan had succeeded. But he would probably have had enough support, both within the country and from England, to avoid the worst consequences of his act of *lèse majesté* and arrange a face-saving compromise. Even if he did not, he would have kept James occupied long enough for the purposes of the English government: the outcome of the Boulogne conference would be known. As it turned out, that outcome came very quickly. Before the end of July the negotiations had collapsed; the English commissioners came home on 2 August, though this (to James) welcome news had not reached Scotland on 5 August. There would be no Anglo-Spanish peace; one of James's greatest fears had been laid to rest.

The behaviour of some of the Edinburgh ministers also turned out to be helpful to James, though that was far from their intention. On 6 August the king's version of the conspiracy, written late at night at Falkland after his return from Perth, reached Edinburgh. The privy council held a public celebration at the market cross; bells were rung and bonfires lit.[50] Almost at once, however, doubts about the king's story began to develop. Differing versions of events appeared, and some of the Edinburgh ministers were openly sceptical, especially Robert Bruce, the king's most outspoken clerical opponent in Edinburgh. The king heartily disliked him, and with good reason. Bruce had preached in support of the unspeakable Bothwell, and had had a major role in the Edinburgh riot of 1596, directed against the king's Catholic officials. 'If the earl and his brother attempted such a treasonable purpose, they had their deaths worthily', Nicolson reported the ministers as saying.[51] [Italics mine.] Another confrontation between king and kirk appeared to be in the making.

In these delicate circumstances James acted promptly and decisively. He returned to Edinburgh on 11 August amid more public rejoicings, and on the following day confronted the Edinburgh ministers at a meeting of the privy

49 Calderwood, *History* vi, 85.
50 6 Aug. 1600, Nicolson to Cecil, *CSPS* xiii, 678–80. Calderwood, *History* vi, 45–7.
51 11 Aug. 1600, Nicolson to Cecil, *CSPS* xiii, 681.

council. Five of them still quibbled; they were ordered to stop preaching altogether, leave Edinburgh within forty-eight hours, and not come within ten miles of the city.[52] In adopting this firm attitude James was taking a calculated risk. He knew that he would be accused of usurping the authority of the church by depriving Edinburgh of its ministers and appointing others to occupy the vacated pulpits temporarily. Nicolson felt that he had acted unwisely, that silencing the ministers would be unpopular and not settle anyone's doubts about what had happened on 5 August.[53] But the king's gamble was successful: the population of Edinburgh did not support its ministers. The five doubters were isolated. Within a month four of them had accepted the king's story; Bruce, who remained doubtful, was banished.[54]

As in the case of the Edinburgh riot of 1596, the king had confronted the church and won, much more easily this time. He pressed home his advantage by settling the question of control of the church in his favour once and for all. Indeed, he had no choice. He planned an early meeting of parliament in order to forfeit Gowrie, the question of clerical representation had to be settled, and the revival of episcopacy was now the only available solution. And so James acted. By the time parliament met in November to forfeit Gowrie and destroy the Ruthvens, three newly appointed bishops were in place; by the end of the year one of them was a member of the privy council. The restoration of diocesan episcopacy was under way.

So James made his political profit from the Gowrie affair, and soon, thanks to the folly of the man he had relied on as his best hope in England, his cup ran over. Essex, in his Christmas letter to James, had asked the king to send an ambassador to England on his behalf by 1 February, and suggested the earl of Mar.[55] James prepared to comply, but fortunately for him the embassy was delayed until after the knowledge of Essex's fiasco had reached Edinburgh. James's great worry now was that he would be publicly associated with Essex, which would greatly damage, if not destroy, his chance of peacefully succeeding Elizabeth. To his relief, and joy, he got everything he wanted. Whatever Elizabeth and Cecil knew about James's dealings with Essex they kept to themselves. And Cecil, through Mar, inaugurated that correspondence with the king which would bring James to the English throne unchallenged and keep Cecil in power until his own death in 1612. Whatever James knew, or suspected, about English instigation of Gowrie's rash action he kept to himself. All he wanted was that Elizabeth and Cecil give no aid and comfort to Gowrie's refugee siblings.

52 *RPCS* vi, 148–9. Calderwood, *History* vi, 56–8, describes the confrontation.
53 14 Aug. 1600, Nicolson to Cecil, *CSPS* xiii, 684.
54 *RPCS* vi, 158–9, 161–2. Calderwood, *History* vi, 86. Bruce's behaviour was positively insulting. In 1602, when he was permitted to return to Scotland, he told James that he was prepared to believe the king's story because Mar had sworn to its accuracy. Pitcairn, *Trials* ii, 305–6. See Lang's account of James's running controversy with Bruce, *Gowrie Mystery*, 99–110.
55 *CSPS* xiii, 755–7.

For the twenty-five years of life that remained to him after what he regarded as a narrow brush with death, King James celebrated 5 August as a famous anniversary and a sure sign of God's favour. The day, along with Essex's self-destruction six months later, was indeed a turning point; had Gowrie succeeded, however briefly, James's grip on the Scottish polity would have been seriously weakened. As it was, one more disobedient aristocrat, who was also a darling of the kirk, had failed to impose his will on the Lord's anointed. The radical leadership of the kirk in Edinburgh had once again played into his hands, and facilitated the restoration of the authority of bishops, which was not only his preferred, but also, now, his only means of controlling those who thought of themselves as God's privy councillors. The king's financial problems remained, of course, but they would vanish when he reached the promised land, a day which now could not be far off.

James was right to celebrate 5 August. Gowrie's conspiracy was the last attempt by a Scottish aristocrat to lay hands violently on his king. Wiser and more experienced men than Gowrie had seen the direction events were taking, and accommodated themselves to it. Those inveterate rivals Huntly and Argyll patched up a truce that neither of them much liked, and Huntly's son married Argyll's daughter. Border brigands like Scott of Bucceleuch and Ker of Cessford turned themselves into agents of law and order; the spoils of the forfeited Bothwell and, eventually, peerages were their reward. In recent years there has been a debate amongst historians about James's attitude toward his nobility and the extent to which he set out consciously to 'tame' them.[56] There can be no argument about the result, however: they were tamed. Gowrie's hopeless attempt to revive the practices of his ancestors was the end of an old song which, with the removal of the court to London in 1603, would henceforth and forever become unsingable.

---

56 See, e.g., M. Lee Jr., 'James VI and the Aristocracy', *Scotia* i (1977), 18–23, and J. Wormald, 'James VI: New Men for Old?' *Scotia* ii (1978), 70–76. K. Brown, 'The Nobility of Jacobean Scotland 1567–1625', in *Scotland Revisited*, ed. J. Wormald (London, 1991), 61–72, is a good brief overview of the position of the aristocracy in James's reign.

8

Scotland and the 'General Crisis' of the Seventeenth Century (1984)

Near the beginning of his elegant brief overview of seventeenth century Europe T. K. Rabb points out that many if not most historians of the period have accepted the notion that, in its middle years at least, the century was one of crisis. 'The term has found its way into most new textbooks,' he writes, 'even when it is not entirely appropriate, and the current generation of students is apparently being taught that the "crisis" can serve as an organizing principle no less powerful than "Reformation" or "Enlightenment".'[1] One of those he cites for corroboration of this view is that brilliant and tireless advocate, practitioner, and (occasionally) progenitor of 'in' history, Lawrence Stone, who accepted the validity of the idea of crisis in 1966, in a review of the first collection of essays on the subject, *Crisis in Europe 1560–1660*, edited by Trevor Aston. Their most recent publications testify to the fact that neither Rabb nor Stone has changed his mind.[2] Nor are they alone. And so it would seem that, in spite of a few nay-sayers like Perez Zagorin, 'the crisis of the seventeenth century' is an historiographical fact of life.

It is, however, a very peculiar fact of life, because no one is quite sure when it began or what it was a crisis of. It is an idea with many fathers, which is not in itself strange, because Clio is a polyandrous muse, especially when she has spawned a new and catchy concept. What is less common is that there is so little agreement as to the nature of the child. To Eric Hobsbawm it is a crisis of the old economic order, to Hugh Trevor-Roper a crisis of the Renaissance court, which led to a struggle between the court and the country, to Roland Mousnier an intellectual and moral crisis, one aspect of which was division within the government itself, to Rabb a widespread cultural malaise, an aspect of what he calls the glacial disintegration of medieval society. J. H. Elliott, on the other hand, argues that there was not a crisis, but rather crises, touched off by the strains of war, a political explanation which appeals to Stone, is not inconsistent with the views of Trevor-Roper, and coincides with those given for the English civil war by the new school of revisionist historians headed by Conrad Russell. Zagorin is unwilling to accept even this: 'There is indeed no way in which the revolutions of Scotland, England,

---

1 T. K. Rabb, *The Struggle for Stability in Early Modern Europe* (New York, 1975), 15. I wish to thank Professor Rabb, and also Professors J. H. Elliott and H. H. Rowen, for their comments on an earlier version of this paper.

2 L. Stone, *The Past and the Present* (Boston, 1981), 133–44. M. Chambers, R. Grew, D. Herlihy, T. K. Rabb, and I. Woloch, *The Western Experience to 1715*, 3rd edn. (New York, 1983), chap.15.

and Ireland, of Catalonia, Portugal, Naples, and Palermo, and of the Fronde in France, can all be accommodated to the same explanatory structure or referred to identical origins.'[3] Not only is there no agreement as to the nature of the crisis, if crisis there was; there is also widespread difference of opinion as to its duration. Mousnier, for example, would have it run from the later sixteenth century to the beginning of the eighteenth; Rabb, by contrast, would limit it to the fifty years or so between the 1620s and about 1670.

What can be made of this? One possible point of departure is that fact that historians as a class are intellectually tidy people and enjoy labels and categories. The seventeenth century was an era in search of an identity: the Reformation was over and the Enlightenment not yet begun. Once upon a time it was the century of Genius, but historians have long since ceased to think of the scientific revolution as the product of genius pure and simple, and in any case genius seemed to be in short supply in other areas of public activity in that century. A second characteristic of historians is that, like humankind in general, they are full of self-esteem and are eager to demonstrate that their own findings, in the area of their own research, have universal significance, and represent some sort of turning point in the human condition. So an historian's own particular 'crisis' becomes expanded into a general 'crisis' – and this idea has been eagerly seized upon, because it is so pleasing to the scholar's self-esteem: who would wish to acknowledge that his or her research was unimportant? And so the seventeenth century found its label: what was once the century of Genius is now the century of Crisis.

One of the advantages of doing research in a history of less-than-major state such as Scotland is that the temptation to magnify findings is minimised. What happened in Scotland was often similar to what happened elsewhere in Europe, and occasionally what happened there was of first-rate importance in European history – the intellectual flowering of the eighteenth century, for example, and the sad career of Mary Queen of Scots because of the significance of her failure for the survival of Protestantism in England and hence in Europe as a whole.[4] Most of the time, however, historians of Scotland are modest about the cosmic significance of their research, perhaps more modest than they should be, and what happened there is a dark mystery to virtually all historians of England, who occasionally cover their ignorance by claiming, as Trevor-Roper did in his seminal essay on the 'general crisis', that Scotland was 'largely irrelevant' to his thesis.[5] But if Scottish historians are understandably reluctant to claim that what happened there may serve as a model for what happened elsewhere in Europe, what did not happen there may be a

3 P. Zagorin, *Rebels and Rulers, 1500–1660* (Cambridge, 1982), i, 139.
4 See, for this argument, M. Lee, Jr., *James Stewart, Earl of Moray* (New York, 1953), 3–6, 278–82.
5 *Crisis in Europe 1560–1660*, ed. T. Aston (New York, 1967), 123. This collection first appeared in 1965. Trevor-Roper has written much on Scotland, but to far from universal applause. See, e.g., W. Ferguson, *Scotland's Relations with England: a Survey to 1707* (Edinburgh, 1977), 110, 118–119.

matter of great significance. The Scottish example effectively torpedoed the Weber thesis, as S. A. Burrell demonstrated some time ago; a recent attempt to confute Burrell's argument is altogether unconvincing.[6] Similarly, what happened, and did not happen, in Scotland is a matter of great importance for the validity of any theory of general crisis.

Scotland was not, of course, a place where nothing happened in the mid-seventeenth century. Those who do not, like Trevor-Roper, dismiss Scotland out of hand tend, like Stone and Zagorin, to lump it together with Catalonia, Ireland, and Portugal as, in Stone's words, 'outlying provinces (which) rebelled against the centralizing process for fear of crushing tax burdens and interference in local liberties'[7] – a generalisation of breathtaking sweep. Elliott draws a cautious parallel with Catalonia in an early article, but his full-scale work on the Catalan revolt makes readers much more aware of the differences than the similarities.[8] There was no ideological component to the Catalan rebellion; David Stevenson, the historian of the Scottish revolution, therefore argues 'that the Scottish revolution had more in common with the revolutions of the 1560s, when the quarrel between state and society was primarily religious in form . . . than with those of the 1640s, which Elliott sees as arising mainly from the fiscal demands of the state'.[9] The closest analogy is that of the Low Countries in the 1560s, with Charles I cast in the role of Philip II, the deracinated son of a native prince who had gone on to a greater crown. But this analogy has its difficulties too, since the strains of wars past and the dread of even greater possible strains from future wars played such a large part in the Netherlanders' thinking, and religious division among the Netherlanders themselves such a large part in the outcome.

It is well known that the massive Scottish uprising against Charles I and his policies began on 23 July 1637, with the celebrated riot in St. Giles Cathedral in Edinburgh on the occasion of the first use of the new prayer book there. Whether distaste for religious innovation was the principal cause of the upheaval was in question even at the time, however. John Spalding, a member of the episcopal bureaucracy in Aberdeen, believed that there was an aristocratic conspiracy. 'They begin at religion as the ground of their quarrel,' he wrote, 'whereas their intention is only bended against the king's majesty and royal prerogative.'[10] Whatever may be conceived as the nature of the causes, there is no doubt that the upheaval in Scotland was the work of

6 S. A. Burrell, 'Calvinism, Capitalism, and the Middle Classes: Some Afterthoughts on an Old Problem', *Journal of Modern History* xxxii (1960), 129–41. G. Marshall, *Presbyterians and Profits: Calvinism and the Development of Capitalism in Scotland 1560–1707* (Oxford, 1980).

7 Stone, *The Past and the Present*, 138.

8 J. H. Elliott, 'The King and the Catalans, 1621–1640', *Cambridge Historical Journal*, xi, no. 3 (1955), 253–71; *The Revolt of the Catalans: A Study of the Decline of Spain 1598–1640* (Cambridge, 1964).

9 D. Stevenson, *The Scottish Revolution 1637–1644* (Newton Abbot, 1973), 326.

10 John Spalding, *Memorialls of the Trubles in Scotland and in England, A.D. 1624–A. D. 1645*, ed. J. Stuart, Spalding Club (Aberdeen, 1850–1), i, 79–80.

the landed classes, the lairds and especially the nobility: they led it and dominated it, though they had support at all levels of Scottish society. The imposition of the much disliked prayer book, 'Laud's liturgy', the Popishness of which was deliberately magnified by the opponents of Charles's religious policy, triggered the upheaval, and religious concern ran very deep and produced the ideological enthusiasm which was necessary to success. But religious discontent by itself, here as elsewhere, could not galvanise enough of the people who counted to produce a successful uprising.[11] The covenanting ideal which became the shibboleth of the Scottish revolution was in existence in the 1590s.[12] The religious discontent of that era was widespread, and was given far more eloquent voice and dynamic leadership by Andrew Melville than by any of the opponents of King Charles, and the monarchy was far weaker in the 1590s than in 1637. But the religious riot in Edinburgh in 1596 was a damp squib, and Andrew Melville ended his days in exile, because in the 1590s the nobility held aloof. By 1637, however, the alliance of magnate and preacher that had played such a large part in the unhappy career of Mary Queen of Scots had formed again. So the question that must be addressed in determining the place of the Scottish evidence in any theory of general crisis is that of the role of the nobility. Had their position undergone so much long-range deterioration by the accession of Charles I that, sooner or later, they would have lashed out at a crown that was steadily and inexorably grinding them down, as the Netherlands' aristocracy had done? Was Charles I Philip II *redivivus*? Or did Charles, by his errors of omission and commission, bring his ruin upon himself?

To answer this question it is necessary to go back at least as far as the Reformation, which had a very profound impact on the perceived nature of the Scottish kingship, the position of the aristocracy in the state and society, and its relations with the crown. Prior to the mid-sixteenth century Scottish monarchy was personal monarchy; everything depended on the person of the king, his character and his abilities. At the national level the magnates welcomed royal leadership, and, if they got it, were prepared to acquiesce in occasional outrageous acts, such as James II's murder of the earl of Douglas. They, in their turn, were leaders, almost petty kings, in their local areas, with their power resting on the tripartite base of kinship, bonds of manrent, and their positions as lords of regality. Their relations with the crown were normally not adversarial, though individual kings were usually at odds with one aristocrat (or aristocratic faction) or another. The crown's ability to survive repeated minorities in the fifteenth and sixteenth centuries and emerge with its strength almost unimpaired is proof of this. Aristocrats feathered their nests during these minorities, but they also acquiesced in the

11 On this point see the interesting discussion by I. Cowan, 'Church and Society in Post-Reformation Scotland', *RSCHS*, xvii (1971), 185–201.
12 On this point see S. A. Burrell, 'The Covenant Idea as a Revolutionary Symbol: Scotland, 1596–1637', *Church History*, xxvii (1958), 341–2, and his 'The Apocalyptic Vision of the Early Covenanters', *SHR*, xlviii (1964), 12–13.

king's right to issue an act of revocation after he came of age, annulling what had been done in his name during his minority. The apogee of the Scottish kingship as personal monarchy came in the reign of James IV, the last of the truly pre-Reformation Scottish kings. His immense popularity with all classes of Scottish society caused his nobles to do what they had never done since David II's disaster at the battle of Neville's Cross in 1346: follow their monarch eagerly on the road to England and, unfortunately, to even worse disaster at Flodden.[13]

The Scottish Reformation would never have succeeded without aristocratic leadership, and in many ways the Reformation strengthened the position of the aristocracy as a class. It rid them of their clerical rivals for office and royal favour. In the absence of a godly prince – and there was none in Scotland for a quarter century after the triumph of the Reformation – it was their duty as godly magistrates to advance the work of the Lord. Protestantism thus provided them with an ideological justification of for their position in the state that they had previously lacked. As is well known, it also enabled them to consolidate their grip on church property, and even the most sincerely religious did so without compunction. John Knox's railing in his *History* at the greed of the aristocracy may have been exaggerated, but it was far from completely unjustified.

In some ways, however, the triumph of the Reformation undermined the position of the nobility. Calvinism was the least hierarchical of all the established forms of sixteenth-century Christianity, both theologically and with respect to polity. By the 1580s a quasi-democratic form of the latter had evolved thanks to Andrew Melville and his followers. For this development the nobility had themselves to blame, to the extent that the Melvillians were reacting against the aristocratic appropriation of church property which the continued existence of an episcopal (and abbatial) structure had permitted. Melville's polity was one with which the aristocracy found it difficult to cope. The godly magistrate loomed large in the plans of the reformers, but his proper function, according to both Knox and Melville, was to follow the lead of God's privy councillors, the clergy. This the nobility would not do, not even genuinely pious men like the Regent Moray, much less the hard-bitten and worldy Morton, during whose regency tulchan bishops became notorious. So the aristocracy held aloof from the kirk sessions, which filled up with lesser proprietors, and as those bodies grew in influence in the localities as administrators of the kirk's discipline, the local influence of the nobility correspondingly diminished. That influence was further weakened owing to the widespread development of the feu farm, which was also a consequence of the religious vicissitudes of the sixteenth century. The possession of a feu meant far greater independence for the holder, many of whom were small

13   For a perceptive analysis of pre-Reformation kingship see J. Brown (now Wormald), 'The Exercise of Power', in *Scottish Society in the Fifteenth Century* ed. J. Brown (Wormald), (London, 1977), 33–65.

men, below the class of laird. 'The beginning of the seventeenth century,' it has been noted, 'was the great age of the portioners and the bonnet lairds, and the feuars who, given the chance, began to climb the social ladder.'[14] It has also been pointed out that all sorts of tenants, not just feuars, were achieving greater security, which 'created an aggressive spirit' among them.[15] The consequence of all these developments was that the lords' grip on their followers began to slacken. It was a portent that in 1568, when Mary Queen of Scots made her futile attempt to recover her throne, more higher aristocrats were to be found on her side than on the Regent Moray's. 'Methinks I see the noblemen's great credit decay in this country,' wrote the English agent Sir Henry Killigrew in 1572 in a remark which is often quoted, 'and the barons, burghs and such-like take more upon them.'[16]

The impact of the Reformation on the position of the crown was much more far-reaching than was the case with the aristocracy. The attitude of John Knox with respect to the right – nay, the duty – of the godly to revolt against an ungodly sovereign is well known. This, taken together with the circumstances surrounding the deposition of Catholic Mary in favour of her prospectively Protestant infant son, led to an appeal to both history and political theory in the writings of George Buchanan, the tutor to the boy king and the propagandist for the new regime, which effectively undermined the idea of personal monarchy. Buchanan also contributed to the blackening of the historical reputation of James III, the last Scottish monarch prior to Mary to be overthrown by his subjects – and the only one, other than John Balliol, since the days of Malcolm Canmore – a process which reached its peak during James VI's minority. As cogently expressed, 'The rebellion of 1488 could be transformed into a great constitutional act. Even more important, so could the events of 1567.'[17] Once the role of the crown became the subject of constitutional definition, and the behaviour of its wearer the subject of clerical scrutiny in the matter of godliness, the automatic loyalty to the king which is the essence of personal monarchy began to disintegrate.

James VI, when he came to govern for himself after 1585, thus faced an unprecedentedly complex situation, the nature of which he understood very well. There was unprecedented opportunity, that of succeeding to the crown of the ageing virgin in Whitehall and the limitless (by Scottish standards) wealth and power that went with it. But there was great danger also: the pupil of Buchanan was well aware of the change in the perception of the nature of Scottish kingship. His nobles had subjected him to a total of seven coups between 1578 and 1585. Suffering as they did from their own new

14 M. Sanderson, *Scottish Rural Society in the Sixteenth Century* (Edinburgh, 1982), 190.
15 *Ibid.*, 188.
16 Quoted in P. H. Brown, *History of Scotland* (Cambridge, 1912), ii, 117.
17 J. Wormald, *Court, Kirk, and Community: Scotland, 1470–1625* (London, 1981), 147. On the legend of James III see N. Macdougall, 'The Sources: a Reappraisal of the Legend', in Brown (Wormald), *Scottish Society*, 10–32, where he compares its growth with the development of the legend of Richard III in England.

insecurities, and queasily aware that if James should become king of England he would be beyond their reach, they might be tempted to treat him as, Buchanan said, the Scots had anciently treated sovereigns whom they regarded as unsatisfactory – as, indeed, they had treated his mother. The temptation would increase if they were repeatedly exposed to sermons from critical preachers who, under the new dispensation, claimed the right to say what they liked from the pulpit without accountability to civil authority.

As is well known, James picked his way through this minefield with great skill. By 1603 he had succeeded not only in making himself more powerful than any king since Robert Bruce, but also in constructing a new theory of kingship and a new basis of loyalty. The treaty of alliance with England which was negotiated in 1586 was the key to his success. From the days of David II and Edward Balliol to those of his own nonage English governments had supported disgruntled Scottish aristocrats, given them refuge and, sometimes, material aid. That process now virtually ceased, and the alliance, since it survived the shock of Mary's execution, greatly enhanced James's chances of being accepted as Elizabeth's successor. James followed the conclusion of the treaty with a rather reluctantly made entente with the kirk in order to free his hands to deal with what he and his political mentor, John Maitland of Thirlestane, agreed were his most pressing political problems: obtaining control of his government and bridling his magnates. By the middle of the 1590s he had succeeded in doing this; he then seized upon the occasion of the clerically-inspired riot in Edinburgh in 1596, directed against his allegedly popish financial advisers, to set about bringing the kirk under control in its turn. This latter process was well under way, though not yet complete, when James became king of England in 1603.[18]

James accompanied his political successes with a new theory of the nature of Scottish kingship, something absolutely essential if he was to justify his policy, particularly with respect to the kirk. Historians of James's reign in England, who rightly praise Queen Elizabeth for remaining silent on such matters – in her circumstances that was by far the wisest course to follow – have been far too prone to criticise James for his discourses to the English parliament on the nature of kingship. What they fail to realise is that in the Scotland of the 1580s and 1590s these theoretical undertakings were essential to the strengthening of James's position as king. He behaved in much the same way as Henry VIII and Thomas Cromwell had in the 1530s, and for much the same reasons, and in this matter, as in so much else, James's Scottish experience determined his behaviour in England. To counter the claim of Andrew Melville and his fellow clerics to membership on God's privy council, James in the *Trew Law of Free Monarchies* espoused the doctrine of

18 For James's policy before 1603 see M. Lee, Jr., *John Maitland of Thirlestane* (Princeton, N. J., 1959) and 'James VI and the Revival of Episcopacy in Scotland, 1596–1600', above; G. Donaldson, *Scotland; James V–James VII* (Edinburgh, 1965), chaps. 10–12; D. H. Willson, *King James VI and I* (London, 1956), chaps. 1–9; Wormald, *Court, Kirk, and Community*, chap. 9.

the divine right of kings. This assertion had the greater impact because Melville and his allies could not deny that, for all his unseemly personal behaviour and regrettable fondness for aristocratic Papists like the earl of Huntly, James was theologically impeccably orthodox. To Buchanan's historical construction James opposed his own version of Scottish history: his ancestor, King Fergus, had come to Scotland as a conqueror. Scottish kingship antedated the law, which, therefore, depended upon the king, not the other way around. A good king will rule justly and in accordance with the law, wrote James, but his position as king depends neither upon the law nor upon the goodwill of his subjects. He is accountable only to God.

In the decades of James's personal rule in Scotland, then, the medieval concept of personal monarchy disappeared in theory; it also vanished in practice. Making use of, among other things, the property placed at his disposal by the annexation of the temporalities of benefices to the crown in 1587, James created a *noblesse de robe* out of the ranks of lairds and lawyers and younger sons and cadet branches of the great houses, councillors and administrators who served him loyally and through whom he governed Scotland both before and after 1603. The magnates were not shut out, however. James insisted that they obey him, that they play the game by his rules; if they refused, they were driven into exile like his cousin Francis Stewart, earl of Bothwell, or even executed, like another cousin, Patrick Stewart, earl of Orkney. The vast majority, however, acquiesced, and they received their reward, in the form of places at the council table – though not, with one or two exceptions, responsible positions in the government – access to the royal ear, a more secure grip on the church property which they or their ancestors had succeeded in acquiring, one way or another, in the course of the last century. And they retained their local power. James was not keen on hereditary sheriffdoms and regalities, occasionally contemplated an attack on them, but never carried one through. Furthermore, the king was gregarious and had the personal touch; he treated the Scottish aristocracy – most of them – as his personal friends. Even after 1603, when it was more difficult to deal directly with the king – James did not encourage visits to London, and anyway it was expensive – there were plenty of Scots as court through whom the king could be approached. And that their king, the man who treated them as old friends, now ruled over the auld enemy was a source of satisfaction, psychic to some, material to others who benefited from the king's generosity with the wealth of his new subjects.

Whatever pride Scottish aristocrats might feel at the enhanced position of their sovereign after 1603, however, their own position was enormously weakened. Sir John Gordon of Gordonstoun saw very clearly what had happened. 'Doubtless our king will do what he can to curb the nobility of Scotland, and to diminish their power, thereby to conform them to the custom of England,' he wrote to his nephew the earl of Sutherland about 1620. 'It is not now with our noblemen as when our king was resident in Scotland. Hardly then could the king's majesty punish any of our greatest nobility when they had offended, by reason of their great dependencies and friendship. But now, he being absolute King of all Great Britain, the cause is altered. He may, when he listeth, daunt the proudest and mightiest of you all.'[19] Conforming them to England worried the nobility, and many others in Scotland as well, because this meant, for James, altering Scottish institutions, procedures, and even manners, in order to bring the 'wild, unruly colt' into tandem, with what he called St George's 'towardly riding horse'.[20] His proposals for union met no overt opposition in Scotland, but evoked no enthusiasm, even amongst his own officials, and there was considerable relief when English opposition killed the project. James was more successful in bringing about greater conformity with England on the part of the Scottish church. He completed the process of restoring diocesan episcopacy, to the accompaniment of some high-handed and arbitrary behaviour on the part of his principal agent, the earl of Dunbar. Having dealt with church polity, James turned to church services, and in 1617 undertook to impose what became known as the five articles of Perth. One of these, the order to take communion kneeling, directly affected everybody, not just the aristocracy, and was very unpopular. Another change, the creation of justices of the peace, threatened the grip of the aristocracy on the local community because it endangered their monopoly of the administration of justice. The steadily increasing burden of taxation affected lairds and burgesses as well as aristocrats, and was as popular as higher taxes always are.

James was a cautious and patient man, however. When faced with unexpected opposition, as with the five articles of Perth, he pulled back. The articles were not withdrawn, but in the last few years of the reign no serious attempt was made to enforce them. After the death of the heavy-handed Dunbar in 1611, the administration in Edinburgh, under the aegis of James's new *eminence grise*, Lord Chancellor Dunfermline, like Dunbar the cadet of an aristocratic house, governed very successfully by means of consensus, conciliation, and compromise. Dunfermline died in 1622, but his colleagues carried on in his tradition. So in James's day the potential strains in the relationship between crown and aristocracy did not develop. In 1625 the position of the crown was far stronger, both in theory and in fact, than it had been in 1567, but the skill of James, and of the men through whom he ruled in Scotland, had succeeded in reconciling the nobility, and the other people who counted, to their diminished position. The transformation of personal monarchy into one which was both bureaucratised and justified by heavenly sanction was complete, and had been accomplished with the acquiescence – nay, the support – of the ruling classes. King James was an

19 Sir W. Fraser, *The Sutherland Book*, 3 vols. (Edinburgh, 1892), ii, 357.
20 *Correspondence of King James VI of Scotland with Sir Robert Cecil and Others in England during the Reign of Queen Elizabeth*, ed. J. Bruce, Camden Society (London, 1861), 31–2.

absolute king who governed with the advice and consent of his important subjects.[21]

In 1604 Secretary of State Balmerino wrote to his English counterpart, Robert Cecil, to indicate his distaste for the king's proposals for union. 'Most of us could be rather content to continue in our wonted condition,' he wrote, than 'to match with so unequal a party, strengthened by the continual presence of our Prince, to whom time and subsequent ages will make us strangers.'[22] Balmerino was prescient, though even he might have been surprised at the rapidity with which his forebodings were justified. Charles I was indeed a stranger in the land of his birth, knew very little about it, and displayed very little interest in remedying that ignorance. But he had a policy: 'the aggrandizement of the crown in wealth and influence, the emancipation of lesser men from the power of the magnates and, perhaps mainly, the material wellbeing of the church.'[23] These objectives were not in themselves unreasonable; what created trouble for Charles was the abruptness of his methods. Without consulting his father's advisers he issued a revocation which called in question all gifts of land which had belonged to either the crown or the kirk made since 1540, as well as all grants of hereditary offices and regalities, a programme which, if carried out, would have adversely affected every major landowner in Scotland and a good many lesser ones as well. The revocation caused a tremendous uproar, on both political and legal grounds: since Charles' minority had only seven months to run when he succeeded to the throne, it was not clear that there was anything that he could legally revoke beyond those made since his accession. Charles's first reaction to the opposition he had generated was to attempt to intimidate it by destroying the political power of its leaders, King James's old councillors and officials. He pointedly ignored them, though keeping them in office to perform routine functions. He separated the privy council from the Edinburgh legal fraternity by insisting that no one should be a member of both the court of session and the council, which he in effect reduced to impotence. The uproar did not subside, however; people feared, as Archbishop Spottiswoode remarked, that the revocation would 'call in question all men's rights since King Fergus'.[24]

Charles did not intend to revolutionise the structure of Scottish landholding. His purposes were to put an end to the feudal superiority of the holders of church and crown lands over those to whom they had feued those lands, to eliminate hereditary offices and regalities, and to improve clerical incomes by arranging for higher stipends out of the teinds, most of which were in private hands. He was not planning to expropriate anybody:

---

21 For James's government of Scotland after 1603 see M. Lee, Jr., *Government by Pen: Scotland under James VI and I* (Urbana, 1980).
22 *Salisbury Mss.* xvi, 98–9.
23 Donaldson, *Scotland: James V–James VII*, 295.
24 13 July 1627, Spottiswoode to the earl of Annandale, J. F. S. Gordon, *Ecclesiastical Chronicle for Scotland*, 4 vols. (London, 1875), i, 487–8.

compensation would be paid for the surrendered rights and privileges. He seems to have imagined, however, that all this could be accomplished simply by issuing the necessary orders. He believed that 'because he was their anointed king his subjects would accept without resentment the curtailment of their power by him.'[25] He did not understand that he had to find a means of governing Scotland, that he could not simply destroy his father's system of conciliar government, as he did during his first eighteen months on the throne, and replace it with nothing, or with nothing more than the advice of a handful of deracinated courtiers and men without influence among the people who counted north of the Tweed.[26] In fact it is arguable that Charles never did understand this. He was saved from the immediate consequences of his stupidity by the emergence of a favourite in the person of William Graham, earl of Menteith, who became Charles's friend and his principal adviser on Scottish affairs from the beginning of 1628 until his own ruin in 1633. Menteith was a member of the old nobility; he shared many of their views and therefore could serve as a link between the king and the land-holding classes in Scotland. His great service to his master was to diffuse the panic which the revocation had caused by arranging that its implementation would be entrusted to a large commission which the people who counted in Scotland could control and whose decisions the king agreed to accept, and, secondly, by having the commissioners concentrate first on the matter of the teinds. This meant that nothing at all was going to be done very quickly: before there could be any change in the status quo it would be necessary to determine the value of the teinds, parish by parish, and that would take time. As the landowning classes saw what was happening, their panic subsided. Their losses would not be great, and would not occur rapidly, because the king, having promised to pay compensation for their surrendered rights, was not, in fact, able to buy very many of them out for lack of resources.[27]

As long as Menteith retained the king's ear Charles's rule in Scotland went well enough. Some of Charles's unpopular innovations were allowed to wither: the effort to revive justice ayres, which if successful would have made inroads on both the judicial power of the aristocracy in the localities and the income of the Edinburgh lawyers, and the proposed commission of grievances of 1625, which Sir James Balfour described as 'nothing else but the star chamber court of England under another name, come down here to play the tyrant, with a specious visor on its face'.[28] The heavy and unpopular taxation

25 D. Mathew, *Scotland under Charles I* (London, 1955), 137.
26 For a full discussion of this matter see M. Lee, Jr., 'Charles I and the End of Conciliar Government in Scotland', below.
27 For the details of Charles's reign in Scotland prior to 1637 see M. Lee, Jr., *The Road to Revolution: Scotland under Charles I, 1625–1637* (Urbana, 1985). There are excellent brief summaries in Donaldson, *Scotland: James V–James VII*, chap. 16, and in Stevenson, *Scottish Revolution*, chap. 1.
28 *The Historical Works of Sir James Balfour*, ed. J. Haig, 4 vols. (Edinburgh, 1825), ii, 131.

continued, to be sure, and the king's enthusiasm for the project led in 1632 to the creation of an Association for the Fishing which the Scots regarded as an attempt on the part of English fishing interests to aggrandise themselves at Scottish expense, though the ostensible purpose was to compete more effectively with the Dutch. But Menteith's supremacy in the king's councils insured relative governmental stability in Scotland, since the nobility trusted him to convey their opinions to the king. Menteith ruined himself, however, by a combination of antiquarianism and vanity. He laid claim to the earldom of Strathearn, by virtue of his descent from one of the sons of Robert II. The claim was in fact sound, and Charles recognised it. The earl's enemies, however, were able to make use of it and of the confusion surrounding the messy marital affairs of Robert II to inform the king that Menteith had all but claimed to be the rightful king of Scotland. The evidence that Menteith ever did such a thing is extremely flimsy, but to a believer in divine right such as Charles even the faintest suggestion of such a claim was damning. Menteith lost his new title, his offices, and his influence, and spent most of the rest of his life fending off his creditors.[29] There was no one to take his place.

Menteith's ruin coincided with Charles's first and only visit to Scotland before the outbreak of the troubles, in the summer of 1633. The visit was an utter disaster. What the Scots learned from the presence of their sovereign was that he was to all intents and purposes an Englishman, that he had a chilly and stand-offish personality, that he would neither listen to nor tolerate those who disagreed with him, that he bore grudges, that his financial exactions would continue at a heavier rate than before, and that he could be expected in the near future to make further changes in the church to bring about greater conformity with the church of England. This last matter was no mere continuation of the policy of his father, however. The church to which the Scots would now be expected to conform was much changed from that of King James owing to the ascendancy of Archbishop Laud and those who thought like him. Furthermore, the instruments of change would be church-men – churchmen of Laud's stripe, who now began to be promoted to Scottish bishoprics. In the days of Menteith, who, like the rest of his class, was hostile to the intrusion of churchmen in politics, Charles had kept the Scottish bishops at arm's length; now he began to favour them, financially and in other ways. Worse still, he began to use them in government, in high office and low: Archbishop Spottiswoode became chancellor, all but three bishops were privy councillors, and many parish ministers sat on the commissions of the peace. The landowning classes, their pipeline to their sovereign gone with Menteith, took alarm once more, their alarm fuelled by the continuing imprisonment without trial of one of their number, Lord

---

29 A fascinating and circumstantial account of Menteith's ruin, written by the unpleasant and unscrupulous Sir John Scott of Scotstarvit, who gleefully took credit for it, is printed in *SHR*, xi (1913–14), 284–96, 395–403.

Ochiltree, for impugning the loyalty of Charles's friend the marquis of Hamilton. The crowning blow was the appalling stupidity of bringing Lord Balmerino to trial in 1635 on a charge of leasing making for having in his possession, and allegedly circulating, a document critical of the king's policy, especially in matters of religion, and full of unflattering comparisons with the behaviour of 'blessed King James'.[30] The charge could not be made to stick; Balmerino was convicted, by an 8–7 vote, of knowing of the document and doing nothing about it, something for which he could hardly be executed, and Charles in fact pardoned him a year or so later. A move designed to intimidate the opposition was thus metamorphosed into a petty and ineffectual act of spite.

By the middle of the 1630s, then, after a decade of Charles's rule, the Scottish aristocracy felt aggrieved and alarmed, but not cowed. They felt no enthusiasm for their Anglicised king, who neither knew them nor consulted with them – where James had summoned the Scottish parliament seven times during his twenty-two years of absentee rule, Charles called it but once, on the occasion of his visit. Although they had hitherto avoided its potentially ruinous consequences, the revocation had an immense psychological impact on them because it made clear to them the weaknesses in their position with respect not only to their king but also to their more independent-minded inferiors. With Menteith gone they felt weak and frozen out, without a role to play. Many of them were in an uncomfortable financial position; like Menteith they had gone into debt in order to acquire property or to engage in expensive building ventures.[31] The hidden agenda that they and the rest of the political nation feared was epitomised in a letter written by Viscount Wentworth, the king's deputy in Ireland, in July 1638, after the troubles began. Wentworth expressed the hope that Charles would subdue the Scots by force and impose not only the English prayer book but also English government and laws, and govern Scotland henceforth as Ireland was governed, by means of the English privy council.[32] The union with England, of which so much had been expected was turning into a real threat to Scotland's continued existence as a separate entity.

So 'Laud's liturgy' became the occasion of resistance. The new service book was not a mere pretext, however. People genuinely believed that it was Popish, a belief strongly reinforced by the increasingly Popish atmosphere of the royal court owing to the growing influence of Queen Henrietta Maria and her entourage, which now included the Pope's new agent, a Scottish priest named George Con. Charles's clerical enemies in Scotland engaged in all sorts of distortions of the content of the service book, and it was never considered

---

30 The document is printed in John Row, *The History of the Kirk of Scotland from the Year 1558 to August 1637*, ed. D. Laing, Wodrow Society (Edinburgh, 1846), 376–81. This Lord Balmerino was the son of the secretary of state mentioned earlier.

31 On this point see ed. J. Imrie and J. G. Dunbar, *Accounts of the Masters of Works*, 2 vols. (Edinburgh, 1982), ii, intro. xx, lxvi–lxxii.

32 R. Bagwell, *Ireland under the Stuarts*, i (London, 1909), 236–7.

on its merits.[33] One reason why it was never so considered was that Charles imposed it by fiat, without consultation with anyone other than the bishops, another example of his utter ineptitude with respect to the means chosen to achieve his ends. 'While the wisdom of Charles's aims might be debated,' it has been observed, 'there is no room for controversy about his methods, which were consistently ill-advised.'[34]

In the space of twelve years, then, Charles's policies had brought about the reconstitution of that alliance of aristocrat and kirkman which had pulled down his unhappy grandmother and which his father had broken in pieces. Charles had done more than that. Mary, for all her shortcomings, retained the support of a substantial minority, perhaps even a majority, of the people who counted in Scotland. Charles in 1637 had almost no support at all. At bottom the crisis he provoked was one of government, fuelled by nationalistic enthusiasm and ideological revulsion. Its principal components were a regime seen as alien and annexationist, an immensely unpopular religious policy, a financial policy regarded as extortionate and likely to get worse, and a ruling class shaken by the perceived weaknesses in its position and anxious to recover the ground it had lost. A speech to the privy council in December 1637 on the part of Lord Loudoun, one of those whose open opposition to the king's policies in 1633 had cost him an earldom, provides an excellent indication of the aristocracy's state of mind:

> The subject of our complaint and controversy is religion, and laws of the kingdom, upon which dependeth both the welfare of the church and commonwealth, our condition of life, our liberty and fortune in this transitory world, and the eternal happiness in the life to come . . . In (the) service book are sown the seeds of diverse superstitions and heresies, that the Roman mass, in many and substantial points, is made up therein; which service book and other innovations have neither warrant of general assembly nor of act of parliament, but contrary to both are introduced by the bishops.[35]

Loudoun's declaration gave pride of place to religion, and repeated the (by then) standard argument that the service book was Popish, but he clearly was more concerned with what he regarded as the illegality of the procedures the king employed to introduce it. Within three months of Loudoun's speech the signing of the National Covenant began, and the mid-century crisis in the British Isles was under way.

This bald and summary gallop through almost a century of Scottish history leads, in this writer's view, to the conclusion that King Charles

33 See the analysis in the introduction to G. Donaldson, *The Making of the Scottish Prayer Book of 1637* (Edinburgh, 1954), especially 70–83. For Charles's court see C. Hibbard, *Charles I and the Popish Plot* (Chapel Hill, 1983), esp. chaps. 2, 3, and 5.
34 Donaldson, *Scotland: James V-James VII*, 295–6.
35 Haig, *Balfour*, ii, 240–1.

brought his ruin upon himself. There was nothing inevitable about the Scottish revolution: the king provoked it by his own ineptitude, and once the resistance began he refused to make any concessions until it was far too late. Had he ruled in the manner of his father, paying heed to interests of the people who counted in Scotland, and governing through them, there need not have been any confrontation, as the relative tranquillity of the Menteith years demonstrated. But Charles never did show any comprehension of the fact that he needed to work at the task of governing Scotland. Menteith's role as a sort of unofficial viceroy devolved upon him by a happy accident. He was not replaced; Sir John Stewart of Traquair, who aspired to the position and in effect acquired it by 1637, along with an earldom and the office of lord treasurer, could not act as a spokesman for the nobility as Menteith had. Or, indeed, for anyone else: Traquair had no natural constituency at all. He achieved his eminence through a combination of bootlicking, bullying, and intrigue, and so mishandled the matter of the service book through his jealousy of the bishops that he contributed substantially to his master's ruin.

Charles's inability to cope with the rebellion he had unnecessarily provoked in Scotland led, of course, to the summons to the Long Parliament and to all that followed from that fateful decision, including the upheaval in Ireland after Strafford's departure from that unhappy land. Ever since the appearance of S. R. Gardiner's magisterial volumes historians of England have argued that the causes of the English civil war stretch back a long way in time, certainly behind the accession of Charles, though, of course, there are many different views as to just how far back they do go, and as to their nature: constitutional, economic, social, intellectual, 'rising' this and 'falling' that. Historians who ventured to think otherwise have been mercilessly trounced; C. V. Wedgwood was dismissed as both frivolous and superficial for beginning her account of the civil war in 1637. Since the rise of Conrad Russell and his school, however, this short-term view no longer seems so foolish. Russell's analysis of the politics of the 1620s concludes that the difficulties of that decade were owing at bottom to the government's inability to fight a successful war.[36] A few more years of Buckingham and blundering in battle might have produced an upheaval in the 1630s. But as long as there was no war, Charles could govern tranquilly and without parliament, as he did after 1629. Though occasionally flirting with them, he avoided continental military entanglements during the most active and critical phase of the Thirty Years War in the 1630s; there is no reason to suppose that he would have become involved as the weary contestants staggered toward peace in the 1640s, and without war there was no need for parliament. There might have been even less need in future: in 1637 the king's opponents feared that a decision favourable to the crown in the ship money case, thus establishing the legality of the tax, would end resistance to payment, which had not been all

36 C. Russell, *Parliaments and English Politics, 1621–1629* (Oxford, 1979).

that effective in any case.[37] In short: if Charles had not himself provoked a rebellion in Scotland, what evidence is there that there would have been an English civil war after all?

Without the British cases the concept of 'general crisis' dissolves into air; what remains is the series of specific crises identified by J. H. Elliott. They had their common features, to be sure. Governments were regarded as inept or oppressive or both – what else, after all, causes political upheaval? – and in many cases, though not all, the reaction took the form of some sort of aristocratic constitutionalism. Sometimes, however, as in Sweden and the Dutch Republic, the crisis was, in H. H. Rowen's phase, a 'revolution that wasn't'.[38] The principal cause of the convulsions that racked the continent was the Thirty Years War, appalling, destructive, exhausting, seemingly endless and unendable owing in large measure to human stupidity, militancy, and miscalculation on all sides,[39] and misleadingly named, because it really did not shudder to a stop until the treaty of Oliva in 1660. This frightful calamity affected the British kingdoms, to be sure, but it was not the cause of what happened there. War had nothing to do with the course of events in Scotland prior to 1637, which makes the Scottish example unique. Scotland was, like Ireland, Catalonia, and Portugal, an outlying area, as Professor Stone says – he might have added Naples too – but in all those other cases it was war which brought about the uprising, as it did in England. The sixteenth-century analogies fit the Scottish example no better, because of the part war played in them. Enthusiasm for comparative history, for finding parallels across space and time, has too often lured its partisans into playing fast and loose with the facts, into brushing aside inconvenient evidence which does not fit into the models and thus threatens the great discovery, into forgetting that the behaviour of individual human beings frequently determines what happens in history. But what happened in Scotland and in King Charles's other kingdoms in the middle of the seventeenth century does not resemble what happened elsewhere in Europe. Like that chimera 'scientific history', so dear to the hearts of the structuralists, the 'general crisis' is a figment of the scholarly imagination. Its common features are too common. Difference of opinion over the nature of the state and the locus of authority, ideological conflict, fiscal pressures – these existed everywhere in seventeenth-century Europe, and in every other period in modern civilisation, with the possible exception of the age of enlightenment. The hypothesis of 'general crisis' is an example of what J. H. Hexter once called historical lumping. As so

37 I owe this point to Dr. Kevin Sharpe, who is at work on a study of the 1630s in England.
38 H. H. Rowen, 'The Revolution that Wasn't: The *Coup d'Etat* of 1650 in Holland', *European Studies Review*, iv, no. 2 (1974), 99–117. M. Roberts, 'Queen Christina and the General Crisis of the Seventeenth Century', in Aston, *Crisis in Europe*, 206–34.
39 For one example see the recent account by R. Bireley, *Religion and Politics in the Age of the Counterreformation: Emperor Ferdinand II, William Lamormaini, S. J., and the Formation of Imperial Policy* (Chapel Hill, 1981).

often happens, however, the imaginative hypothesis of the lumper falls victim to the dogged footnoting of the splitter. Historians of England have often justly been accused of being insular in paying no heed to those parallels to English developments which do exist elsewhere in the world, and perhaps it is their sensitivity to such charges that has led them to embrace the concept of 'general crisis' so eagerly. Here, however, is one case where insularity seems altogether justified.

This essay should end where it started, with the ideas of T. K. Rabb – with, more precisely, the title of his book: *The Struggle for Stability in Early Modern Europe*. Stability of a sort came to western civilisation in the last third of the seventeenth century, thanks in part to the coincidental ending by 1660 of both the insular crisis with the restoration of Charles II and the continental one with the treaties of the Pyrenees and Oliva. This stability is really Rabb's starting point: how to explain the great contrast between the age of Louis XIV and what had gone before? He adopts the hypothesis of crisis in his explanation, but in fact there had been no stability in western civilisation since the age of Thomas Aquinas. Rabb is much nearer the truth when he talks of the glacial disintegration of medieval society. The shattering of the unity of western Christendom by the Reformation, a process which culminated in the great European war which began in 1618, was the final stage of that disintegration. Rabb here may well have fallen victim to his own stylistic virtues: glaciers are not supposed to disintegrate explosively, but this one did – a bang, not a whimper. What the first two-thirds of the seventeenth century witnessed were the death throes of a civilisation, and the birth of much that was new, messily mixed together. Perhaps there is a name for this sort of thing, and an hypothesis that can be constructed to fit it. 'General crisis', however, both in name and in conception, will not do. It is one of those fruitful errors which are of great value because their very provocativeness compels historians to think. This one has now served its purpose, and can, and should, be laid decently to rest.

9

James VI's Government
of Scotland after 1603[1] (1976)

Except for its religious aspects, the domestic political history of Scotland in the last twenty-two years of the reign of James VI has been rather neglected by historians. For this neglect the king's own happy gift for turning a memorable phrase is in some measure responsible. 'This I must say for Scotland, and may truly vaunt it,' he remarked, 'here I sit and govern it with my pen. I write and it is done; and by a clerk of the Council I govern Scotland now, which others could not do by the sword.'[2] James said this in 1607, to a parliamentary body much less obliging than the one he had left behind in Edinburgh. He had every right to feel satisfaction with his accomplishments as king of Scotland, and he had every intention of governing Scotland by his pen. To a certain extent he did so, and his personal responsibility for formulating and ordering the implementation of policy is most apparent in connection with religion. What 'everybody knows' about James's rule in Scotland after 1603 is that he imposed diocesan episcopacy there, and then, later, foolishly insisted on the acceptance of the five articles of Perth. This, though oversimplified, is true enough; and because it is true, historians have tended to take James's remark at face value and assume that he did indeed govern Scotland with his pen, that his officials in Edinburgh were a collection of faceless toadies who unhesitatingly and unquestioningly carried out the royal instructions. The two major contemporary historians, Archbishop John Spottiswoode and the presbyterian David Calderwood – both, be it noted, concerned chiefly with the church – said or implied as much. David Masson, the Milton scholar who edited the relevant volumes of the *Privy Council Register* in the last two decades of the nineteenth century, said so repeatedly, in spite of some of the evidence under his own nose.[3] A careful examination of this evidence suggests that things were really quite different, that the government of Scotland was not merely a matter of unthinking obedience to royal instructions, and that Edinburgh officialdom had rather more independence than is usually supposed.

1 This essay is a revised version of a paper first given at the Conference on Scottish Studies at Old Dominion University, Norfolk, Virginia, in April 1975.
2 Quoted in C. V. Wedgwood, 'Anglo-Scottish relations, 1603–40', *Royal Historical Society Transactions*, 4th series, xxxii (1950), 31. The best modern treatment of Scottish political history, 1603–25, is to be found in the necessarily brief chapters 12 and 15 of G. Donaldson, *Scotland: James V–James VII* (Edinburgh, 1965).
3 Spottiswoode, *History*; Calderwood, *History*. Masson over a twenty-year period starting in 1880 edited thirteen volumes covering the years 1578–1627.

It was obvious in the spring of 1603 that the government of Scotland would henceforth be very different, with an absentee king, but it took some time before the shape of the new regime became apparent. For one thing, James took a lot of important people with him when he went south, including so many officials that at first the government found it difficult to function at all.[4] For another thing, James confidently expected that some form of governmental union would follow closely on the union of the crowns, and therefore that there was no need to make elaborate administrative arrangements for Scotland. About all that was done in the first year was to arrange a postal service, which would be necessary whatever the outcome of union negotiations. It was an efficient system which produced remarkably little complaint. The postmasters were well and promptly paid for their services, which no doubt helped. A letter normally took about a week to pass between London and Edinburgh, often less, sometimes more in winter. An indication that the service worked well is the fact that there is no record of any complaint on the part of King James, who was usually very quick to take notice of any of his servants' real or fancied shortcomings.[5]

With the disappointing outcome of the negotiations between the English and Scottish union commissioners at the end of 1604 it was clear that more permanent arrangements for governing Scotland would have to be made. There were two groups of Scots involved in this matter, the people in London around the king and the ones in Edinburgh. The London Scots comprised three general types, great lords, household and bed-chamber people, and government officials. Most of the officials who went south with James in 1603 returned fairly quickly, like Sir David Murray, the comptroller, or else resigned their positions in the Scottish government, like Lord Kinloss, who became master of the rolls in England and gave up his seat on the court of session. But there was one who neither resigned nor went home, and until his death in 1611 he was to be, after the king, the single most important figure in the Scottish government. This was the lord treasurer, Sir George Home of Spott, soon to be earl of Dunbar. He made his intentions clear in March 1605 when the king appointed Sir John Arnot of Birswick as treasurer-depute to handle the details of business in Edinburgh.[6] Dunbar's influence with the king rested on long personal association – he had been a courtier for years – and on his undoubted efficiency at getting things done. He was not one of those handsome young men one hears so much about in connection with James; he was a fat, superficially affable type in his forties, something of a *faux bonhomme*, and very ambitious. His position at court and in the household – he was master of the wardrobe, and also a member of the

4 See the letters of Dunfermline, still only Lord Fyvie, to the king on 30 May 1603, and to Sir Robert Cecil on 17 July , in *Letters and State Papers during the Reign of King James the Sixth*, ed. J. Maidment (Edinburgh, 1838), 56; PRO, SP 14/2, no. 57.
5 For the postal service see W. Taylor, 'The king's mails, 1603–1625,' *SHR*, xlii (1963), 143–7.
6 *RPCS*, vii, 27.

English privy council, and, briefly, chancellor of the exchequer in England – and the king's confidence in him, gave him the opportunity to dominate Scottish politics as the king's principal agent, if he could find a way both to manage his fellow officials in Edinburgh and to keep his influence at court. He was aware of all of the pitfalls involved in trying to govern at a long distance, all the potential foot-dragging and obfuscation. So he did what he had to do to achieve his goal: he travelled. He went back and forth between London and Edinburgh at least once a year, sometimes oftener, and his appearances had something of the impact of a royal visit. No one doubted that Dunbar was the bearer and interpreter of the king's wishes and that he was prepared to be ruthless about implementing them, and the council treated him accordingly.[7] His occasional employment of the tactics of surprise, of not revealing the king's orders until he judged that the psychological moment had arrived, added to his effectiveness.[8] Dunbar's methods involved a considerable expenditure of time and energy, and may well have shortened his life; from 1607 his health began to deteriorate. But there is no doubt that his tactics were effective. The fact that none of the other London Scots had either the position or the inclination to copy them after his death in 1611 helps to explain the shift in the centre of gravity in the management of Scottish affairs which took place at that time.

Of the many other Scots in London there were five who were politically important, potentially at least. The duke of Lennox, the king's cousin and the only duke in the three kingdoms until the elevation of Buckingham, involved himself very little in Scottish politics, chiefly because he did not wish to leave the court.[9] His great position and his personal closeness to the king made it possible for him to intervene effectively when he wished to, however, and sometimes he did, usually when his personal interests were involved. The earl of Mar, who at this point in his career spent much of his time in England, was rather more politically minded than Lennox, and also had the king's confidence and trust. But Mar was lazy, and often had to be pushed into taking political action. One of those who did the pushing was his kinsman Sir Thomas Erskine, who replaced Sir Walter Raleigh as captain of the king's guard. Erskine was an ambitious man who maintained a considerable correspondence in Scotland; he was a channel through whom to reach the king, and through whom the king kept himself informed. So was John Murray of Lochmaben, the keeper of the privy purse, whose importance

7 See, for instance, the fulsome letter of praise of Dunbar which the council sent to James in Aug. 1605, in Sir W. Fraser, *The Elphinstone Family Book of the Lords Elphinstone, Balmerino, and Coupar*, 2 vols. (Edinburgh, 1897), ii, 152–3, and the letter of the earl of Cassillis to James in 1606, in NLS, Denmilne MS. i, no. 62. This letter makes it very clear that Dunbar was regarded as the king's spokesman.
8 See, for example, his letter of 26 Nov. 1606 to Mar in *Mar and Kellie MSS., Supplementary Report* ed. H. Paton, HMC (London, 1930), 38–9.
9 For Lennox's attitude see his letter of 28 Feb. 1611, in *Laing MSS.*, ed. H. Paton, HMC (London, 1914), i, 123–4.

grew with the years; both Erskine and Murray wound up with earldoms. Finally, there was Alexander Hay of Whitburgh, the 'clerk of the Council' James mentioned in his speech to parliament. Hay was the London secretary for Scottish affairs; in 1608 he was promoted to the position of secretary of state.

And of course there was the most important London Scot of all, King James himself. His correspondence with his ministers in Edinburgh was largely formal; an average of about sixty letters of instruction per year are recorded in the privy council's register of missive letters.[10] More important were the private letters he received from the important people in Scotland: government officials, bishops and nobles. These people could also convey their views indirectly to James by corresponding with English officials and with other Scots around the court. James therefore had ample means of keeping himself informed; it was not possible to mislead him for very long. It was possible to persuade him to change his instructions, but not permanently to deceive him about whether or not they had been carried out.

Of the Edinburgh Scots by far the most important was Alexander Seton, earl of Dunfermline, president of the court of session in 1593 and promoted to lord chancellor as a result of his efforts on the union commission of 1604. His position was a strong one; the king liked him because he was both learned and obsequious, and he had the advantage of coming from a family which had been steadily loyal to the crown and to James's mother – and James put a very high value on loyalty to his mother. The Setons were an aristocratic family, but as a younger son Dunfermline had had to make his way up by service to the government; so he had connections and support among both those who supported and those who opposed the bureaucratising policies of Chancellor Maitland in the 1580s and 1590s.[11] He was the only man who might have challenged Dunbar for pre-eminence with the king, but some incautious behaviour on his part in 1605, which led to his being accused of condoning the holding by the clerical opponents of the bishops of a so-called General Assembly at Aberdeen, almost cost him his office. He was able to hold on, but only by dint of acquiescence in Dunbar's supremacy and abandonment of his rather passive opposition to the king's plan to impose diocesan episcopacy in Scotland. This opposition was not based on religious considerations. Dunfermline officially conformed, but the fact that he was really a Roman Catholic was not a very well kept secret. His opposition was owing to fear that the bishops, once restored to power in the church, would get involved in politics, and to personal dislike of James's chief clerical adviser, Archbishop Spottiswoode.

Dunfermline's possible rivals for pre-eminence among the important Scots who remained in Scotland all suffered from handicaps of one sort or another. Many of the higher aristocracy were either not politically minded, like the

10 SRO, RC 9/1.
11 For Maitland see M. Lee, Jr., *John Maitland of Thirlestane* (Princeton, 1959).

marquis of Hamilton, or else were the chancellor's friends. Among the politically active higher aristocracy, Huntly and Errol suffered from their open Roman Catholicism and constant embroilment with the kirk. Montrose, whom Dunfermline succeeded as chancellor, was angry and jealous, but he was old – he died in 1608 – and he had been tried and found wanting. Argyll was potentially dangerous, but he was preoccupied with highland questions, he mismanaged his personal finances, he ultimately married an English Roman Catholic lady, spent his time in England, and turned Roman Catholic himself, and anyway the king did not much like him. Amongst the chancellor's official colleagues there were three with the influence and connections to be a potential danger. James Elphinstone, Lord Balmerino, the secretary, was one; but he was still expiating various blunders he had made in the conduct of foreign policy in 1600 and 1601. He was clever, but James did not altogether trust him, and he was shortly to fall victim to the king's need for a scapegoat, in the matter of the king's alleged letter to Pope Clement VIII in 1599. His office was now far less important anyway, since there was no longer such a thing as an independent Scottish foreign policy. Sir David Murray, now Lord Scone, the comptroller, was ambitious, greedy, and rather erratic, and temperamentally unsuited to the arts of persuasion – a useful hatchet-man, but not much more. The best brain of the three, Thomas Hamilton, the lord advocate, suffered from his comparatively humble origins, for his immediate forebears had been burgesses in Edinburgh. He was also handicapped by the fact that, as a lawyer, he was a member of the profession of which Dunfermline was the head. Other important officials like the treasurer-depute, Sir John Arnot, and his successor, Gideon Murray of Elibank, could not effectively mount a challenge to the chancellor by themselves, seldom contemplated it, and, indeed, found it to their advantage not to do so. All these men, save Balmerino, who lost much of what he had, got rich from their government service, and were chary of risking what they had gained in an undertaking which would probably be futile.[12]

Bishops did not get rich from government service, or from their dioceses either, and Archbishop Spottiswoode, who became a privy councillor in 1605, was both eager for the chancellor's overthrow and willing to work for it.[13] But he too suffered from various handicaps which in the end rendered his efforts nugatory. For one thing, he was not the primate. George Gledstanes, the archbishop of St Andrews, turned out to be a poor choice. He was fussy, politically naïve, and a nepotist. By the time he died and Spottiswoode succeeded him as primate, in 1615, Dunfermline's position was unassailable. Secondly, very few of Spottiswoode's episcopal colleagues turned out to have much political ability or drive. The two who did, Andrew Knox of the Isles

12　The rewards received by these men and other privy councillors, including Dunfermline, are detailed in William Taylor, 'The Scottish Privy Council 1603–1625' (unpublished Ph.D. thesis, Edinburgh University, 1950), App. D.
13　On the question of clerical incomes see W. R. Foster, *The Church before the Covenants* (Edinburgh, 1975), 43–5.

and Spottiswoode's old friend James Law of Orkney, were both preoccupied with problems peculiar to their dioceses: the messy situation in the western isles on the one hand, and the alleged rapacity and tyranny of Earl Patrick of Orkney on the other. So Spottiswoode could count on very little help within his own organisation. Finally, there was the matter of an issue. Spottiswoode's best chance was to persuade the king that Dunfermline opposed the restoration of diocesan episcopacy. As has been said, there was some truth in this. But once the chancellor gave way on this point, there was very little the archbishop could do.

Spottiswoode and Dunbar worked very closely together between 1606 and 1610 to implement James's policy of restoring diocesan episcopacy, and the archbishop's best chance of becoming James's chief adviser in Scottish affairs would have been on Dunbar's death. Unfortunately for Spottiswoode, Dunbar died at the wrong time, in January 1611; this was too soon after the restoration of episcopacy for the landed classes to acquiesce in a bishop's wielding great power in the state, and anyway Gledstanes was still primate. So Dunfermline succeeded to Dunbar's influence with the king; he was to wield it until his death in 1622. There was one brief challenge at the end of 1612, mounted by Thomas Hamilton, now promoted to be secretary of state, based mostly on the hope that he could make use of the great influence with the king of his kinsman Robert Ker. The chancellor handled this crisis without too much difficulty, and was never seriously threatened again.

Dunfermline's methods were very different from those of Dunbar. In the first place, he could not make his base at Whitehall, as Dunbar had done – nor, indeed, did he want to. Dunfermline disliked travelling, and complained when he had to go to court. So he had to depend on his allies there; he had been carefully cultivating them, and he had a good many. Ever since the union negotiations in 1604 he had been on excellent terms with Salisbury, and his first thought on Dunbar's death was that Salisbury would be his chief channel to the king.[14] But his visit to court in the spring of 1611 convinced him that this would not do. Salisbury's influence was waning after the failure of the Great Contract, and in any case it was far more prudent to work through Scots. Dunfermline's other principal channel to court after 1603 was Queen Anne. Since 1593 he had been the head of the committee which managed her Scottish properties; she liked and trusted him; and her closest female friend, Lady Jean Drummond, was very friendly with Dunfermline, whose first wife, Lilias Drummond, was Lady Jean's sister. For Dunfermline the usefulness of this connection was always limited, and became more so after 1614, when Lady Jean got married and began to spend much of her time away from court. King James did not take political advice from his wife or her friends, and never had; but for the sake of domestic peace he was prepared to pay some attention to the queen's wishes and complaints. She would certainly have complained if Dunfermline, a fellow Roman Catholic, had been dismissed; so

14 See his letter of 8 Feb. 1611 to Salisbury, PRO, SP 14/61, no. 70.

for the chancellor the chief use of this channel was basically negative, to prevent a catastrophe like loss of office.[15] To achieve positive results Dunfermline worked principally through two other people. One was Murray of Lochmaben, who found it useful to co-operate in return for Dunfermline's help in furthering his ambitious estate-building plans in the south-west. The other was Sir Thomas Erskine, now Viscount Fenton, and also the chancellor's kinsman by marriage; Erskine's son and heir was the husband of the chancellor's eldest daughter. The method Dunfermline used was letter-writing – 'Once a week both you and the chancellor shall hear from me,' Fenton wrote to his cousin Mar, now lord treasurer, in September 1617.[16] Dunfermline's and Fenton's secretaries also exchanged letters with some regularity. Fenton was the principal channel, with Lochmaben as a sort of back-up. 'You must excuse me to trouble you with my packets, so long as Lord Fenton is from court,' Dunfermline wrote to Lochmaben in July 1614.[17] Dunfermline also wrote with some regularity to the king, in a tone that ranged from flattering to obsequious, and when he was particularly anxious to convince James of the merits of his arguments he made extensive use of classical analogies and Latin quotations. The preferred technique was for Dunfermline and his allies to agree among themselves and then present the king with an acceptable proposal. 'You know how much it troubles him,' wrote Fenton, 'when matters are in question and don't fall, at such a time, to free himself from pain and trouble.'[18] It is a great pity that so little of this correspondence has survived; we would otherwise know much more than we do about the real 'government by the pen.'

One more aspect of Dunfermline's methods is worth considering here. By contrast with Dunbar, whose favourite device was intimidation, Dunfermline was a committee man. Machiavelli's works were in his library, but he preferred to be loved rather than feared. This was partly a matter of temperament, and partly the result of experience. He had once attempted the politics of confrontation, in 1596, when as the chief of the Octavians he was the principal target of the mob in the famous Edinburgh riot of 17 December of that year. That episode had set back his career very seriously. So his policy now was to make himself so necessary and useful to so many people that his position would become unassailable. One of his assets in this connection, and one which he used with immense skill, was his very large family; the marriage net he created was just about as complicated as that of the Habsburgs, and equally useful. He himself married three times into aristocratic houses; in the process he displayed a taste for very young girls which would certainly have interested Dr. Freud. The result was a large collection of daughters, whom he married not only into aristocratic families

15 For a good brief discussion of Anne's position and relations with James after 1603 see G. P. V. Akrigg, *Jacobean Pageant* (New York, 1967), 207, 264–8.
16 *Mar and Kellie MSS Supplement*, 80.
17 Maidment, *Letters and State Papers*, 223.
18 *Mar and Kellie MSS Supplement*, 64–5.

like the Erskines and the Hays but also into the rising 'official' families which the policy of Chancellor Maitland had created, like the Lindsays of Balcarres and the Maitlands themselves. In addition, Dunfermline arranged the marriages of the children of his older brother, Robert Earl of Winton, who had died in 1603. The result was that by the time he was finished, a very large number of the important families in Scotland were closely connected to him, and therefore naturally had some interest in his retention of power.

None of what has thus far been said, of course, bears upon the proposition suggested at the outset of this article, namely, that Edinburgh officialdom had more influence in the determination of policy after 1603 than has usually been supposed. Highland policy affords an interesting and significant illustration of this influence. This was an area about which James had some definite ideas, set out to implement them by his pen, but after about half a dozen years allowed his councillors in Edinburgh to determine policy – their policy, not his.[19]

The king's attitude towards the highlands had three major facets to it – one undoubted fact and two opinions. The fact was that the crown was getting no money from the area. The two royal beliefs were, first, that the highlands were potentially very rich economically, in foodstuffs and fish and goodness knows what else, and, second, that the highlanders were incorrigibly barbarous. If anything was to be made of the area they had to be either wiped out or subjected to the rule of lowlanders. Until the later 1590s James had had neither the leisure nor the resources to attempt to cope with the highlands; but in the parliament of December 1597 an act was passed authorising the creation of three new towns in Kintyre, Lochaber, and Lewis, and requiring all highland chiefs and landlords to produce their title-deeds in the exchequer by May 1598. In consequence of this legislation the island of Lewis was eventually declared forfeit to the crown, and leased to a group of lowland adventurers headed by the duke of Lennox, whose object was to drive out or subdue the inhabitants and plant the island with lowlanders.[20] The king chose to act via what might be called private enterprise in this matter, largely for financial reasons. It would cost the crown far less this way, and anyhow it was becoming increasingly difficult for the government to get lowlanders either to turn out when summoned for punitive expeditions to the highlands or to pay money in taxes for them.

Thus began an effort on the part of King James to bring the highlands under his control by peopling them with lowlanders and reproducing lowland civilisation there. It turned out to be an utterly impractical policy. The highland chiefs naturally disliked it and did what they could to sabotage it; if the Lewis plantation succeeded, their turn might come next. The earls of

19 Some of the ideas in what follows were first suggested to me in a seminar paper written for me several years ago by Dr. Buchanan Sharp, now a professor at Santa Cruz, whose perceptiveness is herewith gratefully acknowledged.
20 *APS*, iv, 138–9, 160–4; *RPCS*, v, 455; A. Cunningham, *The Loyal Clans* (Cambridge, 1932), 171.

Argyll and Huntly also disliked it. They had been the beneficiaries of the crown's traditional highland policy, traditional since the time of James IV at least, of relying on the Campbells and the Gordons to hold the wild clansmen in check and rewarding them for it. If the new policy succeeded, their great positions in the west and the north-east respectively might be eroded. So the Lewis adventurers never had much of a chance. As early as April 1599 they were in trouble and asking for help,[21] and soon they became discouraged. The local opposition was too strong and the prospect of profit too uncertain, especially once it became apparent that the settlers would have to hold down their acquired property by force. James tried repeatedly over the next ten years to get a successful colonising venture launched, sometimes with the assistance of punitive expeditions which, before 1603, he occasionally promised to lead in person, though he never did. He alternated the colonising policy with occasional reversion to the old system of using Argyll and Huntly to control the area, if they would agree to pay suitable rents on their new acquisitions.

Neither of these policies commended itself to Dunfermline and his fellow councillors. They were convinced that plantation would not work well, and that grants of power to Huntly and Argyll might work only too well. The policy they advocated became clear for the first time in 1605, in the commission issued to Lord Scone, who was to lead one of the many ineffectual punitive expeditions of those years. Scone was to get money out of the highlands by agreement with the local chiefs rather than by coercion. He had the authority to feu crown lands and to issue infeftments and leases on satisfactory terms.[22] Two years later, in 1607, the council tried again. After the collapse of a set of negotiations with Huntly – they could reach no agreement on a suitable rent for the northern Hebrides – the council issued a commission to one of the highland chiefs, the chancellor's friend Kenneth MacKenzie of Kintail, to deal with the inhabitants of the northern Hebrides in the king's name.[23] James was not yet ready to accept the necessity of working through the highland chiefs themselves, however. He annulled Kintail's grant as far as Lewis was concerned, organised one more lowland syndicate, and this time proposed to support the adventurers with a massive armament which would include resources drawn from England and Ireland. This expedition, planned for the summer of 1608, marks the real turning-point in highland policy. James intended that it should finally subjugate what he called the 'rebellious and insolent persons inhabitants within the said Isles.' The lieges were ordered to muster in July, and a convention of estates was summoned to decide 'how the expedition for the Isles may be best prosecuted.'[24] The king's

---

21 14, 20 Apr. 1599, George Nicolson to Sir Robert Cecil, *CSPS*, xiii, 447, 451.

22 *RPCS*, vii, 115–7.

23 *Ibid.*, 336. Dunfermline had been friendly with Kintail for a long time and sold him some property in the 1590s; in 1614 his daughter married Kintail's son and heir.

24 *RPCS*, viii, 59–61, 72, 73.

plan made the council very uneasy; but, an attempt on its part to come to a prompt agreement with two of the major highland chiefs having failed, it had to put the king's wishes before the estates. The convention was recalcitrant; after a long debate there was reluctant agreement to 'serve according to the laws of the country.' But there was to be no tax.[25]

A month or so after this rather unsatisfactory meeting the king appointed Lord Ochiltree as his lieutenant for the forthcoming expedition, with Bishop Knox of the Isles as head of his advisory council. James gave Ochiltree considerable discretion in his instructions, and there was also a subtle shift in their tone. Where, shortly before, James had been writing about the disgrace entailed in having part of his kingdom 'still possessed with [sic] such barbarous cannibals,' he now told Ochiltree to encourage the islesmen to submit and hear the terms on which James would be willing to extend his favour to them. There were no references to barbarism, extirpation, and colonisation. This new royal moderation was probably owing to the persuasiveness of Bishop Knox, whom the council sent to court with a proposal that the king appoint a lieutenant for the expedition.[26] Ochiltree's expedition was a great success, in a curious and unexpected way. He did no fighting to speak of; he obtained the surrenders of two important castles, destroyed a large number of ships, and, most spectacularly of all, lured almost all of the important chiefs of the southern isles aboard his own ship to hear a sermon, and promptly weighed anchor and set sail for Ayr, thus in effect kidnapping them. They were warded in various royal castles while James and his councillors decided what to do with their success.

What the council wanted was made clear in a persuasive letter to the king from Bishop Knox. He had kept a record of Ochiltree's expedition, wrote Knox, so that James would be correctly informed, and 'also understand how easy it is to your Majesty with a little help of the advice of such as has [sic] been there . . . to . . . induce them all, without hostility or opening of your highness' coffers, to accept of such a solid order as may reduce them to a hasty reformation, in no age hereafter to alter.'[27] James was not altogether convinced, but in December 1608 he agreed to appoint a committee to draw up recommendations for him. His instructions indicated a further shift in his attitude. There was still an insistence that with peace and order the highlands could be made to flourish economically, and still a desire to plant towns, presumably with lowlanders, though he did not say so. But the emphasis now was on civilising and Christianising the barbarous inhabitants and collecting the king's rents, and on reducing the power and lands of the chiefs rather than eliminating them. He was loath, he said, to uproot any of the population there

25 *Ibid.*, 73, 93–5, 506–7, 737; *APS*, iv, 404; *State Papers and Miscellaneous Correspondence of Thomas, Earl of Melros*, ed. J. Maidment, 2 vols., Abbotsford Club (Edinburgh, 1837), i, 45–7.

26 *RPCS*, viii, 113–14, 738, 739–40, 766–7.

27 *Original Letters relating to the Ecclesiastical Affairs of Scotland . . . 1603–1625*, ed. D. Laing, 2 vols., Bannatyne Club (Edinburgh, 1851), i, 152–3.

unless absolutely necessary, or to burden his lowland subjects any further with service or taxes for this purpose.[28]

These guidelines amounted to a virtual abandonment by James of his colonisation policy of the last decade, partly because of its demonstrated costliness, for which, it was apparent, his Scottish subjects were utterly unwilling to pay, and partly because a much more fertile field for colonisation had just opened in Ireland. In the spring of 1609 the council sent Bishop Knox to court with the committee's suggestions; he returned in June with the king's authorisation to go to the isles with the comptroller and with one of the captured highland chiefs, Hector MacLean of Duart, who was to be released from ward for the purpose. The king's letter of instructions was very vague, and gave the council considerable discretion, which it now proceeded to use. It ordered Knox to make a survey of royal property in the isles, persuade those chiefs who had not submitted to the government to do so, to hold courts and convoke the lieges if necessary. But it gave Knox very little money, only £2,000, to underline the pacific character of his journey, and it decided not to send the comptroller, whose presence would create the impression that the bishop's purposes were chiefly fiscal and punitive. Furthermore, it released, not just MacLean of Duart, but all the chiefs Ochiltree had swept up, on their finding caution to return to Edinburgh at a fixed date and to co-operate with Knox on his mission.[29]

The result of Knox's journey was the well-known statutes of Icolmkill, agreed to in August 1609 by the bishop and the great majority of the important highland chiefs. There were a large number of specific provisions in these statutes, but by far their greatest significance was that they recognised the chief's authority. He was responsible for his clansmen, and for the observation of these and other laws within his bounds. There was no mention of pains and penalties for violations, no attempt to reduce the chiefs' property holdings, and arrangements were made to improve communication between them and the administration in Edinburgh.[30]

The question now was, would the king accept these statutes, which amounted to a reversal of his policy for the past decade? He finally did so, in the spring of 1610, and with some modifications in later years, they remained the basis of the government's highland policy till the end of the reign. They worked pretty well, because the chiefs now found co-operation both safer and more profitable than resistance. Rory MacLeod of Dunvegan, for instance, built up a flourishing trade in live cattle with the south, and the value of the MacLeod estates in Skye and Glenelg rose substantially.[31] The Icolmkill policy represented a triumph for the council's point of view, the abandonment of the king's ten-year-old colonisation scheme, and in most

28 *RPCS*, viii, 742–6.
29 *RPCS*, ix, 24–33.
30 *Ibid.*, 752–6.
31 S. G. E. Lythe, *The Economy of Scotland in its European Setting, 1550–1625* (Edinburgh, 1960), 11.

areas – Islay and Kintyre are the exceptions – the abandonment of the even older attempt to govern by means of half-feudal, half-patriarchal magnates like Huntly and Argyll. The strength of the government helped to make the chiefs more willing to co-operate, and thus made it possible for the king to live with the clan system and try to amend it rather than wipe it out. At the same time the government's financial weakness led the council in Edinburgh to advocate, and the king finally to accept, a policy which promised to produce some income for the government from the area rather than expenditure, as in the past.

The matter of the highlands is one of the most conspicuous examples of the proposition that it was the council which made policy rather than the king, but not the only one. In economic questions, for instance, by about 1609 the council was making almost all the crucial decisions. Even in religion, there is some evidence that Dunbar and Spottiswoode forced the pace until 1610; after Dunbar's death there was a lull until Spottiswoode became primate in 1615, when the forward march resumed. There is no doubt, however, that in this case the king's wishes were followed, though there are examples of his being successfully dissuaded from an action which his councillors or his bishops, or both, thought unwise. It should be stressed again that there was no overt disobedience to the king. It was a matter of persuasion, or of holding up an order until the objections to it could be pointed out, always very humbly, and with the acknowledgment of the king's superior wisdom. Dunfermline and his colleagues became very expert at persuading James to see things their way, so much so that if the administration of Scotland from 1603 to 1625 is to be described as government-by-pen, one could make an excellent case that the really effective writing was done in Edinburgh rather than in Whitehall.

10
King James's Popish Chancellor (1982)

That the Scottish Reformation was vehemently anti-Catholic from its inception is an historical truism that hardly seems to require demonstration. John Knox declared that one Mass was more dangerous than ten thousand armed men, and lectured his sovereign on the iniquities of the Roman harlot whom she cherished. A generation later Andrew Melville found a large number of Anglopiscopapistical propositions in the writings of his sovereign, King James, who fell far short of Melville's ideal of a godly prince. A generation later still, in July 1637, the first use of a new prayer book alleged to be even more Popish than its English counterpart touched off the famous riot in Edinburgh which led to the civil war. All this is well known. Not so well known is the fact that for almost twenty years Alexander Seton, earl of Dunfermline, a man whom everyone believed to be a Roman Catholic, though he outwardly conformed, held the highest office in the king's gift, the lord chancellorship, and conducted himself in office in such a way that after his death men of all shades of religious opinion combined to praise him and his stewardship. The reasons for his success in overcoming the handicap of his putative Catholicism deserve closer examination; they provide a revealing insight into Jacobean politics and attitudes.

Seton was born in 1556,[1] the third son of George, 5th Lord Seton, a rather stupid man whose great virtue of loyalty, to the ancient faith and to Mary Queen of Scots, created all sorts of problems for himself and his family. As a younger son Alexander was destined for the church. Queen Mary, his godmother, gave him the lands of the priory of Pluscarden as a godbairn's gift, and the title of prior was formally conferred on him at the age of nine. Many members of aristocratic families became commendators of monastic benefices in this period without any expectation that they would become clerics, but in this case it seems likely that Lord Seton genuinely intended Alexander for the church. In 1571, when the boy was about fifteen, he was sent off to Rome and became a student at the Jesuit-run German college, where he acquired that excellent classical education and enthusiasm for books which is so apparent in his letters and which was to be of great help to him in his relations with his equally learned king. How long he stayed in Italy is not clear, but there is no evidence for the assertion that he took holy orders.[2] From Italy he

1 The date usually given is 1555. When he died in June 1622, however, he was described as being in his sixty-seventh year, which would mean that he was born between June 1555 and June 1556. His portrait by Gheeraerts, dated 1610, gives his age as 53. These, taken together, indicate a birth date in the first half of 1556.
2 George Seton, *Memoir of Alexander Seton, Earl of Dunfermline* (Edinburgh, 1882), 19; M. Dilworth, 'Scottish Students at the Collegium Germanicum', *Innes Review*, xix (1968), 20–1.

went to France, where he studied law. He was absent from Scotland for almost a decade in all; he returned late in 1580, when the rise of the king's French cousin Esmé Stuart, who ultimately became duke of Lennox, held out the hope of better days for families like the Setons, doubly pilloried during the regency of the earl of Morton in the 1570s as Catholics and as followers of the fallen queen.[3] Seton managed to keep his footing amid the vicissitudes of Scottish politics in the early 1580s, though he was almost ruined in the spring of 1583 thanks to his father's habit of allowing the family house at Seton to be used almost openly as a headquarters for visiting Catholic priests. One of these, a Jesuit named William Holt, was seized as he was about to depart for France; among the letters he was carrying was one from Seton to his old school master in the seminary at Rome. The duke of Lennox, wrote Seton, had been so successful with the king that James's mind was alienated from the ministers. He expressed the hope that foreign aid would be available to restore the true faith, and reported that Holt's ministrations had provided 'great satisfaction and consolation'.[4] Unfortunately for Seton, Lennox had recently been driven from the country by the ultra-Protestant regime of the Ruthven Raiders. Seton underwent an interrogation, but avoided real unpleasantness when they in their turn fell from power in June 1583. The overthrow of the Ruthven Raiders was no great help to Seton in other respects, however, because the man who came to dominate both king and government was that dazzling and greedy adventurer Captain James Stewart of Bothwellmuir, recently created earl of Arran. This title was regarded as the prerequisite of the Hamiltons; Seton's only sister was the wife of the Catholic Lord Claude Hamilton, one of the two effective heads of the family. Under these circumstances Seton could expect nothing from Arran; he therefore supported the coalition which overthrew Arran in November 1585 and received his reward in the form of a seat on the privy council and, in January 1586, an appointment as an extraordinary lord of session in place of one of Arran's supporters. This appointment was somewhat unusual, since the function of the extraordinary lord of session was to serve as a link between the fifteen ordinary lords, originally thought of as professional judges, and the privy council; the typical appointee to this office was an important aristocratic politician or an official like the lord treasurer, whose seat was virtually *ex officio*. Seton was neither of these things, but he was a lawyer who was expected to be useful to the new administration and his appointment pending a vacancy among the ordinary lords of session may be seen in this light.

With Arran's downfall James VI, now nineteen years old, began to govern in fact as well as in name. The principal domestic political goal of the young king and his political mentor, John Maitland of Thirlestane, secretary of state

3 In 1577 Seton had been deprived of the temporalities of Pluscarden for failure to conform to the established Protestant church; the benefice was conferred on one of Morton's bastard sons. In 1581 Seton got it back again. *RMS*, iv, 717; *APS*, iii, 276, Calderwood, *History*, iv, 400.

4 Calderwood, *History*, iv, 394, 430.

in 1585 and lord chancellor from 1587 till his death in 1595, was to enhance the royal authority by curbing the independent power of the upper aristocracy and the kirk.[5] This entailed, among other things, the creation of a class of reliable government servants. Seton was just the sort of man they needed: a younger son of an aristocratic family, professionally trained, and with his way to make in the world, a man who would find government service rewarding in both a psychic and a material sense. He was also, like his cousin Maitland, one of those by whom James set great store: men who had been loyal to his mother and then transferred that loyalty to him. Seton had done just that, brushing aside the attempts of Mary's agents to involve him in their impractical scheming in the mid-1580s, and making himself as useful as he could. He was faithful in his attendance at council meetings, did his best to persuade Elizabeth's veteran ambassador Sir Thomas Randolph that he was friendly to England, and served on the committee of the articles at the parliament of 1587 which enacted the legislation Maitland devised to implement his policy.

But what of Seton's faith? He was, after all, a Roman Catholic, son of a Catholic father who in 1584 was writing to the Pope with more enthusiasm than sense of his hopes of James's conversion.[6] Seton knew very well that such hopes were chimerical; furthermore, by 1587 the direction of the government's policy was perfectly apparent. Bringing the aristocracy under control had priority; so the government would conciliate and compromise with the kirk in exchange for its support in that campaign – a policy which Maitland advocated and James adopted with some misgivings. Conciliating the kirk meant that no professed Catholic could expect to retain public office: sooner or later Seton would have to make a choice between his career and public acknowledgement of his faith. The moment came early in 1588, when James appointed him an ordinary lord of session. He took the oath of office, but his colleagues were understandably suspicious of his faith. There was no record of his having communicated according to Protestant rites; they insisted that he do so, and he agreed.[7] And from 1588 on there was no public backsliding: until his death he outwardly conformed to the church established by law.

This is not merely another case of a man's wrestling with his conscience and 'winning'. The most powerful motives for his remaining publicly committed to the ancient faith no longer operated. Seton had been fond of his quixotic father, and had been closer to him, in his later years, than any of his other children. But now his father was dead, and so was the queen whom he had served so faithfully. It was no longer possible to reconcile the two great principles of loyalty to the true faith and to the crown, as his father had, by

5 For Maitland see M. Lee, Jr., *John Maitland of Thirlestane* (Princeton, 1959).
6 *Narratives of Scottish Catholics under Mary Stuart and James VI*, ed. W. Forbes-Leith (Edinburgh, 1885), 187.
7 Seton, *Memoir of Alexander Seton*, 23, citing the books of *Sederunt* of the court of session.

working for either Mary's restoration or James's conversion. So Seton chose loyalty to his king. But he read that king aright: he saw that what James wanted of his servants was outward conformity. Like Elizabeth, James believed that it was neither possible nor desirable to make windows into men's souls. Open defiance he would not countenance; but if a person publicly conformed to the established church, what he, or she, chose to believe, or even practise in private, did not greatly concern him. So Seton became, and remained, what was known in England as a church papist. He continued to receive the occasional priest from foreign parts, though far more discreetly than his father had. In 1605, shortly after he became chancellor, he was visited by two Scottish Jesuits, whose reports to the general of their order summarize the situation well:

> He publicly professes the state religion, rendering external obedience to the king and the ministers, and goes occasionally, though rarely, to the sermons, sometimes to their heretical communion. He has also subscribed their confession of faith, without which he would not be able to retain peaceable possession of the rank, office, and estates with which he is so richly endowed . . . Two or three times a year he comes to Catholic confession and communion with his mother, brother, sister, and nephews, who are better Catholics than himself![8]
> Lord Seton often said to me in Scotland, when I urged him to support the Catholic cause, "Be not eager to act before the time comes. I have to live in Scotland, and I must give way to circumstances. When the opportunity presents itself, and there is any hope of success, I shall not be sparing of my goods, my blood, or my life, for the restoration of the Catholic religion." He is now all-powerful in Scotland, but he will attempt nothing until he sees a solid foundation for hope. Meanwhile he takes his portion in this life, though at the risk of that which is eternal.[9]

There is no evidence that Seton ever made any effort to restore the old faith, or even to secure any kind of unofficial toleration for it beyond the sort that he himself enjoyed. But of course he was suspected of far worse. In 1585 the ministers called him 'this papistical prelate and pensioner of the Pope' who 'hath uttered not obscurely his practicing against religion, and in one massacre to cut the throats of the professors thereof'.[10] His hypocritical pretense of conformity was only to be expected of one educated by the Jesuits. The grumbling continued as Seton's career prospered. In 1593 he became president of the court of session and the chairman of the committee to manage Queen Anne's Scottish property for her. This appointment was

8 Forbes-Leith, *Narratives*, 278–9.
9 Ibid., 282.
10 Calderwood, *History*, iv, 430–1.

important because it led to a permanent friendship with Anne, who herself eventually became a Catholic and whose favourite lady-in-waiting, Lady Jean Drummond, was Seton's sister-in-law. Seton and his colleagues were so successful in managing Anne's property that in January 1596, three months after the death of Chancellor Maitland, James made them the nucleus of an eight-man committee entrusted with the considerable task of bringing order out of the chaos of the finances of the crown.

This committee was promptly dubbed the Octavians; Seton was its chairman, and its membership was alarming to the kirk: 'all almost either Papists known or inclining to Popery or malignancy', wrote the presbyterian minister and historian John Row.[11] The great fear of the ministers, and also of the English agents in Scotland, was that Seton, whose ambition for the post was no secret, would succeed Maitland as chancellor and as the king's *eminence grise*. 'If that man should prevail', wrote the English agent Roger Aston in November 1595, 'there were nothing to be looked for but a peril to the good cause'.[12] Aston need not have worried. In the first place, James had no intention of taking on a new *eminence grise*, and he in fact kept the chancellorship vacant for three years. Second, Seton wrecked his own chances by a series of miscalculations in 1596 which almost destroyed his career. His mistakes were not owing to the financial stewardship of the committee, which did a very good job of eliminating unnecessary expenditures and improving the king's revenues, though the courtiers whose pensions were cut naturally had no love for the Octavians and waited for the chance to ruin them. Seton's blunders were political.

The great public issue in 1596 was whether or not George Gordon, earl of Huntly, the most powerful Catholic noble in Scotland, would be allowed to return from the exile into which he had driven the year before, an exile which symbolized the triumph of the policy of curbing the independent power of the higher aristocracy. Andrew Melville and the rest of the dominant faction in the church adamantly opposed Huntly's return. James, on the other hand, wanted him back. He liked the earl, he believed that Huntly had learned his lesson, above all he believed that gentle treatment of Huntly would smooth his path to the English throne by reducing the possibility of Catholic opposition, either domestic or foreign. Seton threw himself into this fray on the king's side, making an eloquent speech in the convention of estates in August 1596 calling for Huntly's return. This speech was a bad mistake; it convinced Huntly's enemies that there was a Popish plot afoot, and that Seton himself was the chief conspirator. Seton compounded his error by urging James to be firm in the matter of the punishment of David Black, the intemperate minister of St. Andrews, who in October 1596 preached a series of outrageous sermons personally attacking James and Anne, and for good

11 John Row, *The History of the Kirk of Scotland*, ed. D. Laing (Edinburgh, 1842), 165. Cf. Calderwood, *History*, v, 394.
12 *CSPS* xii, 60.

measure calling Queen Elizabeth an atheist. The result was, that the famous religious riot in Edinburgh in December 1596 was directed principally against Seton, 'that Romanist president, a shaveling and a priest, more meet to say mass in Salamanca nor (than) bear office in Christian and reformed commonweals'.[13] Seton was not the only target; other suspected Papists among the Octavians were attacked too, and the riot was encouraged – perhaps even precipitated – by the courtiers whose pocketbooks the Octavians' economies had pinched. James dealt with the riot easily enough, but he came to the conclusion that the Octavians, and particularly Seton, were more of a political liability than a fiscal asset. Within a month of the riot the Octavians' power was transferred to the most impeccably Protestant member of the group, Lord Treasurer Blantyre, who proved quite unable to handle it.

Given the embarrassment which his conspicuous advocacy of Huntly's return had caused the king, Seton's losses were not great. He retained the positions he had held before the appointment of the Octavians, and he did not lose the king's favour. In 1598 James made him a lord of parliament in his own right as Lord Fyvie and forced his election as provost of Edinburgh, an office he was to hold for ten years. But his chance for real political power had apparently vanished. Other suspected Catholics among the Octavians could become very influential, as the secretary, James Elphinstone, the future Lord Balmerino, did for a brief time between 1598 and 1600; but not Seton. Like Huntly, he had become a symbol, one who, if given real power, or even the appearance of power, would make James's task that much more difficult.

Seton concluded that he must change both his image and his tactics if he were ever to realize his political ambitions. He had badly underestimated the strength and depth of anti-Catholic feeling, and the suspicion and dislike which his sort of conformity generated. He had also learned that for a man in his religious situation the politics of confrontation were impossible: the advantage his opponents would gain by charging him with Romanism would be too great to overcome. Conciliation and the achievement of consensus would have to be his tactics henceforth, if he ever got another chance. In the meantime, the prudent thing to do was to detach himself somewhat from his allegedly Catholic associates on the Octavians and to cultivate Protestant grandees like the earl of Mar, whom he unsuccessfully supported for the chancellorship in 1598.[14] His second wife, whom he married in 1601, came from an impeccably Protestant family. Two public stands, both of which risked alienating James, were particularly helpful to him. One was his support in 1599 of the legal claim of the Edinburgh minister Robert Bruce to a pension out of the revenues of the abbey of Arbroath when the king, who disliked Bruce, tried to stop it. The second was a speech in the convention of estates in 1600 opposing the levy of a tax to raise an army to make good James's claim to the English throne by force if need be, a proposal whose chief

13 Calderwood, *History*, v, 548.
14 29 Mar. 1598, George Nicolson to Lord Burghley, *CSPS*, xiii, 181.

advocate was Elphinstone.[15] Seton's tactics had some success. Mar became his permanent ally, and by 1599 the suspicious English agent George Nicolson was describing him as an 'honest councillor'.[16] He was also able to take advantage of his position as provost of Edinburgh to look after the town's interests in ways which ultimately earned him the citizens' affection and gratitude.[17]

All this activity made Seton potentially employable again in serious matters of state, but he might never have been so employed had James lived out his days in Edinburgh as a mere king of Scots. It was James's succession to the English throne and the consequent administrative changes which gave Seton a second chance. As president of the court of session he was the most highly placed lawyer in the Scottish government – the chancellor, the earl of Montrose, was an elderly aristocratic nonentity – and so James decided to appoint Seton as the chief Scottish negotiator for the treaty of union between England and Scotland which the king had so much at heart. Seton, who was not too enthusiastic about the king's plans – all the evidence indicates that he, like other Scottish officials, was both suspicious and fearful that the union would open the door to English domination over Scotland – seized his opportunity with both hands. He never uttered a word in public against the proposals, conducted the negotiations both rapidly and skillfully, and in the process made another valuable friend in the person of the chief English commissioner, Robert Cecil. In the event, the union did not come to pass, but Seton had already received the reward for his efforts in the form of an earldom and the office he had coveted for a decade. By the beginning of 1605 he had become earl of Dunfermline and lord chancellor and real power once again lay open to him, because whether or not the treaty was ratified it was apparent that a change in the way King James conducted Scottish affairs was in the offing. Ever since the death of Maitland in 1595 James had in effect been his own chief minister. Even in the first year or so after his removal to London James carried on as much as he had before, paying attention to such details as the wardship of the earl of Atholl and the settlement of a dispute between Edinburgh and Leith. Inevitably, however, the problems and distractions of the king's new situation in London increasingly occupied his attention, while absence blurred his memory for details. The proposals for union did not provide for any amalgamation of the machinery of the two governments; there would be separate administrations in England and Scotland, with the latter being divided between the king in London attempting to govern by his pen with the aid of his advisers there, and the privy council in Edinburgh, obligated to execute the royal orders without question but not in fact always

15 16 Mar. 1599, 29 June 1600, Nicolson to Robert Cecil, *ibid.*, 427–9, 661–4.
    Calderwood, *History*, v, 733–5.
16 *CSPS*, xiii, 542.
17 Seton's career as provost can be followed in *Extracts from the Records of the Burgh of Edinburgh*. ed. M. Wood and others, 7 vols. (London and Edinburgh, 1927–54), vols. v and vi.

doing so. It became increasingly obvious that someone would have to be entrusted with the conduct of Scottish affairs under the King's general supervision and Dunfermline in the light of his new found favour must have had high hopes of being chosen in this capacity.

Once again it was not to be, and once again it was a religious question which stymied Dunfermline. This time, however, his own faith was not at issue. The difficulty stemmed from the religious policy which King James had been following ever since 1600, when he decided to reimpose diocesan episcopacy because it was the only sure means of giving him control of the Scottish church.[18] This decision split the clergy between supporters of the king's policy and the once dominant presbyterians, who believed that episcopacy was unscriptural and that ultimate authority in the church lay in the General Assembly. Dunfermline obviously had no theoretical quarrel with episcopacy, and he was a good enough Erastian; but he had reservations about the king's policy. Part of this was personal: he disliked and distrusted James's chief ecclesiastical adviser, Archbishop Spottiswoode, who cordially reciprocated both sentiments. To Spottiswoode Dunfermline was a dangerous concealed papist, constantly intriguing on behalf of his co-religionists; to Dunfermline Spottiswoode, who had been one of his most active critics in 1596, was an opportunist who hungered for political power. The chancellor feared that once Spottiswoode and his crew were restored to power in the church, they would seek it in the state as well, not only for ambition's sake, but also to employ the powers of the government against their clerical opponents, with the inevitable consequence of political rows and confrontations which Dunfermline was anxious to avoid. The chancellor therefore adopted a conciliatory attitude toward the moderate wing of the presbyterian party, but not because he sympathized with their views on church government. Such a stance might lessen their hostility to him as an individual and persuade them of the genuineness of his Protestantism, but his principal aim was political: to blunt Spottiswoode's anticipated drive for influence in the state.

The most insistent complaint of the bishops' opponents in the church was that the General Assembly was not being allowed to meet. This, they argued, was illegal: the law mandated a meeting once a year at least. Not at all, replied the bishops. The law was clear that the king, or his commissioner, determined the time and place of the meeting; if James chose repeatedly to postpone the meeting, he was within his rights. The Assembly had last met in 1602. The pending union negotiations provided a plausible pretext for the postpone-ment of the Assembly of 1604, but even so, there had been protests, and later in that year the synod of Fife, dominated by the radical wing of the presbyterian party, flatly declared that the Assembly could legally meet without royal permission.[19] Dunfermline had every reason to believe that

18 On this point see 'James VI nd the Revival of Episcopacy in Scotland, 1596–1600', above.
19 Calderwood, *History*, vi, 264–7, 270–1.

another postponement would cause serious trouble. In June 1605 the postponement came, with the king giving no very convincing reason for his
action. The ministers complained; one of them, the moderate John Forbes,
whose account of the affair is the fullest we have,[20] sought out Dunfermline to
indicate his distress. Dunfermline did not want a confrontation on this issue,
and did what he could to meet objections which seemed not unreasonable.
The ministers would be allowed to gather, and would be requested rather
than ordered to disperse. Whether Dunfermline intended that the ministers
should actually constitute themselves an Assembly is unclear; the privy
council's letter was addressed to the ministers 'convened at their Assembly
at Aberdeen' but on the same day the letter was written the council issued
James's proclamation forbidding the meeting.[21] At all events the handful of
ministers who appeared at Aberdeen did constitute themselves an Assembly
and then dissolved, after setting a date for another meeting in violation of the
council's instructions. James was angry; and Dunfermline was in a very
awkward position. Not only had he dealt rather ambiguously with Forbes
before the Assembly, but also, after it was dissolved but before James's anger
became known, he had, according to Forbes, expressed to three ministers who
had been there his satisfaction with the proceedings on learning that there
had been no attack on the bishops.[22] After the conviction of Forbes and five of
his colleagues on a technical charge of treason early in 1606, Archbishop
Spottiswoode, aided and abetted by the earl of Dunbar, the lord treasurer and
Dunfermline's chief rival for the position of James's principal Scottish adviser,
set out 'to procure the Chancellor his disgrace, as suspected to be an enemy to
the estate of bishops'.[23] Once again Dunfermline's career hung in the balance.

For a time it looked as if the king might be angry enough to dismiss his
chancellor. He allowed Spottiswoode and Dunbar to press their charges by
means of a formal hearing before the privy council, and he was reportedly
ready to oust Dunfermline if he could be convicted of 'undutifulness'.[24] But in
the end he decided that Dunfermline's behaviour was owing to miscalculation rather than disloyalty. His temporizing policy was due to a serious
overestimate of the backlash which postponing the General Assembly would
produce – the number of ministers gathered at Aberdeen had been very small.
He had partially redeemed himself by his useful work at Forbes's treason
trial; but the real hero of that occasion, in James's view, was Dunbar, whose
rapid and forceful methods James judged to be best suited for the implementation of his religious policy. Dunfermline had qualms about such tactics.
'I desire not his sacred Majesty to put us oft to such proofs', he wrote to

20 John Forbes, *Certaine Records touching the Estate of the Church of Scotland*, ed. D.
   Laing, Wodrow Society (Edinburgh, 1846), 383ff. Given the treatment meted out to
   Forbes, he is remarkably fair-minded.
21 *Ibid.*, 388–9, 391–2; *RPCS*, vii, 62.
22 Forbes, *Certaine Records*, 401–2.
23 *Ibid.*, 406.
24 *Ibid.*, 513.

Salisbury after the trial, 'for I assure your Lordship in truth in this kingdom the puritanism is very far predominant, and albeit this be done to his Majesty's will and wish, it is not without a greater grudge and malcontentment nor (than) the consequence of it can be of avail. Such diseases in policy will neither so well nor so easily mend, by direct contrariety and opposition, as indirectly and by compass about, specially when the disease is inveterate and has taken hold, as this is here indeed.'[25] James did not agree with this plea for gradualism. He intended to reimpose diocesan episcopacy as rapidly as possible; for that purpose the ruthless Dunbar would be far more suitable than the conciliatory Dunfermline, who, James knew, would do what he was told.

So Dunfermline survived, at the price of acquiescence in both James's religious policy and Dunbar's domination of the Scottish political scene. But the somewhat paradoxical effect of his troubles was to make him much less unpopular with the presbyterian elements in Scottish society, both inside the church and out, because they perceived him as the enemy of their enemy, the bishops. This was enormously helpful to him, because these were precisely the groups that were most likely to criticize what they regarded as simulated conformity. David Calderwood, the presbyterian historian, who was exiled in 1617 for his opposition to the king's religious policy, tells in his *History* a number of what may well be *ben trovato* stories about Dunfermline: poking fun at Archbishop Gledstanes's lack of legal knowledge, grumbling about the concillors' having to play the bishops' hangmen.[26] Attacks on him as a papist after 1606 were not very numerous, were usually politically inspired, and could be safely ignored as long as he retained the king's favour, and this he was able to do. One weapon was flattery: he was effusive in his praise of James, and of Dunbar, whose work in repressing lawlessness on the borders he compared to the cleansing of the Augean stables.[27] Cooperation was another: he worked effectively with Dunbar on a number of issues, notably the ending of free trade between Scotland and England in 1610,[28] and where he was able to take some initiative, as, for instance, in highland matters, he was very successful.

The religious question would be the acid test, however, and here Dunfermline trod very warily. What he deduced from the near-disaster of 1606 was that he should not meddle in religious issues at all if he could possibly help it. For someone in his ambiguous personal position they were far too dangerous; his career had almost been ruined twice on account of them. But of course he could not avoid them altogether. So he worked to further the king's ecclesiastical policy when necessary – at the parliament of 1606, for instance, he

25 PRO, SP 14/18, no. 31.
26 Calderwood, *History*, vi, 699–701, vii, 450.
27 12 Aug. 1609, Dunfermline to James, *Letters and State Papers during the Reign of King James the Sixth*, ed. J. Maidment, Abbotsford Club (Edinburgh, 1838), 171–3.
28 See their joint memorandum on this subject written in October 1610, BL Add. Ms. 24, 275, fos. 9–9b.

strongly advocated the restoration of the temporalities of the bishops, which, according to Spottiswoode, he had previously opposed.[29] He would not, or could not, prevent the occasional harassment of his relatives as suspected Papists, and only occasionally protested when he was himself abused, either by a bishop or at one of the rare meetings of the General Assembly.[30] About all he was willing to do was to try to minimize the influence of bishops, especially bishops like Spottiswoode, in the business of government,[31] to prevent them from using the privy council as an instrument of coercion of their opponents in the church, and occasionally to help those opponents as individuals. Among these individuals was his brother-in-law, John Moray, minister of Leith, who was ousted from his benefice on Spottiswoode's initiative for publishing an allegedly seditious sermon; Dunfermline's efforts could not save him. In only one area was Dunfermline willing voluntarily to involve himself: he was a key figure in the various commissions to improve clerical stipends, a matter on which he saw eye-to-eye with Spottiswoode and the king.[32]

So during Dunbar's years of power Dunfermline made himself as useful as he could, made no effort to unseat the lord treasurer, and mended his fences as carefully as possible. His careful cultivation of all the important individuals and groups in Scottish politics, with the exception of the irreconcilable archbishop, was eventually crowned with success. The all-powerful Dunbar, who was about Dunfermline's age, died in January 1611, at precisely the right moment for Dunfermline's political prospects. The work of restoring diocesan episcopacy had been completed in the previous year; a period of consolidation was now indicated, for which Dunfermline's conciliatory methods were ideally suited. Spottiswoode was eager to be Dunbar's successor, but James knew, if Spottiswoode did not, that the time was far from ripe to give an ecclesiastic that sort of political power. So Dunfermline became the king's *eminence grise* in Scottish affairs, and remained so until his death in 1622. The chancellor saw to it that there

29 Spottiswoode, *History*, iii, 175.
30 See, e.g., 3 Aug. 1608, Dunfermline to James, Maidment, *Letters and State Papers*, 142–4; 13 Oct. 1608, Sir William Seton to James, the baillies of Haddington to James, NLS. Denmilne Mss. ii, nos. 84, 85; 1 Sept. 1610, Margaret Seton, Lady Paisley, to Queen Anne, *Original Letters Relating to the Ecclesiastical Affairs of Scotland . . .1603–1625*, ed. D. Laing 2 vols., Bannatyne Club (Edinburgh, 1851), i, 257.
31 Two exceptions to this generalization should be noted: in Orkney, where Dunfermline's government used Bishop Law against the king's ruffianly cousin Earl Patrick, and in the western highlands, where the chancellor worked closely with Bishop Knox of the Isles in devising the policy which led to the statutes of Icolmkill of 1609. Knox was the one bishop with whom Dunfermline was really friendly.
32 For the Moray episode see Calderwood, *History*, vi, 689–92, 699–702, vii, 19–20, and *RPCS*, viii, 72–3, 270–1, 492–4, 496, 499–500, 563–4. On clerical stipends see W. R. Foster, 'A Constant Platt Achieved: Provision for the Ministry, 1600–1638', in *Reformation and Revolution*, ed. D. Shaw (Edinburgh, 1967), 124–40.

was, in fact, no real challenge to his position during his decade of control by following a cautious and conservative policy designed to upset no one, by using the knowledge gained during his decade as provost of Edinburgh to look after the economic interests of the burghs, and by continuing to avoid religious issues as much as possible – though now, by contrast with Dunbar's day, he was occasionally willing to protect Catholics from harassment, especially if his own household was involved.[33] Though he unhesitatingly conformed to the five articles of Perth, he was not keen on them and showed it – indeed, no one in authority in Scotland, not even Spottiswoode, shared James's enthusiasm for these innovations.[34] Dunfermline also shored up his position through the uses of matrimony. He married three times, always into noble families, and had a large crop of daughters; he was also responsible for the marriages of the children of his older brother Robert, earl of Winton, who died in 1603. Dunfermline arranged a series of politically and socially useful marriages for this brood which connected him with a large number of important families, Catholic and Protestant, aristocratic and official, with the notable exception of the Gordons; Dunfermline wanted no link with the most overtly Popish family in the kingdom. The result was, that there were so many important people with a stake in Dunfermline's continuance in office that James, even if he had so wished, would have found it politically awkward to remove him.[35]

Not that James wanted to. He had always valued the chancellor's intelligence, efficiency, and loyalty, and he found Dunfermline's cautious and conservative variety of consensus politics to his liking in most respects, though he never warmed very much to Dunfermline as a man. From the chancellor's portrait, and from the marvellous painted gallery at his home, Pinkie House, it is easy to see why. Dunfermline's face is that of a reserved, fastidious intellectual; the mottoes on the allegorical paintings in the gallery give evidence of an ironic, sometimes cryptic, sometimes self-deprecatory sense of humour.[36] He was a man who would attract, and be attracted by, the king's genuine intellectualism, but not by James's raffish vulgarity. So Dunfermline was an exception to the general rule that continuous personal access to the king is a *sine qua non* for a ministerial career. He did better at a distance, in part because he knew how to write letters which would please the king: learned, prolix, full of Latin tags and classical references, and of

33 For an example see 28 May 1613, Archbishop Gledstanes to James, Sir W. Fraser, *Memoirs of the Maxwells of Pollok*, 2 vols. (Edinburgh, 1863), ii, 68–71.

34 For the five articles of Perth see I. B. Cowan's assessment in Shaw, *Reformation and Revolution*, 160–77, and P. H. R. Mackay, 'The Reception Given to the Five Articles of Perth', in *RSCHS*, xix (1977).

35 For a fuller discussion of Dunfermline's methods of government see M. Lee, Jr., *Government by Pen: Scotland under James VI and I* (Urbana, Ill., 1980), esp. chap. 4.

36 A few examples of these paintings are reproduced in M. R. Apted , *The Painted Ceilings of Scotland 1550–1650* (Edinburgh, 1966). There is a full description of the gallery in G. Seton, *A History of the Family of Seton through Eight Centuries*, 2 vols. (Edinburgh, 1896), ii, 813–19.

flattery.[37] So Dunfermline reached the height of his power as the agent of an absentee king, power he might never have achieved or retained in the bawdy, Byzantine, corrupt and disorderly surroundings of Jacobean Whitehall.

It is possible to argue that, after his decision to conform, Dunfermline ceased to be a Catholic in any meaningful sense. No matter how one chooses to define a genuine Catholic, however, his fellow countrymen believed Dunfermline to be one. The significance of his remarkable career, therefore, is that in an age of violent public hostility to the ancient faith, he succeeded in overcoming the prejudice aroused by his putative Catholicism, so that Calderwood could write of him in recording his death, 'howsoever he was Popishly disposed in his religion, yet he condemned many abuses and corruptions in the Kirk of Rome. He was a good justiciar, courteous and humane both to strangers and to his own country people, but no good friend to the bishops.'[38] Dunfermline's achievement was considerable for a man who had once been the target of a Protestant mob, but it was not an isolated case. There were other suspected papists like himself, other Octavians indeed, who conformed as he did and had highly successful careers, notably his colleague for thirty years, Thomas Hamilton, the Edinburgh lawyer's son, who died in the next reign, full of years and honours, as earl of Haddington. Dunfermline's success made it easier for others, of course: if the presbyterians refrained from attacking the most prominent church papist in the land because he was the bishops' enemy, it was difficult for them to attack any of the others. It is, of course, true that after the exile of Andrew Melville, the restoration of episcopal power, and the erection of potential engines of repression like the courts of high commission it was much more dangerous for religious dissidents to attack anyone save overt papists like the marquis of Huntly, but it is noteworthy that none of those critical of Dunbar's high-handed tactics during the controversy over the imposition of constant moderators on the presbyteries and synods in 1607–08 or of the five articles of Perth aimed their shafts at Dunfermline. What his career shows is that religious animosities may have run less deeply than has sometimes been supposed,[39] that in the atmosphere provided by what has been called King James's Peace[40] it was possible to defuse the religious issue, to arrive at that sort of unspoken compromise and *de facto* toleration which might, given time, have led to genuine religious peace. But time was not given. How fatally easy it was to reawaken all the old fears and hatreds, King James's inept son and his maladroit agents would discover to their sorrow.

37 There is no collection of Seton papers as such. Most of Dunfermline's surviving letters to James are in the Denmilne Mss. in the National Library of Scotland. Many have been printed in Maidment, *Letters and State Papers* and in Laing, *Original Letters . . . Ecclesiastical Affairs*.
38 Calderwood, *History*, vii, 549.
39 On this point see M. Sanderson, 'Catholic Recusancy in Scotland in the Sixteenth Century', *Innes Review*, xxi (1970), 87–107.
40 Donaldson, *James V-James VII*, ch. 12.

11

Archbishop Spottiswoode as Historian
(1973)

John Spottiswoode, archbishop of Glasgow for more than a decade and then of
St. Andrews for more than two, has by and large enjoyed a good press at the
hands of historians. He was the most important churchman involved in the effort
of James VI to revive the power of bishops in the Scottish church; he served
James and his son Charles I loyally and well, warned them vainly against certain
of their policies which turned out badly, and in the end was driven into exile as a
result of the national revolt in Scotland against the disastrous ecclesiastical
policies of Charles and Archbishop Laud. He was a spokesman for moderation
and charity in a nation where such attitudes became less and less viable, as the
errors of James in his last years and particularly of Charles polarized opinion and
brought about the explosion of the late 1630s. The ruin which overtook
episcopacy in Scotland was not Spottiswoode's fault, and many historians have
concluded that had the government followed Spottiswoode's advice, that
explosion need never have taken place.

This sympathetic view of Spottiswoode as churchman and politician has
extended to the archbishop as historian, the other capacity in which he is
remembered. Spottiswoode's *History of the Church of Scotland* is one of the major
sources for Scottish history for the seventy-odd years from the coming of the
Reformation to the death of James VI in 1625; it was written at the behest of
James, who gave Spottiswoode access to the official records.[1] The archbishop
was not altogether willing to undertake the task, chiefly on account of the
delicate subject of the king's mother, and his book has all the characteristics of
commissioned history. In spite of this, historians have found it praiseworthy.
The verdict of T. F. Henderson is typical: ' His work has the customary defects
of an official history . . . and although, of course, the work of a partisan, is on
the whole written with candour and impartiality'.[2] The impression of candour
and impartiality is owing largely to what W. L. Mathieson, who also praised
the work, called 'its severe restraint of phrase and feeling . . . its enlightened
moderation and its essentially modern spirit'.[3]

In the matter of restraint of phrase Mathieson was quite right. Judiciousness

---

1 The standard edition of Archbishop Spottiswoode, *History of the Church of Scotland*,
   edited by the Rev. Michael Russell and Mark Napier, was published in three
   volumes under the auspices of the Spottiswoode Society (Edinburgh, 1851). All
   references in the notes are to this edition.
2 *Dictionary of National Biography* (London, 1898), liii, 414–5.
3 W. L. Mathieson, *Politics and Religion, A Study in Scottish History from the
   Reformation to the Revolution* 2 vols., (Glasgow, 1902), i, 325.

of tone runs throughout the *History*. Spottiswoode did not employ the scurrility and abuse of the other ecclesiastical partisans who wrote of the Scottish Reformation. To John Knox, for instance, Queen Mary's secretary David Riccio was 'that great abuser of this commonwealth, that poltroon and vile knave Davie' whose murder was 'most worthy of all praise'; Spottiswoode said no more than that Riccio had a 'politic wit' and was vain and arrogant.[4] David Calderwood, a contemporary of Spottiswoode's and an extreme presbyterian, called the archbishop 'a traitor, profane and licentious . . . a profane villain with an impudent face . . . [and] a cauterized conscience'. Spottiswoode's only reference to Calderwood concerned the latter's controversy with King James in 1617: 'carrying himself unreverently and breaking forth into speeches not becoming a subject, [he] was . . . afterwards banished the kingdom'.[5] The language employed even for those whom Spottiswoode unreservedly condemned is hardly very strong by the standards of the day. The earl of Bothwell, for instance, the murderer of Lord Darnley and the abductor of Queen Mary, a thoroughly evil man in Spottiswoode's view, 'made an ignominious and desperate end, such as his wicked and flagitious life had deserved'.[6] The adjectives never get any stronger than that.

In the case of Queen Mary, Spottiswoode was extremely cautious and unwilling to make any judgement whatever. His account of her career was brief, slid round the difficult questions, and tended to lay the blame for her mistakes on others, like Bothwell and the Secretary of State, William Maitland of Lethington – not on her half-brother, the earl of Moray, the future regent, whom the archbishop greatly admired.[7] He did not approve of her religion, of course, but he criticized Knox and the others for attacking the arrangement by which she was to have Mass said in private, on the ground that 'there was hope, by better instruction and humble and courteous behaviour she might be reclaimed' from Popery.[8] Bothwell was assumed to be responsible for the murder of Darnley; all we learn about the famous silver casket is that it contained all the letters Mary ever wrote to Bothwell. 'These letters were afterwards divulged in print, and adjected to a libel entitled, The detection of the doings of Queen Mary, penned with great bitterness by Mr. George Buchanan'.[9] The nearest Spottiswoode got to criticism of the queen was his summary paragraph after his account of her execution (for which, of course, Queen Elizabeth was not responsible – Spottiswoode repeated the official English story). Spottiswoode remarked on Mary's 'many rare virtues' and bad luck; her reign began auspiciously, 'but then giving ear to some wicked

---

4 Spottiswoode, *History*, ii, 27, 35. *John Knox's History of the Reformation in Scotland*, ed. W. C. Dickinson, 2 vols., (New York, 1950), i, 112.

5 Spottiswoode, *History*, iii, 247. Calderwood, *History*, vii, 395.

6 Spottiswoode, *History*, ii, 82.

7 *Ibid.*, 121.

8 *Ibid.*, 7.

9 *Ibid.*, 62. George Buchanan was a famous humanist turned Protestant propagandist, who became tutor to the young James VI.

persons, and transported with the passion of revenge for the indignity done unto her in the murder of David Rizzio her secretary, she fell into a labyrinth of troubles' which only ended with her death.[10] Nothing could be more careful and tactful than that.

The queen's great antagonist John Knox received equally gingerly treatment. Knox was, of course, a hero to Scottish Protestantism and could be criticized very little, if at all. Spottiswoode solved his most serious problems by denying the authenticity of Knox's *History*; this allowed him to omit a number of inconvenient matters such as the great confrontations between Knox and Mary which the reformer made so much of in his writings. Knox's involvement in the destruction of churches (which Spottiswoode unreservedly condemned) was dismissed as a rumor.[11] As with Mary, most of the references are bland; Spottiswoode's chief concerns were to censure Knox rather gently for his views as to the authority of princes and to demonstrate that he was not a presbyterian: 'yet was he far from those dotages wherein some that would have been thought his followers did afterwards fall; for never was any man more observant of church authority than he, always urging the obedience of ministers to their superintendents'.[12] On this point Spottiswoode was quite right; in fact, if anything, he understated his case.[13] The archbishop's discomfort in having to write about Knox is nevertheless apparent; the great reformer was much too independent-minded, too willing to meddle in politics, too prepared to talk back to the powers-that-be for the Erastian episcopal courtier's taste. So, as with Queen Mary, caution prevailed.

Judiciousness of tone and moderation in the characterization of individuals are not the same thing as impartiality of spirit, however. Spottiswoode knew that he would be charged with bias; in his address to his readers he denied showing any in his writing, and urged his readers to suspend judgement until they had read. In the next paragraph, however, and in the prefatory letter he wrote to King Charles, his real intentions became apparent. He had originally planned, he said to his readers, to confine himself to the history of the church in his own time, but then he decided to go back to the beginnings of Christianity in Scotland for a number of reasons, the most important of which was this: 'that they who are possessed with a misconceit of the present policie of the church, might possibly be wonne from their opinions, when they should see the forme of government now established to be the same that was observed in the Church in the most pure and uncorrupt times'.[14] The people who possessed that misconceit, he wrote in his letter to King Charles, would not hold it if they knew their history: 'for did men understand how things went at our Reformation, and since

---

10 *Ibid.*, 361.
11 *Ibid.*, i, 373.
12 *Ibid.*, ii, 184.
13 See for instance, G. Donaldson, *The Scottish Reformation* (Cambridge, 1960), chap. 5.
14 Spottiswoode, *History*, i, p. xxiii. Spottiswoode very nearly fulfilled his original intention at that; over three-fourths of his text deals with events between 1558 and 1625.

that time, they would never have been moved to think that Episcopacy was against the constitutions of this Church, one of the first things done in it being the placing of Superintendents with Episcopal power in the same . . . Then for the Consistorial Discipline brought from Geneva some sixteen years after the Reformation – did men know the troubles raised thereby both in the Church and State, with the necessity that your Majesty's father, of blessed memory, was put to for reforming that confused government, they would never magnify nor cry it up as they do. To remedy this want . . . I took the pains to collect this History'.[15] In other words, his work was to be one long defense of episcopacy, a defense based, not on any Laudian doctrine of divine right, but on historical and practical grounds. Episcopacy was beneficial to both church and state.[16] Furthermore, John Knox's generation was not hostile to episcopalian principles; it was the innovators of the second generation led by Andrew Melville who attacked episcopacy as unscriptual and insisted that only a presbyterian polity was in accord with the word of the Lord.

The title Spottiswoode gave to his work is, therefore, somewhat misleading. This is not a history of the Church of Scotland from the year 203 A.D., as his subtitle says, or even from the Reformation. There is no discussion of theology at all; Spottiswoode contented himself with reprinting the Book of Discipline of 1560, and his account of the doctrinal ideas of the reformers is skimpy at best. He points out the fact that the old church had fallen on evil days, but the internal problems of the post-Reformation church get very little discussion – always excepting, of course, the vexed question of episcopacy and presbytery. The recurring financial problem, for instance, which occupied a great deal of the time and thought of a good many people in both church and government, is mentioned only occasionally, possibly because no one emerged from involvement in it with any credit, not even the king. Laymen grasped at church lands; the solution of 1561, that bishops and the holders of abbey lands should contribute one-third of the income from the temporalities of these benefices for the payment of clerical salaries, worked badly for many reasons; nominees to the bishoprics engaged in simoniacal transactions, like Archbishop Montgomerie of Glasgow, or granted damaging leases like Spottiswoode's predecessor in St. Andrews, George Gledstanes; the king's major error was to listen to those who persuaded him in 1587 that the annexation of the temporalities of benefices to the crown would benefit both church and state, an action he later regretted.[17] What

15 *Ibid.*, pp. cxxxvii–cxxxviii.
16 See, for instance, the argument, *ibid.* ii, 272–3, that the abolition of episcopacy would have very adverse effects on the material welfare of the remaining ministers, because the temporalities of the bishoprics would be swallowed up by laymen, as those of the monasteries had been.
17 *Ibid.*, i, 327, 373; ii, 15, 282, 376–7; iii, 227. Robert Montgomerie held the archbishopric of Glasgow briefly in the 1580s as a result of a corrupt transaction with King James's favorite, Esmé Stuart, duke of Lennox. George Gledstanes was archbishop of St. Andrews from 1604 to 1615. The 1587 Act of Annexation of the temporalities of benefices to the crown was repealed in 1606.

Spottiswoode did write about, what occupies most of his pages, is politics, the politics of the period from 1558 to 1625, with particular emphasis on the relations of church and state, the role of ministers in politics, and the matter of church government, all from the royalist and episcopal point of view.

It is hardly surprising that a man who when he wrote his *History* had been an archbishop for between twenty and thirty years, should defend his calling and the view of church polity which it implied. His enthusiasm was in part the zeal of the convert. His father was a distinguished churchman, an associate of John Knox and one of the original superintendents. He himself was intended for a career in the church from the beginning; perhaps owing to the fact that he studied at Glasgow under James and Andrew Melville, he began his career as one of the supporters of their presbyterian view of church polity. Gradually, however, his views began to change, – how rapidly, and why, must remain conjectural, since his *History*, unlike Knox's, is not in the least autobiographical, and he in fact minimized his own importance in the history of his time. Family influence may have been important to his change of view. His father, before his death in 1585, allegedly became alarmed by 'the disorders raised in the Church through that confused parity which men labored to introduce, as likewise the irritations the king received by a sort of foolish preachers'; the elder Spottiswoode 'therefore wished some to be placed in authority over them to keep them in awe', lest the king be alienated.[18] Then there was his wife: in 1589 Spottiswoode married the daughter of David Lindsay, minister of Leith, James's chaplain, and himself a future bishop; Lindsay was one of the most prominent of the clerical moderates. Spottiswoode apparently continued to feel some lingering sympathy for the Melvilles as late as 1596, possibly owing to fear of a possible resurgence of Catholicism. By 1600, however, Spottiswoode had broken with the extremists in the church over the issue of the clerical role in Parliament;[19] he became not only a believer in episcopacy but also in monarchy, a spokesman for the doctrine of the divine right of kings.

If there is a hero in Spottiswoode's history, it is King James. 'He was the Solomon of this age, admired for his wise government. And for his knowledge in all manner of learning. For his wisdom, moderation, love of justice, for his patience and piety (which shined above all his other virtues, and is witnessed in the learned works he left to posterity), his name shall never be forgotten, but remain in honour so long as the world endureth. We that have had the honour and happiness many times to hear him discourse of the most weighty matters, as well as of policy as divinity, now that he is gone, must comfort ourselves with the remembrance of these excellencies, and reckon it not the least part of our happiness to have lived in his days'.[20] Spottiswoode tells the whole history of the church, and of relations between the church and

18 *Ibid.,* ii, 336–7.
19 Calderwood, *History*, vi, 2.
20 Spottiswoode, *History*, iii, 270.

state, as the king would have wished it told – which is, after all, what an official historian is supposed to do. Peace, justice and good order in church and state were James's constant goals; the chief obstacles to the achievement of these laudable ends were those meddlesome ministers who constantly and improperly interfered in politics, and who therefore had to be restrained by the revival of a strong episcopal polity, which, said Spottiswoode, was James's purpose from the beginning.[21] In his dealings with his obstreperous clergy, King James was always reasonable, rational, theologically expert, conciliatory – and right;[22] those churchmen who talked back to him and who defended such assaults on kingly authority as the Raid of Ruthven were wrong.[23] Furthermore, James was even willing to save the ministers from the consequences of their own excesses, to restrain them lest they become so unpopular that the people would rise up and drive them from the country, since he placed the welfare of the church above his own momentary political advantage.[24] If the king made mistakes they were the consequence of his clement and peace-loving nature, which led him too readily to pardon those who had offended him, politicians like the Master of Gray, murderers like the countess of Somerset, and disobedient ministers like those who balked at the acceptance of the five articles of Perth.[25] In all this Spottiswoode was painting a misleading picture; for example, we know from other evidence that he himself disapproved of the five articles of Perth, would have avoided enforcing them if he could, and regarded them as a serious error.[26] But this was not so much as hinted in his *History*. The king can do no wrong. Calderwood – and Mathieson, too, who quotes him – attributed this to the cynicism of the Erastian. 'I tell you', Calderwood quoted the archbishop as saying to a minister who was being examined for non-compliance with the

21 See his critical comments on the compromise of 1586 which was to contribute to the triumph of presbyterianism in 1592; *ibid.*, ii, 341–2.

22 As one example among many, see the exchange between the young king and the General Assembly in October 1583, *ibid.*, 303–5.

23 The Raid of Ruthven, a coup d'état engineered in 1582 by the Protestant faction of the Scottish aristocracy with the wholehearted support of the dominant element among the clergy, put an end to the influence of James's French cousin and favorite, Lennox.

24 Spottiswoode, *History*, ii, 343. It should be pointed out, however, that in the most spectacular confrontation between king and ministers, that which led to the riot of December 1596, Spottiswoode lays much of the blame on a court clique which deliberately misled both sides in an attempt to pull down the group of officials known as the Octavians. *Ibid.*, iii, 8 ff, esp. p. 27.

25 *Ibid.*, ii, 373; iii, 230, 250. Patrick, Master of Gray, played a sinister role in the negotiations preceding the execution of Mary Queen of Scots. Frances Howard, countess of Somerset, was the central figure in the famous Overbury poisoning case. The five articles of Perth, imposed on the Scottish church by King James in 1618, were regarded as Popish by the majority of the Scottish clergy.

26 See Mathieson, *Politics and Religion*, i, 316–20, 324. Compare Spottiswoode's account, *History*, iii, 241–57.

articles, 'the King is Pope now, and so shall be'.[27] This does less than justice to the archbishop. There is no reason to doubt his sincerity; he came genuinely to accept James's views as to the nature of the state and of the kingly office.

Spottiswoode's opinions are made clear in his treatment of the discussions inside the Protestant camp in 1559 over renunciation of allegiance to the queen regent, Mary of Guise, James V's widow, the mother of Mary Queen of Scots. Knox and John Willock persuaded their fellows to take this step, citing numerous Scriptural examples. Spottiswoode commented rather sadly, 'It had been a better and wiser part in these preachers to have excused themselves from giving any opinion in those matters, for they might be sure to have it cast in their teeth, to the scandal of their profession. Neither was the opinion they gave sound in itself, nor had it any warrant in the Word of God. For howbeit the power of the magistrates be limited, and their office prescribed by God, and that they may likewise fall into great offences; yet it is nowhere permitted to subjects to call their princes in question, or to make insurrections against them, God having reserved the punishment of princes to himself'.[28] The treatment of Mary of Guise in Knox's *History* scandalized him; 'to detract from the fame of princes, and miscensure their words and actions, savoureth of malice, and no way becometh a Christian, much less a minister of Christ'.[29] For this reason, among others, Spottiswoode declared that Knox could not have written the *History*: 'A greater injury could not be done to the fame of that worthy man, than to father upon him the ridiculous toys and malicious detractions contained in that book'.[30] He was equally critical of the humanist George Buchanan, whom he otherwise highly praised, on the same ground: 'Only in this is he justly blamed, that led by the factions of the time, and to justify the proceedings of the noblemen against the queen, he went too far in depressing the royal authority of princes, and allowing their controlment by subjects'.[31] Papists, of course, were even more reprehensible, since they would not render any obedience to a king who did not acknowledge the Pope's authority: 'If the king', said the Jesuit John Ogilvie to his interrogators, 'play the runnagate from God, as he and you all do, I will not acknowledge him more than this old hat'.[32] Ogilvie was duly hanged, not for Popery but for sedition.[33] Not only was absolute obedience to the prince enjoined by Spottiswoode, so also was absolute honesty. In commenting on the fall of Secretary Balmerino, who confessed that he deluded James into signing a flattering letter to the Pope unwittingly, Spottiswoode said, 'It is not for those that serve princes and are trusted by them in the greatest affairs, to deal deceitfully with their masters; for

27　Calderwood, *History*, vii, 421.
28　Spottiswoode, *History*, i, 301–2.
29　*Ibid.*, 321.
30　*Ibid.*, ii, 184–5. See also i, 320–1.
31　*Ibid.*, ii, 300. James's dislike of Buchanan's political views was notorious.
32　*Ibid.*, iii, 225.
33　*Ibid.*, 227. Ogilvie was the only Scottish Jesuit martyr.

seldom have any taken that course, and have not in the end found the smart thereof'.[34]

If King James, the spokesman of divine right and the champion of episcopacy, was Spottiswoode's hero, then, necessarily, the villains of his story were the clerical radicals, particularly Andrew Melville, the supporter of prebyterianism and the advocate of the doctrine of the two kingdoms. It was with Melville's return from Geneva in 1574 that 'the innovations' began 'to break forth that to this day have kept it [the church] in a continual unquietness'.[35] Spottiswoode's picture of Melville is overdrawm almost to the point of caricature. He belittled Melville's scholarship, and charged him with mismanagement of the affairs of his St. Andrews college – and with teaching Buchanan-style politics there, which he undoubtedly did. Far worse, of course, were Melville's views on ecclesiastical polity and the proper relations of church and state. Melville perverted Scripture to arrive at his anti-episcopal position, he was disrespectful to bishops, he refused to acknowledge the right of the secular authority to original jurisdiction over ministers for what they said in the pulpit, 'though the speeches were treasonable', his nephew and close associate James Melville diverted money intended for the relief of the churches of Geneva into the pockets of the rebel earl of Bothwell, he stirred up other churchmen to follow his own radical line, and he would not even keep to the rules he himself had laid down: when he found himself outvoted in the presbytery of St. Andrews, he and a small minority seceded, arguing that votes should be weighed and not counted.[36] Spottiswoode was eager to find stories which would discredit Melville, and occasionally repeated one for which there is no evidence, such as the report that Melville advocated the destruction of Glasgow Cathedral.[37] Melville was not, of course, the only troublemaker; there were several other ministers who unwarrantably meddled in politics as he did, and contumaciously refused to obey the king, such as Robert Bruce of Edinburgh, who had trouble swallowing James's story of the affair at Gowrie House, and David Black of St. Andrews, who allegedly vilified James, Queen Anne, and Elizabeth from the pulpit, and whose refusal to admit the jurisdiction of the Privy Council touched off the chain of events which led to the riot in Edinburgh in December, 1596, which was the turning point in James's struggle to get

---

34 *Ibid.*, 205. James Elphinstone, Lord Balmerino, was Secretary of State from 1598 until his fall in 1609. It seems likely that he made his confession largely to allow the king to save face.

35 *Ibid.*, ii, 200.

36 *Ibid.*, ii, 200–3, 257, 308–9, 416–7, 448; iii, 65. Francis Stewart, earl of Bothwell, nephew of Queen Mary's Bothwell, kept Scotland in turmoil in the early 1590s. He posed as a champion of Protestantism, and received support from those ministers who thought James was too lenient with Catholics in general and George Gordon, earl of Huntly, in particular.

37 *Ibid.*, ii, 258–9. Cf. T. McCrie, *Life of Andrew Melville*, 2nd edn., 2 vols. (Edinburgh, 1824), i, 84–5. McCrie has noted a number of other inaccuracies in Spottiswoode's account of Melville.

control of the church. The number of mischief-makers, however, was not large – Spottiswoode's tendency always was to play down the extent and the seriousness of the opposition to James's policies.

Spottiswoode's description of church-state relations during the Melville era does considerably less than justice to the presbyterian party. It is true that Melville and his friends were stiff-necked and obstinate, and that the king's frequent efforts at compromise were usually rejected: Spottiswoode was unwilling to admit, however, that there was anything at all to be said for Melville and his supporters – that, for instance, they had any reason for concern about James's temporizing policy toward the Catholic party, particularly the earl of Huntly – and the archbishop minimised the amount of opposition within the church to the restoration of episcopacy. Consider, for instance, Spottiswoode's account of the General Assembly of the church held at Montrose in early 1600, the last held before the appointment later that year of three prominent moderates (including Spottiswoode's father-in-law David Lindsay) to three vacant sees marked James's final decision to adopt an episcopal polity. The question of the restoration of the clerical vote in Parliament had been under discussion for some time; James was eager to find a formula which would allow him to restore a modified form of episcopacy with the consent of the General Assembly. He was utterly unsuccessful; the Montrose meeting insisted on imposing all sorts of restrictions on the church's parliamentary representatives which would insure their accountability to the Assembly, and it would not even allow them the name of bishop – they were to be called commissioners. Spottiswoode touched briefly on some of this, and treated the outcome as a royal victory: 'And now there rested no more but to nominate persons to the bishoprics that were void'.[38] It is clear enough from contemporary accounts that neither the king nor anyone else believed that the decisions of this Assembly represented a royal victory.[39]

Radical Protestants were not the only enemies, of course. There were also the Papists, who in the last evil days of their power had behaved very badly indeed. The bishops had prevented King James V from reaching an amicable agreement with Henry VIII; Cardinal Beaton forged James V's will and fell victim to his own cruelties and excesses; John Hamilton, the last Catholic archbishop of St. Andrews, was talented but dissolute, and was suspected of having a hand in the murders of both Darnley and the regent Moray.[40] The old religion was overturned, of course, as a result of the revolution of 1559–60;

38 Spottiswoode, *History*, iii, 82. For the Montrose Assembly cf. the much fuller account in Calderwood, *History*, vi, 1–26; see also Mathieson, *Politics and Religion*, i, 279–80.

39 See, for example, 25 March 1600, George Nicolson to Sir Robert Cecil, *CSPS* xiii, 629–30.

40 Spottiswoode, *History*, i, 140–1, 165; ii, 156. Cardinal David Beaton, the leader of the pro-French party in the late 1530s and early 1540s, was assassinated in 1546 by men whose motives were a mixture of personal grievances, politics, and religion.

Spottiswoode, in describing that upheaval, adopted a very cautious line. The religious results of the revolution he could not but applaud; but he played down the religious causes as much as he could, in favor of a nationalist explanation. The queen regent's subservience to France, her filling of government offices with Frenchmen, her use of French troops – these are the factors which Spottiswoode stressed.[41] Knowing what some of the religious radicals of his own day thought of Charles I and Laud, and even of himself, he was at pains to avoid even the faintest suggestion of approval of Knox's doctrine about the obedience due to an idolatrous magistrate.

In the days of James VI the Popish menace took a rather different form. There were, first, the missionary priests, some of whom, like Ogilvie, met what Spottiswoode considered a well-deserved fate, others being merely deported. Then there were the Catholic aristocrats, people like James's favorite, the earl of Huntly, whose treasonable and murderous behavior in the 1590s was repeatedly overlooked by the king. Spottiswoode had nothing good to say about Huntly, but he dutifully accepted the king's explanation, given to the Edinburgh minister Robert Bruce, that James wanted to conciliate all factions at home in order to be as prepared as possible for the day when Elizabeth died and he put forward his claim to the English throne. Bruce's retort, that the king had to choose between restoring Huntly and retaining his, Bruce's, support, which Spottiswoode called 'saucy', marked the beginning of Bruce's fall from favor, which he never did regain.[42]

The third sort of Papist was more dangerous still, perhaps, because concealed. The most notable example in Spottiswoode's pages was Alexander Seton, earl of Dunfermline, the chief of the Octavians, president of the court of session, and finally Lord Chancellor from 1604 to his death in 1622. Spottiswoode neither liked nor trusted Seton; the impression which emerges from his occasional references to Seton is that of an ambitious, time-serving hypocrite.[43] In 1608, at the Linlithgow General Assembly, Spottiswoode was one of the chief supporters of a series of resolutions on Papists, in government and out; Seton, wrote Spottiswoode, supposed himself 'to be specially aimed at in all that business (wherein he was not mistaken)'.[44] But Seton was high in the king's favor, and so in reporting his death Spottiswoode was full of praise: the chancellor was 'very observant of good order, and one that hated lying and dissimulation, and above all things studied to maintain peace and quietness'.[45]

In his address to his readers Spottiswoode described his methods as follows: 'Whatsoever my private opinion is of matters, I studied to keep an indifference in writing, and so, contented to propound the causes,

41 See, e.g., his summary of the career of Mary of Guise, *ibid.*, i, 320.
42 *Ibid.*, iii, 6–8.
43 See, for instance, the account of Seton's role in the meeting of the illegal Aberdeen assembly of 1605, *ibid.*, 174–5.
44 *Ibid.*, 193–7. The quotation is on p. 197.
45 *Ibid.*, 263.

counsels, and success of every business, I leave to each man his liberty of approving or disapproving things as he shall have reason.'[46] The archbishop was, however, by no means as impartial as he would have us believe. Most of the tricks he played on the dead are those of omission and silence: he simply ignored, or mentioned fleetingly and refused to discuss, whatever failed to contribute to the picture of Scotland in the seventy-odd-years since the Reformation which he wished his readers to see. To be sure, he was no more biased than those other Scots who wrote of the church in this period: Knox, Calderwood, John Row, Buchanan – and he was far more charitable toward individuals. Robert Reid, bishop of Orkney, died, said Knox, clinging desperately to 'his god, the gold'; to Spottiswoode, Reid was 'a man of singular wisdom and experience' – and Spottiswoode's verdict is far nearer the truth.[47] So it is fatally easy to take the archbishop at his own valuation, and believe in his 'indifferencie'. This would be a serious mistake. Spottiswoode's *History* is not 'indifferent'; it must be used carefully, even more carefully than the writings of Knox or Calderwood, because of its deceptively smooth and moderate surface. This book is partisan history, written to defend a view of church and state which was crumbling even before the author had finished his labors. His dedicatory letter to Charles I was written after the revolutionary Glasgow Assembly of 1638 had declared episcopacy abolished and the archbishop had gone into exile. It is dated 'from the place of my peregrination, 15 Novemb. 1639'.[48] Within a month he was dead; his royal master gave him a state funeral in Westminster Abbey, where he was interred with Anglican rites. Since this was the king's wish, no doubt the archbishop would not have seriously objected.

46 *Ibid.*, i, p. xxii.
47 *Ibid.*, 188. Knox, *History*, i, 130.
48 Spottiswoode, *History*, i, p. cxxxix.

12

Charles I and the End of Conciliar Government in Scotland (1980)

That complex problems like the causes of the English civil war are constantly subject to reinterpretation is an obvious truism. Twenty years ago we were all embroiled in the gentry controversy; now it is the fashion to lay more stress on the blunders and failures of the government of Charles I. Lawrence Stone's recent survey is a case in point. Though his title, *The Causes of the English Revolution 1529–1642*, promises a long running start, this quondam disciple of R. H. Tawney places a surprising amount of emphasis on what he calls precipitants and triggers, which, it turns out, are the blunders and failures of the government of Charles I. Among these is the mishandling of the situation in Scotland. It is well known, of course, that the attempt to impose the new service book in 1637 touched off the chain of events which led to the Long Parliament, but historians have pointed out that this was by no means the first of Charles's errors there. At the very beginning of his reign came the act of revocation, which among other things rescinded 'all grants made of crown property since 1540, . . . all disposition of ecclesiastical property and the erections of such property into temporal lordships'.[1] No such sweeping change came about, of course, but in the view of most scholars this act, though in some sense successful, since it achieved the purpose both of increasing clerical stipends and of providing a machinery for their continuing adjustment, made the Scottish landed classes so mistrustful and fearful for their property that Charles could never gain their confidence. The comment of Sir James Balfour is always quoted: the act 'in effect was the ground stone of all the mischief that followed after'.[2]

Historians also generally agree that most of Charles's errors, and especially these two, were easily avoidable. Even the supporters of that currently fashionable version of the inevitability theory, the so-called 'general crisis', declare that Scotland is an exception to their general rule–and indeed they know very little about Scotland–though they have not yet explained in any very satisfactory way why a series of avoidable acts touched off an inevitable revolution.[3] It is not at all

1 G. Donaldson, *Scotland: James V – James VII* (Edinburgh, 1965), 296.
2 *The Historical Works of Sir James Balfour*, ed., James Haig, 4 vols. (Edinburgh, 1824), ii, 128 (hereafter *Balfour*).
3 H. R. Trevor-Roper, 'The General Crisis of the Seventeenth Century', in *Crisis in Europe 1560–1660*, ed. Trevor Aston (New York, 1965), 59–95, and his comment in a symposium on his article, *ibid.*, 116. For a withering exposure of the wrongheadedness of Trevor-Roper's views on Scottish history see W. Ferguson, *Scotland's Relations with England: A Survey to 1707* (Edinburgh, 1977), 77, 110, 118–9, 123.

clear, however, that Charles could easily avoid trouble in Scotland. Gordon Donaldson has suggested that some sort of confrontation between the crown and the Scottish aristocracy was very probable at some time or other. The nobility had only recently been brought under control by James VI, they had a long tradition of independent action and local supremacy, they were under-employed, and their king, the son of the king Scotland had given to its greater neighbour, was a stranger to them.[4] The parallel to the Low Countries in the days of Philip II was apparent to the Scots, who had numerous links with the Dutch republic.[5]

It can, in fact, be argued that there was a 'general crisis' in the Scotland of Charles I, though of a kind different from that suggested by Trevor-Roper, or even by David Stevenson's remark that after 1603 'Scotland was virtually all country and no court'.[6] The crisis was one of government, and it began almost as soon as Charles became king, though not merely because of the act of revocation. The impact of this act has been exaggerated; Balfour's comment has been taken too literally. Though certainly the most widely resented of Charles's decisions during the first phase of his rule because of the number of important people it affected, it was simply the most striking of a series of actions and attitudes which virtually destroyed the Jacobean system of government.

James's reign in Scotland had been a long and remarkably successful one. During his forty years of governance he had brought its fractious aristocracy and its stubbornly independent-minded kirk under control, provided peace and economic prosperity, and more law and order than ever before, even in the highlands. He had built up a loyal and efficient corps of officials composed mostly of younger sons and members of cadet branches of the aristocracy, lairds, and Edinburgh lawyers, whom he rewarded with pieces of the church property which had been annexed to the crown in 1587, and he had achieved the great ambition of his life when he peacefully succeeded to the English throne. His only major setback was the failure of his plan for Anglo-Scottish union after 1603, a failure that owed more to English than to Scottish opposition, though the plan was popular in neither country. James digested his defeat, and, being a patient man, he set about preparing for possible future unification by bringing Scottish institutions and practices in church and state into line with those of England–where the two countries differed, James almost always opted for the English model.

In the first years of his personal rule James had a political mentor in the person of his lord chancellor, John Maitland of Thirlestane; after Maitland passed from the scene James was, in effect, his own chief minister. After his removal to London and the failure of the union treaty, however, it was apparent that some new system of governance would have to be devised: the

4 Donaldson, *Scotland*, 299–300.

5 On this point see D. Stevenson, *The Scottish Revolution 1637–44* (Newton Abbot, 1973), 321.

6 *Ibid.*, 324. It should be added that Stevenson is skeptical about the validity of Trevor-Roper's theory.

king would be a permanent absentee, and would no longer have either the time or the command of detail which had been his before 1603. James would continue to make policy, but others would see to its implementation. The first pattern that emerged was that operated by the lord treasurer, the earl of Dunbar, who dominated Scottish politics from 1606 to 1611. Dunbar made his base at court, where he could be sure of always having the king's ear. He intimidated the privy council in Edinburgh and successfully reduced it to dependence on himself, and in the interest of maintaining his grip and of keeping in touch with the crosscurrents of Scottish politics, he travelled constantly between London and Edinburgh. After his death in 1611 his rival, the lord chancellor, the earl of Dunfermline, became James's chief political adviser and inaugurated a very different system. Dunfermline was a conciliator; he operated from Edinburgh and his method was to work out a consensus on policy in the council and present the results to the king as the opinion of virtually all the important people in Scotland. Dunfermline was a master of the fine art of literary flattery, and was careful to secure allies for himself among the important Scots at court. If, as often happened, the king sent instructions which Dunfermline and his associates on the council did not care for, they were usually able to persuade James to alter them, either by writing to him directly or by using one of their friends at court as a spokesman. Dunfermline and his colleagues in effect governed Scotland for James, and he let them do so, because he knew them all personally; they had been his friends and servants for decades. Dunfermline's death in 1622 made little difference to the system. No one man replaced him; instead, power was shared by a triumvirate of his former associates, the earl of Mar, the lord treasurer, the earl of Melrose, who was both secretary and president of the court of session, the highest Scottish civil court, and Sir George Hay, the new lord chancellor, the protégé of a courtier Scot, the marquis of Hamilton, who was a close friend of the great duke of Buckingham. Like King James they were elderly men, unadventurous, rather tired, and by now rather inflexible; they might well find it difficult to work with a new master.[7]

James's death on 27 March, 1625, came at a very awkward time. Scotland was just beginning to emerge from three awful years of crop failure, floods, murrain, and famine, what one scholar has called 'the most serious demographic crisis of seventeenth-century Scotland'.[8] War with Spain was apparently imminent, though no one had formally said so; the country had not been at war for more than two generations, and officialdom's response was understandably uncertain. The three leading Scottish officials were men whom neither Charles nor Buckingham knew very well; for whatever reason, the great duke had thus far made no effort to engross Scottish patronage.

7 For James's reign see M. Lee, Jr., *John Maitland of Thirlestane* (Princeton, 1959), and *Government by Pen: The Scotland of James VI and I* (Urbana, 1980).
8 R. Mitchison, 'The Making of the Old Scottish Poor Law', *Past and Present* lxiii, (1974), 65.

Another complication was the sudden death of Buckingham's friend, Hamilton, at the early age of 35, just a few weeks before that of the king; this meant that there was no London Scot who both possessed the new king's confidence and knew the leading men in Edinburgh.

Prior to his accession Charles had shown very little interest in Scotland– 'your nation', he called it in a letter to the council in October 1625, a phrase James never would have used[9]–and he knew nothing about the Scottish political scene. He knew the courtier Scots, of course, and did not much care for most of them. But there were some Scottish courtiers to whom Charles did pay attention. Two of these were more important than the others. One was Robert Maxwell, earl of Nithsdale, a Catholic, who had restored the family fortunes after the execution of his elder brother by marrying one of Buckingham's cousins. He was arrogant, quarrelsome, and stupid, deeply in debt, and much disliked by the ruling triumvirate in Edinburgh. The other was the poet Sir William Alexander of Menstrie, the principal promoter of the scheme for the colonization of Nova Scotia, which was to be forwarded, financially and otherwise, by the sale of baronetcies on the Ulster model. Alexander's closest Scottish associate in this scheme was the director of the chancery, Sir John Scott of Scotstarvit. He was a greedy man and a troublemaker–in Balfour's words, 'A busy man in foul weather, and one whose covetousness far exceeded his honesty'–but a learned and plausible debater.[10]

Charles was known to be interested in the Nova Scotia scheme: Alexander dedicated a promotional pamphlet to him, and he had written to the privy council in its support.[11] He had also been making inquiries into the rights of the various sorts of landholders in the Principality of Scotland and was planning to issue an act of revocation some time before he reached his 25th birthday in November 1625.[12] It was generally understood that a king, in order to protect himself from the consequences of misgovernment during a minority–and for two centuries every Scottish ruler without exception had succeeded as a minor–could, before he reached 25, revoke anything done in his name before he had reached the age of 21. Charles apparently was planning to extend that principle to the property included in the Principality of Scotland. Apart from these two matters no one in Edinburgh knew what Charles's intentions were, or what his policy would be, when word of James's death arrived. So little was known of the new king's views that some of the opponents of James's ecclesiastical measures were briefly hopeful that Charles would alter the

9 *RPCS* 2nd ser., i., 160–2. Italics mine.
10 *Balfour*, ii, 147.
11 17 Mar. 1625, Charles to the council, *RPCS* xiii, 720–1. T. H. McGrail, *Sir William Alexander* (Edinburgh, 1940), 48.
12 *RPCS* xiii, 558–63, 716–8. 24 Jan. 1625, the earl of Kellie to Mar, HMC, *Report on the Manuscripts of the Earl of Mar and Kellie, Supplement,* (hereafter *M&K Supplement*), ed. H. Paton (London, 1930), 218.

policy of what one of them called the 'imposing of certain novations upon the Kirk'.[13]

Under these circumstances it behooved the Scottish leadership to get to London promptly, both to make themselves known to their new master and to pay their last respects to the old. Superficially the visit went well enough; Charles was cordial and had already continued them in their offices.[14] But there were a number of indications of trouble to come. Despite his councillors' request that he act, Charles postponed his decision on the makeup of the new council, and it was reported that he planned to drop the judges of the court of session from its membership.[15] Lord Chancellor Hay, under some pressure, and vulnerable now because of the death of his patron Hamilton, surrendered his profitable lease of the Orkneys.[16] At King James's funeral Archbishop Spottiswoode of St. Andrews was a conspicuous absentee. He insisted that he would march in the procession only beside his fellow primate of Canterbury; this point conceded, Charles ordered him to wear an English surplice. He refused, and did not march at all. 'This carriage of his is much commended here, and I doubt not but will endear him to his country', commented Gilbert Primrose in a letter to his father James.[17] Charles's order was an indication that he was not going to reverse his father's policy of assimilation of the Scottish church to that of England—that, if anything, he would intensify it.

It also became apparent that Charles was not going to abandon the revocation. One of Gilbert Primrose's tasks in London was to draw up a draft under Melrose's supervision.[18] The substantive clauses of this document, which applied only to the Principality of Scotland, were straightforward enough, but the preamble asserted that the king had the power to revoke grants made during his minority, 'or by our predecessors in their times', which were prejudicial to the kingdom.[19] Whether this was a rhetorical flourish or a portent of further action was not at all clear, and contributed to the sense of uncertainty and unease. So too, in a different way, did Charles's unsympathetic comments on and responses to a proposal from the magistrates of Edinburgh on the question of the organization of the town's churches; a long and bitter dispute ensued, ultimately mediated by Archbishop Spottiswoode. The general uncertainty had not been dispelled when the convention of estates met on 27 October 1625. Charles's letter

---

13 14 Apr. 1625, the earl of Rothes to Sir Robert Ker, in *Correspondence of Sir Robert Kerr, First Earl of Ancram, and his son William, third Earl of Lothian*, ed. David Laing, 2 vols. (Edinburgh, 1875), 35–8.

14 Sir W. Fraser, *Memorials of the Earls of Haddington*, 2 vols. (Edinburgh, 1889), ii, 88–9.

15 *RPCS*, 2nd ser. i, 10–11, 13–16, 649–51.

16 21 May 1625, Gilbert Primrose to James Primrose, *ibid.*, 654–5.

17 *Ibid.*, 649–51.

18 17 May 1625, G. Primrose to J. Primrose, *ibid.*, 651–3.

19 The revocation is dated 14 July 1625, *ibid.*, 81–2.

ordering the meeting had given no indication of his purposes,[20] though it was generally expected that he would ask for money. This was indeed the first order of business; Charles requested a tax to pay his father's debts, the expenses of his anticipated coronation, and the costs resulting from the current 'estate of the affairs of Christendom'–i.e., the war. The estates promptly voted the same very large tax that had been adopted in 1621, and the council immediately wrote Charles a fawning letter informing him of that fact.[21] Both the swiftness of the estates' action and the letter were unfortunate. There had been no bargaining; the estates had not even waited to discover what else Charles wanted before voting the tax. The letter was the kind which the council had become accustomed to writing King James, who was very fond of hearing his praises sung, but never lost touch with the realities of Scottish political life. Since Charles was ignorant of those realities, the vote and the letter, taken together, led him to assume that in Scotland all he had to do was to issue orders, issue them firmly, and obedience would follow.

Charles might have learned the erroneousness of this opinion from the way the estates treated the rest of his program. They instantly rejected his proposal to forego the tax, except for the amount needed to pay for his coronation, in return for paying for the maintenance for three years of 2,000 men, with the shipping necessary to transport them; the country, they said, was much too poor to afford that. The controversial items on a long list of royal proposals, mostly having to do with economic issues and the way in which the court of session conducted its business, were referred to the appropriate bodies for action or advice, save two, which were rejected. The geography of Edinburgh militated against the judges' coming to court on horseback, they explained– James would not have needed to be told that–and the proposed duty on coal exported in foreign ships would ruin the trade: foreign buyers would go elsewhere. The estates did not say so, but the implication was that this proposal was designed to benefit English coal owners. The estates also took a number of actions on their own initiative, three of which, adopted at the request of the lairds, were apt to anger Charles. Scotstarvit was accused of extortion and publicly ordered to adhere to the approved schedule of fees for the work of his office. The lairds bitterly complained of the precedence the king had granted to the Nova Scotia baronets. And, finally, the estates addressed themselves to the rumour that Charles was planning some alteration in the court of session, whose meeting had been repeatedly postponed on Charles's orders. Since the court had been established by act of parliament, the estates asked Charles to proceed in the same way if he proposed to make any changes.[22]

More was to come. On 3 November, the day after the estates adjourned, the

---

20 *Ibid.*, 132–3. A convention of estates was a less formal version of parliament, with the same categories of membership and much the same legislative powers.
21 28 Oct. 1625, the council to Charles, *ibid.*, 151–3.
22 For the proceedings of the estates see *ibid.*, xxv–xxxiii, 150–80. The official text of their acts is in *APS* v, 166–88.

council received the king's commission for the new council and promptly decided to return it to him with a request for three changes. The quorum, which called for eight members plus the officers of state, was too large; it should be cut to five. The councillors did not want immunity from legal action for non-payment of debt; this would set a bad example, and anyhow it would be harder for them to raise loans if their potential creditors had no redress at law. Finally, the king had named Melrose president of the council, with precedence over everyone save the chancellor, the two archbishops, and the treasurer. Melrose did not want this job: the nobility would be jealous of him, and the king's business would suffer as a result. He could do better from his accustomed place at the council table.[23]

Two weeks later, on 17 November, while Charles was still digesting all this, the council wrote again, a letter very different in tone from that of three weeks before reporting the vote on the tax. The chancellor had produced a series of documents to which the great seal was to be attached, among them, apparently, a statement authorizing a new act of revocation, perhaps summarizing it, but providing no text. On 12 October the revocation had apparently passed the privy seal in just this way.[24] Hay and his colleagues protested. No one knew exactly what was in the document, and there was universal fear that 'all . . . former securities granted by your Majesty and your royal progenitors were thereby intended to be annulled, and that no right hereafter to be made in the majority of kings could be valid'. They hinted very strongly that they believed the revocation to be illegal, except as it applied to the Principality. All but one of the other documents were also illegal, in their opinion; they asked the king to designate one or two of the councillors who had served under James to come to London to confer with him. And, finally, they protested against Charles's designation of the laird of Thornton, one of the first Nova Scotia baronets, as a member of the council and of the various commissions which Charles was planning to continue or create. This was indeed a bizarre appointment, given Thornton's reputation. He had seduced the second wife of the fifth earl Marischal, persuaded her to live with him, and with the aid of her son by Marischal had looted Dunnottar Castle of its tapestries, furnishings, and valuables during the earl's absence. So thorough were they that when the old man returned he had even had to borrow a bed to sleep in. After her husband's death Thornton married the lady, and was sued by the sixth earl, the son of his father's first marriage, for, among other

23 *RPCS*, 2nd ser. i, 182–5.
24 The date is given in the parliamentary record for 1633, *APS* V, 23. No trace of the document has been found in the privy seal register, and the keeper of the privy seal, Sir Richard Cockburn of Clerkington, seems to have been in Edinburgh in October. Whether or not a text was read in council at this time is not clear. On 7 Jan. 1626, Mar said that he had heard the document read once there, HMC, *Report on the Manuscripts of the Earl of Mar and Kellie* (hereafter *M&K*), ed. H. Paton (London, 1904), 135. The council's letter of 17 November, however, says that 'none as yet has seen the same', which seems plain enough.

things, having committed these acts of robbery. The suit had been settled
before James's death, but there had been a tremendous scandal, and the
councillors felt aggrieved at having to associate with such a character, whose
'sincerity in religion', they said, was also in doubt.[25]

That the councillors should write such a letter, in the face of the recent
warning to Mar's eldest son that 'when he [Charles] has once resolved to
follow any course, there is no means to draw him from it, or alter the least jot
of his resolution', indicates the depth of their anger and concern.[26] The full
scope of Charles's plans was now apparent. Though they had not seen the
revocation, their information as to its contents was accurate enough. The
king's plan was to revoke all gifts of land which had belonged to either the
crown or the kirk made since 1540, whether or not the gift had been made
during a royal minority. The amount of property involved was enormous;
virtually every landowner of any consequence would be adversely affected if
the king carried through on his scheme. Among the most seriously threatened
were the families of men like Melrose, the loyal servants of the crown upon
whom James had depended to run his government and whose support
Charles could ill afford to lose.

Charles had no intention of revolutionizing the structure of Scottish land-
holding, however. His purpose was to use the act as a lever to bring about
changes which he regarded as desirable: improvement in clerical stipends via
the teinds [tithes], the elimination of the feudal superiority of the holders of
church and crown lands over those tenants to whom they had set those lands
in feu, the alteration of the tenure of certain lands held of the crown, and the
right to revoke grants of hereditary offices and regalities, which had long
been regarded as an obstacle to good government but upon which James had
always been too cautious to launch a frontal assault. Charles intended to pay
compensation for most of the losses entailed, and to leave most of the land
concerned in the hands of its present holders. But the councillors and their
fellow landholders knew nothing of this. They were panicky and mistrustful,
and their mood was not improved by Charles's order of 22 October that all
recipients of pensions appear before the council to disclose the cause and the
amount of the grant.[27] This kind of order usually foreshadowed a winnowing
of the list.

The king's other changes, though nowhere near as widely resented, were
also unpalatable to those whom they affected. There was to be a complete
separation between the council and the court of session; furthermore, no
nobleman was to sit on the court any more.[28] There was to be a commission of
grievances, with wider authority and greater power than that created by
James in 1623, which had dealt almost exclusively with economic issues. The

25 *Ibid.*, 137–8. *RPCS*, 2nd ser. i, 193–5.
26 *M&K*, 132–3.
27 *RPCS*, 2nd ser. i, 187–8.
28 5 Oct. 1625, Kellie to Mar, *M&K Supp.*, 234. 22 Oct., J. Douglas to Lord Erskine, *M&K*, 132–3.

new commission's principal functions were to hear complaints of official misconduct and to investigate people who spoke or wrote against the government. It was, wrote Sir James Balfour, 'nothing else but the star chamber court of England under another name, come down here to play the tyrant, with a specious visor on its face'.[29] There was to be an exchequer commission with the power to do exchequer and treasury business; Mar and the treasurer depute, Sir Archibald Napier of Merchiston, could not act without the consent of the commission, but the commission could act without them.[30] Mar, who evidently had not known of this until Hay produced the commission in council on 17 November, vehemently protested to the king. He had warned Charles that his enemies would try to blacken his reputation, he wrote, and evidently they had succeeded. This commission would destroy his credit, 'and yet never put a penny in your purse'. This was no way to treat an honest old servant: he hoped the king would reconsider. Mar's sense of grievance was the more acute because he had just been informed that Charles had promised to give him a hearing before giving credence to any unfriendly reports—and now this![31]

The attitude of the Scottish leadership did not sit well with Charles, who was now receiving the first indications of the disaster at Cadiz. At first he expressed surprise that some proposals which he thought would be popular evidently were not, and complained that during their visit to London none of his officials had reminded him to make a revocation, which had to be issued before November.[32] Charles's surprise soon gave way to anger, however. He was convinced that the councillors were deliberately fanning popular fears respecting the revocation,[33] and he ordered their leaders to come to London to explain themselves. 'The humor of our leading men continueth to oppose the king's directions', wrote Nithsdale to one of the signers of the letter of protest of 17 November. 'Let them answer, when they come here, for it'.[34]

In the king's opinion the chief culprit was Melrose. His refusal of the presidency of the council was insulting. He was the most active of the triumvirate—Mar and Hay suffered from periods of bad health—his was the legal brain, and he was behind all the protests, which dwelt on the legal issues raised by Charles's actions. He stood to lose the most if the king's plans went through; he was president of the court of session, where his two brothers also sat, and his landed wealth and his very title derived from church property. He had inspired the demand that changes in the session be made in parliament and the protest over the Nova Scotia baronetcies, he could be expected to challenge the legality of the revocation—and it was absolutely unprecedented

29 *Balfour*, ii, 131.
30 22 Oct. 1625, Charles to Hay, *M&K*, 131–2.
31 18 Nov. 1625, Mar to Charles *ibid.*, 133. 7 Nov., Kellie to Mar, *M&K Supp.*, 235–6.
32 13 Nov. 1625, Kellie to Mar, *M&K Supp.*, 238.
33 On this point see *M&K*, 146.
34 28 Nov. 1625, Nithsdale to Annandale, in *State Papers and Miscellaneous Correspondence of Thomas, Earl of Melros*, ed. J. Maidment (Edinburgh, 1837), 593–4.

to attempt to nullify the actions of sovereigns of full age. So also was the removal of judges from the court of session; they had their appointments for life–*ad vitam aut culpam*–and all the precedents of James's reign indicated that a king could not remove a judge merely because he wished to.[35] Charles believed, however, that if he was to accomplish anything at all via his revocation, he had to break the grip of the great landowners on the court of session, where, so he had been told, the key legal issues would be decided.[36] They not only had to be excluded from the court themselves, but their influence over it had also to be attenuated to as great a degree as possible. Hence the decision that in future neither noblemen nor privy councillors should be members of the court.

The exclusion of the councillors from the session was thus the key to the implementation of Charles's Scottish policy. The experience of James's reign, especially during Dunfermline's years of power, had shown that the council's authority, cohesiveness, and independent-mindedness grew in proportion to the number of judges sitting there. These men were lawyers, likely to follow the lead of the country's principal lawyer, as Dunfermline had been and as Melrose, who had been president of the court since 1616, now was. A weak and docile council was what Charles now wanted, not the sort which would habitually write him the kind of letter it had recently sent, indicating unwillingness to approve a royal warrant on the ground that a special privilege it granted would set a bad precedent and cost the treasury £30,000, and implying that Charles was ignorant of the financial consequences of his action.[37] So court and council were to be separated, and the power of Melrose, the most important link between the two, was to be broken.

The meetings between the king and the Scottish leaders began on 7 January 1626, and lasted for a fortnight. They were acrimonious and unproductive. The military situation made the timing unfortunate. Charles's frame of mind, after Cadiz, could not have been of the best; the councillors had left behind a country with invasion jitters of its own and hopelessly unprepared, desperately short of gunpowder, and 'not a craftsman to make a steel bonnet in all the land'.[38] Melrose and his colleagues made very little impression on Charles, who seemed simply not to hear anything he did not want to hear; the old men returned home defeated and resentful–'in dudgeon', wrote the Venetian ambassador.[39] Only Archbishop Spottiswoode emerged with an

---

35 See, on this point, P. G. B. McNeill, 'The Independence of the Scottish Judiciary', *Judicial Review* n.s. iii. (1958), 140.

36 See the council's letter to him on 15 Mar. 1625, on the affairs of the Principality, *RPCS*, xiii, 716–8.

37 27 Sept. 1625, the council to Charles, *ibid.*, 2nd ser. i, 144.

38 *Ibid.*, 185–7, 191–2. 7 Dec. 1625, Patrick Home of Polwarth to Sir Robert Kerr, *Ancram and Lothian Corr.*, ii, 481–2.

39 *Calendar of State Papers relating to English Affairs existing in the Archives and Collections of Venice . . .* ed. A. B. Hinds, xix (London, 1913), 335. The Venetian reports must be used with caution; the remarks about Scotland are occasionally very inaccurate.

improved position. He had not been present at the meetings of the council that had offended Charles; he had always been a strong supporter of the prerogative, and he now took advantage of various opportunities to endorse Charles's views. The king was obviously pleased.[40]

The discord began almost at once. Charles thanked his councillors for the prompt vote on the tax, but then charged that the rest of his program had failed, not on its merits, but because its spokesmen, notably Nithsdale, were unpopular. Hay, 'in great choler' rejoined that the cost of supporting 2000 men, on the basis of figures he had collected from sea captains, was so great that the estates would not hear of sending the matter to committee to work out some sort of compromise, as the king had thought could be done. Spottiswoode disputed Hay's memory of the sequence of events, claiming 'in some little passion' that the leadership had decided not to send the proposal to committee before, not after, they put it to the estates, and a wrangle between the two ensued.[41] So the sessions went, with the triumvirate justifying its actions and engaging in sharp exchanges with the king's supporters: Spottiswoode, Nithsdale, Scotstarvit, the bishop of Ross, and with most of the participants, including the king, making frequent displays of touchiness and vanity.

On the revocation Charles proved to be very ill-informed. He believed that he had done nothing more than his father and grandmother had done, save for one clause he could not remember, and was astonished that there should be such a fuss. Mar pointed out that since he became king at age twenty-four, he had done nothing as king which he could properly revoke. The text of Charles's revocation was at last produced and compared with James's; the point upon which Hay and Mar harped over and over again was that Charles was attempting to revoke acts of his predecessors made in their full age. If this act was ratified by parliament, no one could be sure of his property, now or in the future: Charles's successors could revoke his acts. At the session at which the texts were compared, the only one from which the king was absent– Buckingham was there–the only speech in favor of the revocation came, Mar wrote, from 'that worthy judicious lawyer the bishop of Ross, who babbled all the time so far without sense or reason, as every indifferent man who heard him might easily perceive that his judgment was far short of that which the gravity of his beard did promise'.[42] Hay, in summing up, boldly told the king

40 The sources on which the following paragraphs are based are the notes made at the time by Mar, *M&K*, 133–46, 153–5, and an account written thirty-five years later by Scotstarvit, dealing mostly with his controversy with Melrose over the tenure of the members of the session, printed in *SHR* xi (1914), 164–91. The king's interviews with Mar in Feb. 1626 (*M&K*, 144–6), show how little his mind had changed; he repeated many of the allegations his councillors had been at pains to refute. For Spottiswoode's views see his letter of 14 Nov. 1625, to Annandale, in Sir W. Fraser, *The Book of Caerlaverock*, 2 vols. (Edinburgh, 1873) ii, 72–3.

41 *M&K*, 133–4.

42 *Ibid.*, 139.

that those who had advised him to issue the revocation had 'made shipwreck of their own estates, and would now fish in drumlie waters by shaking all things loose that they may get some part to themselves; some of them having no wit at all, some of them but half witted, and neither of them [of] great honesty',[43] a shaft aimed chiefly at Nithsdale and Scotstarvit.

The second great matter, having to do with the court of session, was left to Melrose, who, to avoid any charge of special pleading, indicated in advance that he was personally prepared to resign from the court as the king wished. The king's line was that all offices vacated with the demise of the crown, and that he could therefore appoint whom he liked to the court. He also claimed that since the council was superior to the session, and no one disputed his right to appoint and dismiss councillors, his right to appoint and dismiss judges should be equally obvious. This case was argued by Scotstarvit, who by his own account had had his arguments endorsed ahead of time by Sir James Skene, a member of the court and a man with no love for Melrose; Skene was Charles's choice to succeed Melrose as president.[44] Scotstarvit argued that when the court was founded nothing was said about lifetime tenures, and that only two of the commissions issued before 1581 contained such a clause. Melrose's reply was based on precedent: there were no wholesale renewals on the accession of new monarchs in 1542 and 1567, and previous deprivations of individuals could be regarded as *ad culpam*. There was no clear-cut winner. Scotstarvit, in his account, naturally gave himself the better of the argument. He also candidly admitted that personal animus against the current judges, especially Melrose, fueled his zeal–Scotstarvit disliked practically everybody, and made no bones about it. Mar, equally naturally, regarded Scotstarvit's reasoning as 'feckless and to no purpose'.[45]

Other matters took less time but were no less controverted. Charles was irritated that the council had sent the commission for the new council back instead of accepting it and asking for revisions. Mar and Melrose rejoined that it could not be accepted because the clause granting the councillors immunity directly contravened an act of parliament. The king's spokesmen could not make good on their claims that both council and session had ignored the statute in the past. The king's animus toward Melrose surfaced during this discussion, and also in his references to Melrose's refusal of the presidency of the council; he made it clear that he was going to fill this office. The egregious Thornton attempted to recover something of his lost reputation by accusing the lord chancellor of taking bribes. The alleged briber promptly denied this, and Hay struck back by accusing Thornton of arranging a bigamous marriage for his sister. Thornton's attempt to accuse Mar of oppressing him also backfired when Mar revealed the whole sordid story of his robbery of

43 *Ibid.*, 140.
44 In 1612 Melrose, then lord advocate, had prevented Skene from succeeding his father as clerk register and briefly occupied the office himself.
45 *M&K*, 143.

Marischal. Hay attacked the commission for grievances as being in certain aspects illegal; Mar declared that the treasury commission was not only illegal but also a slur on him: 'I cannot but sorrow that in my old age that mark of distrust should be put upon me'.[46] Nithsdale attacked Mar's handling of his office; Mar replied by accusing Nithsdale of oppression and corruption as a border commissioner. A slanging match ensued which Buckingham did his best to quiet down.

The last of the meetings took place on 22 January 1626. It dealt mostly with the court of session, and ended on a note of compromise sounded by Spottiswoode. There were seven judges whom the king wanted to replace: five officials, including Melrose, and two nobles, Lords Lauderdale and Carnegy, both of whom had claimed that they were entitled to remain on the bench. Hay had argued for the retention of Lauderdale and Carnegy on the basis of merit, and, indeed, their merit was not in dispute. Spottiswoode suggested that they be offered places as extraordinary lords. Charles, who had previously indicated that he wanted no aristocrats as extraordinary lords either,[47] thought well of this idea. But it quickly appeared that he was not willing to compromise on much of anything else. On 26 January a spate of letters, proclamations, and instructions went northward. A minatory letter went to the officers of state who were members of the court of session: resign from the latter or lose both jobs. The letter to Lauderdale and Carnegy was less harsh but equally firm. Charles got his way: all the justices resigned, and the eight whom Charles wished to retain were readmitted. Oddly enough, their letters of renewal, and the commissions of the new appointees, made no mention of the question of tenure.[48]

With respect to the revocation Charles attempted to allay his subjects' fears, which, he was now persuaded, were genuine if misguided. He ordered the council to proclaim that his action was taken out of zeal for religion, to reduce the burden of taxation on his subjects by recovering property rightfully belonging to the crown, and to put an end to the confusion and oppression to which the current condition of the teinds gave rise by 'procuring . . . that every man may have his own teinds upon reasonable conditions', which, he said, had been his father's intention. He also wanted to 'free the gentry . . . from all those bonds which may force them to depend upon any other than upon his Majesty'. He had no intention of wronging anybody, he said; he issued the sort of revocation he did because, not having had a minority during which the crown's patrimony could suffer damage, he felt obligated

46 *Ibid.*, 142.
47 25 Oct. 1625, J. Douglas to Lord Erskine, *M&K Supp.*, 132–3. Extraordinary lords of session, now four in number, were royal nominees who possessed no legal qualifications, received no pay, and sat with the court when they pleased. They were almost always privy councillors, and often high officials. There were fifteen ordinary lords, who were supposed to have professional legal training.
48 *RCPS*, 2nd ser. i, 220–1, 234–6. *The Earl of Stirling's Register of Royal Letters . . .* ed. Charles Rogers (Edinburgh, 1885), i, 13, 15–6. McNeill, 'Scottish Judiciary', 143–4.

'for keeping of his royal prerogative to revoke what his predecessors had done to the hurt of the same'.[49] But just what he intended to do, and how, was not disclosed; the disquiet, not surprisingly, did not diminish.[50] So in July 1626 Charles at last became specific, indicated the types of property to which the revocation applied, and created a commission to work out appropriate compensation for those who surrendered their rights by 1 January 1627. Charles also promised to make a specific declaration as to the patrimony of the crown at the next parliament. Any revocation issued by his successors could apply only to that patrimony; all other property would be secure.[51]

This statement was helpful in some ways. Though the amount of property encompassed in it was vast and the commission's powers limited, the principle of compensation had been conceded, and the promised act of parliament delineating the crown's patrimony would allay the fears for the future which Mar and others had so strongly emphasized. But almost everyone concerned found the statement disquieting in some way. The magnates would lose both income and power if regalities and heritable offices were eliminated; even the king's supporters had some qualms on this score. The reformed church from the very beginning of its existence had laid claim to the whole of the teinds as its rightful possession; on this point there was no disagreement between bishop and presbyter. It was now apparent that Charles did not intend that this should happen, that bargains were to be struck with the current possessors of the right to collect teinds, whoever they might be, which would leave a considerable proportion thereof in lay hands. Even the heritors, for whose benefit Charles said he was acting, were dubious; the king's talk about increasing his revenues out of the teinds suggested their new freedom from what Charles regarded as aristocratic oppression was going to cost them something.

Then, a month later, Charles reverted to authoritarian tactics. He had asked the lords advocate to provide him with a plan for implementing his intentions; apparently without waiting for a reply he ordered the preparation of a summons of reduction (i.e., nullification) against all holders of church property, regalities, and hereditary offices.[52] The holders of such property thus faced a nasty dilemma: make a voluntary surrender by January and get compensation, or take their chances in court—either the council or Charles's newly created bench of sessioners—with the prospect of no compensation if they lost. So there was further protest, fueled still further by Charles's order that the revocation be entered in the session's books of *sederunt*, thus giving it the strength of a judicial decree. There were calls for a parliament, especially from Melrose, and an aristocratic deputation made its way to London at the end of 1626 to present its complaints.[53] After some hesitation Charles received

49 *RPCS*, 2nd ser. i, 227–9.
50 See, e.g. 25 Mar. 1626, Charles to Mar, *Stirling's Register* i, 31.
51 *RPCS*, 2nd ser. i, 351–3.
52 *Stirling's Register*, i, 57–8, 72.
53 *Ibid.*, 86–7, 103. *M&K*, 151–3.

it graciously, and once again shifted his tactics, probably at the suggestion of William Graham, earl of Menteith, who was then at court and about to begin his rapid rise in Charles's favour.[54] The threat of immediate legal action was laid aside. Charles instead appointed a much larger commission than that of July 1626, made up, like its predecessor, of the four elements that constituted the convention of estates; at least three members of each group had to be present to constitute a quorum. The new commission had far broader powers than its predecessor, and Charles promised to accept its recommendations, which he had not done in July. It was made clear that its major task was to deal with the teinds.[55] This was an immensely complicated question, since it involved securing an adequate stipend for the parish minister, making it possible for the heritors to possess the teinds of their own lands, and obtaining a percentage of the teinds for the crown. None of these things could be done until the value of the teinds for each parish was known; a long administrative task lay before the commission. The work was necessarily slow, and far from complete when the storm broke in 1637.[56]

On the other matters raised at the January meetings Charles made adjustments to meet specific objections but gave no ground as to principle. He reiterated his insistence on the precedence of the Nova Scotia baronets.[57] The commission for grievances went forward, still with its broadly defined powers independent of those of the council, including the authority to appoint agents in each shire. The commission did provide, however, that the same person could not act both as informer and as a supposedly independent witness, which, as Hay had pointed out, the provision for anonymous informing in the first draft would have made possible.[58] The exchequer commission, of which Spottiswoode was president, also had wide powers, in the sense that the lord treasurer and his deputy could do nothing of any importance without its approval. The commission could not act without one or the other of them being present, however; the king thus met the most vehement of Mar's objections.[59] The new council, weakened by the creation of these commissions and shorn of the sessioners, was constituted on 23 March 1626. Archbishop Spottiswoode's name led all the rest, even the chancellor's, and there was a lord president in the person of the earl of

---

54 On 27 Dec. 1626, Charles made him a privy councillor; *RPCS*, 2nd ser. i, 495–6. For Menteith's part in this incident see *ibid.*, pp. clxxvii–clxxviii, citing Forbes's *Treatise of Church Lands and Tithes*. The Venetian ambassador mentions the intervention of a Scottish nobleman, unnamed; the context suggests Menteith. *Calendar of State Papers, Venetian*, xx, 78.

55 26 Mar. 1627, Charles to the commissioners, *Stirling's Register*, i, 145.

56 The text of Charles's proclamation appointing the commission is in *RPCS*, 2nd ser. i, 509–16. For a good brief account of the revocation see Stevenson, *Scottish Revolution*, 35–42.

57 12 Feb. 28 July 1626, Charles to the council, *Stirling's Register*, i, 18–9, 68–9. 13 July, the council to Charles, *RPCS*, 2nd ser. i, 343–4.

58 *Ibid.*, 241–3. *M&K*, 141.

59 *RPCS*, 2nd ser. ii, 265–7.

Montrose.[60] The quorum was not changed from that stipulated in the rejected commission of November 1625. It was unreasonably large and, as predicted, caused repeated difficulties in the ensuing years; Charles gradually and reluctantly whittled it down.

The council's powers were still further attenuated in July 1626 when Charles created a council of war to manage the feeble and underfinanced Scottish war effort.[61] Montrose presided over it, and the triumvirate was excluded. It was not very effective, save in the matter of raising regiments to follow various aristocratic captains overseas, and even here it had great trouble finding the money to keep the recruits from deserting. Once the invasion scare had passed, it was impossible to persuade anyone to make the kinds of financial sacrifices which Charles, remembering the alacrity of the vote on the tax, optimistically expected of his subjects.[62] The burghs, the element in Scottish society most directly affected by the war, since their trade suffered and the king pressed them hardest for financial contributions, expressed their distaste for the king's whole policy by asking him 'to make the seas peacable, that trade and navigation may flourish'.[63]

It was also apparent that the January meetings had not caused Charles to lose confidence in those he had chosen as his Scottish advisers. He did refrain from appointing the offensive Thornton to the council, but Thornton was a member of both the exchequer and grievance commissions. The almost equally offensive Nithsdale Charles appointed collector of the recently voted taxation.[64] The king continued to find Scotstarvit's schemes plausible; the council had continually to intervene in defense of the king's subjects, whom Scotstarvit was attempting to gouge on a really massive scale, allegedly charging fifty or sixty pounds for what used to cost two.[65] Archbishop Spottiswoode continued to enjoy an increasing measure of the king's favour, in spite of his and his episcopal colleagues' doubts as to the effect on the church of the king's revocation. The archbishop carefully separated himself from the triumvirate and made a confidant of the Catholic Nithsdale. 'All things are loose here', he wrote in March 1626, 'and the combination holds firm, which your lordship saw at court, which his Majesty's service will hardly endure'.[66]

King Charles agreed. The chief target of his wrath was Melrose, who besides losing his presidency of the session was omitted from the commissions for the exchequer and for grievances, and in January 1626 was forced to accept Sir William Alexander as joint secretary, with Alexander to be resident

60 Ibid., 248–51.
61 Ibid., 337–8. Charles further jolted his councillors by absent-mindedly sending instructions to the council of war before naming it. Ibid., 333–5.
62 28 July 1626, Charles to the council, Stirling's Register, i, 67.
63 RPCS, 2nd ser i, 386–9.
64 Ibid., 233–4.
65 Stirling's Register, i, 17, 84–5. RPCS, 2nd ser. i, 517–8.
66 Fraser, Caerlaverock, ii, 73–4.

at court. Melrose was left with nothing of the office but an empty title; he displayed his annoyance by rebuffing Alexander's friendly overtures and treating him very frigidly.[67] In time his temper cooled and he tried to recover. He wrote fawningly to Buckingham;[68] he praised Charles's instructions to the commission of revocation, contrasting the present situation with that which had obtained earlier, when the king was listening to men who had ruined themselves and were trying to recoup 'by undoing of his Majesty father's faithful servants, by depriving them of the gracious recompenses of their services bestowed upon them by that blessed king'.[69] He was even willing to change his title, from Melrose to Haddington—'to humor the King because it is an erection', wrote his wife to her eldest son.[70] In vain: his decline continued.

The same fate overtook his fellow triumvirs, though more gradually. Mar, the ancient aristocrat, could not be handled as roughly as Haddington the *arriviste*, but by the beginning of 1627 it was apparent that he would have to leave office sooner or later; the inevitable occurred in 1630. Hay was less of a problem because he had no real power base. Archbishop Spottiswoode, who was ambitious for the chancellorship, cultivated Nithsdale, fed him stories that the council was sabotaging his efforts as tax collector, and urged him, for the good of the country, to move against Hay.[71] In the autumn of 1626 Nithsdale tried, and utterly failed; the charges were 'so frivolous and of so small consequence', the archbishop wrote disgustedly to Viscount Stormont, that Hay's position was actually strengthened.[72] But the attempt frightened Hay, who now, according to the Venetian ambassador, allowed himself to be bought.[73] Charles raised him to the peerage as Viscount Dupplin in May 1627; from that time on he did as he was bidden. He was virtually a cipher, and he and everyone else knew it.

The net result of all this activity was that by the end of 1626 Charles had seriously jeopardized his chances of ruling Scotland successfully—jeopardized, but not destroyed. He made the fact that he had little interest in Scotland, and no desire to learn about it, painfully apparent. Treasurer-

---

67 See Alexander's letters to Melrose in Mar. 1626, Fraser, *Haddington* ii, 145–7, and to the earl of Morton, 6 Oct. 1630, *NLS*, MS 80, no. 40.

68 See, e.g., his letter of 26 Feb. 1627, in *Calendar of State Papers, Domestic Series, Charles I, 1627–8*, ed. J. Bruce, (London, 1858), 52.

69 6 Mar. 1627, Melrose to the earl of Roxburgh, in Fraser, *Haddington* ii, 148–51. This letter, to a man who had the king's ear, was written a few weeks after Nithdale was replaced as collector of the taxation.

70 16 Sept. 1627, Lady Melrose to the laird of Polwarth, HMC, 14th Report, pt. 3 (London, 1894), 108. She said this was her guess; Melrose had not told her, 'nor I did not sper [ask]'.

71 See his letters of 14 Mar., 4 Apr., 12 Aug., 1626, to Nithsdale, in Fraser, *Caerlaverock*, ii, 73–6.

72 HMC, *Report on the Laing Manuscripts*, i, ed. H Paton (London, 1914), 173–4. See also the correspondence of the Venetian ambassadors, *Calendar of State Papers, Venetian*, xix, 559, 577, 594; xx, 24.

73 2/12 Feb. 1627, Contarini to the Doge and Senate, *ibid.*, xx, 119–20.

depute Napier offered to create and manage a network of correspondents to supply Charles with the information he needed, in return for a lucrative post at court; Charles showed no interest.[74] He expected the Scots to obey his orders and give advice only when asked. The bishop of Ross, whose long-winded speeches infuriated Mar and Melrose, was Charles's kind of man; Ross had said, at the last of the conferences in January 1626, 'that he wondered that any subject should deny the King's prerogative, for who doth so, he was no loyal subject'.[75] Charles made him a privy councillor and an extraordinary lord of session. Charles had no use for his father's servants or his father's methods, and did not like to be reminded of them; he became weary of hearing about Mar's grey hairs. These old men, he felt, were presuming on age and experience, talking down to the young and inexperienced man he was. They would not have defied his father's orders so, he said to Mar in February 1626. 'Alas sir', replied James's old friend, 'a hundred times your worthy father has sent down directions unto us which we have stayed, and he has given us thanks for it when we have informed him of the truth'.[76] Charles found that state of affairs most unwelcome.

Charles meant to rule as well as reign; he, not the council, would make the decisions. His central decision as to policy was contained in the various versions of the revocation; his councillors found it unpalatable; their power to obstruct his plans had therefore to be eliminated. And so it was, in that the morale and prestige and cohesiveness of the council as a body, and the *ex officio* power of the officers of state as individuals, were effectively destroyed, in behalf of a policy so unpopular that no one ever took responsibility for recommending it to the king. Instead of listening to his traditional advisers, the king now took counsel with men who were either unknown in Scotland and without influence there, like Alexander, or else well enough known to be disliked, like Nithsdale, Scotstarvit, and Thornton. The discontent was general. The country, wrote Sir Robert Gordon of Lochinvar to the council in August 1626, is 'so much grieved, what with revocations and yearly taxations, and now with penal statutes, that your Lordships can hardly believe how the people doth grudge.'[77] Lochinvar was a new-made Nova Scotia baronet, and so not likely to exaggerate out of distaste for the regime. Even those whom Charles wished to help were dubious. 'It was a measure of Charles's incompetence as a politician', writes David Stevenson, 'that he received no gratitude for the revocation even from those who stood to benefit by it'.[78]

The destruction of the council's capacity to govern did not necessarily entail the end of all possibility of Charles's ruling Scotland successfully,

74 *Memorials of Montrose and his Times*, ed. M Napier, 2 vols, Maitland Club (Edinburgh, 1848), i, 25–7.
75 *M&K*, 144.
76 *Ibid.*, 146.
77 *RPCS*, 2nd ser. i, 678–9.
78 Stevenson, *Scottish Revolution*, 40.

however. In the years of absentee government since 1603 the council had been politically impotent once before, during Dunbar's hegemony from 1606 to 1611. What Charles needed was a Dunbar of his own: a man who knew the ins and outs of Scottish politics, was politically acceptable to the people who counted, forceful enough successfully to implement the king's policy, and willing to undertake the labor necessary to achieve that success by travelling back and forth between Edinburgh and Whitehall. Another measure of Charles's incompetence as a politician is that he destroyed his father's system of government before he had found his Dunbar. It was pure folly to rely on the egregiously incompetent Nithsdale, whom he repeatedly had to protect from both his creditors and from the penalties for recusancy, and the deracinated Alexander, who had been at court since at least 1608 and whose annual summer visits to Scotland had something of the character of a vacation.[79] By happy accident, Charles, late in 1626, stumbled upon a sort of Dunbar in the person of Menteith, an ancient aristocrat whose influence with the king and willingness to undertake the travelling necessary to explain the views of the king and the Scottish political classes to each other helped for a time to defuse the tensions which Charles's destruction of the council's authority had created. But Menteith's personal ambition brought him to ruin in 1633, and Charles, showing utter lack of understanding of the importance of what Menteith was doing for him, made no effort to find a successor. Government by council had been deliberately wrecked; government by strong man had failed. Once Menteith was gone Charles's government in Scotland headed straight for disaster.

The conclusion to be drawn from this cautionary tale of the beginning of Charles's Scottish kingship is that the traditional view of Charles as an inept blunderer is accurate enough, but not for the traditional reasons. Charles inherited a situation that had its difficulties—what new monarch did not? – and, given his unfamiliarity with the Scottish scene, some changes in the system bequeathed to him by James were very likely to come about sooner or later. But Charles's actions betrayed his lack of understanding, not only of how his father had governed Scotland, but also of the fact that he needed a governmental system there at all. Perhaps he took too literally James's famous boast that he governed Scotland with his pen; certainly Charles, in Scotland as in England, imagined that all he needed to do was to issue orders to have them obeyed. What he saw in his first year as king was that his father's councillors opposed his plans; so their power was broken, as was that of the institution through which they governed. By this act, as much as and perhaps more than by the revocation, the dangers of which those affected by it managed mostly to avoid, Charles lost the confidence of the Scottish ruling class. He thus took the first step along the road to a rebellion, by making possible the recreation of that coalition of landowner and kirkman which had destroyed Queen Mary and which King James had successfully broken up. It

79 *Stirling's Register*, i, 62–3. *Balfour*, ii, 144. McGrail, *Alexander*, 172–3.

was his complete ignorance of how to govern, rather than the policies he was attempting to implement, which doomed Charles's Scottish kingship. His problems there were not of the same order of magnitude as those which confronted Louis XVI or Nicholas II, or, indeed, as those which he himself faced in his southern kingdom. All the evidence suggests they were not insoluble; very few of the conditions of revolution which Stone has found in the England of the 1620s obtained in Scotland.[80] Charles, like his own unhappy grandmother, must bear most of the responsibility for the fate that overtook him.

80 See Lawrence Stone's summary in *The Causes of the English Revolution 1529–1642* (New York, 1972), 114–7.

13

Scotland, the Union, and
the Idea of a 'General Crisis' (1994)

The nature of what historians, over the last thirty years or so, have agreed to call the 'General Crisis' of the seventeenth century has prompted a certain amount of sporadic and genteel debate. It is a subject that has aroused interest but not passion, unlike the gentry controversy and, more recently, the 'revisionist' version of the causes of the English civil war. My own previous contribution to the debate, an article published in 1984 called 'Scotland and the "General Crisis" of the Seventeenth Century', argued that 'general crisis' as a way of explaining what happened in Europe in those years, though appealing, was unsound.[1] The article demonstrated, at least to its author's satisfaction, that the Scottish case was an exception to all of the many hypotheses that scholars had floated as to the nature of that supposed crisis, and therefore, since events in Scotland precipitated what happened in England, clearly 'Exhibit A' in any crisis theory, the whole idea was fatally flawed. It goes without saying that what transpired in Scotland and England, and Ireland too, would not have happened as it did, or perhaps at all, had it not been for the Anglo-Scottish union of 1603. Alas for authorial pride, however: the idea of a 'general crisis' still seems to be alive and well, though rather less written about in the last few years. So what follows is a reconsideration of the nature of the seventeenth-century 'crisis', if that is the proper word, once again from the Scottish vantage point, and some suggestions which may provide a new starting-place for discussion.

One of the impediments to thought weighing upon historians, especially political historians, is our agreed-upon chronology. We all accept the existence of something called the seventeenth century, which is in one sense true and in another profoundly false. The crisis theorists have told us that the general crisis, whatever it was, happened in that century, although some argue that it began earlier. This has led to narrow, rather tunnel-minded thinking about it, focused on two major phenomena, the domestic upheavals of the 1640s and 1650s, and the international-cum-domestic unpleasantness in central Europe which we call the Thirty Years' War. (This tidy label is another impediment to thought: if the Peace of Westphalia had been signed a little sooner, or a little later, we might realize more clearly than we now do that the German tragedy was one facet of a much larger phenomenon.) The obvious difficulty with this double focus is that the major domestic upheaval, and the only successful one, that in Charles I's three kingdoms, had only tenuous

1 *SHR*, lxiii (1984), 136–54, reprinted above.

connections with the continental conflicts that were so obvious a factor in the revolts elsewhere. So R. B. Merriman's six contemporaneous revolutions[2] remain just that, without a satisfactory common explanation.

It may seem presumptuous for a nit-picking scholar to accuse other historians of not thinking big, but in this case the charge seems justified. Of all those who have grappled with this intractable problem the one who has come nearest to a solution is T. K. Rabb. In his elegant little book on the 'general crisis'[3] he has asked one of the right questions: why did stability return to Europe in the last third of the seventeenth century? And he has gone on, in passing, to suggest the right answer, though unfortunately he does not follow it up. Had he done so, this essay probably would not have been written.

Rabb is certainly right in saying that Europe in 1700 was vastly different from Europe in 1600. One can say that about any of those hundred-year periods we agree to call centuries, to be sure. But the difference between 1600 and 1700 is arguably greater than that between any other such hundred-year interval before or since in the history of western civilization. The case, briefly, is this. Western civilization began in Europe with the collapse of Roman authority in the west–a standard textbook observation. In the fifteen hundred years of its existence our civilization has had two organizing principles–two paradigms, to use a fashionable word–within which we have operated. The first was the idea of Christendom. The second is the idea of the omnicompetent, centralized, bureaucratic state. In 1600 the old idea was still alive, though in its death throes. In 1700 it was dead and the current organizing principle had triumphed, though there were still patches of instability in areas as widely separate as England and Russia.

In its first phase this newly triumphant organizing principle most commonly took a dynastic form, typified by that devout prince, Louis XIV, the self-proclaimed embodiment of the state. The French Revolution, an event whose significance has sometimes been exaggerated, made two major changes in it. In the first place the Revolution undermined–some might say destroyed–the principle's dynastic component. (The Americans, to be sure, had already rejected dynasticism, but they, like the Scots, were on the fringes of the civilized world. What happened there was not decisive.) After 1793 a king was no longer necessary, or even desirable, as a symbol of the state. In the place of the crown there arose other symbols: Marianne, John Bull, Uncle Sam, the flag, whose burning has become such an unspeakably depraved action to some people in the United States. Second, and more important, the French Revolution added a fourth necessary qualifying adjective. The omnicompetent, centralized, bureaucratic state must now also be the national state. So over the course of the last two hundred years fragmented nationalities have come together, as in Italy and Germany, and multinational empires have come unglued, whether based on dynastic principle

2 R. B. Merriman, *Six Contemporaneous Revolutions* (Oxford, 1938).
3 T. K. Rabb, *The Struggle for Stability in Early Modern Europe* (Oxford, 1975).

such as those of the Hapsburgs and Romanovs (whose policies in this respect the various Soviet autocrats from Lenin to Gorbachev did not change in any significant way), or on racial superiority and the 'White Man's Burden', such as the British. And from Ottawa to Belgrade to Moscow the problem is still very much with us.

The other two great principles of the French Revolution, liberty and equality, have tended to cut in opposite directions in their impact on the state, with the result that one has often been sacrificed to the other. In 1789 equality was a new idea, born of the Enlightenment; its enforcement depended upon the power of the omnicompetent state, whose power was always greatly enhanced thereby. One need look no further than the history of the United States since the presidency of Abraham Lincoln for an illustration of the truth of that statement. Liberty was a much older idea, stemming from the contractual nature of medieval government and the rights, mostly property rights, of the privileged and unequal: their 'liberties'. It is an idea that is potentially highly subversive of the organizing principle of the omnicompetent state, particularly in our own time, when it is indissolubly associated with the principle of democratic elections. So in many states liberty was, and is, suppressed, sometimes in the name of equality, sometimes in the name of inequality. In others, such as the United Kingdom, ingenious ways have been found to get around it, by arranging for the periodic election of an autocrat who, once installed in power, can behave in much the same way as Frederick the Great. In still other places, thanks very often to the principle of proportional representation, liberty has produced a replication of the Polish diet. In the United States yet another pattern obtains. Its founding fathers were concerned to preserve liberty; so they wrote a constitution designed to prevent the erection of an omnicompetent, centralized, bureaucratic state. Their success has been only partial. The government of the United States is indeed omnicompetent, centralized, bureaucratic, and at the same time subject to periodic fits of deadlock and paralysis, like the England of Charles II. Since the electorate is able to put an end to this situation if it wishes to do so, however, Americans have not yet had to call upon a Dutch saviour other than Franklin D. Roosevelt.

The all-powerful state was a matter of slow growth. The government of Louis XIV was not born in the crucible of the wars of the earlier part of the century; its roots go back at least to the days of Louis XI, or even to those of Philip the Fair, when the first signs of the weakening of the idea of Christendom began to appear. Significantly, the French government's attack upon the papacy in the person of Boniface VIII was formulated by the new men, lawyer-bureaucrats such as Guillaume de Nogaret. While the papacy was undergoing first, assault, and then virtual subordination at the hands of the French monarchy, Dante was eloquently expounding his Gelasian vision of pope and emperor together leading mankind to spiritual and temporal felicity. Coming from a man who was himself the victim of the strife of Guelf and Ghibelline in his beloved Florence, it was a vision more Utopian than Thomas More's. Yet behind it lay the reality of belief. It would be a daring person indeed in the Western Europe of Dante's time who would deny that, in the words of Pope Boniface in 1302, 'it is altogether necessary to salvation for every human creature to be subject to the Roman Pontiff'.[4] The men and women of Western Europe thought of themselves as Christians; they believed in the all-encompassing nature of the Christian message; they believed that outside the church there was no salvation.

The erosion of the grip of the church on the minds and imaginations of the faithful over the next two centuries is a familiar story that need not be repeated here. Yet the ideal of a united Christendom remained, as deeply held by Luther and Calvin as by Erasmus and More and Loyola, yet corresponding less and less to reality. The great turning point was the Schism, a disaster which in no way could be fitted in with any conceivable version of God's plan for the universe and which could only be ended by the action of secular governments. From that moment the balance began irrevocably to shift. Hus was burned in 1415; the heresiarchs of the next century died in their beds. Universalists though they were, self-proclaimed reformers rather than revolutionaries, Luther and Calvin had shattered the unity of Christendom beyond recall.

In the middle of the sixteenth century, however, almost no one was prepared to accept the finality of that break-up. Nor, as it turned out, were large numbers of people prepared to accept the mounting power of the dynastic state, its growing centralization, its bureaucracy's steady assaults upon localism and the independence and liberties of the privileged, its increasing interference in and regulation of economic life, its more frequent and more extensive forays into people's pocketbooks, forays made more necessary and more grievous by inflation and war. What resulted was a century of conflict on two fronts, which frequently intertwined with each other: throughout all of western civilization, intermittent attempts to restore the unity of Christendom through the elimination of papists or heretics, depending on one's point of view, and, almost everywhere, attempts to check the steadily growing power of the centralizing bureaucratic state before it achieved omnicompetence. 'Crisis', as Rabb has pointed out, is not an entirely satisfactory word for what happened, since it usually implies intensity and brevity, followed by resolution.[5] So the title of the first collection of essays on the problem, *Crisis in Europe 1560–1660*, is something of a contradiction in terms.[6] (Ironically, whoever invented the title of this collection got the dates pretty much right, though none of the essays discusses the significance of that hundred-year period as a whole.) Rabb's own title, however, conjures up an incomplete vision, since the two struggles envisaged two different sorts of stability that were incompatible with each other–or rather, those who struggled against the encroaching

4 The bull *Unam Sanctam*, in Columbia University, *Introduction to Contemporary Civilization in the West*, 2nd ed., 2 vols., (New York, 1954), i, 322–3.
5 Rabb, *Struggle for stability*, 29–33.
6 *Crisis in Europe 1560–1660*, ed. T. Aston (New York, 1967).

state wanted to preserve the sort of instability that their view of liberty entailed and that the dynasts were determined to wipe out. Both struggles failed, and the result was caesaropapism, exemplified in all sorts of different ways, from the revocation of the Edict of Nantes to the first amendment to the constitution of the United States. The organizing principle within which western civilization had operated since its inception was dead, on earth and in heaven too. One of the ornaments of the new age was Sir Isaac Newton, appropriately enough master of the mint to King William III and II, the Calvinist king who, having ousted his Catholic father-in-law from the thrones of his three kingdoms, made an ally of the pope in his long and ultimately successful effort to thwart the ambitions of the Most Christian King of France.

The so-called 'General Crisis', then, was of a rather larger order of magnitude than those who have previously grappled with it have indicated, save Rabb, who wrote of the 'larger development' into which his analysis fits as 'the glacial disintegration of medieval society'.[7] This is almost right, though, as is sketchily indicated in the preceding pages, it was more than a society that was dying. Where, then, does Scotland fit into this large scheme of things? At the beginning it played a prominent part, far more prominent than one might expect of a kingdom whose role in the affairs of western civilization had always been peripheral at best. Historians like to date the beginnings of the wars of religion in 1560 with the tumult of Amboise. There were the Schmalkaldic wars, to be sure, but they were a sort of curtain raiser, quickly overshadowed by the last installment of the Hapsburg-Valois conflict, which ended with the Treaty of Câteau-Cambrésis in March 1559. In fact the wars of religion began with the riots that took place in Perth in May 1559, when the Protestant opponents of the Catholic regent, Mary of Guise, responded with violence to what they regarded as her violation of a promise not to outlaw certain Protestant preachers. Indeed one might argue that the greatest significance of the tumult of Amboise was that it, and a Protestant wind which scattered a relieving force, kept the distracted French government from coming to the aid of the beleaguered regent, who was the mother of its own, and Scotland's, queen. So the Protestant party won its provisional triumph in Scotland in 1560, a triumph that became permanent thirteen years later with the surrender of Edinburgh Castle, the stronghold of the last armed supporters of the now deposed and fugitive Mary Queen of Scots.

The Scotland of Queen Mary was hardly the model of a centralized, omnicompetent, bureaucratic state. The great aristocrats were petty kings in their own regalities, they and their followers controlled local government in both town and country, there was no bureaucracy–though a nucleus of legal talent, the essential element of a bureaucracy, was beginning to collect in Edinburgh–and the crown's military and financial resources were meagre.

7 Rabb, *Struggle for stability*, 35.

Scottish monarchs were not without assets, however.[8] The dynasty was an old one and commanded loyalty, as its ability to weather the difficulties created by repeated minorities demonstrated. A king who knew how to lead would be obeyed: English invasions, often threatened and frequently suffered, reminded almost every generation of Scots of the awful consequences of being without a king. The very lack of central governmental institutions that could apply any legal check to royal authority was in fact a potential asset to a king if—and it was a big *if*—he could find a way of making himself independent of the magnates. James IV did not try. He was a magnates' king despite his destruction of the greatest of them, the lord of the Isles, and a Crusader who wore an iron chain to atone for his sins, sexual and other. James V, who wore no iron chain to atone for his incessant womanizing and was anything but a magnates' king, did try. His instrument was the church, from which he extorted large sums of money. But the patron of the anticlerical poet-dramatist Sir David Lindsay did nothing for the church in return, and he self-indulgently spent the money mostly on buildings. Unlike his father, he had no vision of the unity of Christendom—he was too much of a Tudor. His one permanent governmental legacy was a professional court, the college of justice. His hapless daughter, absorbed in her dynastic calculations and confronted by a religious situation unique in Europe, with the papal church the church *de jure*, and the new dispensation actually in control and financed in large measure by a tax on the legal church, not only could not solve her problems, she could not even provide leadership. So she went under, and the old church went under with her.

The deposition of Mary had repercussions far beyond the borders of Scotland. It was a major event in the century-long 'crisis' that was gripping western civilization, because it meant the end of the possibility of the restoration of the authority of the old church in the British Isles from within; after 1573 that could be accomplished only by foreign invasion. Had the Catholic queen of Scots succeeded or displaced her cousin on the English throne, to which, in Catholic eyes, she was already entitled, had English support for Dutch and Huguenot rebels never materialized, there would have been no need for the Invincible Armada, and we might all be writing of the triumphs of that new Constantine, King Philip the Great, the reunifier of Christendom.

But Mary failed, and eventually paid for her plotting with her life. Her execution brought the possibility of peaceful dynastic union between Scotland and England, which seemed utterly remote when James IV married Margaret Tudor, ever closer as Elizabeth continued to dwell in single blessedness. (It should be remembered that James IV was far from being

8 On this point, see especially the works of J. Wormald: *Court, kirk and community: Scotland 1470–1625* (London, 1981); *Lords and men in Scotland: bonds of manrent 1442–1603* (Edinburgh, 1985); *Mary Queen of Scots: a study in failure* (London, 1988); and many articles, especially 'James VI and I: two kings or one?', *History*, lxviii, (1983), 187–209.

the first Scottish king to marry an English princess. Like his father-in-law, James IV was a descendant of John of Gaunt, and arguably had as good a claim to the English throne as did Henry VII.) So James VI, when he came to govern for himself, faced a set of circumstances unique in the annals of Scottish kingship. The English throne might one day be his, ought to be his when Elizabeth died by the rules of primogeniture; it became the great object of his life to sit upon it. At the same time he was confronted by a church with a mission, a church that had a covenant with God. Of all of God's reformed churches it was the purest. It had won through against great odds thanks to God's special favour. If it maintained its purity, if indeed it became purer still, then, with God's help, it could and would carry its message through Christendom. The Scots were a blessed people, the Lord's chosen instruments—an idea that can be found, arguably as early as the Declaration of Arbroath.[9] Their prince must be godly too, that is, he must listen to, and obey, the spokesmen of the Lord. James believed in himself as a godly prince, and the vision of a unified Christendom caught his imagination also, provided that it took place under his auspices. In his early years on the English throne he and his publicists conjured up the image of James as the new Constantine who would preside over an ecumenical council to achieve reunification. While he was still only James VI, however, he had to deal with the kirk's overarching vision of the kingdom of Christ Jesus, in which he was only a member. So he created a vision of his own, that of the free monarch, God's vicegerent, answerable only to Him and not to those who imagined themselves to be God's privy councillors. Furthermore he had the resources to help him implement his vision, resources in men, the educated laymen, mostly lawyers, to create a bureaucracy, and resources in wealth, in the form of church lands annexed to the crown in 1587, to reward them. He was also mercifully free of institutional checks on his authority. Scotland, as Arthur Williamson accurately remarks, had no 'ancient constitution',[10] and its parliament was amenable to royal control thanks to that peculiar institution known as the committee of the articles. The checks on royal authority were political and economic: the entrenched power of the magnates, especially at the local level, the intransigence of God's privy councillors, Andrew Melville and his ilk, the limited, though growing, national wealth available for taxation, and the political dangers inherent in James's attempting to tax too heavily or too often in his delicate circumstances. There is no need to repeat the familiar story of James's success in dealing with his problems.[11] By 1603

9 G. Donaldson, *The faith of the Scots* (London, 1990), 88.
10 A. H. Williamson, *Scottish national consciousness in the age of James VI* (Edinburgh, 1979), 146.
11 See the works of Wormald cited in note 8 above, and also G. Donaldson, *Scotland: James V–James VII* (Edinburgh, 1965), chs. 8–15; M. Lee, Jr, *John Maitland of Thirlestane* (Princeton, 1959) and *Government by pen: Scotland under James VI and I* (Urbana, 1980); and K. Brown, *Bloodfeud in Scotland 1573–1625* (Edinburgh, 1986).

the outlines of the all-powerful state that was to be the wave of the future were visible in Scotland. There was a modern theory of monarchy and a central bureaucracy in place, though hardly as yet a centralized or omnicompetent regime. But the lineaments of the latter could be perceived.

The union transformed the Scottish scene, and the circumstances of King James. It put at his disposal the resources of a far wealthier kingdom, which he might use to complete the implementation of his vision of free monarchy in Scotland, and it insulated him from clerical and aristocratic backlash. At the same time, as James I of England, he found himself having to deal with a polity that, by comparison with Scotland's, was medieval and decidedly backward. The benevolent (for a monarch) principles of Roman law were unavailable in England. Parliament was a medieval anachronism that his Tudor predecessors had failed to emasculate when they had the chance. Henry VIII might have done so had he used the wealth of the monasteries as Thomas Cromwell had evidently wished him to. Cromwell was the man who represented the future: a centralizing bureaucrat whose fingers reached into every aspect of English life, a thoroughly secular-minded politician who had no use for the idea of Christendom and stressed the ancient (and quite mythical) autonomy of the *ecclesia Anglicana* in his anti-papal propaganda. But Henry foolishly dispensed with Cromwell, plunging headlong into continental war once again (thus demonstrating that he had learned nothing from the military failures of the 1520s), sold monastic lands to pay for these wars, which gained him nothing, and in so doing threw away the chance to rid the English monarchy of its medieval incubus, parliament, this 'rotten seed of Egypt', as James called it after seven years of unsatisfactory experience with it. But James was not about to undertake the task that Henry had failed to perform. As he remarked to the Spanish ambassador, the count of Gondomar, 'I . . . found it here when I arrived, so that I am obliged to put up with what I cannot get rid of'.[12] He did not wish to provoke constitutional confrontation. On the two major constitutional issues between James and parliament, James was in the right: the judges upheld his right to levy impositions, and foreign policy had always been the province of the crown.

The political bigamy that the union entailed was bound to cause trouble sooner or later. James avoided it. He continued to consolidate the power of the 'new' monarchy in Scotland, executing even his own cousin, Earl Patrick of Orkney, when that ruffianly and self-willed magnate carried his defiance too far. He drew back from his one major misstep, the five articles of Perth; the damage that blunder caused need not have been permanent. The creation of the omnicompetent, centralized, bureaucratic state would take time; the process was further advanced in Scotland than in England when James died. Charles had no patience with obstacles, and no sense that patience was a

12 Quoted in M. Lee Jr, *Great Britain's Solomon: James VI and I in his three kingdoms* (Urbana and Chicago, 1990), 93.

necessary monarchical virtue. The tale of his unwisdom need not be retold.[13] But the nature of the backlash he provoked must be spelled out; it is crucial to the larger analysis of this essay.

In Scotland Charles behaved like a modern king, a 'new' monarch. He forced annual and increasing taxes through meetings of the convention of estates and his one pre-1637 meeting of parliament. He put an end to the *de facto* autonomy of the privy council that had obtained in the last fifteen years of James's reign, and weakened its influence by excluding members of the college of justice from it. His Act of Revocation, itself of questionable legality, threatened the grip of most magnates and many lairds on property rights and superiorities in so far as these had been acquired from crown or church. Men feared, wrote Archbishop Spottiswoode, that the revocation would 'call in question all men's rights since King Fergus'.[14] Charles tolerated no opposition, and tried a member of the nobility, Lord Balmerino, on a capital charge for allegedly circulating a paper critical of his policies. He behaved like the foreigner he was: his foreign and economic policies were perceived as damaging to Scotland's welfare. His principal agent after 1633, the earl of Traquair, was a self-made bureaucrat with no constituency among the people who counted. And, of course, Charles attempted to impose a religious change that was deeply offensive to the vast majority of the Scottish people.

The upheaval, when it came, took place under aristocratic leadership. It was, wrote the disapproving clerk of the Aberdeen city council, 'the nobility's covenant'[15]–though of course not all of the nobility turned against the king. Scottish aristocrats as a class had good reason to worry about their position. The union threatened Scottish national identity, a matter of concern for many Scots besides nobles, of course. It also greatly reduced most aristocrats' political influence and their expectations of favour at the hands of a now-distant monarch. King James's political skills had disguised many of these harsh realities and kept discontent in check; the very different policy and behaviour of his son made the noblemen's new situation painfully apparent.

There is also the question of the aristocracy's economic position. Walter Makey's analysis of the 'silent revolution'–a combination of inflation, fixed monetary rentals from feued lands, and the threat posed by Charles's Act of Revocation to the nobility's possession of the teinds, which, when paid in kind, were inflation proof–has given rise to the hypothesis that this was a revolt of downwardly mobile 'mere' aristocrats for whom debt was more alarming than royal absolutism or religious radicalism and who, in Keith

---

13 See R. Mitchison, *Lordship to patronage: Scotland 1603–1745* (London, 1983); M. Lee., Jr *The road to revolution: Scotland under Charles I 1625–1637* (Urbana and Chicago, 1985); Donaldson, *Scotland: James V–James VII*, ch. 16; and A. I. Macinnes, *Charles I and the making of the covenanting movement 1625–1641* (Edinburgh, 1991).

14 13 July 1627, Spottiswoode to the earl of Annandale, in J. F. S. Gordon, *Ecclesiastical chronicle for Scotland*, 3 vols. (London, 1875), i, 487–8.

15 *Extracts from the council register of the burgh of Aberdeen 1625–1642* ed. J. Stuart (Edinburgh, 1871), 157.

Brown's words, 'following a long hard look at their accounts', rode off to Greyfriars Kirk to sign the covenant and join the revolution.[16] Brown's own researches demonstrate, however, that although aristocratic indebtedness was indeed a fact of life, nobles were frequently able to stave off their creditors for long periods of time. Furthermore they, like their English counterparts whom Lawrence Stone analysed in his famous book,[17] were worse off in the years between 1590 and 1610 than they were thereafter, though the later 1630s were difficult owing to a combination of bad harvests, heavy taxation and Lord Treasurer Traquair's policies of retrenchment. Yet some of the nobles in dire financial straits, like the earl of Morton, were royalists, while one of the richest of all, the young of earl of Buccleuch, was an enthusiastic covenanter who in 1642 bought the lands and lordship of Dalkeith from the bankrupt Morton for the enormous sum of £320,000.[18] The extent to which a landed man, whether noble or laird, was impelled to ride off to sign the covenant after an inspection of his account books remains unknown and, given the state of the records, is likely to remain so.[19]

It is clear enough, however, that when 'Laud's liturgy', as the new prayer book was called, touched off the explosion in July 1637, the powder keg had much in it besides fear of popery. Indeed, it had to contain more; religious discontent by itself would not have provoked the alliance among the people who counted in Scotland that was the necessary preliminary to successful resistance to the king's policies. That was true in England as well, though Caroline Hibbard has persuasively demonstrated how significant a factor fear of popery was in precipitating the upheaval there.[20] To the extent that this was a war of religion, however, it was a very peculiar one, quite unlike those on the continent or the wars of the Congregation, analogous only to what was going on in Muscovy, in that in both England and Scotland it was a war in defence of the existing system of belief against innovation on the part of the crown. The same observation applies to most of the other aspects of the opposition to Charles on both sides of the Tweed. The king was the modernizer, the innovator, the man moving, however ineptly and clumsily, along the road travelled by all the 'new' monarchs of the continent. His opponents, covenanters and parliamentarians alike–and, one might add, like Catalans and defenestrators and Frondeurs in other contexts–were defenders of the old ways, of their liberties in the medieval sense. The power and

---

16 Brown's analysis is contained in two articles, 'Noble indebtedness in Scotland
    between the Reformation and the Revolution', *Historical Research*, lxii (1989), 260–
    75, and 'Aristocratic finances and the origins of the Scottish revolution', EHR, civ
    (1989), 46–87. The quoted phrase is on p. 87 of the latter article. Walter Makey's
    discussion occurs in the first chapter of his *The church of the covenant 1637–1651*
    (Edinburgh, 1979).
17 L. Stone, *The crisis of the aristocracy* (Oxford, 1965).
18 Sir W. Fraser, *The Scotts of Buccleuch*, 2 vols. (Edinburgh, 1878), i, 279.
19 Brown makes this point: 'Aristocratic finances', 48–9.
20 C. Hibbard, *Charles I and the Popish plot* (Chapel Hill, 1983).

privilege of the medieval ruling class was at stake. (Let no one be fooled by the leadership of King Pym and later, of Oliver Cromwell, those quintessential country gentlemen, south of the Tweed. The eclipse of aristocratic leadership in England was a temporary condition. The ultimate triumph of parliament there meant the triumph of the aristocracy, whose grip on government in the eighteenth century was as tight as ever it was in the days of the feeble house of Lancaster.) The twin crises of the breakup of the medieval, and the imposition of the modern, organizing principle, which in Scotland had flared briefly into violence under Mary and been quieted by the skills of James VI, and so long deferred in England by the conservatism and inertia of Elizabeth and James I, now erupted in full force.

There was an eruption in Ireland as well, of a rather different kind, which considerations of space preclude discussing here. It was precipitated by events in the larger island, and had a profound impact on what happened there, from its outbreak in October 1641 until Cromwell brutally ended it almost a decade later. The 1640s saw a war of three kingdoms, not merely a civil war in each. We are all greatly in the debt of, among others, J. G. A. Pocock, Conrad Russell and David Stevenson for their valuable work on what is now called, properly, the 'British' problem (shorthand for 'British Isles', not 'Great Britain').[21]

The rapid collapse of royal authority in Scotland sparked the revival of covenanting enthusiasm. The prompt sweeping away of the episcopal structure, and the apparently united religious zeal of the triumphant covenanting party gave rise, in some quarters at least, to the vision of the Scots as God's chosen people, carrying their crusade out of Scotland to–who knew where? The Day of the Lord might well be at hand. The Solemn League and Covenant spoke grandiloquently of encouraging other Christian churches 'groaning under, or in danger of, the yoke of anti-Christian tyranny' to follow the island kingdoms' example.[22] David Stevenson, whose work constitutes the standard account of the Scottish revolution,[23] has persuasively argued that the motives of most of those who made the alliance with the English parliamentary leadership in 1643 were defensive. This was especially true of the aristocratic politicians, who were concerned primarily with retaining what they had already won by the parliamentary legislation of 1641. But if they were preoccupied with their medieval liberties, some of their apocalyptically

21 J. G. A. Pocock, 'The limits and divisions of British history: in search of the unknown subject', *American Historical Review*, lxxxvii (1982), 311–36; C. Russell, *The causes of the English civil war* (Oxford, 1990), *The fall of the British monarchies 1637–1642* (Oxford, 1991), and many articles, especially 'The British background to the Irish rebellion of 1641', *Historical Research*, lxi (1988), 166–82; D. Stevenson, *Alasdair MacColla and the Highland problem in the seventeenth century* (Edinburgh, 1980), and *Scottish covenanters and Irish confederates* (Belfast, 1981).

22 E. J. Cowan, 'The Solemn League and Covenant', in *Scotland and England 1286–1815*, ed. R. A. Mason (Edinburgh, 1987), 193.

23 D. Stevenson, *The Scottish revolution 1637–1644* (Newton Abbot, 1973), and *Revolution and counter-revolution in Scotland 1644–1651* (London, 1977).

minded allies fed on the equally medieval vision of a Christendom reunited under the aegis of that best of all the best-reformed churches, their own. No such vision existed in England. God might speak first to his Englishmen, but since He said such different things to different individuals amongst them, the religious vision that triumphed there was the appalling one (to the covenanters) of Independency. The idea of a united Christendom had died in England at the hands of Henry VIII and Cromwell, who sent its spokesman, Thomas More, to the block. It is paradoxical that the same king who shattered the medieval organizing principle in England also greatly deferred the creation of the modern one there by following policies that necessitated the retention of a powerful parliament.

One of the remarkable aspects of the upheaval in Scotland was that it produced no separatist movement among the king's enemies. Nor, by contrast with England, did it spawn any republican sentiment. The covenanters believed in union with England, a federal union, which would limit the power of the royal executive and thus produce all the advantages brought about by the great event of 1603 and mitigate its disadvantages. The marquis of Argyll, that hard-bitten pragmatist, pleaded eloquently for continuance of the union 'so happily established betwixt us' in a speech to the House of Lords in 1646.[24] And when Charles I was executed, those then in power in Scotland, the most radical elements amongst the king's opponents, at once proclaimed his son king of England and Ireland as well as Scotland. This fateful decision, which precipitated the Cromwellian conquest, was taken without any consideration of possible alternatives, such as proclaiming Charles II king of Scotland only, or not proclaiming him at all.

The radical wing of the covenanting movement was in power in 1649 on account of the disastrous failure of the Engagement of 1647. The Engagement, which represented the effort of many of the great magnates still in opposition to the king to rescue him from his English captors and at the same time preserve their own authority, was ruinous in every respect. It was the decisive step in the shattering both of the vision of a reunified Christendom and of the aristocratic polity enshrined in the legislation of 1641. It split the aristocracy, already weakened by the defection of the now-defeated Montrose and his associates, between the Engager majority and the sizeable minority headed by Argyll. The defeat of the Engager army broke the aristocracy's grip on the government, which for two years fell into the hands of the radical leadership in the kirk and its cowed aristocratic spokesmen, until its army in turn was routed at Dunbar. The kirk party itself then split apart, between Resolutioners and Protesters; the final result was effective English military conquest and occupation. Oliver Cromwell accomplished what neither Edward I nor any of

24 E. J. Cowan, 'The union of the crowns and the crisis of the constitution in seventeenth-century Scotland', in *The satellite state*, S. Dyrvik *et al*, eds. (Bergen, 1979), 133.

his successors down through Edward VI's Lord Protector Somerset had been able to achieve.

The four years between the signing of the Engagement and the battle of Worcester marked the end of medieval Scotland. Gone was the vision of a united Christendom. Gone was the vision of the Scots as a chosen people, especially dear to God. Gone too was the willingness of the aristocracy to defy the king in defence of their liberties. The awful years between 1649 and 1651 showed them where rebellion led: to humiliation before their inferiors, and to the real possibility that major financial exactions would be added to that humiliation. Lay patronage was abolished, royal grants of superiorities of kirklands were cancelled, the committee of estates could tax the heritors of a parish or presbytery if voluntary contributions to succour the poor were inadequate, with heritors who gouged their tenants paying extra, ministers' stipends were to be augmented, and a parliamentary committee was set up to look into the sufferings of all oppressed tenants, whose troubles were owing to 'the guiltiness and sins of your Lordships and such as rule in the land'.[25] Even after the weakening of its influence after Dunbar the kirk was still powerful enough to compel Engager nobles such as Lauderdale to do public penance for the iniquity of their past behaviour before it would consent to their readmission to public service. The aristocracy had learned that 'No bishop, no king' was only part of the truth; the rest of the truth was 'no nobility either'. And there followed nine years of alien military dictatorship, during which the magnates were, if lucky, merely reduced to helplessness and bootlicking if they wanted a favour; if unlucky, they were heavily fined or imprisoned or in exile. Small wonder that as a class the Scottish aristocracy embraced the returned Charles II with such fervent enthusiasm in 1660. The despotism of an absentee king, a vastly unattractive prospect in 1637, now seemed to them far preferable to any repetition of the ghastly indignities they had undergone since the destruction of the Engager army at Cromwell's hands twelve years before.

For Scotland, then, Rabb's 'struggle for stability' was over after 1660. The covenanters' vision was dead. The polity of the kingdom was recognizably modern in many ways, with a government that rested to a very substantial degree on military force. The burden of taxation was heavy and permanent, and soldiers were employed to make life unpleasant for delinquents. The magnates did not venture to oppose the king's will. They often intrigued viciously against one another, but the purpose of the intrigues was invariably to persuade Charles either to retain or dismiss those who governed in his name. Parliament, when it met, carried out his wishes and was usually very active—given the amount of legislation the parliament of 1661–3 enacted, and its heavy work schedule, it is difficult to understand how it could have been so steeped in alcohol as the opponents of the re-established episcopal church claimed. Judges were equally subservient; when Sir John Gilmour, president

25 Stevenson, *Revolution and Counter-revolution*, 137–40.

of the court of session, expressed an opinion on the law of entail displeasing to the king, it was thought that Charles might dismiss him.[26] The southwest was disaffected in religion and was the scene of the two rebellions against Charles's government. Both were minor affairs and easily put down. The aristocracy took no part in them, and some of their members were frightened out of all proportion to the danger they presented–Lord Treasurer Rothes, for instance, was in a state of panic in the aftermath of Rullion Green. There was still lawlessness in Scotland, but much less than before, even in the Highlands, where magnates' quarrels over jurisdiction were often the cause of the trouble. Magnates' power in their local areas was still great–there were no *intendants* sent out from Edinburgh–but with the lessons of 1649–51 fresh in their minds, they did not disobey the king. Lauderdale's frequently quoted comment to Charles in November 1669 that 'never was king so absolute as you are in poor old Scotland' was an accurate assessment.[27] The aristocracy was content to acquiesce, provided that its own position of superiority over everybody else in Scotland was not endangered.

By contrast England after 1660 remained governmentally medieval–there had been nothing like the experience of 1649–51 in Scotland to frighten the English landed classes. The struggle for stability there was very far from over. None of the issues that had precipitated the uprising against Charles I was settled in 1660 save for fiscal feudalism and prerogative courts; the consequence was potential deadlock between the demands of an executive that needed the wherewithal to govern according to the new organizing principle and a medieval-minded legislature, whose only real weapon was fiscal strangulation. Toward the end of his life Charles II found a way out of the deadlock by reconstructing parliament and rendering it subservient by a combination of ideology and patronage and a government paid for by the expansion of the hereditary excise and customs duties. His foolish brother threw it all away, and the result was the triumph of that medieval anachronism, parliament. What this meant was further delay in the creation of the omnicompetent, centralized, bureaucratic state, and the necessity for the invention of a new principle on which it could operate, since the medieval instrument of resistance had triumphed over the modern dynastic absolutist.

The victory of the English landed classes in their long contest with the crown had a bizarre consequence in Scotland, in the form of the creation of an unprecedented and artificial medievalism. That hitherto docile tool of those in power, the Scottish parliament, was completely changed in character by abolition of the committee of the articles. Parliament promptly became a new arena, a most desirable arena, in which the magnates could intrigue against one another. Parliamentary debate was vigorous, and sessions were often dramatic. But the real game was the same as it had been before 1688: the favour of the crown, or, with Queen Anne, of those who wielded the power of

26 29 Sept. 1663, Thomas Ross to the countess of Wemyss, in Fraser, *Scotts*, ii, 390–1.
27 *The Lauderdale papers*, ed. O. Airy (Camden Society, 1884–5), ii, 164.

the crown. The English government was not pleased: present circumstances–
the war to contain the ambitions of Louis XIV–made the game too dangerous
to allow it to continue. So, after seventeen years, it was ended. The magnates
acquiesced in the abolition of their new playing field in the hope and
expectation that they–and perhaps the country as well, but certainly they–
would benefit. The union of 1707 made little difference for a generation, and
the disappointment in Scotland was correspondingly great. But many of the
magnates flourished under the new rules. They learned to intrigue in the
antechambers of the Harleys and Walpoles and Newcastles as they had in
those of Charles II, and those who were disappointed and became Jacobites
paid for it. The state north of the Tweed was indeed omnicompetent,
centralized, bureaucratic, and sufficiently Scottish, with its distinctive church
and legal system, to keep the vast majority of the patriotic from rebellion.

In due course the new organizing principle took hold south of the Tweed as
well. Parliament, that medieval anomaly, gradually worked out the mechan-
ism by which to transform itself into an engine of modern government: the
cabinet. If any one man can lay claim to being the progenitor of the cabinet
system, it is that untrustworthy Machiavellian, ever fertile in expedients,
Robert Spencer, earl of Sunderland, the last chief minister of the last would-be
absolutist king. Thomas Cromwell and he stand at the beginning and the end
of the English story, as William and John Maitland and the latter's grandson
Lauderdale stand at the beginning and the end of the Scottish. The man who
implemented Sunderland's vision was his fellow Chit, Sidney Godolphin.
The fierce factional struggles of Anne's reign deceived J. H. Plumb, among
others, into imagining that stability had not yet been achieved, but it had:
these were the quarrels of the victors over the spoils, resembling the behaviour of the Scottish magnates after 1660.[28] Eventually one faction triumphed,
on both sides of the Tweed: the 'Venetian oligarchy' of Walpole in the south
and the voracious Campbells in the north. The political marriage they
ultimately consummated was blessed, not in St. Paul's, but in the new
cathedral in Threadneedle Street. Walpole and Islay were the heirs of Godolphin and Lauderdale. The government ran in the name of the sovereign,
and recent research has rescued both Anne and her Hanoverian successors
from the caricature of incompetence and incomprehension once drawn by
Whig historiography.[29] The leadership in parliament nevertheless became the
executive; it gradually transformed the royal bureaucracy into its bureaucracy, and reached its hand into every facet of British life: omnicompetent and
centralized.

There was, then, no 'general crisis', as usually defined, in the Europe of the
seventeenth century. What there was, was the death of one organizing

28 J. H. Plumb, *The growth of political stability in England 1675–1725* (Baltimore, 1969).
29 For example, E. Gregg, *Queen Anne* (London, 1980); R. Hatton, *George I: elector and
    king* (Cambridge, Mass., 1978); and the many works of Jeremy Black on foreign
    policy which stress the crucial role of George II.

principle and the triumph of another. The whole process took a very long time, and Scotland, like every other state in Christendom, was involved. The timetable in Scotland approximated the dates in the Aston book: 1560–1660. The union of 1603 both accelerated the process and created circumstances which made possible a sharp backlash. In due course the backlash came, and brought about further acceleration. At the same time the union tied Scotland to a far wealthier and more powerful kingdom where the process began sooner, in the 1530s, ended later, early in the eighteenth century, and created a new and different form of modern state that, after 1707, encompassed both. From that time on the consolidation of ministerial authority has proceeded, not without its ups and downs. It is now possible for a prime minister to govern like Frederick the Great. If he or she shows signs of turning into Charles I, however, it is, happily, still possible for the Jenny Geddeses on the back benches to bring about an overturn without hurling anything more damaging than epithets.

14

Annus Horribilis:
Charles II in Scotland, 1650–1651

The best known episode in the life of King Charles II prior to 1660 is the year he spent in Scotland in 1650–1651, a year of misery which culminated in military disaster and a fortunate and romantic escape. Historians from Clarendon onward have discussed it, some at considerable length, from one of three points of view: as an episode in the wars of the three kingdoms, or in the history of Scotland, or in the story of the king's life. Two recent accounts are excellent: those of David Stevenson, the leading historian of the Scottish revolution, and of Ronald Hutton in his biography of Charles, while J. R. Jones, in his brief political study of the king, stresses the impact of Charles's experiences during this year on his education as a politician.[1] One would hardly think that the tale needed retelling. Two aspects of it have been very largely neglected, however. One is what it shows about the differing views of the nature of Scottish kingship. The other is its significance for the character of Scottish politics after 1660 and the nature of the Restoration regime in Scotland.

When one thinks of the government of Restoration Scotland one thinks first of Lauderdale, the violence-prone satrap, the Scottish member of the Cabal, hated by the king's opponents in the English parliament, who vainly endeavoured to force the king to get rid of him. Lauderdale was Charles's favourite Scot, one of the handful of members of that otherwise deplorable race whom he actually liked. In 1660 he had known Lauderdale for a long time, twelve years, longer than any other prominent Scottish politician. He was under obligation to Lauderdale, who had spent nine years in various English prisons after his capture following the battle of Worcester. At the same time Charles had good reason to doubt the soundness of Lauderdale's political judgment and, perhaps, his reliability, doubts fed by his principal adviser, Edward Hyde, earl of Clarendon, who hated Lauderdale. Lauderdale, after all, was a Covenanter from the beginning, a leader of the rebellion from a very early age, the leading Scottish member of the Committee of Both Kingdoms at the age of 28. Clarendon admitted that he was intelligent and industrious, but he was also a bootlicker and a dissembler who would stop at nothing to get what he wanted.[2]

1 D. Stevenson, *Revolution and Counter-revolution in Scotland 1644–1651* (London, 1977). R. Hutton, *Charles II, King of England, Scotland, and Ireland* (Oxford, 1989). J. R. Jones, *Charles II: Royal Politician* (London, 1987).
2 Edward, Earl of Clarendon, *The History of the Rebellion and Civil Wars in England*, ed. W. D. Macray (Oxford, 1888), iv, 320–1.

Lauderdale was one of the principal promoters of the Engagement of 1647, the agreement between the Scottish government and Charles I which brought about the Scottish invasion of England that ended in disaster at Preston in August 1648. It was in order to discuss the terms on which Prince Charles might come to Scotland to join the campaign to liberate his father that Lauderdale first met him in that same month of August. Given Lauderdale's past record, many people in Scotland expected a chilly reception for him; they were surprised that the prince welcomed him 'and used him with familiarity and respect enough'.[3] Lauderdale wrote to the Scottish secretary, the earl of Lanark, that he had 'a very gracious reception', and, nine days later, that 'we are like to be very happy in him'. Charles was 'most impatient' to be with the Engager army, so impatient that he repudiated the terms that, two months earlier, he and his mother had stipulated for if he were to come to Scotland.[4] The experienced politician of thirty-two and the young man of eighteen got on well together, and Lauderdale made one very valuable discovery: that personal contact with Charles was the key to having influence with him. From the beginning Lauderdale tangled with Hyde, who did not want the prince to go to Scotland. Lauderdale in his turn made clear his opposition to Englishmen's making policy for Scotland, a position that at this time was certainly sincerely held and that Lauderdale always publicly maintained, for public relations purposes at the very least, throughout his career.[5]

The disaster at Preston changed everything: Charles would not now go to Scotland. Lauderdale returned there, wrote Hyde, 'with as much rage and malice against the council about the Prince as against Cromwell himself'.[6] This was hardly just. The prince sent Lauderdale to see how the land lay in the wake of the fiasco of the Engagement. Lauderdale's stay was brief. He found the clerical extremists firmly in control, and by the terms of the new Act of Classes there would be no room in public life for him and the other Engagers. Even Lord Chancellor Loudoun, whose willingness to cooperate with the Engagers had lasted scarcely longer than that of the political leader of the kirk party, the marquis of Argyll, was forced to 'make a solemn repentance' in church. He did so amidst an orgy of weeping in which Argyll, the radical lawyer Archibald Johnston of Wariston, and the moderator of the General Assembly of the kirk Robert Douglas, joined. Even those aristocrats who had not been active in the Engagement, like the earl of Abercorn, were fined because they had not opposed it; how much more of a penalty would be exacted from a

3 Henry Guthry, *Memoirs* (London, 1702), 233–4.
4 10, 19 Aug. 1648, Lauderdale to Lanark, *The Hamilton Papers*, ed. S. R. Gardiner, Camden Society (London, 1880), 237–8, 244–7. 20 Aug., Lauderdale to Hamilton, SRO, GD 406/1/2479.
5 Clarendon, *History* iv, 375–8.
6 *Ibid.*, 378.

backslider like Lauderdale![7] So he, and the equally delinquent Lanark, soon to be duke of Hamilton on the execution of his elder brother by the English, quietly slipped away to what was, by the time they reached it in February 1649, the court of a king in exile at The Hague.

Within days of the arrival in Edinburgh of the news of the execution of Charles I the Scottish parliament had proclaimed his son king – king not only of Scotland, but of England and Ireland as well. This decision was extremely provocative to the government of the newly proclaimed English Commonwealth, yet it was taken apparently without any consideration of the possible alternatives: proclaiming Charles king of Scots only, or not proclaiming him at all. By contrast with England, there was no republican sentiment in Scotland, and Covenanters of all sorts, aristocrats and kirkmen both, favored continuing union with England, provided that the terms were to their liking. In March Robert Baillie dismissed the story that some noblemen did not support the proclamation of Charles II as a false rumour spread by Cromwell and his 'brethren in evil'.[8] Whatever Argyll may have thought about the wisdom of the decision – there is no evidence that he questioned it – he could hardly have done anything else. The execution of Charles I led, as it had in England, to a backlash of sentimental royalism, compounded by the outrage felt by Scots of all political hues at the English having executed a king of Scots without so much as a by-your-leave. Lauderdale understood very well that Argyll and his friends needed the king if they were to retain their grip on power. So Lauderdale urged Charles to go to Scotland on whatever terms the ruling party chose to make; once there, he would be able to alter them to his advantage.

William Spang, Baillie's kinsman and correspondent in the Netherlands, regarded the stance of Lauderdale and other Engagers in urging Charles to go to Scotland even if it meant signing the Covenants as self-sacrificing, since they had been 'grievously censured' by the Scottish parliament.[9] It was anything but that. The Engagement represented the effort of the moderate Covenanters among the aristocracy, led by the greatest aristocrat of all, the duke of Hamilton, to hang onto the power they had acquired in the years after 1637. As a class the aristocracy had already been weakened by the defection of Montrose and his associates, now branded as Malignants and hopelessly discredited by, among other things, their association with wild Irishmen. The Engagement fissured the aristocracy again, with a minority, led by Argyll,

7 27 Dec. 1648, Abercorn to Lauderdale, *State Papers Collected by Edward, Earl of Clarendon*, ed. R. Scrope (Oxford, 1767–86), ii, 462–4. At the same time Lord Balmerino warned Lauderdale that 'There will be a penitential speech expected of yourself before your reconcilement to the Kirk'. *Calendar of the Clarendon State Papers preserved in the Bodleian Library*, 5 vols. ed. O. Ogle and W. H. Bliss, *et al* (Oxford, 1869–1970), i, 460.

8 *The Letters and Journals of Robert Baillie*, ed. D. Laing, 3 vols., Bannatyne Club (Edinburgh, 1841–2), iii, 68.

9 *Ibid.*, 72–3.

opposing it because of the leniency of the terms it offered to Charles I: a violation of the Covenants. Its failure threw power into the hands of the radicals. 'Leadership still nominally lay in the hands of Argyll and his few noble supporters', writes David Stevenson, 'but now as never before they had to consider and give way to the opinions of the other estates and, above all, to those of the more extreme ministers'.[10]

The result was something new in Scottish history: a regime in which the influence of the upper aristocracy was gone. The original leadership was replaced by 'new leaders from lower in the social structure, men who have not previously taken a prominent part in national politics and who support more radical policies than their predecessors' – a common revolutionary phenomenon, as Stevenson points out.[11] There followed a series of parliamentary enactments designed to punish 'the guiltiness and sins of your lordships and such as rule in the land', by compelling them to contribute to the relief of the poor, with especially oppressive landlords paying extra. There was to be no more lay patronage, and ministers were to receive higher stipends.[12] The humiliated magnates were appalled. It appeared to Lauderdale and the other Engager aristocrats that only the king could save them. Only he could restore the traditional social and political order, and he could do this only if he were there, in person. Once he got there, he could set things right.

If the Engager aristocrats needed the king, so did their opponents, who themselves were badly fractured. The radical clerics and their parliamentary allies, men like Johnston of Wariston, were temporarily triumphant, but their unprecedented position of power was precarious, and they knew it. They could no longer count on the wholehearted support of Argyll and the rest of the anti-Engager aristocracy, given their recent decision to punish the sins of such as rule in the land. Furthermore, they had to deal with the revulsion of feeling that had swept Scotland with the execution of Charles I. The newly proclaimed Charles II was an unknown quantity, who had no enemies. If he could be turned into a Covenanted king, the vision of Andrew Melville, of two kings and two kingdoms in Scotland, so memorably uttered to James VI half a century ago, might become a reality. Not all members of the party were convinced. Montrose and other Malignants had frequented Charles's court-in-exile. Cromwell, with all his shortcomings, would be preferable to a Malignant king. The majority of the kirk party was well aware of this sentiment. What they needed, and badly, was a Covenanted Doge.

Argyll and his dwindling band of aristocratic allies were in a cleft stick. Many of them were as appalled as the Engagers at the behaviour of the new parliamentary majority – the young earl of Buccleuch walked out and boycotted parliament for three months after the passage of the bill abolishing

10 Stevenson, *Revolution and Counter-revolution*, 135.
11 *Ibid.*, 136.
12 *Ibid.*, 137–140.

lay patronage. But Argyll was not prepared to eat humble pie, throw in his lot with the Engagers, and accept the leadership of Hamilton and Lauderdale. He would be finished as a politician if he did, and he was much too ambitious for that. He could not afford to disown the radical leadership, but if the king came back, he might well be able to turn the young man into his ally, and thus shore up his tottering authority.

All three major groups in Scottish politics, then, saw Charles as a potentially useful tool. They envisaged him as a *tabula rasa* on which they could write their own message. To the Engagers he would be a new James VI, governing by consensus among the nobility, old and new – it is symbolic that their leaders were Hamilton, the greatest of the old aristo-crats, and Lauderdale, the grandson of James's two great chancellor-bureau-crats. To the kirkmen he would be a member of the kingdom of Christ Jesus, whose privy councillors they were. To Argyll he would be a con-stitutional king, a king governing in accordance with the settlement enacted in the parliament of 1641, arguably Argyll's greatest achievement, which in effect put power into the hands of a parliamentary majority. This kind of constitutionalism was a variation of that of George Buchanan, who had argued that an unsatisfactory king could be deposed if his actions (or inaction) displeased a majority of his subjects. Argyll's variation turned the king into the agent of the parliamentary majority, with no capacity for independent action. Argyll had no doubt of his ability to manage a parliamentary majority, as long as the king acquiesced in his vision and his leadership. As for what Charles himself might want – well, he was young, and, no doubt, teachable.

So in March 1650 Charles, at Lauderdale's and Hamilton's urging, and because he had no other very attractive option, negotiated with a set of commissioners sent from Edinburgh and, step by step, gave way to their demands. The hypocrisy of both parties was apparent. The king's flamboyant lifestyle was disconcerting to the commissioners: 'Many nights there was dancing and balling till near day'.[13] He wanted to take his English chaplains to Scotland and was told that he could not; so he provoked the commissioners by taking communion kneeling before he left.[14] 'They [the commissioners] say they find nothing but vanity and lightness in him', wrote one observer shortly before the final agreement was signed, 'and that he will never prove a strenuous defender of their Faith. And 'tis evident . . . that he perfectly hates them, and neither of them can so dissemble it but each other knows it'.[15] Back in Scotland a fast was proclaimed in order to pray, among other things, 'for delivery of the King from malignant counsels'.[16] Alexander Jaffray, provost of

13 *The Life of Mr. Robert Blair*, ed T. McCrie, Wodrow Society (Edinburgh, 1848), 226.
14 *Ibid.*, 227.
15 *Letters and Papers Illustrating the Relations between Charles the Second and Scotland in 1650*, ed. S. R. Gardiner, SHS (Edinburgh, 1894), 74.
16 John Nicoll, *A Diary of Public Transactions*, ed. D. Laing, Bannatyne Club (Edinburgh, 1836), 6.

Aberdeen, one of the commissioners and a hard-line member of the kirk party, later reflected sadly on the responsibility of all sides for the disastrous results. 'We did sinfully both entangle and engage the Nation and ourselves, and that poor young Prince to whom we were sent, making him sign and swear a Covenant which we knew, from clear and demonstrable reasons, that he hated in his heart. Yet, finding that upon these terms only could he be admitted to rule over us . . . he sinfully complied with what we most sinfully pressed upon him'.[17]

During the negotiations some of the commissioners obliquely hinted, not directly to Charles but in a letter to his brother-in-law, the prince of Orange, that if the terms they were compelled to insist upon were not to Charles's liking, he would no doubt be able to get them modified after his arrival, 'where his royal presence will obtain more than we are warranted to grant' – precisely Lauderdale's line.[18] And indeed they made some few concessions in their agreement with Charles. The government in Edinburgh promptly rejected these and insisted that Charles accept their original demands. The commissioners waited until Charles was under way, and thus unable to turn back without serious loss of face, before informing him of this. He was furious, but after ten days of argument he gave way. When he reached the Scottish coast he was not permitted to land until he had not only signed the Covenants but also promised to embody the ideals of the Solemn League in future acts of parliament, a further humiliation for the young man. His distaste for what he had been compelled to do was obvious. To the extent that he believed that, once in Scotland, he would not be held to the promises he had made, he was in for a terrible shock.

Lauderdale and Hamilton had completely miscalculated. Argyll, forced to choose between his partisans and the king, had to support the men who gave him his power. Within two days of their arrival Hamilton and Lauderdale were forced to leave the king's side. Parliament on 28 June 1650 flatly refused to reverse a vote it had taken less than four weeks previously to reaffirm the Act of Classes. The most vehement speeches, wrote the earl of Balcarres, were made against Lauderdale and the duke of Buckingham, Charles's oldest friend, whom he had brought with him, 'because he is called Buckingham, the only crime some lays (sic) to his charge'. Argyll, greatly exerting himself, managed to get permission for nine Englishmen to attend the king. Among them was Buckingham, who, said Gilbert Burnet, toadied to Argyll and the ministers and advised Charles to follow their lead. But no exceptions to the Act of Classes were permitted. Hamilton and Lauderdale were not exiled, but Lauderdale was ordered to go live in his house, and Hamilton in Arran – 'this ugly place',

---

17 Quoted in *Correspondence of Sir Robert Kerr, First Earl of Ancram, and his son William, Third Earl of Lothian*, ed. D. Laing, Bannatyne Club (Edinburgh, 1875), i, p. xc.
18 Gardiner, *Charles II and Scotland*, 67. The prince of Orange encouraged Charles to pursue the Scottish venture.

he called it.[19] Neither of them had given the young king much reason to have confidence in their political astuteness.

The forced departure of Hamilton and Lauderdale was only the beginning of Charles's troubles. This was his first independent political undertaking, and nothing in his experience or education had prepared him for the revolutionary regime with which he had to deal. Argyll and the others 'made great show of outward reverence to him', wrote Clarendon, who clearly got his information from the king himself after it was all over, but Charles was in fact both uninformed and powerless: 'he had nothing of a prince but might very well be looked upon as a prisoner'. The servants he brought with him were dismissed and replaced by people 'whose names he had never heard of, but for their notorious crimes against his blessed father'.[20] 'They are so watchful over me that I do nothing but they observe it', he wrote to Hamilton in August.[21] He went where he was told. Shortly after he landed, while he was staying at the marquis of Huntly's house at Bogiegicht, Arthur Erskine of Scotscraig, one of Argyll's agents, came to fetch him. 'Sore against his will' he was taken to Falkland, where he could be more closely watched. About the only advantage he derived from his first weeks in Scotland was that he became acquainted with a good many of the Scottish aristocracy, including the future earl of Tweeddale and the young earl of Rothes, both of whom were to be significant figures after 1660.[22] On 29 July 1650, after a month of doing nothing, Charles undertook to visit the Scottish army, which was defending Edinburgh from Cromwell's attack. The army received him with such enthusiasm that his captors, alarmed, put pressure on him to leave. The commissioners of the kirk were responsible for this, because of their hostility to the 'carnal confidence' – Wariston's phrase – that Charles's presence induced in the troops. Even the earl of Cassillis, an uncompromising Covenanter, thought he should stay, for the sake of the army's morale and his own reputation. But Charles gave

19 *Ancram and Lothian Corr.* ii, 269–71. *The Works of Sir James Balfour*, ed. J. Haig, 4 vols, (Edinburgh, 1825), iv, 64–4, 76–7. Gilbert Burnet, *History of His Own Time*, ed. M. J. Routh, 6 vols. (Oxford, 1823), i, 91. Sir Edward Walker, *Historical Discourses upon Several Occasions* (London, 1705), 159. Walker was Garter King of Arms and the clerk of Charles's council. He accompanied Charles to Scotland and was promptly ordered to leave the court. Hamilton's description of Arran is in his letter to Lothian, 10 Aug. 1650, *Ancram and Lothian Corr.* ii, 278–9. Clarendon, *History*, v, 133, described Arran as 'for the most part inhabited with wild beasts'.

20 Clarendon, *History* v, 134–5. 15/25 Jan. 1651, Nicholas to Ormonde, *A Collection of Original Letters and Papers concerning the Affairs of England from the Year 1641 to 1660*, ed. T. Carte, 2 vols. (London, 1739) i, 400–1.

21 SRO, GD 406/1/10574.

22 Walker, *Discourses*, 159–60. *The Diary of Mr. John Lamont of Newton*, ed. G. R. Kinloch, Maitland Club (Edinburgh, 1830), 20. By his own account Tweeddale, an Engager, had to visit the king surreptitiously at Dunfermline; he managed because his uncle, the earl of Dunfermline, was keeper of the palace there. John Hay, earl of Tweeddale, 'Autobiography, 1626–1670', ed. M. Lee, Jr, SHS *Miscellany XII* (Edinburgh, 1994), 80.

way, 'sore against his own mind'. After five days his first attempt at asserting his independence was over.[23]

The troops' friendly reception was not the first evidence of the young king's popularity. When the news of his landing reached Edinburgh in June there was a big celebration, with bonfires and 'dancing almost all that night through the streets'.[24] The commission of the kirk, with the reluctant acquiescence of Argyll and his associates, determined to show the Covenanted king that he must toe their line. They began a purge of the army, which was to contribute to the military disaster at Dunbar in the following month. The ostensible reason for this was that God would favour an army free of Malignants and Engagers; as Gardiner wryly remarks, 'there was at any rate less chance of its falling under the influence of Charles'.[25] Among the purged was the troop of the earl of Eglinton, a veteran Covenanter and an opponent of the Engagement; he was suspect, apparently, because it was at his suggestion that Charles had visited the army.[26]

Not only was Charles not to have the opportunity of engineering a military coup; he was also to sign a declaration admitting and bemoaning his past and present failings and those of his father and mother. There would be a day of public humiliation for the sins of the royal family, going back to Charles's ancestors' opposition to the Reformation, King James's installation of 'geniculation' at communion, and Charles I's penchant for Popery and arbitrary government. In addition Charles must abandon his contacts with those Malignants whom – so Cromwell had informed the committee of estates – he had been seeing![27] Charles must have been hard put to it to decide which was more disgraceful: the public denunciation of his parents, or having his behaviour monitored and determined by the enemy commander. He resisted as best he could, and in the process attended a formal meeting of the privy council on 13 August, the first such meeting since his arrival seven weeks before.[28] It did no good. The commissioners of the kirk, dragging the committee of estates with them, declared that the king must sign or they would no longer fight for him, and so informed Cromwell. Charles signed, on 16 August. Even Argyll was dismayed at the intransigence of his clerical allies, 'these madmen', he called them to Charles.[29] He might well have been willing to heed the warning of his old enemy, the earl of Crawford, who as early as 2 July cautioned the earl of Lothian, now secretary, that the

23 *Diary of Sir Archibald Johnston of Wariston 1650–1654*, ed. D. H. Fleming, SHS (Edinburgh, 1919), 6. *Balfour* iv, 87. For Cassillis's views see *The Nicholas Papers*, ed. G. F. Warner, 4 vols (London, 1886–1920), i, 188–9.
24 Nicoll, *Diary*, 16–17.
25 Walker, *Discourses*, 162–3. S. R. Gardiner, *History of the Commonwealth and Protectorate*, new edn., 4 vols. (London, 1903) i, 275.
26 Walker, *Discourses*, 179.
27 14 Aug. 1650, Loudoun to Argyll *et al*, *Ancram and Lothian Corr.* ii, 280–2. Walker, *Discourses*, 178–9.
28 *Balfour* iv, 90–1.
29 John Willcock, *The Great Marquess* (Edinburgh, 1903), 248.

government's policy toward Charles was too rigid. 'Greater union and less rigour were fitter, and let some of the greatest look to it', lest in the long run they suffer themselves.[30] This was prescient. But Argyll was the nominal leader of the 'madmen', and so he had to follow them. Andrew Melville's vision was being made reality, and in its most extreme form.

Charles himself became increasingly unhappy and desperate. In mid-July he wrote to Hamilton, lamenting the rigidity and 'cruelty' of both church and state toward the duke; a few weeks later he excused his delay in replying to Hamilton's letter on the ground that 'I have been so narrowly watched by the severe Christians'. There was to be no mercy for the duke, though his request to be admitted to penance was so humble that Charles 'said the meanest of his subjects would not have made so low a petition to him'.[31] In August Charles managed to see an agent of the marquis of Ormonde, whom he told that 'the Scots have dealt very ill with me, very ill', and that he had feared for his life if he refused to sign the declaration.[32] By early September he was ready to flee. He wanted the prince of Orange to send a ship to Montrose harbour – he was now at Perth – 'pretending it is to carry over a messenger', and railed at the hypocrisy of his clerical jailers, whose 'villainy' confirmed him in his attachment to the Church of England.[33] The military debacle at Dunbar, which Cromwell thought would allow the king to assert himself, helped Charles not a whit, save to prompt Argyll to take up the matter of arranging for his coronation. Three days after the battle Lord Chancellor Loudoun informed the king that they would search out the causes of the Lord's anger and do what was necessary; when they had decided what that was, the king would be informed.[34] Charles wanted an end to the prohibition of the employment of Engagers. This proposal had some support among the clergy, but the commission of the kirk flatly rejected it. Such a step would be 'very scandalous and offensive to God's people in the land'. The commissioners further informed the king that the public humiliation for his guilt and that of the rest of the royal family would follow in due course. They also speculated on the causes of the Lord's anger: Charles had signed the Covenants for the wrong reasons; he consorted with Malignants and had not sufficiently purged his family and court. Predictably, they blamed the defeat at Dunbar on the sinfulness of the king and the worldliness of the nobility. At the same time the committee of estates ordered a purge of Charles's horse guard on account of 'diverse odious complaints' against them.[35] As the diarist John Nicoll later observed, 'Much

---

30 *Ancram and Lothian Corr.* ii, 272.
31 Gardiner, *Hamilton Papers*, 254, 255. *Clarendon Calendar*, ii, 77.
32 Carte, *Original Letters* i, 391, 397.
33 *The Diary and Correspondence of John Evelyn*, ed. W. Bray, 4 vols. (London, 1863–70), iv, 105–6.
34 *Ancram and Lothian Corr.* ii, 298–9, 301.
35 *Ibid.*, 301–3, 497–9. *Balfour* iv, 98–107. *The Records of the Commissions of the General Assemblies . . .* ed. J. Christie, SHS (Edinburgh, 1909), 46–8, 57–8.

was taught against the sins of the King and the subjects, but little against the ministry and their faults'.[36]

Charles demonstrated his ability to learn from his foes. He adopted their canting language in requesting the committee of estates to come to Perth to consult with him, and said that he trusted 'that the Lord will return again, that hath smitten us, and will bless our consultations'. He promised to make Argyll a duke and a knight of the Garter – Argyll, evidently believing that the defeat of the kirk's newly purged army gave him greater room for manoeuvre, was now prepared to admit some moderate Engagers to the fold. The extremists who controlled the commission of the kirk remained vehemently and publicly intransigent, however, and they now had a military force to back up their demands, in the revived army of the radical Western Association, which was as much opposed to Malignants around the king as it was to the English. So on 27 September the committee of estates ordered that the king's household be thoroughly and finally purged.[37] Charles's situation, wrote Sir Edward Walker, was 'sad and dangerous': if he repudiated the party in power, it would surrender Edinburgh and Stirling to Cromwell. He was 'not much above a prisoner, sentinels being every night set about his lodging, few daring to speak freely or privately to him, and spies set on his words and actions'. Even his bedroom was not private: ministers thrust in almost daily to catechise him. He knew only what the committee of estates chose to tell him about the doings of the government. Unless something changed, Walker went on, 'he shall at the best be but the shadow of a king, without power or authority to defend himself or protect his subjects'.[38]

Something did happen, early in October: the botched military coup known as the Start. Clarendon declares that the organizer was the king's physician, Dr. Alexander Fraser, a follower of Hamilton who had been barred from the court for advising the king not to sign the August declaration. Fraser had been in touch with royalist aristocrats like Huntly and Atholl and Engagers like Lauderdale and General Middleton. Men were to be gathered, Charles was to flee northeastward from Perth to join them, and the country, thoroughly sick by now of Argyll and the clerical extremists, would rise in their support. The plan had a chance. It was reminiscent of the way Scottish politics had worked in the youth of Charles's grandfather: it was, after all, nothing new for a young king of Scots to shake off the tutelage of one aristocratic faction with the aid of another. But 1650 was not 1579 or 1583. The ideological differences were far more acute, and there was Cromwell to contend with. Charles ruined whatever chance the scheme had by his own indecision. Too many people learned about the plan, including Buckingham, who, pursuing his courtship of Argyll, threw his weight against it. So Charles dithered. 'By

36 Nicoll, *Diary*, 60.
37 *Ancram and Lothian Corr.* ii, 499–500. Gardiner, *Commonwealth and Protectorate* i, 334–5. *Balfour* iv, 109–12. For the Western Association see Stevenson, *Revolution and Counter-revolution*, 175.
38 Walker, *Discourses*, 195.

the counsels of these about him [he] was so various in giving order for that rising, sometimes commanding and then countermanding to rise, that all the party was put in a confusion'.[39] And then he suddenly bolted from Perth with a few followers and rode east. At Dundee, on the first leg of his flight, he met Lauderdale, by prearrangement; Lauderdale was cool, and 'seemingly persuaded him to return'.[40] But Charles pressed on, turning north and going up Glen Clova, which, given the nature of the country, trackless mountains still, seems a very odd choice. He spent an uncomfortable night at Clova, 'lying in a nasty room, on an old bolster above a mat of segges and rushes, overwearied and very fearful'. The agents of the committee of estates caught up with him there. Charles, 'either overcome with importunity, or seeing no visible power to resist, and distracted with variety of opinions', threw in his hand and agreed to accompany them back to Perth.[41]

The Start was, wrote Walker, 'an unexpected action', which should have been pursued; Walker feared that its abandonment would be disastrous.[42] At first disaster seemed the likely outcome. Charles had to eat crow again, to explain that he had fled because he feared that he would be betrayed into Cromwell's hands, that it had been 'folly and madness' to have listened to 'some wicked persons'.[43] But unlike the equally botched flight to Varennes, Charles's escapade 'proved, contrary to the expectation of wise men, very much to his majesty's advantage'.[44] What saved Charles was the resolute behaviour of his followers, especially General Middleton. After Charles abandoned the Start, many of them, with Middleton taking the lead, refused to lay down their arms without an act of indemnity. The army was ordered to chastise them for their impudence, and Charles was expected to endorse this and express his 'detestation of their way'.[45] Had this happened, the Start would have been a complete fiasco for Charles. But it did not: the Royalists were able to extract their act of indemnity out of the committee of estates, thanks in large part to a successful night attack on a regiment sent to punish them and Middleton's resolute leadership of an aristocratic coalition that included Huntly, Atholl, and Seaforth. It was Middleton more than any other individual who allowed Charles to benefit from his aborted coup and recover some freedom of action. 'Had not this party of the Nobility kept themselves on foot, and Middleton been prosperous in the first encounter, I fear His Majesty's condition would have been . . . very sad and full of danger'.[46] Middleton's recent record was exemplary from Charles's point of view: it was

---

39 2 Jan. 1651, Baillie to Dickson and Spang, Laing, *Baillie* iii, 117.
40 Walker, *Discourses*, 199.
41 *Balfour* iv, 114. Walker, *Discourses*, 199–200.
42 Walker, *Discourses*, 196.
43 *Ancram and Lothian Corr.* ii, 500–1. *Balfour* iv, 139–41. 2 Jan. 1651, Baillie to Dickson and Spang, Laing, *Baillie* iii, 117–8.
44 Clarendon, *History* v, 171.
45 22 Oct. 1650, Loudoun to Lothian, *Ancram and Lothian Corr.* ii, 317.
46 On this point see Walker, *Discourses*, 198–204. The quotation is on p. 204.

he who had brought the bulk of the army over to the side of the Engagement in 1648.[47] The extremist minister James Guthrie knew what he was about when he singled out Middleton for excommunication in spite of Charles's request that he not do so.[48] Charles owed Middleton a debt. It would be paid after 1660.

After the Start Charles met regularly with the committee of estates, was consulted, and was kept informed. Gradually Engagers were readmitted to the royal service, provided they displayed proper contrition for their past behaviour: first less prominent people such as the earls of Linlithgow and Dunfermline; then Lauderdale, who did his penance the day after Christmas in the church at Largo, with Rothes an interested spectator, then Hamilton, and finally even Middleton, who was released from excommunication on 12 January 1651, after he had done penance in sackcloth in the church at Dundee. In March the forfeiture of the royalist marquis of Huntly, whom the kirk party had executed in 1649, was reduced and his son restored. 'Behold, a fearful sin!' wrote the Engager Sir James Turner. 'The ministers of the Gospel received all our repentances as unfeigned, though they knew well enough they were but counterfeit; and we on the other hand made no scruple to declare that engagement to be unlawful and sinful, deceitfully speaking against the dictates of our own consciences and judgments'.[49] The list of regimental colonels drawn up in parliament in December was the subject of a protest by Chancellor Loudoun, who complained that it contained too many Engagers and former friends of Montrose. But the influence of Loudoun, a Campbell and a close ally of his chief the great marquis, was waning: in June 1651 he was haled before the commission of the kirk to face a charge of adultery.[50] Parliament, and even the commission of the kirk, denounced the radicals' so-called Remonstrance attacking the king, and Cromwell did Charles the favour of destroying the Remonstrants' army of the Western Association in December 1650. There was, Gardiner says, 'a substitution of the national for the covenanting cause',[51] climaxed by the repeal of the Act of Classes in June 1651. Argyll tried to shore up his increasingly shaky position by proposing that Charles should marry his daughter. Charles adroitly shifted the onus of refusal onto his mother, who declined her permission when asked. The Campbells' star was setting; it would not rise again until after the revolution of 1688.

Still, the king's path was thorny. He had to continue apologizing for the Start.[52] The kirk was powerful enough to insist on two pre-coronation fasts in

47   26 June 1648, Baillie to Spang, Laing, *Baillie* iii, 45.
48   McCrie, *Blair*, 244–5. It is not an accident that Guthrie was one of those executed after 1660.
49   *Balfour* iv, 125, 188–9, 199, 200, 205, 240, 269. Fleming, *Wariston Diary*, p. xxxv. Turner's remark is quoted in Gardiner, *Commonwealth and Protectorate* ii, 24.
50   *Balfour* iv, 210–14. Kinloch, *Lamont*, 31.
51   Gardiner, *Commonwealth and Protectorate* i, 339.
52   See, e.g., *Balfour* iv, 139–41, 185–6.

December, one for contempt of the gospel, one 'for the sins of the King, his family, and nobility'.[53] On the latter day John Menzies preached a sermon on the text, 'And the Lord said unto Samuel, How long wilt thou mourn for Saul, seeing I have rejected him from reigning over Israel?' (I Samuel xvi, 1.) Charles, compliant though he was, was outraged – 'I think I must repent too that ever I was born', he allegedly remarked – and Menzies later apologized for picking that text.[54] The belated coronation, which took place on 1 January 1651, could not have been very joyful either. Charles had to submit to being crowned by Argyll, and forego anointing on the ground that it was superstitious. He had to take an elaborate oath to observe the Covenants, never to try to change them, and to enforce them in his three kingdoms. And, finally he had to listen to Robert Douglas's long sermon on the limitations of kingly power and the right of subjects to revolt if a king attempts to subvert their religion, liberties, and laws. What this sermon suggests is that with the destruction of the army of the Western Association the leadership of the kirk had abandoned the vision of Andrew Melville and replaced it with that of George Buchanan. The monitoring of Charles's behaviour would not cease merely because he was now a crowned, if unanointed, king. A memorandum of Secretary Lothian's on 9 January required 'That the King have constantly a proportion of his guards to wait upon him and to guard at the church, as also when he goeth to the fields to walk or goff'.[55] One wonders how often Charles 'goffed' in January. Still, our ancestors may have been hardier than we: people noted with disapproval that Charles's great-grandmother Queen Mary, far from showing any regret at the explosive demise of her husband Darnley, allegedly golfed, and won an archery match at Seton, in February 1567.

Like his grandfather King James, Charles found Buchanan's vision of kingship as distasteful as Melville's. His frame of mind shows clearly enough in a gloomy letter he wrote to Ormonde in November bemoaning 'the distracted and miserable condition of this kingdom' and the reneging on their premises of those who had asked him to come, especially respecting money. This, coupled with his own failures, discouraged his friends elsewhere who had promised money when he set out: so, he could do nothing to help Ormonde.[56] The same message reached his court-in-exile on the continent. 'The King is in a very sad condition there', wrote Secretary Nicholas on 27 November, 'the Kirkmen and their faction adhering still very rigidly to their mad principles'. In Nicholas's view Argyll would sooner trust Cromwell than his king.[57] John Nicoll the diarist commented in April that 'The King with a patient spirit did behold and

---

53 *Ibid.,* 188.
54 McCrie, *Blair,* 255, 262. Gardiner, *Commonwealth and Protectorate* i, 346.
55 *Ancram and Lothian Corr.* ii, 332.
56 *The Letters . . . of King Charles II* ed. A. Bryant (London, 1935), 20–21. Scotland's miserable condition was not due entirely to Charles's enemies. The weather was awful, prices were high, and smallpox carried off a large number of children. *Balfour* iv, 163–4.
57 *Nicholas Papers* i, 203, 205.

suffer much of some of those traitors who, under pretext of piety and religion did wish his overthrow'. Charles was learning to keep his own counsel, as James VI had during his tumultuous adolescence. He 'very prudently seems to trust all men,' wrote Secretary Nicholas, 'but hath his own thoughts and wisely passes by many indignities'. Nicoll was suspicious of the aristocracy as a class. Charles's coronation was delayed, he wrote, not only by clerical opposition, but also by 'the nobles having their own ends to govern the Kingdom'. This sentiment echoed that of one of Secretary Nicholas's intelligencers, who wrote in March that 'Our Grandees who govern intend never their King shall be more master of Scotland'. Argyll and his faction, desperately trying to retain their parliamentary influence, which was slipping away with the restoration of the civil rights of so many Engagers, resorted to open criticism of the king in parliament. Balfour reported that they 'did check the King much for his inconstancy, (as they called it) in deserting his best friends that brought him to this country [and] put the crown on his head'. 'Alas!', wrote Baillie, 'that so good a King should have come among us to be destroyed by our own hands, most by traitors and dividers'.[58] Suspicion and defeatism ran rampant. Sir John Hope of Craighall and his brother, sons of Sir Thomas Hope, the late Lord Advocate, who had played such a major role in the drafting of the National Covenant, and the earl of Roxburgh, a veteran royalist politician, separately proposed that Charles should deal with Cromwell. The Hope brothers, one of whom had been made a gentleman usher of the privy chamber, made Charles angry, but Roxburgh filled him with despair: 'He said to a confident (*sic*), since Roxburgh was so, he did not well know whom to trust'.[59]

Charles's coronation may not have dispelled the gloom he felt, but he did have greater freedom of action now, which he used to augment the army, of which he formally became commander-in-chief on 31 March 1651. His success was limited. Supplies were scarce – the wet weather of 1650 meant a poor harvest – and Charles met with as many excuses as volunteers.[60] The army that finally assembled at Stirling in May was not very large, perhaps 10,000 men. In June Charles had his first taste of military command, and may have botched it. Hoping to provoke an engagement Cromwell moved out of Edinburgh toward Stirling, and found the Scots entrenched on rising ground at Torwood, on the other side of the Carron. 'The English advancing near the water side the Scots General of the Artillery Colonel Weems undertook to the king to cannonade them out of their quarters and if a party of horse were commanded to cross the water a little above, and fall in upon their rear in the confusion they would be into and the army attacking them in the front they might have been routed. The march of which party being drawn out was

58 Carte, *Original Letters* i, 445–6, 454. Nicoll, *Diary*, 41, 52. *Balfour* iv, 275. Laing, *Baillie* iii, 145.
59 Carte, *Original Letters* i, 410–1. *Balfour* iv, 249. See also Stevenson, *Revolution and Counter-revolution*, 196.
60 Nicoll, *Diary*, 31–2. 8 Feb. 1651, Sir John Drummond to Charles, *Ancram and Lothian Corr.* ii, 503–4. *Balfour* iv, 281.

countermanded by the King'. It seems likely that General Leslie, who was the commander in fact at Torwood, though Charles might be commander in name, had much to do with this: he had no desire to repeat the mistake he had made at Dunbar. The account goes on: 'The cannon and army nevertheless were drawn out, and cannonaded them out of their camp and put them in great confusion. This being done about daylight, and the two armies stood in view of one another all that day. In the evening Oliver marched to Leith again, and the Scots army to Stirling'.[61] Shortly thereafter Cromwell launched the attack upon Inverkeithing which ultimately led to the desperate gamble that ended at Worcester on 3 September 1651.

The Worcester campaign, a crowning mercy for Cromwell, was a kind of catharsis for Charles. No matter that defeat stared him in the face, and that he and his followers all knew it. We 'are all laughing at the ridiculousness of our condition', wrote Hamilton, 'but we have one stout argument, despair; for we must now either stoutly fight it or die'.[62] The small and ever-dwindling army was Charles's army; he was surrounded now by Engagers and Malignants and no one else. The hated Argyll, whose nose had been out of joint for some time, had opposed the planned march into England and refused to join it, thereby, perhaps, losing his last chance to save himself if Charles ever really came into his own again. 'All the rogues have left us', commented Hamilton.[63] The king fought bravely at Worcester and afterwards made that marvelous escape that promptly went into legend and, heavily embroidered, became the stuff of his dinner-table conversation for more than thirty years. He was ever grateful to those who helped him escape, and to those who were with him at Worcester and suffered on his behalf – Lauderdale, Middleton, the feckless Buckingham. Hamilton would have shared in this too, but he was one of those who died. For Charles it was an honorable and redemptive ending to an episode characterized mostly by impotence, frustration, hypocrisy, and blunders.

Charles learned from this squalid year that he could trust aristocratic Engagers, and this he did after 1660. Indeed he could, and not merely Engagers. The Scottish aristocracy became perfervid royalists. Like Puritan gentlemen in England who were horrified by Levellers, they turned to monarchy after 1660 as their best defense against social upheaval. None of the magnates ventured to oppose the restored king's will. They often intrigued viciously against one another, but the purpose of the intrigues was invariably to persuade Charles to dismiss or retain those who governed in his name. The despotism of an absentee monarch, a vastly unattractive prospect in 1637, now seemed to them far preferable to any repetition of the ghastly indignities they had undergone since the destruction of the Engager

---

61 Tweedale, 'Autobiography', 82. For the skirmishing around Torwood see Gardiner, *Commonwealth and Protectorate* ii, 25–8.
62 Quoted in Stevenson, *Revolution and Counter-revolution*, 207.
63 Quoted in Gardiner, *Commonwealth and Protectorate* ii, 34.

army at Oliver's hands at Preston twelve years before. So they accepted a government that rested to a very substantial degree on military force, and begged for commands in the standing army or the militia.

Charles recognized the aristocracy's new temper, and save for Argyll, whom he clearly loathed, he made no effort to punish those who had been officeholders in the radical regime, apart from depriving them of office. For two there might have been royal favour: the veteran Eglinton, who died in January 1661, and the stiff-necked and rigidly honest Cassillis, whom Charles made a privy councillor and a lord of session, but who had to be suspended for refusing to take the oaths of allegiance and supremacy unless he could explain the sense in which he was taking them.

Along with Argyll the chief objects of Charles's detestation were the radicals among the presbyterian clergy, who, wrote Clarendon, clearly reflecting the opinions of his master, never freed him from their importunities, 'under pretence of instructing him in religion: and so they obliged him to their constant hours of their long prayers, and made him observe the Sundays with more rigour than the Jews accustomed to do; and reprehended him very sharply if he smiled on those days, and if his looks and gestures did not please them, whilst all their prayers and sermons, at which he was compelled to be present, were libels and bitter invectives against all the actions of his father, the idolatry of his mother, and his own malignity'.[64] The future bishop Gilbert Burnet wrote hyperbolically of remembering that on 'one fast day there were six sermons preached without intermission'[65] – an unlikely tale, since he was about eight years old at the time, and no doubt any long sermon seemed like six. It must have seemed so to Charles as well. The clergy had treated him shamefully, deceitfully, and hypocritically, and so, when he had a chance, he took his revenge. His instrument was James Sharp, a moderate member of the commission of the kirk in 1650–1 who had spent a year in prison after the king's defeat. In 1660 Sharp was the spokesman in London of the so-called Resolutioner clergy, those who had broken with their radical brethren over the Remonstrance and the repeal of the Act of Classes, to the restored – and, be it remembered, Covenanted – king in behalf of the presbyterian polity. Sharp's metamorphosis from presbytr to archbishop in less than a year no doubt appealed to Charles's rather grim sense of humour where Scots were concerned, and has left Sharp's biographer, who is unwilling to believe that he simply sold out, rather at a loss.[66] None of the other

64 Clarendon, *History* v, 134.
65 Burnet, *History* i, 92.
66 Julia Buckroyd, *The Life of James Sharp* (Edinburgh, 1987). The best she can do is this: 'There were two possibilities: either he could maintain his presbyterian views and retire ignominiously, sacrificing no doubt his post as Royal Chaplain, his position in St. Andrews University and any hope of advancement in public life; or he could resign himself to the inevitable, go along with the change and try to ensure that it conformed at least to some extent with the desires of Scots churchmen. He chose the latter course'. p. 71.

thirteen bishops had been at all prominent in the church of the Covenant, though one, the irenic Robert Leighton, was principal of Edinburgh University. Only one of the bishops of 1638, Thomas Sydserf, was restored. Three of the new appointees had spent many years in exile. Others had served quietly in their parishes. What they all had in common was a willingness to obey, which a number of them demonstrated by preaching suitable sermons before parliament in 1661. Some Charles knew from his stay in Scotland. Others were the beneficiaries of patronage: that of Middleton, now an earl, and his political allies.[67]

It was Middleton, the professional soldier, rather than Lauderdale the professional politician, whom the restored king chose to govern Scotland. Middleton became the royal commissioner. Lauderdale, who on his release from prison in the spring of 1660 hastened to Breda to renew his ties with Charles, became secretary of state over the opposition of Middleton and Hyde: his reward for his sufferings. Lauderdale was to build his great career from this office, as his grandfather and namesake had done before him. But for now Middleton was the king's man. This was not merely because Charles was prepared to govern by force. Middleton had emerged with far more credit from Charles's awful year in Scotland than had Lauderdale, whose political judgments had been very wide of the mark. 'Middleton', said Charles to Hyde when it was all over, 'had the least in him of any infirmities most incident to the nation that he knew, and . . . he would find him a man of great honour and ingenuity'.[68] Furthermore Middleton had managed to escape from the Tower after Worcester. He eventually made his way to the exiled court; Charles made him commander of the royalist military forces in Scotland, now or in the future. Charles recognized that the failure of the rebellion in Scotland in 1654–5 was not Middleton's fault, and that he had done all that he could.[69] Hence the decision in 1660 that Middleton be the agent for the erection of an irresistible royal power in Scotland by whatever methods were necessary. Only thus could Charles wipe out the memory of the humiliation he had suffered.

The unhappy year revealed a good deal about Charles himself. He was pliant and adaptable, to the point of hypocrisy. He repeatedly gave way under pressure. In the face of conflicting advice he could not make up his mind. His troubles showed him at his worst, and, if anything, made his character even less attractive. After 1660 he was cynical, unreliable, and ungrateful, save to those who shared the only creditable episodes of that awful time, those at the end. For those who had humiliated him there was vengeance. There is an element of personal vendetta lacking in his treatment of his defeated enemies in England and Ireland in his decision to send Argyll, Wariston, and Guthrie to the scaffold.

67 For the bishops see J. Buckroyd, *Church and State in Scotland 1660–1681* (Edinburgh, 1980), 41–5.
68 Clarendon, *History* v, 242.
69 For the royalist rebellion, usually called Glencairn's Rising, see F. D. Dow, *Cromwellian Scotland* (Edinburgh, 1979), 123–42.

When it was suggested to Charles after his successful escape to France that he might return to Scotland, he retorted that he would rather be hanged.[70] He meant it. Scotland was an embarrassment as well as a humiliation. When he was king indeed, it could suffer in its turn. If Scotland could be used in the pursuit of his larger schemes, well and good. But he would leave its business in the hands of those few Scots he trusted, and when they had all, one way or another, failed him, in those of his arbitrary brother. He did not wish to bring Scotland to mind.

What came to pass in Scotland after the Restoration was a new sort of kingship, quite unlike anything the Stewarts had previously practiced there. It was not theocratic, not parliamentary, not constitutional, not Jacobean government by consensus, though it was certainly government by pen. The amount of correspondence passing between Edinburgh and Whitehall was enormous, especially after 1667, when Lauderdale achieved his position of supremacy in Scottish affairs. But it was very different from the previous great period of government by pen, in the days of Lord Chancellor Dunfermline. From Edinburgh came reports and requests, from Whitehall orders and decisions, which the royal agents in Edinburgh did not venture to dispute. Charles I had been accused of being a despot, Charles II really was one, with the full cooperation of his chastened and fearful aristocracy. Gone were the visions of George Buchanan, of Andrew Melville, even of the *Trew Law of Free Monarchies*; what had emerged was Leviathan. Counterfactual history is always problematic, but it is quite possible to suppose that if Charles II had never gone to Scotland, never suffered through the trauma of his *annus horribilis*, his government of his ancient kingdom might have been quite different.

---

70 Gardiner, *Commonwealth and Protectorate* ii, 57.

15

The Buccleuch Marriage Contract: An Unknown Episode in Scottish Politics (1993)

On 5 October 1663 the Scottish parliament took an action unique in its long and variegated history. It ratified a marriage contract between two of the king's subjects. Not ordinary subjects, to be sure – they were the duke of Monmouth, Charles II's eldest bastard, a lad of fourteen, and Anna Scott, countess of Buccleuch, aged twelve, who had been married the previous April. Persuading Parliament to ratify this contract was potentially a very tricky business; the king entrusted the handling of it to the earl of Lauderdale, the secretary of state, normally resident in Whitehall, who had been sent to Scotland to manage this session of parliament. The ratification was a private act, one of a large number passed at each session of the Scottish parliament in favor of private individuals and corporations: towns, universities, etc. Because it was a private act Osmund Airy, the editor of the Lauderdale papers, our principal source for the day-to-day doings of this parliament, ignored it in making his selection from the vast Lauderdale correspondence. So the episode has gone completely unnoticed by historians.[1] This is a pity, not only because the story of the marriage contract and its ratification is fascinating in itself, but also because it was important for Lauderdale's political future. Lauderdale's success in getting the ratification passed without backlash helped to convince King Charles that he was the man to manage Scottish business from now on.

The political history of Restoration Scotland has been largely neglected by historians. Lauderdale was the dominant figure for most of Charles's reign, but it was some years before he achieved that eminence. Lord Chancellor Clarendon, until his fall in 1667, was Charles's principal adviser for all of his three kingdoms, a fact that Lauderdale resented but had to live with. Clarendon did not like Lauderdale, who, he wrote, had been a leader of the Covenanters' rebellion 'when he was scarce of age, and prosecuted it to the end with the most eminent fierceness and animosity'. Clarendon granted Lauderdale's intelligence and diligence but thought him 'insolent, imperious,

---

1 *Lauderdale Papers* (hereafter *LP*), ed. O. Airy, 3 vols., Camden Society (London, 1884–85). For convenience's sake this edition will sometimes be cited below. In addition to omitting many letters Airy does not always indicate that the texts he prints are incomplete. In every case the original manuscript has been checked. Sir W. Fraser, *The Scotts of Buccleuch*, 2 vols. (Edinburgh, 1878), i, 417–22, does discuss the ratification, but only as an episode in family history.

flattering and dissembling', and with 'no impediment of honour to restrain him from doing anything that might gratify any of his passions'.[2] So Clarendon tried to prevent his appointment as secretary in 1660 and failed, although all the other major Scottish offices were filled by men satisfactory to the chancellor. It was a crucial failure, because the appointment gave Lauderdale personal access to the king, and personal access was the only route to influence with a ruler who loathed paperwork and much preferred to do business in meetings and conversations.[3]

Charles rejected Clarendon's advice in this case because he liked Lauderdale, who was both learned and witty. The two had been thrown together a good deal in the years between 1648 and 1651, and had gotten on well together from the beginning. And Lauderdale was a 'Worcester' Scot, one of those who had accompanied Charles on his forlorn military adventure in the summer of 1651 that had ended in military disaster at Worcester and the king's subsequent miraculous escape. Lauderdale was not so lucky. He spent nine years in various English prisons between 1651 and 1660, and was, perhaps, fortunate not to be executed. Charles loathed Scotland and disliked most Scots, but he made an exception for those who were with him at Worcester. He felt permanently in their debt, and never turned his back on them.

Charles's and Clarendon's principal agent for Scottish affairs after 1660 was the royal commissioner, the earl of Middleton, another Worcester Scot, a soldier whom Charles liked and admired[4], but who proved to be an inept politician. Middleton and Clarendon were exasperated by Lauderdale's positions on two of the major issues of 1661, the immediate restoration of episcopacy in the church, which Lauderdale opposed, and the removal of the English garrisons in Scotland, which he favored. Lauderdale lost on the first point, and won on the second. So Middleton determined to be rid of him. In the parliamentary session of 1662 an act was passed requiring all office-holders to take an oath abjuring the Covenants. According to the lawyer Sir George Mackenzie, Lauderdale only laughed. He was prepared 'to sign a cartful of such oaths before he would lose his place'.[5] So another device had to be found. What Middleton came up with was too clever by half.

Lauderdale had been arguing that an act of indemnity and oblivion for the past, similar to that adopted by the English parliament within three months of Charles's return, should also be enacted for Scotland. The fairness of this

2 Edward, Earl of Clarendon, *The History of the Rebellion and Civil Wars in England*, ed. W. D. Macray, 6 vols. (Oxford, 1888), iv, 320–1.
3 See the illuminating comments of Ronald Hutton on this point in *Charles II, King of England, Scotland, and Ireland* (Oxford, 1989), especially ch. 16. Hutton rightly stresses that, contrary to the popular impression, Charles was not lazy; he spent a lot of time in meetings of the privy council and of its policy-making arm, the foreign affairs committee.
4 See Clarendon, *History*, v, 242.
5 Sir George Mackenzie, *Memoirs of the Affairs of Scotland from the Restoration of King Charles II*, ed. T. Thomson (Edinburgh, 1821), 165.

proposal could hardly be denied. In September 1662 such an act was passed, with an additional clause excluding from public office up to twelve people. The whipsaw technique was used here: the king accepted this clause because he thought parliament wanted it, and vice versa. The twelve were to be selected by a process of 'billeting': each member of parliament would draw up a list in secret, and the twelve whose names appeared most frequently would be excluded. Lauderdale's name headed the list.

Charles was enraged by this effort to deprive him of Lauderdale's services without his permission. But Middleton proved difficult to dislodge. He still had Clarendon's wholehearted support, and Charles still remembered what he owed him. Middleton came to London to defend himself; it was not until Charles discovered that Middleton had also taken it upon himself to delay issuing a royal proclaimation, contrary to orders, that Charles finally decided, in May 1663, to deprive him of his office as royal commissioner.[6]

Parliament had passed the billeting act; therefore parliament had to undo it. A new session was necessary; it formally opened on 18 June 1663. Charles sent Lauderdale north to manage it – his first visit to his native land since he took the road to Worcester in Charles's company in 1651. He left behind him as acting secretary in Whitehall his and the king's friend Sir Robert Moray, an old soldier of great charm who shared Charles's interest in science; Moray was the first president of the Royal Society, which Charles chartered in 1662. Middleton was still in London, intriguing to recover his position. Lauderdale had confidence in the dependability of Moray, another of those who had been on Middleton's enemies list, but not, perhaps, in Moray's ability to handle all the intrigue at court. Since he had to rely on Moray, however, he professed not to worry. There were 'great brags' circulating in Edinburgh about Charles's favor to Middleton, Lauderdale wrote shortly after his arrival there, but 'I am sure he [Charles] will not let me be bit to death by a duck'.[7]

Lauderdale had to walk a fine line at the parliamentary session. The billeting business had to be cleared up and the act repealed, but there could not be too many victims. Middleton had had many collaborators, including the king's cousin, the duke of Lennox, and Lord Chancellor Glencairn; these people had to be allowed to escape punishment. Lauderdale himself handled the investigating committee and managed well; in the end only Middleton, his close ally the earl of Newburgh, and his intermediary, Sir George Mackenzie of Tarbat, who had been caught in entirely too many lies, paid any political penalty. The whole business took a great deal of time, and dominated the correspondence between Edinburgh and London. Charles was reluctant to abandon Middleton entirely, so additional charges were brought

---

6 There is a brief, straightforward account of the billeting episode and what preceded it in W. C. Mackenzie, *The Life and Times of John Maitland, Duke of Lauderdale* (London, 1923), 241–58.

7 23 June 1663, Lauderdale to Moray, BL, Add. Ms. 23119, fos. 51–52.

against him: corruption and disobedience to royal orders. Final parliamentary action was not taken until 9 September.[8]

The billeting issue was far from Lauderdale's only problem. He was suspect to the bishops as an old Covenanter who had argued against the reestablishment of episcopacy in 1661. So he made a major speech to parliament apologizing for his Covenanting past and specifically endorsing the legislation of 1662 restoring the bishops' powers. This legislation was ratified, and the privy council authorized to pursue those ministers who were in violation of it. People were required to attend their parish church on pain of being treated as seditious. Men in public office had to sign a declaration renouncing the Covenant. The act of 1661 giving the court of session, the highest Scottish court, the power to review excommunications was repealed as being prejudicial to episcopal authority. If the General Assembly of the church should be summoned – it was called the 'national synod' in the legislation – it would be allowed to consider only what the king set before it, and could adopt nothing contrary to law or the royal prerogative. This act left so much power in the hands of the bishops that, according to Gilbert Burnet, their opponents ceased to want the Assembly to meet – which may have been the idea. All the bishops, wrote Lauderdale, thanked him for his speech. Charles was most pleased, wrote Moray, and said, 'Sure, nobody that repines at church government will reckon you of his side'.[9]

Lauderdale was suspect to many English, including Clarendon, not only on the score of the bishops but also because he had succeeded in getting the English garrisons in Scotland removed. So he now had to prove that he was not 'soft' on defense. Parliament therefore authorized the creation of a militia of 20,000 foot and 2,000 horse, which could be sent anywhere in the king's domains for the purpose of dealing with either domestic disturbance or foreign invasion, a clause Charles very much wanted in the act.[10] The creation of this armed force was very important to Charles, who was in the process of successfully doing the same sort of thing in England.[11] There was much else for Lauderdale besides: economic legislation, including one act, which bothered Charles, that put duties on English imports;[12] the ratification of former legislation compelling vagabonds to work and assigning poor children to

8 APS, vii, 450–1, 458–61, 471–2. 21 July 1663, Lauderdale to Moray, 31 July, the earl of Rothes to Moray, 15, 21 Aug., Moray to Lauderdale, 10 Sept., Lauderdale to Charles, BL, Add. Ms. 23119, fos. 99–100, 142–3, 167, 173–5; Add. Ms. 23120, fo. 10.
9 13 July 1663, Lauderdale to Charles, 21–23 July, Moray to Lauderdale, BL, Add. Ms. 23119, fos. 86–7, 101–2, APS vii, 455–6, 465, 502. Bishop Burnet's History of His Own Time, 6 vols. (Oxford, 1823), i, 353–4.
10 APS, vii, 480–1. 21 Aug 1663, Moray to Lauderdale, BL, Add. Ms. 23119, fos. 173–5.
11 On this point see Joyce Malcolm, 'Charles II and the Reconstruction of Royal Power', Historical Journal, xxxv (1992), 307–30.
12 APS vii, 465–6. Moray explained to Charles that this was an old problem, dating back to King James's time; Charles agreed to await Lauderdale's oral report after the end of the session before taking any action (7 Sept. 1663, Moray to Lauderdale, BL, Add. Ms. 23120, fos. 8–9).

masters until they reached the age of thirty; the creation of a commission to deal with the problem of the debts of landowners, Lauderdale among them, whose estates had been confiscated during the recent troubles, and of another to value teinds and raise the stipends of ministers insufficiently provided for; a five-year tax on the clergy to help fund the universities; the repeal of those clauses in an act of 1662 that limited the Crown's power to pardon the sons of forfeited people, which had annoyed Charles, and so on.[13] Lauderdale was exhausted. 'No dog leads so busy a life', he wrote early in July. 'Torment of visitors in crowds, not companies, and incessant meetings . . . I am perfectly dazed'. A day or two later he asked Moray to send him his spectacles and repeated that he was utterly worn out. By the middle of the month he was afflicted by a stomach ailment that caused him to let blood and by rumors from London that he had spoken impertinently of General Monck and was plotting against Clarendon. 'These are damned insipid lies', he wrote to Moray. The earl of Bristol, in the course of his misguided campaign against Clarendon, was sniping at him in the House of Lords, which irritated him considerably. He longed to be back in London: 'God send me . . . to Whitehall again'.[14]

It was in the midst of all this hectic activity that Lauderdale received a letter from Moray dated 2 July. He had seen the king that day, Moray wrote, and 'the first thing his Majesty said to me was that there was a paper presented to him (which he put into my hand) wherein it was desired that Contract of the D. of Monmouth's marriage might be confirmed by an Act of Parlt. in the terms you see in . . . the paper . . . He said the thing is perhaps not necessary, yet abundance of law does not break it. You will soon see what is to be done in the case'.[15]

This proposal was absolute dynamite. Parliament was to be asked to ratify a marriage contract that every lawyer who had seen it had said was illegal because it violated an entail. The lawyers further agreed that parliament had no right to do such a thing. Parliament might legislate on the subject of entails in general, but it had not done so, and would not until 1685. What was involved here was the destruction of the private right of an individual, that of a landowner to determine the succession to his estates. Only the court of session was competent to rule in such a case. Parliament itself had recognized that fact in 1592, when it provided for the enactment at the end of every parliament of an act called *Salvo jure cuiuslibet*. This act gave anyone who believed that his or her rights had been prejudiced by one of the private acts passed during that session the right to sue in court. Further clarification was provided in 1633: 'The lords of session and all other judges shall be obliged to judge betwix [sic] the parties according to their rights standing in their person

13 *APS* vii, 463–4, 468–9, 474–6, 485–6, 491. 11 Aug. 1663, Lauderdale to Moray, *LP* i, 175–7. One of the beneficiaries of the last-mentioned measure was Lauderdale's friend the son of the marquis of Argyll.
14 *LP* i, 148–9, 157–8, 159–61. BL, Add. Ms. 23119, fo. 72.
15 BL, Add. Ms. 23119, fos. 65–6.

before the making of the said particular acts'. That was clear enough: a private ratification passed by parliament could not deprive an individual, such as a designated contingent heir to an entailed estate, of his or her legal rights.[16] This is precisely what the Scottish parliament, a parliament made up predominantly of landowners, was being asked to do. Lauderdale shuddered at the prospect. Yet, he knew that if the king insisted that the contract be ratified, he would have to accomplish it. His political future hung in the balance. He knew – or if he did not know, he soon learned from Moray's letters – how deeply Charles cared about this. All of Lauderdale's other accomplishments at this parliament would be disregarded if he failed in this, because the interest of the king's beloved son was involved.

The entail that the marriage contract breached was that made by Francis Scott, second earl of Buccleuch, in 1650, the year before his death. He entailed his estates, first to his sons – he had none – then to his daughters, of whom, by 1663, only one, Anna, had survived. The entail restricted what a female successor might do. She had to marry a Scott or a man who would take the surname of Scott. There were limits placed on her ability to raise cash by mortgaging her lands. Above all, she must make no effort to alter the entail in any way. Any such attempt *ipso facto* condemned her to lose the estate at once; it would pass to the next heir.[17] And there was a next heir specified in the entail, Earl Francis's only surviving sibling, his sister Jean, who was married to the earl of Tweeddale and was the mother of several children, including a son who, in the eyes of his parents, would make an ideal husband for the young countess of Buccleuch, first Anna's elder sister Mary, who inherited on Earl Francis's death, and then Anna.

Mary's and Anna's mother did not think so. She regarded her Tweeddale in-laws with a combination of horror, hatred, and fright. The root of the problem was money. To settle some of his father's obligations Tweeddale had borrowed a large sum from his brother-in-law Buccleuch; by 1660 his debt, with accumulated interest, stood at at least £44,000.[18] This was a huge sum of money, worth well over a million dollars today. Tweeddale had no intention of paying it if he could help it; hence his desire to have his eldest son marry Countess Mary. He was disappointed not to have been named to Mary's

---

16 R. S. Rait, *The Parliaments of Scotland* (Glasgow, 1924), 449–51. The quotation is on p 450.

17 Fraser, *Scotts* i, 312. 'An Information of the Condition of the Family of Buccleuch', SRO, GD 157/3079, pp. 1–2. The author of this document, as the context makes clear, was Sir Gideon Scott of Haychesters. Earl Francis's entail was recorded in the books of the Lords of Council and Session on 24 June 1650.

18 This is the figure given in the codicil to Countess Mary's will, dated 4 May 1660, SRO, GD 157/3193. A memorandum on the money owing to the estate on Mary's death the following March lists the debt at £52,027; one note in Tweeddale's own papers gives the amount as £48,000; another, as £54,734, still another as £65,292. SRO, GD 224/924/43; NLS Ms. 14542, fos. 63–64, 14543, fos. 238, 242. Money is given in pounds Scots. Twelve pounds Scots equalled £1 sterling.

council of tutors in Earl Francis's will.[19] In 1654, when he accepted a commission to go to London to negotiate a reduction in the fine levied on the Buccleuch estate by the government of the Protectorate, he made his intentions clear. He wrote to Mary's and Anna's mother, Margaret Leslie, who had remarried and was now countess of Wemyss, that 'hitherto I have been made a cipher as to all things concern[ing] that family'. He hoped 'that I may for the future have this satisfaction, that by my advice those children may only be disposed of', and that she and Wemyss would regard him and his wife as among their nearest friends.[20]

Lady Wemyss was unpersuaded. 'There is no less aimed at', she wrote of Tweeddale, 'than the ruin of my young children'.[21] In February 1659 she became so fearful of Tweeddale's influence, through his friend General Lambert, with the new Protector, Richard Cromwell, that she married Mary off to the eldest son of Gideon Scott of Haychesters, a member of the council of tutors, the one who had been the most active in poisoning her mind against Tweeddale. Mary was under age, however – not yet twelve – and Tweeddale promptly challenged the marriage in court. After many months of tension the situation was resolved in Lady Wemyss's favor: Mary turned twelve and declared that she loved her husband – and perhaps went through a second marriage ceremony with him. Sadly, however, the little girl died on 12 March 1661, at the age of thirteen. Anna, the new countess of Buccleuch, the last of Earl Francis's children, was ten years old. Lady Tweeddale was now only one life away from the vast Buccleuch inheritance and its income of approximately £120,000 a year.[22]

Lady Wemyss once again faced the problem of keeping the detested Tweeddale from laying hands on the heiress. The political atmosphere of 1661 made her uneasy. She had cultivated General Monck, and urged him to further the king's restoration; Monck himself allegedly said that she and her husband had persuaded him to follow this course. But about all this had accomplished was to dissuade Charles from treating her husband harshly. The earl of Wemyss had been a radical Covenanter, one of those whose behavior Charles found personally offensive during the awful year he spent in Scotland in 1650–51.[23] Charles had received Tweeddale well, in spite of his Cromwellian past, and made him a privy councillor.[24] Above all there was

---

19 'Information', SRO, GD 157/3079, p. 2. It was customary to exclude the next prospective heir from the guardianship of children who inherited property; hence, Tweeddale's exclusion, even though it was his wife, not he, who stood to inherit.

20 SRO, GD 157/3088.

21 Fraser, *Scotts* i, 336.

22 'Information', SRO, GD 157/3079, p. 27. For Mary's brief life see Fraser, *Scotts* i, 320–84.

23 Sir W. Fraser, *Memorials of the Family of Wemyss of Wemyss*, 3 vols. (Edinburgh, 1888), i, 258–9, 271, iii, 261. See also 31 Jan. 1661, Robert Baillie to William Spang, *The Letters and Journals of Robert Baillie*, ed. D Laing, 3 vols., Bannatyne Club (Edinburgh, 1842), iii, 438.

24 NLS Ms. 7109, p. 44.

Lady Wemyss's own brother, John Leslie, earl of Rothes, affable, charming, a delightful talker, a drinker and a womanizer, another Worcester Scot, and as far as any Scot could be, the king's friend. He was also greedy and treacherous, and in the spring of 1661 he double-crossed his sister.

In Scotland, unlike England, wardship had not been abolished. When the king was restored Rothes had asked for, and received, a gift of the wardship of Mary and Anna, his nieces. Lady Wemyss was angry. In the summer of 1660 she hastened to London with Mary (who was 'touched' by Charles in a vain effort to cure her) to get the king to make Wemyss joint guardian, which he did.[25] Rothes, when he learned of Mary's death, wrote a wonderfully hypocritical letter to, among others, Wemyss and Mary's widowed husband and his father, saying that he had informed Secretary Lauderdale, 'with undeniable pressing reasons for a ratification of his Majesty's former gift of the ward of . . . lady Anna . . . in the same way as it was formerly', in order to nip in the bud the designs of 'those we apprehend to be our enemies'.[26] What he really wanted, and what he had been planning well before Mary's death, was that, as before, the king grant the wardship to him alone. He was successful, and thanked Lauderdale profusely for his help.[27] Lord and Lady Wemyss appealed to Monck, who replied that he found it hard to believe that Rothes would 'do so unhandsome a thing', but that, unless Rothes could be persuaded to ask that Wemyss be joined with him in the guardianship, Monck could do nothing for them.[28]

Lady Wemyss was shaken. She had provided well for her brother through her deceased daughter's will, which – if they could get away with it – would provide Rothes and Wemyss, as coexecutors, with an enormous sum, in the neighborhood of £48,000 apiece. Her brother's greed was apparently limitless, and, Lady Wemyss thought, he was much too friendly with Tweeddale. He could now, as guardian, sell Anna in marriage to Tweeddale's son. Haychesters, who hated them both, wrote, after the event, that this was what Rothes intended to do.[29] The size of Rothes's eventual payoff, £12,000 a year for nine years plus the cancellation of a £36,000 debt, suggests that he may have hinted as much.[30] Lady Wemyss may have thought so. Unbeknownst to her Tweeddale was up to something even more devastating. He asked his kinsman, the lawyer Sir John Nisbet, if the language of Earl

25 Fraser, *Scotts* i, 373–7. NLS Ms. 14543, fos. 140–1.
26 12 Mar. 1661, Rothes to Wemyss, *et al*, SRO, GD 157/3188.
27 SRO, GD 224/402/9. N.d. but before Mary's death, and 13 Oct. 1661, Rothes to Lauderdale, BL, Add. Ms. 23116, fo. 142. The content of the letter dated 13 Oct. suggests that it might have been written earlier in the year. It has no year date.
28 23 April 1661, Monck to Wemyss, Fraser, *Wemyss* iii, 107.
29 'Information', SRO, GD 157/3079, pp. 18, 24. Countess Mary's will is in Fraser, *Scotts* ii, 307–13.
30 The arrangement between Rothes and Anna, which was formalized in March 1663, is printed in 'Letters . . . to Sir John Gilmour', ed. H. M. Paton, *SHS Miscellany V* (Edinburgh, 1933), 159–61. 'Information', SRO, GD 157/3079, pp. 25–27. SRO, GD 224/924/40, 224/924/43. Fraser, *Scotts* i, 411.

Francis's will, which spoke of the 'heir female' – singular – could be construed to mean that Lady Tweeddale was the heir to the deceased Countess Mary, thus cutting out Anna altogether. Nisbet replied firmly in the negative.[31]

The situation seemed to Lady Wemyss to be dangerous in the extreme. So she thought of a brilliant ploy, against which no one could prevail. On 28 May 1661, she wrote to the king offering Anna as a bride to Charles's bastard son, James Crofts, a boy of twelve. Charles was delighted, and wrote at once to accept the offer.[32] This was such a shrewd idea that contemporary observers, without any evidence at all, attributed it to others – to Lauderdale (Clarendon), or Rothes (Mackenzie) – as though a mere woman could never have imagined anything so clever. But Lady Wemyss was far from a 'mere' anything – Mackenzie himself described her as 'a person of much wit and subtlety', and that shrewd cleric Robert Baillie called her 'a witty, active woman'.[33] She was a veteran intriguer who had shown her ability to wriggle out of difficulties in the past, and she was adept at double-dealing. Having induced all the tutors, including Haychesters, to endorse Anna's proposed marriage, she saw to it that her deceased child's widower, Haychesters' son, got nothing from the estate, precisely on the ground that the marriage, which while Mary was alive she had fought so hard to uphold, was illegal. He never got a penny.[34] This was a manoeuvre that, save for the unfortunate young man and his father, pleased everyone, including Tweeddale, who otherwise was, for the moment, foiled. Lady Wemyss's only failure was that the king would not alter the terms of Rothes's wardship. 'I am confident', wrote Charles blandly, 'you will not mislike it, when you consider it is for the advantage of the family you are come of, and for a person I have so great kindness for'. Rothes had given the king the necessary assurances: 'I shall not meddle as to the disposal of my niece without your Majesty's commands'. Rothes would have to be paid off. Lady Wemyss was not pleased, and her relations with her brother remained rather stormy for some time.[35]

No one thought of asking the children what they thought about the marriage

31 NLS, Ms. 14543, fo. 165.
32 The king's letter, dated 14 June 1661, is printed in Fraser, *Scotts* i, 403–4.
33 *The Life of Edward, Earl of Clarendon, Continuation*, 2 vols. (Oxford, 1760), ii, 25. Mackenzie, *Memoirs*, 113–4. Laing, *Baillie* iii, 438.
34 Fraser, *Scotts* i, 383, 397. 'Information', SRO, GD 157/3079, pp. 23–5; GD 157/3228, 157/3091. Lady Wemyss was not above suggesting that those involved in the management of the estate during Mary's marriage – not, of course, including herself – might be prosecuted for embezzlement. SRO, GD 157/3208.
35 25 Aug. 1661, Charles to Lady Wemyss, Fraser, *Scotts* i, 404. 1 Feb. 1662, Gilmour to Tweeddale, NLS, Ms. 14543, fo. 199. Rothes's letter to Charles is printed in Fraser, *Scotts* i, 411–2, where it is dated 1663. This is clearly wrong; the letter belongs to the summer of 1661.There was considerable doubt as to whether the Buccleuch estate was subject to wardship. Tweeddale and his allies among Countess Anna's tutors made the argument at the time in a petition to the king, and in 1692 Anna's lawyers took Rothes's heirs to court, on the ground that Earl Francis had sold all the lands held *cum maritagio* (NLS, Ms. 14543, fos. 185–6; SRO, GD 224/924/43). When Mary succeeded in November 1651 the question of wardship did not arise, for obvious reasons.

they were being hurried into. What suited the adults was all that mattered – though Lady Wemyss, when she wanted to rush Anna's elder sister into marriage at an illegally early age, had claimed that it was Mary herself who insisted on being married at once.[36] Lady Wemyss and the king were not being cruel or thoughtless. That was how aristocratic marriages normally worked in Scotland, especially where women were concerned, though most girls married at fifteen or sixteen rather than at twelve. The marriage was a disaster, though it ultimately produced the requisite heirs to the Buccleuch estate. Anna turned into a serious and intelligent woman; her husband's fecklessness and folly are well known. Yet it was he who provided the most telling commentary on such marriages when he remarked, in his later years, that he regarded his mistress, Lady Henrietta Wentworth, as his real wife because he was too young to know what he was doing when he married Anna.[37]

The marriage could not take place before April 1663 at the earliest, when Anna and James would have reached the legally appropriate ages of twelve and fourteen respectively; there would be no repetition of the fiasco of 1659. In the meantime there was much to do. Tweeddale received a warning, when in September 1661 the king ordered him to prison in Edinburgh castle. The ostensible reason was that in the recently adjourned session of parliament he had spoken against imposing the death penalty on the radical minister James Guthrie, who was nevertheless executed. Tweeddale spent a couple of weeks in the castle and eight months under house arrest. His punishment far outweighed his alleged offense – he was, he wrote Lauderdale, 'thunderstruck' by Charles's order.[38] Tweeddale was being warned to make no trouble over the intended marriage.

Lauderdale's involvement with the proposed marriage began in January 1662, when Charles asked him to find out about the invalidation of Mary's marriage contract. If this happened it would, by cutting Mary's husband out of any share of the estate, leave that much more for James and Anna. 'I neither know what was in the contract nor who proposes the reduction [invalidation]', he wrote to Sir John Gilmour, the president of the court of session. Gilmour supplied a satisfactory report.[39] A rather more delicate

36 'Information', SRO, GD 157/3079, p. 9.
37 A. Fraser, *Royal Charles* (New York, 1979), 371. For marriage in this period see her *The Weaker Vessel* (London, 1984), chs. 14–15, and R. Marshall, *Virgins and Viragos* (Chicago, 1983), chs. 3–7.
38 14 Sept. 1661, Tweeddale to Lauderdale, and to Charles, *LP* i, 99–101. For this episode see J. Buckroyd, *Church and State in Scotland 1660–1681* (Edinburgh, 1980), 47–8. At the same time Anna was ordered served heir to her estates, whatever the wardship situation might be: Rothes was not to be in a position to make trouble either. *RPCS*, 3rd ser., i, 33.
39 Paton, 'Gilmour', 131–33. In the end, Mary's widower and his father let the legal case go by default by failing to appear when summoned. They thus avoided a definitive pronouncement on the merits of the contract, hoping, vainly as it turned out, that they might be able to revive their claims in the future ('Information', SRO, GD 157/3079, p. 25).

question involved the illegitimacy of the intended bridegroom. This issue seems to have been raised by Lady Wemyss in the summer of 1662, when she brought Anna to London to present her to the king, in part to put paid to rumors that the girl was afflicted with 'low stature, weakness and infirmities of body, and uncomeliness'.[40] Could a bastard make a valid will under Scots law? Could his children inherit the estate? Lady Wemyss had had advice that they could not.[41] This was a touchy question because any effort to legitimize the young man would deeply offend the king's brother. Charles was sufficiently concerned to summon Gilmour to London to discuss the matter in the fall of 1662.[42] Gilmour's reports, after investigation, were reassuring. There was no record that any king of Scotland had ever legitimated any of his bastards. The descendant of the most famous of recent royal bastards, the earl of Moray, ransacked his charter chest on demand and could find nothing. Legitimation was not necessary for young James to enjoy a peerage, or hold public office, or make a will. His children could inherit, provided they were legitimate. Even illegitimate children could be provided for by will. Only if James died both intestate and without lawful issue would his property revert to the Crown. Lauderdale wrote to Gilmour in January 1663 that Charles was well pleased, 'and is resolved to do nothing in the business'. Even Lady Wemyss, who was very nervous about this, and kept pressing Charles to get as much favorable legal opinion in writing as possible, eventually subsided.[43]

The next question was that of the marriage contract itself. From the beginning the king's requirements were plain. If, after the marriage, Anna predeceased her husband and left no heirs, James was to have the estate. Charles's attitude was understandable. Anna was apparently healthy enough, and had recently survived a bout of smallpox[44] that, happily, left her unmarked, but the track record of the Scott family with respect to longevity was very bad. Anna's father had died young, as had three of his four siblings and three of his four children. In October 1662 Anna's lawyers attempted to satisfy Charles with a carefully drafted proposal that in certain respects did not conform to Scottish law and custom but did not immediately fracture the entail. A marriage normally had to last a year and a day before a surviving spouse could lay claim to a liferent in the deceased spouse's estate. This rule might be waived in James's favor, 'providing that the granting thereof infer not her and her heirs their losing of the estate', and when Anna reached her majority she could dispose of the estate to James's heirs, failing offspring of

40 Quoted in Fraser, *Scotts* i, 406–7.
41 'Information', SRO, GD 157/3079, p. 33, N.d., but probably late 1662, Haychesters to Lady Wemyss, SRO, GD 157/3233.
42 Paton, 'Gilmour', 139. John Nicoll, *A Diary of Public Transactions*, ed. D. Laing, Bannatyne Club (Edinburgh, 1836), 386.
43 The relevant correspondence is in Paton, 'Gilmour', 144–59. See also 'Information', SRO, GD 157/3079, pp. 33–5.
44 15 Feb. 1662 Rothes to Lauderdale, BL, Add. Ms. 23115, fo. 71.

her own, under the same conditions.[45] This was cloudy, indeed contradictory, language; how could James's heirs inherit without rupturing the entail? The proposal did not satisfy the king; if Anna died childless before reaching her majority, James could not inherit. As for Lady Wemyss, she did not care what happened to the estate if Anna died childless, as long as Tweeddale did not get it. A counter-proposal, dated 4 November 1662, appeared: James and his subsequent children would inherit if Anna died childless. If James, too, died childless, then his heirs – presumably the king – and not Anna's would have the estate. Though the estate was now Anna's, she was obligated to give it up to the heir if she and James had children and he predeceased her, though she was guaranteed an income of £60,000 a year, about half the normal income of the estate. All this was eventually written into the marriage contract.[46] Thus was Earl Francis's entail destroyed, though in other respects it was adhered to; young James took the name and arms of Scott of Buccleuch. The king, for his part, promised to spend £480,000 on Scottish land for James and his descendents. This land would revert to the crown if James died childless, though Anna might keep the income for her lifetime if she survived him – an academic provision, as it turned out, since Charles never bought any land. He did give his son a less expensive wedding present in November 1662 by making him a duke, duke of Monmouth in the English peerage, ignoring the advice of Clarendon, who thought the title of earl of Buccleuch sufficient. Clarendon sourly commented that Lady Castlemaine (who had royal bastards of her own to consider) was enthusiastic for the higher title.[47]

The terms of the proposed contract produced instant reactions. Haychesters, still hoping to ingratiate himself with Lady Wemyss and get something for his son, warned her that because the contract violated the entail it could activate the 'clause irritant', the clause extruding Anna from the estate at once and putting it into the hands of Tweeddale's wife and children. Haychesters advised Lady Wemyss to be very careful, and get legal advice from people not beholden to Tweeddale, whose friends would lead her down the garden path by making light of her fears.[48] When asked by Haychesters the leading lawyers in Edinburgh, including Sir John Gilmour, were unanimous that the proposed contract broke the entail, and that when Anna could be held legally responsible for her signature – which, since she was a minor, would not happen yet – the clause irritant would apply. The next heir would then have

45 SRO, GD 157/3230.
46 SRO, GD, 157/3232. The marriage contract is printed in full in Fraser, *Scotts* ii, 461–82.
47 *Calendar of State Papers, Domestic Series. 1663–1664*, ed. M. A. E. Green (London, 1862), 18. *Clarendon, Continuation*, ii, 25–7. Anna was still merely a countess, and is so described in the marriage contract. On the day of the wedding Charles made his son duke of Buccleuch; in 1666 he made Anna duchess of Buccleuch (though not of Monmouth) in her own right. Thus in 1685, when her husband was executed as a traitor, Anna ceased to be duchess of Monmouth but remained duchess of Buccleuch; her descendents still hold the title.
48 SRO, GD 157/3233.

the option either of suing to nullify Monmouth's rights under the contract, thus restoring the original entail, or of suing Anna's curators and all those who consented to the contract for damages equal to the total value of the estate.[49] If Anna died without heirs the heir under the entail would no doubt pursue the latter course rather than tangle with the king's son. The only recourse the lawyers could see was that the king might use his powers of revocation to quash the entail, which had been drawn up during his minority, on the ground that it violated the ancient practice of the Scotts of Buccleuch, by which the estates devolved upon heirs male. The only trouble with this was that the male heir of the first earl of Buccleuch was Tweeddale's eldest son. Unsurprisingly, the suggestion went nowhere.[50]

Anna's curators were nervous, especially those who had been on the former council of tutors and were thus obliged by Earl Francis's will to maintain the entail. On 15 April 1663, five days before the wedding, Gilmour reported to Lauderdale that he had attended a meeting of Anna's curators and lawyers called by Lord Chancellor Glencairn, and that some of the curators expressed their unwillingness to sign the contract. Gilmour himself was in an equivocal position. The king had assigned him and Lauderdale to look after Monmouth's interests in the drafting of the contract – Monmouth had no curators as yet because he had no estate. The document was so favorable to Monmouth that Gilmour could not fail to support it, but he could not sign it because, as the drafter of Earl Francis's entail in 1650 he could not 'be witness against my own witnessing'. This was extraordinary. Even the implacable Lady Wemyss, who, said Gilmour, favoured Monmouth 'not without some odium to others', showed some nervousness about having the entail 'disturbed'.[51] Pressure was applied, and in the end all but two of Anna's curators signed the contract.

On 20 April 1663, Anna and Monmouth were married. It was the social event of the season, attended by the king and queen and all the court,[52] but no amount of nuptial jollification could disguise the fact that the marriage

49 On 11 Feb. 1663, Anna, on her twelfth birthday, formally named her curators, thirteen in all and mostly relatives headed by her uncle Rothes and her stepfather Wemyss. They were officially responsible for the management of Anna's affairs until she turned twenty-one.

50 SRO, GD 157/3234, 3235.

51 15 Apr. 1663, Gilmour to Lauderdale, Paton, 'Gilmour', 167–70. Lauderdale also did not witness the contract, for other reasons. He had a claim to the teinds of the parish of Sheriffhall, which, he claimed, his father had reserved when in 1641 he granted the superiority of Sheriffhall to the earl of Morton, who in the following year sold this, and much else, to Anna's father. The teinds are specifically mentioned in the contract as part of the Buccleuch estate (Fraser, *Scotts* ii, 472. 8 Apr. 1663, Lauderdale to Gilmour, Paton, 'Gilmour', 166–7).

52 The observant Samuel Pepys noted that the coat of arms at the tail of Monmouth's coach had no bar sinister. Whether or not the error was deliberate, it would have been mightily offensive to Charles's brother. It was corrected two days later. *The Diary of Samuel Pepys*, eds. R. Latham and W. Matthews, 11 vols. (London, 1970–83), iv, 107.

contract was, to say the least, open to legal challenge. What might Tweeddale do? What might be done to prevent him from doing anything?

Tweeddale had been mending his fences. On 4 February 1662 he had written to Gilmour, asking him to intercede with Rothes on his behalf and to see that justice was done in the 'intended match'. He would do everything 'just', if only Lady Wemyss could be persuaded to 'lay aside this implacable disposition'. Tweeddale's hopes of Rothes were badly misplaced. The latter's recent display of friendship for him was pretense. Rothes feared, and with reason, that Tweeddale might try to spoil his plan to profit from the wardship, and even if he had been inclined to intercede with his sister, she was in no mood to do him favors, especially for Tweeddale. On the same day that her husband wrote Gilmour Lady Tweeddale addressed Lauderdale, apologizing for having given him so much trouble lately on his cousin's account – Lauderdale and Tweeddale were first cousins – and saying that she would now have to trouble him again for her own sake. 'I have long borne the reproach of my father's family by the practices of the mother and the servants of it, and now . . . I . . . hear of the diligent endeavors used to stop the prosecution of justice and the laws'. She could not believe that so just a prince would authorize such a thing.[53] By the end of June 1662 Tweeddale was free from his detention and sitting on the privy council once again. Then, in September, he had a piece of great good fortune. He, like Lauderdale, had a prominent place on Lord Commissioner Middleton's enemies list in the billeting episode. Lauderdale, in saving himself, found himself thrown into alliance with his cousin, who shared his views on a number of political issues. By the middle of 1663 Tweeddale was once more president of the privy council, an office he had held briefly before his incarceration in 1661.[54]

All this made Lady Wemyss nervous again. She was further disconcerted to discover that the king would not acquiesce in the plans she had for the young married couple. Her proposal was that Monmouth be sent overseas to complete his education at Charles's expense, while Anna returned with her to Wemyss Castle, to remain until she turned twenty-one, thus allowing Lady Wemyss and her husband nine more years to enjoy the huge income from the Buccleuch estates.[55] This was not Charles's idea at all. He had no intention of permitting James and Anna, to whom both he and his brother took an instant liking, to leave court, and as for the money, that would be for the young couple to enjoy – though Lady Wemyss eventually got a pension of £6,000 a year.[56]

53 Paton, 'Gilmour', 133–4. BL, Add. Ms. 23117, fo. 27. 28 Feb., 5 Oct. 1661, 15 Feb. 1662, Rothes to Lauderdale, BL, Add. Ms. 23115, fos. 71, 85, 23116, fos. 136–37. In Tweeddale's papers there is an unsigned memorandum of advice, probably written in June 1662, urging Tweeddale to approach Lady Wemyss directly. There is no evidence that he did this. NLS, Ms. 14543, fos. 156–7.
54 NLS, Ms. 7109, pp. 45–6. Nicoll, *Diary*, 393.
55 'Information', SRO, GD 157/3079, pp. 29–30.
56 Fraser, *Wemyss* i, 274. This had been her formal allowance for the expenses of raising the children, but in fact it was about one third of what she had been pocketing from the estate. SRO, GD 157/3208. Fraser, *Scotts* i, 374.

So Lady Wemyss picked up a suggestion that had been advanced back in January 1663.[57] Since parliament was now in session, let it ratify the contract – and not only ratify it, but also take whatever steps were necessary to block any legal challenge through the act *Salvo*, by denying its use to Lady Tweeddale and her heirs. Then the entail would remain broken, and Tweeddale's hopes obliterated forever. Lady Wemyss therefore presented the king with that piece of paper Moray spoke of in his letter to Lauderdale on 2 July. What Lauderdale received was only a copy; the original, Moray wrote, was being sent to Rothes.[58] Because it was Rothes, not Lauderdale, who was the royal commissioner to this parliament. Charles expected Lauderdale to do the work, but did not entrust him with the authority of the office of commissioner. The secretary was still very much on probation.

When Lauderdale and Rothes received Lady Wemyss's proposal they at once consulted Sir John Gilmour, who 'admired at the proposition' and said that he wanted to lay it before the full court of session. The judges were unanimous 'that such an act could not pass in parliament to make void entails, as to be excepted out of the act *salvo juris cuiuslibet*, which is the security of subjects in cases of ratification of private rights'. Parliament would be acting unfairly if it did this, since it would not hear all sides of the question; it was an action 'most unfit to be pressed by his majesty'. Lauderdale was much relieved, and expected that this would 'prevent further importunities upon his majesty'.[59] When the judges' written opinion was delivered to Charles, he apparently accepted it, 'and so I think hath rid himself of the lady's importunity,' which, said Moray, weighs on him 'as much as anything but her humor and way of dealing'. Charles clearly did not like Lady Wemyss, a bossy and persistent battleaxe who was in every respect the opposite of the beautiful Lady Frances Stuart, currently Charles's idea of the *pièce de résistance* of womanhood. He told Moray that Lady Wemyss was the source of the slanders against Lauderdale that were going around the court. But he did love his son, whom Lady Wemyss prodded into writing to her husband, who was attending parliament, urging the ratification of his marriage contract.[60] After a day or two, Charles returned to the subject with Moray. He did not understand the judges' reasoning, he said, since in England parliament could break an entail. And he did not understand the problem of the act *Salvo*. Moray tried again, arguing against the usefulness of any parliamentary action, since what one parliament did another could undo, an argument, Moray thought, Lauderdale might repeat in writing to the king, who would be 'glad to see it'. Moray also urged Lauderdale to get one of the judges or another lawyer to provide a

---

57 SRO, GD 157/ 3234.
58 BL, Add. Ms. 23119, fos. 65–6.
59 7, 14 July 1663, Lauderdale to Moray, BL, Add. Ms. 23119, fos. 78, 88.
60 11 July 1663, Monmouth to Wemyss, Fraser, *Wemyss* iii: 64. It was difficult to get Monmouth to pay attention to anything; see, e.g. 16 Jan. 1663, Lady Wemyss to Gilmour, Paton, 'Gilmour', 145–6.

clarification of the act *Salvo* for the king: it needed 'a better lawyer than myself to make it perfectly clear to him'.[61]

In mid-August, after a pause while he paid a visit to his wife at Tunbridge Wells and then the docks at Portsmouth, Charles brought the matter up again. He was not satisfied with Moray's explanations, he said, and he understood that Lauderdale himself had had a confirmation passed by parliament 'secluding the Act *Salvo*', involving his lordship of Musselburgh. Moray looked through Lauderdale's papers but did not find the relevant ones. He urged Lauderdale to 'provide for clearing the case, and the nature of the Act both . . . against the time the Duke's case be insisted on'. Moray repeated that nothing could be clearer than what the judges had already said. 'After that his Majesty did not insist, but I expect he will be pressed to drive it on further'.[62]

Before Lauderdale could respond to this Charles had made up his mind. On 20 August he sent a cross letter, not to Rothes or Lauderdale, but to Lord Chancellor Glencairn, who as one of Middleton's allies was not in good odor, in effect blaming him for not having proposed a way to get the contract ratified, since he and the judges thought 'the way proposed inconsistent with law'. Charles made his displeasure, and his purpose, plain: he wanted the contract ratified before parliament rose. 'I see', he went on, 'that the exception of the act *salvo jure* is passed in some cases, and therefore I do expect in this'. He also wanted an accounting of 'that great fortune from the time it ought to be accounted for'. Whatever quibbles the lawyers might have, the king wanted parliament to act.[63]

Glencairn and Gilmour were thunderstruck, and frightened. Gilmour at once sent a defensive letter to Moray, to be shown to Charles, protesting that he had always had only Monmouth's interests at heart, sending a copy of his letter of 15 April explaining why he had not signed the marriage contract, and adding that he could not 'be thought to have gratified any pretended heirs of tailzie, to whose prejudice (if law will allow it) the contract of marriage is concluded'.[64]

The judges, however, stood their ground. After some ten days of deliberation they reiterated that the marriage contract could not secure the estate to Monmouth failing heirs to the marriage, though he could enjoy the income for life if the marriage lasted a year and a day. Parliamentary ratification would 'altogether invert the fundamental law of the kingdom', even if Tweeddale consented to it; unless the law were changed, 'Tweeddale's son or any other the next heir of tailzie might justly challenge' the parliamentary act. At the same time, Sir John Nisbet's opinion on the act *Salvo* was sent to the king. The Musselburgh case was not relevant, wrote Nisbet, because the lordship of

61 21–23 July 1663, Moray to Lauderdale, BL, Add. Mss. 23119, fos. 101–2.
62 15, 21 Aug. 1663, Moray to Lauderdale, *ibid.*, fos. 167, 175b.
63 Paton, 'Gilmour', 172–4.
64 3 Sept. 1663, Gilmour to Moray, *ibid.*, 174–6.

Musselburgh, which belonged to the abbey of Dunfermline, was being excepted from a general act of annexation of church property to the Crown. In other words, the king was acting to his own prejudice in excepting Musselburgh from the act *Salvo*; he could do that, but he could not similarly prejudice the rights of his subjects.[65]

Lauderdale and Rothes clearly hoped that these weighty legal opinions might cause Charles to change his mind. If they had to force this through parliament, the session would be prolonged, and they wanted it over with as soon as possible, among other reasons in order to get to London and scotch Middleton once and for all.[66] Lauderdale, in sending the judges' opinion to the king, explained that no one could act on something 'so positively illegal' as the marriage contract without a clear order; now that they had one from the king, it would be obeyed – unless, of course, went the unspoken thought, the king withdrew it. Rothes hinted as much in asking for Charles's speedy resolution on the matter.[67] On 16 September Moray reported that the king was wavering. Moray had presented him with the documents; Charles looked at them and then commanded Moray to speak. Moray put the case in the strongest possible terms. An act confirming the contract would be meaningless unless another act was passed first, declaring that parliament has the power to dispose of the property of any subject without his consent and contrary to his declared will. Moray added that this was not said to 'sway him beyond what he thought fit' – which, of course, it was – and said that he had prepared some drafts of statements the king might send to parliament if he decided to go ahead anyway.[68]

Charles paused. He was not angry at Gilmour, he said, and did not want to have Moray read him Gilmour's letter, much to the annoyance of Lady Wemyss, who hoped that Charles would fire Gilmour for his impudence.[69] Charles ordered Moray to consult with Clarendon; 'I could do nothing but submit, having already said to himself all I could upon the subject'.[70] The intervention of English officialdom was decisive. Clarendon, Secretary Bennet, and the duke of York all told Charles to go ahead, and that he should

65 10 Sept. 1663, Patrick Scott of Langshaw to Sir William Scott of Harden, SRO, GD 157/3237. Nisbet's opinion, dated 6 Sept., can be found in the Tweeddale family papers, NLS, Ms. 14543, fos. 218–9. Nisbet, Tweeddale's legal advisor, evidently supplied Tweeddale with the copy.
66 See, e.g., 21 Aug. 1663, Moray to Lauderdale, BL, Add. Ms. 23119, fos. 173–5. Middleton eventually received the dubious consolation prize of the governorship of Tangier.
67 10 Sept. 1663, Lauderdale to Charles, 11 Sept., Rothes to Charles, BL, Add. Ms. 23120, fos. 12, 14.
68 15–16 Sept. 1663, Moray to Lauderdale, *ibid.*, fos. 27–29a.
69 10 Sept. 1663, Moray to Lauderdale, *ibid.*, fos. 19–20. 29 Sept., Thomas Ross (Monmouth's governor) to Lady Wemyss, Fraser, *Scotts* ii, 390–91. Lady Wemyss had disliked Gilmour ever since he pronounced against the legality of Countess Mary's marriage in 1659.
70 21 Sept. 1663, Moray to Lauderdale, BL, Add. Ms. 23120, fo. 40.

adjourn parliament and order Glencairn and various judges and lawyers to come to London to figure out how to proceed. Moray protested that this would go over very badly in Scotland: it would look like English dictation. Parliament should not be adjourned. Moray went to the 'necessary room', found pen and paper, and drafted a statement for Charles to send to Rothes. The king put everything off for a day to go fox-hunting, which, said Charles, would make Lauderdale, no devotee of the chase, think he was as mad as other people.[71] But now there was no turning back.

On 28 September Moray covered seven pages of paper in his small, spidery handwriting with his account of the drafting of the act that parliament was to pass and the instructions that were to accompany it.[72] The basic texts were the work of Secretary Bennet; Moray's long conferences with him, held in the king's 'necessary room', a place with many uses, produced only one major change. There was to be no formal statement that the act was the result of a royal command; rather, the king was acting in response to advice from persons unspecified. This would save face if, as Moray thought possible, the act did not pass. On all other points Bennet's draft was preferred, evidently owing to Clarendon; Moray made it clear that Bennet himself was prepared to accept Moray's amendments. Clarendon cared nothing for Monmouth, although he knew that the king did; it seems likely that he pushed for the most extreme version of the act in order to make trouble for Lauderdale. The principal change Moray wanted was that if Monmouth as well as Anna should die childless, the estate would revert to the next heir of entail, with title of duke of Buccleuch. This, Moray argued, would make what he called the 'hard clause' – the breach of the entail – much more acceptable, since the breach would not be absolute, but rather would amount to the 'splendid adoption' of a new person into it.

Moray failed, however, and the provisions of the contract were not altered. The language of the act of confirmation was blunt: the contract violated the entail, but – and this, said Moray, was the main point of the narrative – this was not the king's idea. The violation was the result of the initiative of 'the friends and curators of the said duchess'. Furthermore, the chief purpose of 'the irritant and resolutive clauses in the said tailzie' was to insure that a female heir 'should not have power to marry at her pleasure, but to the honor, dignity, and estate of Buccleuch'. Therefore, to prevent anyone from challenging the contract 'upon pretext of any irritant clause or provision mentioned in the foresaid band of tailzie . . . or any other pretext whatsoever', parliament would ratify the entire contract, 'and especially that clause . . . whereby it is provided that failing heirs of the Duchess' own body the said Duke and his heirs shall have right to the honor, dignity, and estate of Buccleuch in manner as is therein expressed'. The irritant clauses in

---

71 25–26 Sept. 1663, Moray to Lauderdale, *ibid.*, fos. 29b-31.
72 *Ibid.*, fos. 31–34. The next few paragraphs are based on this letter and the documents cited in the following notes.

the entail did not apply to this marriage contract. No Scottish court could ever allow a challenge to be raised; the judges were prohibited 'in all time coming' to hear any plea based on the irritant clause in Earl Francis's entail. The act *Salvo* did not apply, and the one passed at the end of this parliament so stated.[73] As Moray commented, 'The business of *salvo jure* must not be minced'.

The instructions to be sent forward with this act caused the conferees as much trouble as the act itself. Charles, who watched everything very closely through a long Sunday in Oxford – he heard the first draft 'still not fully dressed' in the morning, and supper was on the table long before they finished – was concerned to stress the 'good and valuable' nature of the marriage contract and the great advantages it brought to the house of Buccleuch. The clauses irritant in the entail were clearly designed to keep an heiress from marrying beneath her, and therefore did not apply. The act was 'not contrary to indispensable justice'. If it did not pass, Rothes was authorised to prorogue parliament for a maximum of three months and order Glencairn, Lauderdale, Gilmour, and the rest of the legal fraternity to get the contract through. Charles would 'be not a little troubled' if the act failed – language which Moray found not impossible as an expression of royal displeasure, though he would have preferred that Charles speak of how 'much concerned' he was that the ratification should pass. Finally, Charles ordered that the unfavorable opinion of the court of session on the contract that he had received earlier in the month be razed from the record, on the ground that it was irregularly arrived at.[74]

This is 'a cloudy and knotty business', wrote Moray, but there was no way to stop it. Monmouth's people thought so too. 'Sir Robert Moray found us such work here, that although the King was fully . . . resolved to do the thing, yet Sir Robert's diligence to divert him from it suspended it all the time we were at Bath', wrote Monmouth's governor to Wemyss, but at Oxford Clarendon, 'who hath taken a great deal of pains to effect all your desires', took things in hand. Moray's 'paper of advice how the act should be drawn' was rejected in favour of Clarendon's and Bennet's draft. 'We shall expect with impatience the issue'.[75]

If there were to be any parliamentary opposition to the confirmation, the initiative would have to come from Tweeddale, and everybody knew it. At the end of his screed, Moray floated an idea that Lauderdale might think absurd, 'yet out it comes': Tweeddale should support the act, if 'he could find it in his heart to do it'. He could get anything he wanted from the king if he did, and he would be doing a great service to his country, 'a more handsome

73 *APS* vii, 494–5, 526.
74 The instructions, and Moray's comments and proposed emendations, are in BL, Add. Ms. 23120, fos. 35–7.
75 Fraser, *Scotts* ii, 391–2.

sacrifice than the Roman did (I have forgot his name) that saved Rome by leaping into the Gap'. The 'service to his country' that Moray had in mind, given the nature of the act, was the preservation of Lauderdale's political career. Moray was on tenterhooks. On 1 October he wrote Lauderdale that the proposed act gave the members of parliament an admirable opportunity to show their loyalty and zeal by voting for it, since they would not be acting in response to a direct royal command. If there were trouble, however, Moray suggested that an act might be drafted permitting the breaking of an entail in favour of a royal child who married an heir with the consent of the curators. This would cover Monmouth's situation, but only Monmouth's, and prevent Tweeddale from getting support from other landowners. Furthermore, it would not be a private act, and therefore not subject to challenge through the act *Salvo*.[76]

Moray need not have worried. Tweeddale did nothing, and within a week of the king's sending of his instructions the act was passed. What Lauderdale may have said to Tweeddale is unknown; after all the many letters of September there is nothing on the marriage contract in Lauderdale's correspondence after 1 October, not even the letter to the king announcing parliament's action, although presumably Lauderdale wrote one. Contemporary observers were no wiser. 'How far it [the ratification] may import as to some who have been silent to it', wrote one of Haychesters' correspondents the next day, 'I confess with me is a mystery of State, which, in its own time, may be visible and evident'.[77] Haychesters' own bitter gloss was that what the king promised Tweeddale 'is not well known nor safe to be inquired into'.[78] Burnet regarded Tweeddale's 'compliance' in the 'robbing' of his children as having 'brought a great cloud upon him'.[79] But in Restoration Scotland the favour of the king was all that counted in the minds of the aristocracy. Tweeddale by his inaction had assured himself of that, and he had not yet given up hope that the estate might one day fall to his heirs. He was absent from the formal parliamentary vote, took the precaution of having witnesses to his presence elsewhere, and had the fact notarised.[80] If in future he or his heirs challenged the contract, no one could argue that he had voted to confirm it. But Tweeddale took care that his precautions were taken quietly and passed unnoticed. When he went to London in January 1664 Lauderdale took him 'in his riding posture' to the king, who 'gave him as kind a reception as I think he could desire'.[81] In February 1664 Charles agreed to do what Moray had suggested back in September and put Lady Tweeddale back in line for the estate; if both duke and duchess died without children, she and her heirs would have it, as an

---

76 1 Oct. 1663, Moray to Lauderdale, BL. Add. Ms. 23120, fos. 48–9.
77 6 Oct. 1663, George Lockhart to Haychesters, SRO, GD 157/3239.
78 'Information', SRO, GD 157/3079, p. 46.
79 *Burnet's History*, i, 176.
80 NLS, Ms. 14543, fo. 214.
81 7 Jan. 1664, Lauderdale to Gilmour, Paton, 'Gilmour', 178–9.

earldom.[82] It is possible, though unprovable, that this was what Tweeddale was promised in return for his inaction.

Tweeddale may have earned the king's gratitude and insured his political future, but the great gainer from the parliamentary session was Lauderdale. The king followed developments very carefully. In spite of his dislike of paperwork, Charles read Lauderdale's dispatches at once. 'He leaves all other things to do it as soon as they are presented to him', wrote Moray, 'except it be his dinner'.[83] Moray passed on Charles's comment that 'if you write not upon better paper and with better pens, we will have you billeted again' – and Lauderdale complied, for which historians can be thankful. Moray urged Lauderdale to be sure to report regularly, and Lauderdale needed no prompting.[84] He worked hand-in-glove with Rothes, with whom he had cooperated, not without suspicion of double-dealing on both sides, for a long time.[85] They were careful to see to it that good news from Edinburgh about such matters as the passage of the confirmation of the marriage contract reached Charles first from them.[86] The king was delighted by the results they achieved. He told Rothes and Lauderdale when they made their personal report that the session had gone even better than he expected.[87] The royal prerogative had been strengthened and extended. The position of the official church had been secured, and dissenters could now be pursued under legislation that the disapproving Robert Wodrow characterised as 'the bishops' drag-net'.[88] The armed force by which Charles set such store had been authorised. Yet, Moray's letters made it abundantly clear that Charles paid even closer attention to the question of the marriage contract than to anything else, even the billeting mess. It is not unreasonable to suppose that if

82 NLS, Ms. 14543, fo. 223b. SRO, GD 28/1791A. In 1680, after the birth of three children to Anna and Monmouth made the matter irrelevant the marriage contract was formally 'reduced' (invalidated) to the extent that it violated Earl Francis's entail, SRO, GD 28/2137A. Fraser, *Scotts* i, 438–9.

83 30 June 1664, Moray to Lauderdale, *LP* i, 141–2.

84 25 June 1663, Moray to Lauderdale, BL, Add. Ms. 23119, fos. 54–5. Airy also expressed his gratitude for Charles's comment (*LP* i, 136). It might be added that Moray's handwriting leaves much to be desired.

85 See, e.g., 21 Sept. 1663, Moray to Lauderdale, BL, Add. Ms. 23120, fo. 24. *Burnet's History*, i, 206–7. As early as Nov. 1660 Rothes and Lauderdale worked out a code: if Rothes passed on a request from someone in Scotland in a holograph letter, Lauderdale was to take it seriously. If Rothes used an amanuensis, Lauderdale could disregard it. 13 Nov. 1660, Rothes to Lauderdale, *LP* i, 37–8.

86 The Edinburgh informant of Henry Muddiman the newswriter wrote on 8 Oct. that they had prevented Glancairn's message with these glad tidings from leaving until after their messenger had gone. *Calendar of State Papers, Domestic Series 1663–1664*, 291.

87 30 Dec. 1663, Lauderdale's memorandum of events since his return to London., BL, Add. Ms. 23120, fos. 140–1.

88 Robert Wodrow, *The History of the Sufferings of the Church of Scotland*, 2 vols. (Edinburgh, 1721–22), i, 169. 'All along', he wrote, 'we shall find our prelates screw everything higher than the English laws go', *ibid.*, 164.

Lauderdale and Rothes had failed to deliver the ratification, Charles would not have been satisfied at all.

So Lauderdale's success with Monmouth's contract made his future career as Charles's principal agent in Scottish affairs possible. It did not make it inevitable. His enemy, Clarendon, who would have been delighted to see him stumble over the ratification, was still the king's principal adviser. The untrustworthy Rothes also basked in the king's favour, and was accumulating offices. He was already lord treasurer; and with the death of Lord Chancellor Glencairn in 1664 he was made keeper of the great seal. Even though parliament had been dissolved, the king allowed him to retain the title of royal commissioner, with its financial perquisites, which had never happened before. Rothes, with the backing of Clarendon and the double-dealing Archbishop Sharp of St. Andrews, supported a policy of repression of religious dissidents that Lauderdale thought mistaken. Not until this policy provoked a rebellion did Rothes lose the king's confidence. At about the same time, early in 1667, the king was losing confidence in Clarendon as well. By the middle of that year Lauderdale was firmly in the saddle, and remained there until ill health forced his resignation in 1680.

This story has a wider significance than its impact on the career of one aristocratic politician, no matter how important. It also says a great deal about the attitude of Scottish aristocracy as a class in years after 1660. The fathers of these men – and some of these men themselves, like Lauderdale – had risen in rebellion against what they regarded as the tyranny of an absentee king; what they wrought was indeed, in the words of the disapproving clerk of the burgh of Aberdeen, 'the nobility's covenant'.[89] The result was in every way disastrous for them. Of all the many groups and classes that made up the society of Charles II's three kingdoms, none was happier at his restoration than the Scottish aristocracy. Their utter silence in the face of the assault contained in the ratification on the property rights of one of their number made it perfectly clear that they would accept from Charles II arbitrary government of a kind that had provoked the revolt against his father. Only thus could they be sure of maintaining their position in society and the state.

Too much must not be read into a single episode, the character of which was not likely to be frequently replicated for all of Charles's activity among the ladies of his court and his playhouses. It was, however, one more indication, and a most striking one, that the Scottish aristocracy was cowed and would cause the king no trouble. As Lauderdale himself put it in a report to his master while this parliament was in session: 'There is so little reason to apprehend the least disturbance to his affairs from hence that if his Majesty's service in any of his dominions do require the assistance of this kingdom, he may confidently promise to himself a more universal

89 On this point see M. Lee, Jr, *The Road to Revolution: Scotland Under Charles I, 1625–1637* (Urbana, 1985), ch. 7.

concurrence of the body of this kingdom for maintenance of his authority either within Scotland or in any other of his dominions . . . than any of his predecessors could have done'.[90] The ratification of the marriage contract supported that judgement.

90 *LP* i, 169.

16

The Troubles of a Family Man:
the Earl of Tweeddale and his Kin

The political history of Restoration Scotland is a kind of black hole which has been little investigated and from which little light has emerged. The recent surge of interest in Scotland's 'long' seventeenth century has passed it by. One reason for this neglect is that historians have whiggishly assumed that the only political issue that mattered was that of religious dissent, because the only permanent result for Scotland of the 'Glorious' (though far from Bloodless) Revolution was the establishment of the presbyterian church. So the religious issue has received a lot of attention.[1] The other potentially permanent result, the creation of a truly independent parliament with the abolition of the committee of the articles, caused so much political difficulty for the crown that the parliament was eliminated with the union of 1707.[2] So historians have tended to regard Restoration politics as an irrelevant interlude between the upheaval that began in 1637 and the antecedents of the treaty of union, which determined Scotland's political future from that day forward. And a distasteful interlude as well, dominated by the despotic satrap Lauderdale and then by James VII and his (probably) hypocritical and bootlicking Catholic agents the Drummond brothers.

Another cause for the historians' neglect of the politics of the period is the nature of the sources. Apart from the acts of parliament and the privy council register, very little of the government record is in print. The printed register of the great seal ends in 1668. There is nothing for the privy seal for these years.

1 E.g., W. R. Foster, *Bishop and Presbytery* (London, 1958). I. B. Cowan, *The Scottish Covenanters 1660–1688* (London, 1976); see also his review article on the Covenanters in *SHR* xlvii (1968), 35–52. J. Buckroyd, *Church and State in Scotland 1660–1681* (Edinburgh, 1980) and *The Life of James Sharp, Archbishop of St. Andrews* (Edinburgh, 1987).
2 Historians of Scotland have shamefully neglected the history of parliament, largely because they believed that the existence of the committee of articles made parliament the puppet of the executive, and therefore uninteresting. The standard treatment is still that of R. S. Rait, *The Parliaments of Scotland* (Glasgow, 1924), a good book in many ways but very out of date. Jenny Wormald [e.g., *Court, Kirk, and Community: Scotland 1470–1625* (London, 1981), 156–8] has pointed out that parliament was anything but a puppet, but no one has taken up her implicit suggestion that the subject needs attention. There are some hopeful signs, however. The journal *Parliamentary History* has published a special volume of articles, *The Scots and Parliament*, ed. Clyve Jones (Edinburgh, 1996), and there is one large-scale study, J. R. Young, *The Scottish Parliament 1639–1661: A Political and Constitutional Analysis* (Edinburgh, 1996); unfortunately, it is a relentlessly tedious chronicle.

In 1905 the Scottish History Society published a two-volume edition of a manuscript of books of adjournal of the justiciary court, running from 1661 to 1678. There are a few diarists, and the well-known accounts of two prominent contemporaries, Bishop Gilbert Burnet and Sir George Mackenzie of Rosehaugh, the 'bloody' lord advocate. Not much political correspondence is in print; the most extensive, and extensively used, collection is the three-volume set of Lauderdale papers which Osmund Airy edited for the Camden Society in 1884–85. Unfortunately Airy was a very bad editor, and selected letters mostly for what they contained about the religious issue. So all his texts must be checked against the original manuscript before a citation can be made with any confidence.

The would-be historian of Restoration politics, therefore, faces the daunting task of tackling the unprinted government record available in Register House and, in addition, several huge piles of papers. There are three particularly important piles: the Lauderdale papers in the British Library, some thirty-five volumes of Additional Manuscripts, the enormous collection of Yester manuscripts in the National Library of Scotland, containing the correspondence of the second earl of Tweeddale, Lauderdale's cousin, collaborator, and then bitter enemy, and the Hamilton papers at Lennoxlove, the only one of the three for which there is a calendar, thanks to the work of Rosalind Marshall, whom we can all bless for her toil. It is not surprising that no one has had the courage to attempt a large-scale political history. It is a task that can only be performed in Britain; the material is not available elsewhere.[3] But it should be done. John Pocock, Conrad Russell, David Stevenson, and others have taught us all that the history of the three kingdoms of the British Isles cannot be understood if each is considered in isolation. Historians of Scotland and Ireland have known this for a long time, and the historians of England are now paying heed. Restoration politics in England have received a lot of attention in recent years. Until there have been thorough studies of Scottish and Irish politics in their own rights, however, the nature of the governments of Charles II and James VII and II, and the politics of England in their reigns, cannot be properly understood.

As an illustration of this point, consider the following remark of Ronald Hutton in his recent biography of Charles II. In the early 1670s, he writes, 'Lauderdale ... turned unilaterally upon his two close friends [the earl of Tweeddale and Sir Robert Moray] and snubbed, bullied and insulted them until they withdrew, *bewildered and upset*, from government. He seems simply to have grown jealous of their obvious ability and fearful that it might come to eclipse his own'.[4] [Italics mine] Hutton, as the title of the biography implies, has made a serious and in many ways successful effort to write about Charles

3 To the best of my knowledge nothing exists in the United States except a microfilm copy of the Lauderdale mss. in the British Library, which I obtained for the Alexander Library of Rutgers University some years ago.
4 R. Hutton, *Charles II, King of England, Scotland, and Ireland* (Oxford, 1989), 310.

as king of three kingdoms. But he is an historian of England, whose politics were quite different from those of Scotland, and the above quotation indicates that he has failed to grasp the difference. Lauderdale's behaviour certainly upset Tweeddale and Moray, but it did not bewilder them in the least. They knew exactly why Lauderdale did what he did. Tweeddale and Lauderdale had their political differences, over important issues such as the best way to handle the collection of customs and excise duties, and Tweeddale's constant complaints of overwork got on Lauderdale's nerves – he, too, often felt overburdened. But politics did not cause the breach between the two men. Nor did jealousy of Moray's and Tweeddale's ability: Lauderdale worried about no one's ability as long as he monopolized the king's ear. What caused the rupture between Tweeddale and Lauderdale – Moray sided with Tweeddale – was a family matter.

The high aristocracy dominated Scottish politics between 1660 and 1707 more thoroughly than at any time since the days of the Regent Albany, and one key to understanding their political behaviour in both periods is family considerations. With an absentee king family connections are apt to count for much more than when the king is present. One of the first politicians to understand this was Alexander Seton, earl of Dunfermline, lord chancellor from 1604 until his death in 1622. The younger son of a lord, he rose to prominence as a government servant; he was not a great lord in his own right. But he arranged his own marriages and those of his large crop of daughters, nephews, and nieces to such good effect that he was kin to virtually every important family in the land save the Campbells and the Gordons. His political position was unassailable in consequence, as long as he retained the confidence of his master the king.

That master, King James VI and I, was a careful and well-informed overseer, the only Stewart absentee of whom that statement can be made. The high aristocracy's dominance was even more pronounced when the king was a cipher or, though powerful, ignorant and uncaring, like Charles II. During the dotage of Robert III and the captivity of James I the duke of Albany created a Stewart family monopoly so threatening to the crown that James I had to destroy it when he returned, cousins though they were – and an uncle whom he spared had a hand in his murder.[5] In Lauderdale's Scotland the marquis of Atholl declined to marry his son and heir to Lauderdale's stepdaughter, who married the earl of Moray's heir instead. Atholl and Lauderdale became political enemies; Lauderdale arranged for Moray to succeed him as secretary of state when he finally resigned his great office. The one absentee king who attempted to rule without the cooperation of the aristocracy was Charles I, and disaster was the result.

John Hay, second earl of Tweeddale, was a politically ambitious man. He was genuinely talented – 'the ablest and worthiest man of the nobility', Bishop Burnet, who knew him well, called him, and modern historians have for the

---

5 For James I see the biography by Michael Brown (Edinburgh, 1994).

most part agreed.[6] One of Shaftesbury's correspondents, writing in 1679, called him 'selfish and plyant',[7] which is really no more than saying that he was a politician; they were all selfish and pliant, none more so that the top politician of them all, King Charles II. Tweeddale's ability, coupled with his family connections, might have resulted in a great political career. His ability he never lost. His family connections gave him his chance at power, but in the end they led him to political ruin and financial disaster. Two of these relationships were by far the most important, that with Lauderdale, his first cousin, whose only child married Tweeddale's eldest son, and that with the duchess of Monmouth and Buccleuch: Tweeddale's wife, Jean Scott, was Duchess Anna's aunt. These relationships are the subject of the following discussion, which I regard as a preliminary, and an accompaniment, to a larger study of Tweeddale's truncated political career in the reign of Charles II on which I am currently engaged.[8]

The defining event in Tweeddale's political career was a death in the family. On 6 December 1671 Lauderdale's estranged wife, the mother-in-law of Tweeddale's son and heir, died in Paris. Anne Home, countess of Lauderdale, was a wealthy woman, one of the two co-heiresses (with her sister) of her father and brother the first and second earls of Home and of her wealthy mother. When she married the young John Maitland in 1632 she brought with her a considerable fortune in jewels,[9] books, and London real estate, including the house in Highgate where the couple lived after the Restoration. Their one surviving child, their daughter Mary, who had married Tweeddale's eldest son John Hay, Lord Yester, five years previously, was her mother's sole heir. Yet in the end Mary got very little, and what she did get, she, her husband, and her in-laws had to fight doggedly to obtain. Much of her inheritance was stolen from her, and the thief was her own father.

Mary Maitland was not the wife Tweeddale had envisaged for his eldest son. He had desperately wanted to marry the boy to his niece the countess of Buccleuch, the heiress of his wife's brother Francis Scott, second earl of

6 There is a good summary of contemporary and present-day opinion of Tweeddale in P. W. J. Riley, *King William and the Scottish Politicians* (Edinburgh, 1979), 48–9, where Burnet's remark is cited. Riley, who was writing about the last stages of Tweeddale's career – he died in 1697 – thinks well of him.

7 J. R. Jones, 'The Scottish Constitutional Opposition in 1679', *SHR* xxxvii (1958), 39.

8 Another part of the story told below can be found in my book, *The Heiresses of Buccleuch* (East Linton, 1996). What follows here is based on the research done for that book, which also led to the writing of the article on the Buccleuch marriage contract reprinted above, and to the editing of two documents of Tweeddale's own composition, his 'Autobiography, 1626–1670', SHS *Miscellany* XII (Edinburgh, 1994), 58–98, and 'Relatione of the Wrangs done to the Ladie Yester, 1683' [henceforth 'Wrangs'], SHS *Miscellany* XIII (forthcoming).

9 One valuation of the jewelry after Lady Lauderdale's death put its worth at £96,000, another at over £100,000, still another at £156,000. NLS, Ms. 14548, fos. 84, 92–3, 123. One of the compilations made for Tweeddale at the time stated that Lauderdale had gotten a total of some £289,000 from his marriage. *Ibid.*, fos. 88–9.

Buccleuch, who had died young in 1651. But both of the young countesses – Mary, the elder, had died at thirteen in 1661 – had slipped through his fingers. What was worse, he had to remain quiet while the king destroyed Lady Tweeddale's chance of inheriting the Buccleuch estates if the current countess, Anna, died childless. Such had been the stipulation in the entail Earl Francis had made shortly before his death: Lady Tweeddale was his sole surviving sibling. But Francis's widow, now countess of Wemyss, detested her former brother-in-law. To make sure that he could not lay hands on Anna for his heir, she had offered the ten-year-old child to King Charles in 1661 as a bride for his beloved bastard Monmouth, and the king had happily accepted. The marriage contract stipulated that Monmouth, not Jean Tweeddale, would be the heir of a childless Anna, and Charles arranged for the Scottish parliament to ratify the contract, an unprecedented act. All Tweeddale could do was to absent himself when the vote in favour of ratification took place.[10]

Tweeddale's eagerness to secure the Buccleuch estates for his son by marriage or his wife by inheritance was not merely because of the large Buccleuch rent roll, some £120,000 a year. He also wanted – indeed, desperately needed – to escape a staggering debt to the Buccleuch estate inherited from his father, which had been incurred for family reasons. Tweeddale's father (like Lauderdale's) had married a daughter of Lord Chancellor Dunfermline; his father's sister had married the lord chancellor himself, as his third wife. The son of this last marriage, Charles Seton, the current earl of Dunfermline, was thus both Tweeddale's uncle and his first cousin. He was also a massive spender. He persuaded Tweeddale's father and two other kinsmen, the earl of Callander and the son of the earl of Eglinton, to guarantee his borrowings; when he could not pay, they were liable. Tweeddale's father had promised Eglinton that his son would come to no harm from this arrangement, and felt obligated to honour this commitment. He borrowed £40,000 for this purpose, with his son's brother-in-law the earl of Buccleuch as *his* guarantor; when he could not pay, Buccleuch had to. So from 1650 the Tweeddales owed the Buccleuchs £40,000 plus 6% annual interest. By 1665 the debt amounted to more than £65,000.[11]

10 For details see Lee, *Heiresses*, and the article on the Buccleuch marriage contract above.
11 For the amount of the debt in 1665 see NLS Ms. 14543, fo. 242. The story of Dunfermline's finances is far too complicated even for summary here. As guarantor of two thirds of Dunfermline's debt Tweeddale perforce owed various creditors a lot of money, which he did his best to avoid paying. In 1659, when Tweeddale obtained possession of most of the Dunfermline estates after a bargain with the third guarantor, the earl of Callander, Dunfermline's debt amounted to over £293,000; in 1691 Tweeddale still owed over £290,000. Yester writs, SRO, GD 28, nos. 2013, 2016, 2018, 2204. Some of the property Tweeddale obtained was very valuable, especially the Pinkie estate and the tack of the lordship and regality of Dunfermline. A document of 1683 estimated the value of Pinkie at over £90,000, and of the tack at £14,000 a year. NLS, Ms. 14550, fos. 191–2. I have not attempted to provide an account of Tweeddale's dealings with Dunfermline and his debt, since they had little bearing on his political career.

Tweeddale had no intention of paying this debt if he could possibly help it, an attitude he shared with most aristocratic debtors in the 1660s. Countess (now Duchess) Anna's marriage contract was certainly open to legal challenge which, if successful, might even result in her being ousted forthwith from the Buccleuch title and estates in favour of Lady Tweeddale. But such a challenge could not be mounted until, at the earliest, February 1676, when Anna turned twenty-five, nor could it possibly succeed if Monmouth was still the apple of his father's eye. Tweeddale's best hope was to work his way somehow into the king's good graces and then renegotiate the debt, using two claims he and his wife could make against the Buccleuch estate as bargaining chips. At first this strategy worked well. Political circumstance threw him and the influential Lauderdale together, and they agreed on many public issues. Tweeddale's discreet behaviour over the Buccleuch marriage contract commended him to King Charles, who hitherto had had no reason to favour him; he had, after all, served in two of the parliaments of the Protectorate. 'Though his children were . . . by this [the marriage contract] robbed of their right', wrote Burnet, Tweeddale 'had given way to it so frank a manner that the king was enough inclined both to oblige and to trust him'.[12] Tweeddale's zealous service as one of Monmouth's curators, an appointment Lauderdale helped to arrange, also pleased the king.[13] The Buccleuch estate needed managing: the duchess and her husband were immensely extravagant and, young as they were, heedless. (Monmouth always was; Anna, in time, came to be somewhat less so.) Anna's step-father, the earl of Wemyss, and her uncle, the earl of Rothes, her mother's brother, had pillaged the estate by getting Anna's older sister, on her deathbed, to sign a will outrageously favourable to them. In addition Rothes had obtained a gift of Anna's wardship and marriage from the restored Charles II, who liked him; he sold his consent to the marriage for £12,000 sterling, more than the annual income of the Buccleuch estate. Tweeddale, after his appointment as curator, took the lead in negotiating new terms with Rothes and Wemyss – there were many grounds on which both the will and the wardship could be challenged. By 1667 settlements had been reached on both questions which saved the estate substantial amounts of money. For example, the wardship payment was cut to £8,000, and the king agreed to pay half of the £5,000 outstanding. Still, the settlements were so costly to the estate that in the 1690s, after her mother, stepfather, and uncle were all dead, Anna took the heirs to court to recover some of what had been lost.[14]

---

12 G. Burnet, *History of My Own Time*, 2 vols., ed. O. Airy (Oxford, 1897–1900), i, 373.

13 14 May 1665, Lauderdale to Tweeddale, NLS Ms. 7023, fo. 18.

14 For Charles's decision on the payoffs to Rothes and Wemyss see SRO, GD 224/924/40 and Sir W. Fraser, *The Scotts of Buccleuch*, 2 vols. (Edinburgh, 1878), i, 434, ii, 487–8. For the wardship see *ibid.*, i, 411. The final settlement is in NLS, Ms. 14544, fo. 45. The course of the negotiations on both issues can be traced in Rothes's letters to Lauderdale between 1664 and 1667, in BL Add. Mss. 23122–26. For Anna's subsequent lawsuits see SRO GD 224/924/43.

While the curators' negotiations with Rothes and Wemyss were going on Tweeddale was carefully preparing his own case for the reduction of his enormous debt to the Buccleuch estate. He had two counterclaims to make. One involved the lands of Easter Hassenden, in the barony of Hassenden in Roxburghshire, now in Duchess Anna's possession. The lands had once been held by the Cunninghams of Belton, whose heiress had married the first Lord Yester in 1468. Her claims had been inadvertently swallowed up when the barony of Hassenden passed into the hands of the Scotts in the reign of James IV. In 1629 Tweeddale's father revived his family's claim, and got a favourable ruling in 1633. Before he could take further action, however, the holder, Anna's grandfather Walter Scott, first earl of Buccleuch, died, and the legal process stopped because the new earl was a minor. By the time Earl Francis reached his majority, in 1647, the families were knit together by marriage and the matter was not pursued. After Francis's death the minorities of Mary, and then Anna, continued to preclude legal action. Now Tweeddale proposed to revive the claim, even though Anna was still a minor, and to claim arrears of rent from 1629. If he won this case, Tweeddale, by his own figures as to the value of the estate, would be entitled to some £72,000, even without interest charges: more than his debt to the Buccleuch estate. Easter Hassenden was a potential gold mine, but a settlement might be beyond reach because the duke and duchess were still minors.[15]

The Tweeddales' second claim on the Buccleuch estate was very different, and did not require any waiting. This was Lady Jean's alleged rights as heiress to her long-deceased brother David Scott, who had died in 1648. By the terms of her father's will his estate was to be divided into two equal parts: half to his heir Earl Francis, the other to be divided equally among his four other children, all of whom save Lady Jean were now dead. In 1644, by her marriage contract, Lady Jean had renounced her claims to share in the estate of her father and of her deceased sister Mary. Her eldest sister had also renounced her claims when she married, and had died without heirs. But Lady Jean had not renounced any claim she might have to inherit from her brother David, whose share amounted to more than one quarter of her father's estate, which had been valued at over £200,000 on his death in 1633. Lady Jean – or rather, Tweeddale in her name – now laid claim to David's inheritance, well over £60,000. He had died intestate and she, his sole surviving sibling, was his nearest of kin.

Tweeddale outlined the case to Lauderdale in June 1666. He forestalled the obvious question by saying that he had not raised the matter before because he had only recently looked into the details. Lauderdale thought the claim was sound, unless Lady Jean's renunciation of anything befalling her through

---

15 For a convenient summary of Tweeddale's claim to Easter Hassenden and what he thought it was worth see his letter of 14 Apr. 1666 and the attached memorandum, NLS Ms. 14542, fos. 22–5. The business featured extensively in the Tweeddale-Lauderdale correspondence in 1665 and 1666.

her father's death might invalidate it. 'Subtle lawyers may argue' that, he warned. He went on to advise 'that you do not enter into any suit at law wherein the Duke of Monmouth is concerned without first acquainting the king and getting his leave'. Tweeddale nevertheless went to the commissary court in Edinburgh and on 7 August 1666 got a favourable judgement. The court ruled that Lady Jean was her brother's heir; she was entitled to the sum of £63,338, 17 shillings.[16]

This was a major breakthrough. Tweeddale knew better than to expect that bags of money would be turned over to him; the judgement was a bargaining chip. His lawyers and Monmouth's would now work out a proposal for the curators and report it to the king. Serious negotiation began when Tweeddale came to London in the autumn of 1666. By February 1667 a settlement emerged. Tweeddale did not get everything he claimed; he hardly expected to. If Lady Jean had received everything to which she was entitled as her brother's heir, plus interest, she would have gotten £68,400; what she got was £52,663, 15 shillings, 10 pence. The Hassenden settlement was much less favourable. Tweeddale's total claim, thirty-six years of rentals plus the value of the property at eighteen years' purchase, amounted to over £97,000; he got £13,396, 9 shillings, 6 pence. His debt was calculated at £81,660, 6 shillings, 4 pence, both principal and interest. So he owed £15,600. The king endorsed the settlement and promised that Monmouth and Anna would ratify it when they reached their majority.

The financial result was hardly generous to Tweeddale, but given the king's interest in the matter he could hardly insist on all that he claimed was owing to him and his wife. Charles had set the figure that Tweeddale was to pay; he would, therefore, pay it – or, as was his wont, owe it. It was, at least, a manageable sum. He had made one bad mistake, however, which would come back to haunt him. This was a memorandum stating that Earl Francis, having turned twenty-five, had given a discharge to his tutors and curators, which meant that he had laid no claim to his brother David's estate. Since Francis never did turn twenty-five, the claim was false.[17]

Tweeddale had come to London in the autumn of 1666 not only to work out the settlement of his debt but also to be present at his son's marriage to Mary Maitland. In his bland and otherwise uninformative account of the business in his autobiography Tweeddale indicates that the couple came together by accident. He had intended that the young Lord Yester, aged eighteen, should go to France to continue his study of the French language, but when Yester got

16 For Lady Jean's inheritance see Tweeddale's letter to his agent in London, NLS Ms. 7024, fos. 31–2, and Lauderdale's letter to Tweeddale, 23 June 1666, in 'Letters from . . . Lauderdale to . . . Tweeddale and Others', ed. H. M. Paton, SHS *Miscellany* VI (1939), 130–4. The claim is laid out in a petition to the king on 28 Aug. 1666, NLS Ms. 14544, fo. 15. See also Fraser, *Scotts* ii, 317–8. The court ruling is in SRO, GD 224/402/10/1.
17 There is a convenient summary of the settlement (in pounds sterling) in NLS Ms. 14544, fos. 17–8. The memorandum with the false statement about Earl Francis is in *ibid.*, fo. 21. See also SRO, GD 224/924/43.

to London early in 1666 he discovered that the quarantine imposed in France in consequence of the great plague of 1665 would keep him from going. So he stayed with his father's friend Sir Robert Moray, where he was expected to improve his skills in dancing, fencing, and mathematics, and perhaps try to learn Italian. He was also to go to see Sir Peter Lely, who had promised to paint his portrait. Moray introduced him to Mary and zealously promoted their marriage.[18] But by his other account, written considerably later, Tweeddale indicated that he and his wife were very dubious about this suggestion. For one thing, Mary was at least ten years older than Yester.[19] She had been shopped around to a good many people as a prospective bride, without success – Tweeddale himself had been involved in one such effort in the mid-1650s, when Lauderdale was in an English prison. She was evidently very unattractive. Tweeddale and Lady Jean feared that her physical infirmities would prevent her having children, and 'her other defects would be small inducement to engage a young a man's affection'. But they left the decision to their son, who gradually succumbed to Lauderdale's and Moray's blandishments. Yester wrote to his father about his hopes of preferment and 'the pleasures of a court'. Lauderdale and Moray were so persuasive 'as to render him, as he wrote, more ambitious than amorous'. Tweeddale finally 'put as good a face as he could upon it'. So the marriage took place, on 11 December 1666, in the presence of the king and court. A French observer who 'was forced to be there' was not kind. The bride 'is very homely and like a monkey, clothed with gold and silver. He seemeth to deserve such a wife and no more'. In spite of everything the marriage was very successful and produced plenty of children, seven in all, five of whom survived to maturity.[20]

One may take leave to doubt that Tweeddale was so opposed to the marriage. At the time he appeared eager for it. His letters to his son do not hint at any reservations. He did not know the lady, he said, having seldom seen her and never talked to her, and in a letter to Moray he asked if Moray believed the two were compatible. Moray's reply was convincing; so on 2 August Tweeddale asked him to find out if Lauderdale would welcome Yester as a suitor for Mary. On receiving a positive answer Tweeddale wrote a cheerful letter to Lauderdale about the families' future.[21] Whatever Mary's

18 'Autobiography', 92. 25 May, 1 June 1666, Tweeddale to Yester, NLS Ms. 7001, pp. 119–20, 123–4.
19 Yester was born in 1648, 'Autobiography', 77–8. Mary Maitland is mentioned in her grandmother's will, dated 1638. NLS Ms. 14547, fos. 11–14.
20 Tweeddale wrote of his doubts about the marriage in some notes for an account he was drafting describing his rupture with Lauderdale and the latter's villainies. He subsequently decided to omit from the document everything preceding the marriage itself. The finished project, 'Wrangs', NLS Ms. 14547, fos. 1–8, is the document to be published in the forthcoming volume of SHS *Miscellany*. Tweeddale's notes are in NLS Ms. 3134, no. 120. The French observer's comment is quoted in J. B. Paul, *The Scots Peerage*, 9 vols. (Edinburgh, 1904–14), viii, 458.
21 Tweeddale's letters to Yester, Moray, and Lauderdale in the summer of 1666 are in his copybook, NLS Ms. 7001, pp. 110 ff.

drawbacks, she was an heiress, after all, with very substantial prospects. The marriage contract called for a dowry of £60,000, to be paid in ten yearly installments. The second son of the marriage was to succeed to Lauderdale's title and estates. If for whatever reason Lauderdale diverted the succession – and he had the right to do just that – then the second son would get £84,000 from Lauderdale's estate at death.[22] Politically the match was by far the best that Tweeddale could hope to make. Lauderdale was now his close kinsman – in their frequent correspondence his 'dearest brother' (usually abbreviated to 'd. b.'). Tweeddale's political future was assured. Furthermore, Lauderdale could now be expected to interest himself in Tweeddale's affairs, and in those of the Buccleuch estate: his grandson, after all, would be the heir to Lady Jean's claims. In a letter of 10 September 1666 to Lauderdale Tweeddale rejoiced that the marriage was now settled, and remarked that Monmouth's curators would meet the next day to discuss Easter Hassenden and Lady Jean's claim to be her brother's heir.[23] The juxtaposition could hardly have been entirely coincidental.

All went swimmingly for three or four years. The whole of the dowry was paid ahead of schedule.[24] Within half a year of the marriage Lauderdale was all-powerful in Scotland and Tweeddale was his chief agent in Edinburgh. On the whole the government ran well, in part because Tweeddale was very competent, in part because the end of the Dutch war in June 1667 was beneficial to the Scottish economy. As has been said, there was some friction between the two men, and one major personal disappointment for Tweeddale. He wanted to be appointed treasurer-depute when the incumbent, the aging and querulous Lord Bellenden of Broughton, was finally pushed out. He felt that he had earned the promotion. But Lauderdale had earmarked the office for his younger brother, Charles Maitland of Halton, the master of the mint, and Tweeddale knew it. In February 1671 Halton got the post.[25] Tweeddale thought Halton to be both incompetent and crooked. No sooner did he get into office, Tweeddale later wrote, than he began to make illegal gifts to people like his son-in-law.[26] Tweeddale's protests got nowhere.

The grant of office to Halton was a portent of trouble for Tweeddale. In a memorandum of 1671 on his visit to London for the negotiations on Anglo-Scottish union in the last months of 1670 Tweeddale noted that Lauderdale

22 The terms of the marriage contract are in NLS Ms. 14548, fos. 62–3. In Jan. 1665 Lauderdale had entailed his estate to Mary, with the proviso that he could redeem the entail on payment of a rose noble. NLS Ms. 14549, fos. 113–4.

23 NLS Ms. 7001, pp. 142–4.

24 NLS Ms. 14549, fos. 79–80.

25 19 Oct. 1668, Halton to Lauderdale, BL Add. Ms. 23130, fo. 74. 17 Nov. Lauderdale to Tweeddale, Paton, 'Lauderdale Letters', 168–9. 31 Jan. 1671, Elizabeth Murray to Lady Tweeddale, printed in D. Cripps, *Elizabeth of the Sealed Knot* (Kinston, 1975), 93–4.

26 In 1673 Lauderdale had to acquiesce in parliament's abolition of three of the most egregious of these grants; *APS* viii, 210–12.

was cool and unpleasant. Halton was always present at their conversations, and Lauderdale always sided with his brother. He 'called me in derision his tutor, saying he would not be tutored in England as he had been in Scotland', perhaps a reference to Tweeddale's great enthusiasm for union, which Lauderdale did not share.[27] The political and personal atmosphere was changing. In his bitter account of his rupture with Lauderdale Tweeddale ascribed his troubles to the malign influence of Elizabeth Murray, the chief author of his family's woes.[28] Elizabeth Murray was a fascinating woman, forty-five years old in 1671 and at, or slightly past, the peak of her lush, red-headed beauty. She was countess of Dysart in her own right, and well connected at court: her father had been a favourite of Charles I. She had known Lauderdale for a long time. In the early 1660s, according to Bishop Burnet, there was some coolness between them because Elizabeth felt that Lauderdale had not been sufficiently appreciative of her efforts to save his life after his capture at the battle of Worcester. But by 1668 at least, when Elizabeth's husband betook himself to France for his health, the coolness was gone. Lauderdale began to call on her at Ham House; his visits became more frequent after her husband died in January 1669. No one made any effort to be discreet – that was not necessary in Charles II's England – and eventually Lady Lauderdale took umbrage. She too resolved to go to France for her health, which in fact was not good; she departed in April 1670. Her decision set many wheels to turning.[29]

In January 1670, as Lord Yester later recalled, his father-in-law came to him with a proposition. Lady Lauderdale was annoyed at Yester because he had been more sympathetic to Lauderdale than to her in their domestic jars. She might therefore 'out of the pique she had at me defraud my wife and children' of their inheritance.[30] To forestall this possibility Lauderdale proposed to give Yester a bond for 200,000 merks, which would cover the value of Lady Lauderdale's jewels and movables. Yester in return would give a back-bond for 120,000 merks, guaranteeing that the value of the jewels and movables would be used to pay Lauderdale's debts and 'for the relief of his estate'. The back-bond would be paid to whomever Lauderdale should designate: the name was to be left blank. In this way Lady Lauderdale's hands would be tied. He had consulted the Lord

27 NLS Ms. 7001, pp. 314–22.
28 'Wrangs' (see above, n. 8). Tweeddale first drafted this document in 1679, and rewrote the final section after Lauderdale's death in 1682. In what follows, information not otherwise footnoted comes from this account, which is very one-sided but for the most part factually accurate.
29 Cripps' biography of Elizabeth Murray, from which most of this paragraph is taken, is very competent. For Lady Lauderdale's health see 16 Jan. 1669, Lauderdale to Tweeddale, Paton, 'Lauderdale Letters', 192–3.
30 NLS Ms. 14547, fos. 141–2. In 'Wrangs' there is a different version of Lauderdale's argument. He might predecease his wife, said Lauderdale, and if he did, his widow might fall into the hands of adventurers and strangers, who might persuade her to disinherit her daughter.

Advocate, said Lauderdale, and this seemed the best solution. The back-bond, he added, 'was only for the fashion, that being the usual form in such cases'. Yester and his father, who had no reason to doubt Lauderdale's good faith, acquiesced. The bonds were to be drawn up in Scotland, so that Lady Lauderdale would learn nothing about them. Lauderdale came to Scotland in the summer of 1670; the exchange was arranged for Yester House in late August, as Lauderdale started for London.[31] The day arrived; Yester produced his bond; Lauderdale fumbled through his pockets and declared that he must have left his bond in another suit, 'having shifted his clothes that morning'.[32] Pocketing Yester's bond, he promised that he would send his up from London. He never sent it. It took Yester almost a year, after he had experienced some 'dryness' at Lauderdale's hands, to become suspicious: he was not very bright. He had given Lauderdale a very dangerous weapon, should Lauderdale choose to use it.

There was another straw in the wind. Lady Lauderdale's decision to go to France meant the breakup of the household at Highgate, where Mary and Yester had lived after their marriage. Lauderdale asked Lady Tweeddale to come to London to help move her daughter-in-law and grandchildren back to Scotland. One evening, at supper in Lauderdale's Whitehall lodgings, Lady Dysart heaped praise on Halton's eldest son Richard, who was also present. She was evidently thinking of a possible marriage between Richard and her eldest daughter; in time they would succeed to Lauderdale's estate – if he chose to disinherit Mary Yester. With wife and daughter both far from London, and no grandchildren present to beguile him, Lady Dysart had the field to herself with Lauderdale, and she took full advantage of her opportunity. It came at the end of 1671. When Lauderdale heard that his wife was seriously ill in Paris, he sent an agent over, and then a second on the word of her death. They were to secure all her papers, jewels, and movables, on the ground that by French law no foreign woman could make a valid will without her husband's consent – Lauderdale knew that his wife would leave everything to their daughter. The government of Louis XIV, now preparing to launch a war against the Dutch in alliance with that of King Charles, was not about to offend one of Charles's most influential ministers. By chance William Hay of Drumelzier, Tweeddale's younger half-brother, was in Paris and prepared to act on Yester's behalf, but Yester's instructions came too late, because, he alleged, Lauderdale had interfered with the posts. By the time they arrived, in mid-January 1672, Lauderdale's agents had bullied Lady Lauderdale's confidante, Lady Boghall, into turning over everything to them. They had the invaluable help of George Douglas, the commander of a regiment in French service, who got Lady Lauderdale's coach and horses

---

31 Yester's memorandum, NLS Ms. 14547, fos. 141–2, dates the meeting in Sept.;
    Lauderdale was in Morpeth on 1 Sept., however (Paton, 'Lauderdale Letters', 227),
    so it must have taken place in late Aug.

32 This detail comes from 'Wrangs'; Yester's memorandum is silent on the subject of
    Lauderdale's wardrobe.

for his trouble; his mistress was busied in buying clothes for Lady Dysart's *trousseau*. 'It seems my L. Lauderdale intends that somebody shall rejoice, mourn who pleaseth', commented Drumelzier.[33]

Yester, who had gone to London to condole with his father-in-law, played his cards very badly. He allowed his and his father's irritation at Lauderdale's behaviour to show, but he did nothing useful about Lady Lauderdale's real estate or getting the necessary inventories of her jewels and movables. Lauderdale was blandly reassuring. Mary would not suffer, he said. She should trust his generosity, and she would get more than she would have under her mother's will. But he would not surrender the back-bond, though its *raison d'être* had vanished with Lady Lauderdale's death.[34] 'Let not uncertain expectations move you to do anything prejudicial to your own family', wrote Yester's anxious mother on 16 January 1672,[35] but Yester allowed himself to be gulled once again: he told Lauderdale that he would leave everything in his hands. Tweeddale berated his son for his weakness and stupidity, and told him to come home before he did any more damage.[36] Yester did so, still in an unruffled frame of mind.[37] His parents were very worried, but Tweeddale dared not remonstrate with Lauderdale. He had written Lauderdale that Yester and Mary have 'perfect confidence in your kindness'. In spite of the recent 'dryness' between them, in spite of his failure to receive the coveted office of Lord Privy Seal when its holder died – Lauderdale had once dangled it in front of him – Tweeddale still hoped that relations could be patched up and the old, easy intimacy resumed.[38] It was not to be.

The blow fell in the summer of 1672, when Lauderdale and his new wife, now duke and duchess,[39] made a very vice-regal appearance in Scotland for a session of parliament. Mary, just out of childbed, and Yester were summoned to appear in court; Lauderdale demanded that they surrender

---

33 Drumelzier's letters to Yester from 8 Dec. 1671 to 23 Feb. 1672 are in NLS Ms. 14414, fos. 5–17. The quoted comment is in that of 27 Jan., fo. 15. See also Yester's memorandum, NLS Ms. 14547, fos. 141–2.

34 3 Feb. 1672, Yester to Tweeddale, NLS Ms. 14403, fo. 62. NLS Ms. 14547, fos. 141–2.

35 NLS Ms. 14413, fos. 22–3.

36 9 Jan. 1672, Yester to Tweeddale, 16 Jan., Tweeddale to Yester, NLS Mss. 14403, fos. 50–1, 14413, fos. 12–13.

37 NLS Ms. 14403, fo. 70.

38 29 Sept, 9 Nov. 1671, Lauderdale to Tweeddale, 31 Oct, 26 Dec, Tweeddale to Lauderdale, 9 Jan. 1672, Tweeddale to Yester, 5 Feb, Yester to Tweeddale, NLS Ms. 7023, fos. 281, 285, BL Add. Ms. 23135, fo. 101, NLS Mss. 14407, fo. 334, 14413, fo. 10, 14403, fo. 64. The reversion of the office of Lord Privy Seal had in fact been promised by Charles I to the earl of Dunfermline, as the latter reminded Lauderdale on 2 Dec. 1671, NLS Ms. 2955, fo. 39.

39 Tweeddale wrote Lauderdale a congratulatory note on his elevation and his receipt of the Garter; 9 May 1672, Lauderdale to Tweeddale, Paton, 'Lauderdale Letters', 239–40.

their rights to anything they might claim from her mother's estate save the London properties, on the ground that the jewels and movables were pledged in the back-bond to cover Lauderdale's debts. They were also required to renounce all claims to Lauderdale's own estate save the £84,000 to which their second son was entitled under Mary's marriage contract if he were not Lauderdale's heir. Lauderdale continued to profess that Mary would get everything to which she was entitled, and more: he wanted her to receive her inheritance as a gift from him. So they signed. They did not yet know that Lauderdale intended to disinherit them completely, and they had no hope of fighting him in a court packed with judicial sycophants. They hoped that, in return for their acquiescence, Lauderdale would discharge the back-bond, and drew up a draft to that effect. Lauderdale refused, and cut off discussion by referring everything to their respective lawyers. All he would sign was a discharge of any financial obligations they might incur arising from Lady Lauderdale's estate, a derisory document since there were none.[40]

In 1673 came the final break. Tweeddale had hoped that Sir Robert Moray might be able to act as a peacemaker, but Moray's own relations with Lauderdale were cool by then, and all hope of his mediation ended with his death in July.[41] So Tweeddale openly joined the duke of Hamilton and the other opponents of Lauderdale in the session of parliament that began in November of that year.[42] He compounded his offence in Lauderdale's eyes by suggesting to the king that Lauderdale's fees as royal commissioner were excessive, which, said Tweeddale in his narrative, Lauderdale regarded as an 'unpardonable crime'. The duke's revenge was swift. By June 1674 Tweeddale lost all his government offices and, seven months later, his commission in the militia. His political career, apparently, was over.

Lauderdale's animus extended even to his grandchildren, of whom he had apparently been so fond. He used to love to play with them, and worried about their health; now, he would not even visit them when he came to Scotland. The family lived with Lady Tweeddale, who had come to loathe Lauderdale for what he had done to them. 'I may assure you', she wrote her

40 The relevant documents are in NLS Ms. 14548, fos. 102–7. See also Mss. 14547, fos. 141–2, 14549, fos. 170–1.
41 J. Patrick, 'The origins of the opposition to Lauderdale in the Scottish parliament of 1673', *SHR* liii (1974), 16–17. A. Robertson, *The Life of Sir Robert Moray* (London, 1922), 146. Moray died unexpectedly after a dinner with Lord Chancellor Shaftesbury. Lauderdale commented callously in a letter to the earl of Kincardine that he was not troubled by Moray's death, 'but one use I shall make of it: I shall be very unwilling to dine with the Lord Chancellor, seeing his meat digests very ill'. *Ibid.*, 146–7.
42 See Patrick, 'Opposition', 1–21, for an excellent account of the formation of the anti-Lauderdale coalition. The parliamentary session was a failure for Lauderdale, but his enemies failed to dislodge him, since he kept the confidence of King Charles.

husband, then in London, in April 1674, as one of Lauderdale's visits to Scotland was coming to an end, 'they see that person so seldom that they can receive no prejudice by example if it come not by nature'. And a few weeks later, 'I am astonished to think from whence all this hatred can come'.[43]

In that same November of 1673 when Tweeddale's political opposition to Lauderdale became public, another blow fell upon him. The duke and duchess of Monmouth formally repudiated the settlement of Tweeddale's debt to them which had been negotiated during their minority; they were going to pursue him for the full amount, which by now came to over £86,000. This action was, wrote Tweeddale, 'doubtless encouraged and fomented by the Duchess of Lawderdale, and the King's allowance thereof upon very sinistrous and undue suggestions of the Duke'. There had been intimations, however, that the advisers of the young couple, as they neared their majority – Anna was now twenty-two and her husband twenty-four – were taking steps to shore up their legal position. Anna was still in violation of the terms of her father's entail, since the Buccleuch estate was still destined for Monmouth, not Lady Tweeddale, if Anna died childless, as she still was. There was legal danger here, since the entail stipulated that, should a female heir attempt to alter its terms, she would *ipso facto* be dispossessed and the estate pass at once to Lady Tweeddale as the next heir. Since Anna could not be sued until she turned twenty-five, when her tutelary status would legally end, the lawyers advised her to start legal action to nullify the clauses of the marriage contract and a regrant of the estate in 1666 which violated the entail, and then stall, thus blocking any legal action against her. Then negotiations could take place with Lady Tweeddale and her heirs, to get their consent to the regrant of 1666. So on 4 April 1672 a formal summons went to Tweeddale, ordering the production of the relevant documents in his possession, in order to proceed with the nullification of any document that violated Earl Francis's entail. It was a propitious time for such a move: at last Anna was pregnant. Her first son would be born in August.[44]

Before any legal settlement was reached on the violation of the entail – and, indeed, none was intended – the Monmouths launched their suit to recover Tweeddale's debt, in June 1674, the month Tweeddale was pitched out of office. It dragged on for almost five years. Tweeddale made three basic arguments. First, the settlement of 1667 was very favourable to the duke and

43 NLS Ms. 14402, fos. 119–20, 144. Lady Tweeddale's bitterness was undoubtedly owing in part to what she regarded as betrayal by the duchess of Lauderdale, with whom she had been friendly before Lauderdale married her. See Cripps, *Elizabeth*, chaps. 10–11.

44 The little boy died young, early in 1674, when Anna was again pregnant. Lady Tweeddale, who did not bear a grudge against her niece, wrote Tweeddale, who was in London, 'I pray God comfort his mother under so sad an affliction and preserve her from hurt by it in the condition she is in', and when Anna was delivered of another son a few months later, wishing her 'much joy and comfort'. NLS Ms. 14402, fos. 67, 167. A selfish woman would have wished her barren.

duchess, since what the Tweeddales were owed, from Hassenden and Lady Jean's inheritance from her brother, far outweighed the amount of Tweeddale's debt, yet Tweeddale had agreed to pay £15,600. Second, the size of Lady Jean's father's estate on his death in 1633 was far larger than had been stated at the time, larger by at least £190,000. Hence her inheritance from her brother David was larger than had been calculated in 1667. Tweeddale repeatedly stressed that Lady Jean had given up far more under her marriage contract, drawn up when she was a minor, than in all fairness she should have been asked to surrender. Third, the king had given his word that Anna and Monmouth would ratify the agreement when they reached their majority. The king had determined that £15,600 was the amount Tweeddale was to pay, and Tweeddale had agreed, even though in fact the Monmouths owed him money. He had relied on the king's word, and now the king was reneging on his promise. In repeated petitions to the king Tweeddale pointed all this out and declared that he would abide by the agreement and pay what he owed under it, even though it was disadvantageous to him, if the promised ratifications were forthcoming.[45]

Monmouth's lawyers had the courts on their side, however. They admitted that Tweeddale had some claim to Easter Hassenden, but disputed Tweeddale's assertions as to its value. Lady Jean's right to inherit from her brother David they challenged. They wondered why Lady Jean and Tweeddale had taken so long to raise the question, since they claimed that her inheritance was larger than Tweeddale's debt. They fastened on a weak spot in Tweeddale's case: the statement that Earl Francis, when he reached twenty-five, had ratified the actions of his tutors and curators and thus laid no claim to his brother David's estate. They correctly pointed out that Francis never reached his twenty-fifth birthday. This did not mean that Lady Jean was not David's heir – the judges in fact found in her favour on this point. What it did mean was that the king was acting on incorrect information when he made his promise to Tweeddale in 1667. The promise therefore was not binding. The court's rulings went overwhelmingly against Tweeddale. One of them, Tweeddale wrote with considerable bitterness, was decided by one vote, that of a relative of Lauderdale's, Lord Pittrichie, who died that following day. He was 'brought to the house that day only in a chair for that effect, when he was not in a condition to understand sense, as he never was to understand law, much less the point in question'.[46]

In the latter part of 1678 Tweeddale, in desperation, journeyed to London with a number of questions to the lawyers and to plead his case with whoever he thought would listen, and even with some who, he believed, would not.

45 For Tweeddale's arguments see NLS Mss. 14542, fos. 77–8, 14544, fos. 73, 76–9, 82–3, 91–2, 7025, fos. 142–4, 149, SRO, GD 224/924/44.
46 The Monmouths' case is summarized in SRO, GD 224/402/10/2. See also GD 224/924/41–44, NLS Ms. 14544, fo. 58, 24 Jan. 1677, William Pringle to Tweeddale, NLS Ms. 7008, fo. 16.

Once more he petitioned the king, who was unsympathetic. Duchess Anna was even chillier. 'My Lord Tweeddale has not been to see me since the day we scolded', she wrote her half-sister's husband Lord Melville, 'and looks very grim on me when he meets me . . . The Duke of Monmouth tells me that my Lord Tweeddale torments the Duke of Lauderdale about our business, but he is not likely to persuade the Duke of Lauderdale to be more his friend than ours' – Anna was on excellent terms with both the Lauderdales. Lady Jean, who from Yester House bombarded her husband with advice, declared that she did not believe a word Lauderdale said, or that there was 'any spunk of natural affection or concern' for his grandchildren in him, but that it might be wise to show him the petition intended for the king. Lauderdale was coolly polite and altogether unhelpful. Archibald Murray, an old friend, urged Tweeddale to send for Lady Jean, who might be able to soften up Lauderdale. Perhaps even Lady Wemyss might be helpful, he went on; she had been civil to Yester, and 'would take off the edge of her daughter'. This was a counsel of despair, and Tweeddale knew it. He could do nothing but submit.[47]

The final settlement was reached on 6 March 1679. Tweeddale's debt at that point had reached £111,853, 15 shillings, of which over £67,000 was interest. Easter Hassenden was valued at only £12,341, 10 shillings, far below the £32,400 Tweeddale claimed, and less than the £13,396 allowed for in 1667. Lady Jean, as heir to David Scott, received £37,112, 5 shillings, again, far less than the figures of 1667; the courts had ruled that she had no title to any part of her sister Mary's estate. So Tweeddale owed £62,400.[48] In return the Monmouths granted him what he must have regarded as a non-existent boon. In February 1680 the court of session formally nullified those clauses in Anna's marriage contract, the parliamentary confirmation of 1663, and the subsequent regrants of the Buccleuch estate that violated Earl Francis's entail.[49] Now that Anna and Monmouth were the parents of three apparently healthy children, it was safe to restore Lady Jean to her place in the succession to the great estate. Tweeddale's hope that at some future time, in more favourable political circumstances, he might be able to strike at Duchess Anna in court vanished forever.

This time Tweeddale found it difficult to avoid payment on a debt he had evaded for almost thirty years. He tried working on Duchess Anna's sympathies, thanking her for restoring his grandchildren's rights under her father's entail, talking of the welfare of the family and how fond her father had been of Lady Jean. He would cheerfully pay the principal on his debt, he said, if she would forgive the interest. The duchess was not moved. 'As to my

47 SRO, GD 224/924/41. NLS Ms. 14544, fo. 126. NLS Ms. 14402, fos. 187–239, contains Lady Tweeddale's letters; the quoted phrase is in the letter of 28 Dec. 1678, fo. 239. Anna's letter to Melville is in Fraser, *Scotts* i, 438–9. Tweeddale's last appeal to Lauderdale, dated 6 Feb. 1679, is in SRO, GD 224/173/2/10a. Lady Wemyss had hardly been civil to Yester, according to his mother; see her letter of 28 Sept. 1678 to Tweeddale, NLS Ms. 14402, fo. 201.

48 SRO, GD 224/924/43.

49 NLS Ms. 14544, fo. 156. SRO, GD 28/2137A. Fraser, *Scotts* i, 438–9.

Lord Tweeddale's great merits to me to induce me to forgive him the interest
of a debt which his delaying to pay has swelled to a considerable sum', she
wrote to her friend the future earl of Cromarty, 'I must tell you I have never
heard of such a way as he has to ask forgiveness, either for debts or injuries,
for when he was last in England he printed the basest and falsest paper his
overgrown malice could invent'. She would not be 'unnatural to my kindred',
she went on, but she would not 'be persuaded to live in debt and miserably all
my life to please him'. Tweeddale must pay.[50]

While Tweeddale struggled with the Monmouths Lauderdale continued
his assault on his daughter and her family. He reluctantly turned over the
London real estate Mary had inherited from her mother, which legally he
could not hang onto, after collecting nine months' rent to which he was not
entitled and, according to Yester, neglecting repairs, selling the furniture,
and digging up all the best fruit trees at Highgate for transportation to
Ham House, where he and the duchess now lived.[51] He made a will
leaving his movables to his new wife and his title and estates to his brother
Halton, and demanded that Mary specifically renounce the lands that he
had earmarked for her in his entail of 1665 and her marriage contract, and
her claim to his earldom. Once again the threat of the back-bond was
raised. Mary rejoined that she must be guaranteed the £84,000 promised in
her contract if her second son did not inherit the title and estates, and held
harmless for her father's debts, but in the end she had to sign.[52] Lauderdale
pursued Tweeddale at law for the right to collect the teinds of Pinkie,
which Tweeddale now possessed, on the ground that Pinkie lay within
Lauderdale's lordship of Musselburgh. He helped to persuade the childless earl of Erroll not to leave his title and estates to Tweeddale's second
son. In the legal dispute between Tweeddale and his half-brother Hay of
Drumelzier over their father's debts he helped prevent Tweeddale from
making a settlement on favourable terms. And, of course, he would do
nothing to help Tweeddale in his negotiations over his debt to the Monmouths.

At the same time, perplexingly for Tweeddale, the atmosphere was
changing. In the summer of 1677 Lauderdale and his duchess paid an
extended visit to Scotland, Lauderdale's last, as it turned out. Lauderdale
launched his suit over the teinds of Pinkie, but at the same time he actually
visited his grandchildren. And at long last he made known his willingness
to destroy the back-bond, which, with the original bond that he had kept for
all these years, was consigned to the flames in front of witnesses in
Holyroodhouse on 7 August 1677.[53] There was much puzzlement. 'His
cajoling Yester's children' and his other moves were 'all mistries', wrote the

50 NLS Mss. 7008, fo. 169, 14403, fo. 248. Anna's letter to Cromarty is in Sir William
   Fraser, *The Earls of Cromartie*, 2 vols. (Edinburgh, 1876), ii, 260–1.
51 NLS Mss. 14547, fos. 141–2, 14549, fos. 225–6.
52 NLS Mss. 14548, fo. 225, 14549, fos. 113–5, 137.
53 NLS Mss. 14549, fo. 138.

duke of Hamilton.[54] What had happened was not so mysterious: the duchess and Halton, the beneficiary named in the back-bond, had had a falling-out, principally because Halton's eldest son flatly refused to marry the duchess's eldest daughter. The duchess quickly made other, very satisfactory arrangements, but her attitude to Halton was now one of chilly contempt.[55] And, now that she had gotten her daughter's future settled, her principal purpose was to engross as much of the Lauderdale estate as she could. So for the next few years she played a complicated game, with her husband first acquiescing in her manoeuvres and then, after his stroke in 1680, being a puppet in her hands. Her dislike of Tweeddale and Yester did not abate – they were irreconcilable, she wrote in September 1679, 'because they have done [me] so much wrong',[56] and Yester, in her eyes, remained 'a most contemptible creature'.[57] But she was outwardly polite, and the duke, whose political base was eroding by early 1679, was being much less unfriendly. Tweeddale, who desperately wanted Lauderdale's support for his petitions to the king in the Monmouth business, was prepared to accept Lauderdale's gestures at face value.[58]

The duchess proceeded to profit from the changed circumstances of 1679–80. Tweeddale dared not be hostile. Halton's financial misbehaviour had at last caught up with him; his stewardship as treasurer-depute and master of the mint was under investigation, and he was politically isolated and in deep trouble. So in 1681 the duchess got her enfeebled husband to sign a conveyance of his titles and estates to Yester's and Mary's second son,[59] as stipulated in Mary's marriage contract, and then she began to bargain. Her terms appalled Yester and Tweeddale. She wanted the whole of Lauderdale's movable and personal estate, and the better part of his lands, free and clear of debt. The heir would be responsible for the duke's debts, estimated at £164,000; until they were paid, a committee of trustees dominated by the duchess would administer the estates and allow the heir a pittance, £6,000 a year, to live on. Furthermore she wanted Tweeddale to give her the Pinkie estate, the most valuable of his acquisitions from his spendthrift uncle

54 HMC, *Report on the Mss. of the Duke of Buccleuch and Queensberry*, ed. Sir W. Fraser and W. Scott, 2 vols. (London, 1897–1903), i, 222–3.
55 See e.g., Rothes's letter to Queensberry in May 1679, in M. Napier, *Memorials and Letters Illustrative of the Life and Times of John Graham of Claverhouse, Viscount Dundee*, 3 vols. (Edinburgh, 1859), i, 264–7. For a rather benign version of the duchess's marital manoeuvres see Cripps, *Elizabeth*, chap. 16. In the event her daughter married the earl of Argyll's heir, whose sister married young Halton. Conversation at the dinner table at Inveraray must have been difficult sometimes.
56 The recipient of this extraordinary statement was the earl of Moray, the new father-in-law of her younger daughter. Cripps, *Elizabeth*, 231–2.
57 *Ibid.*, 235.
58 NLS Ms. 14403, fo. 273. What Tweeddale wanted was some financial help from the king in meeting his payments to the Monmouths. See, e.g., his petition of June 1682, NLS Ms. 14407, fo. 83. He got nothing.
59 NLS Ms. 14548, fo. 225.

Dunfermline. In return for all this she would ask the king to make the heir a marquis – the dukedom would die with Lauderdale.[60] Tweeddale and Yester unhesitatingly rejected the offer. They believed, as Tweeddale wrote, 'that she made use of that feint, only to make the better bargain with Halton and his son'. So Halton succeeded to his brother's earldom, and the duchess got most of what she wanted, even the Maitlands' ancestral house and lands of Lethington.

After Lauderdale's death in August 1682 the Tweeddales tried to recover part of what Mary and Yester had lost. The 'Relation of the Wrangs done to the Ladie Yester' was given to the duke of York, who had been friendly, for presentation to the king. Accompanying it was a long petition from Mary detailing the wrongs that her father, under the baleful influence of her wicked stepmother, had inflicted upon her, and asking for justice. Lauderdale, she said, had promised her his estate; the clause in the marriage contract allowing him to disinherit her she dismissed as a routine sort of thing, designed 'to be a tie upon daughters and their husbands to be dutiful'. The renunciation she and Yester had signed was obtained under false pretenses: no sooner was the ink dry than Lauderdale disinherited his grandson in favour of his brother at the duchess's behest. The duchess had embezzled property which rightfully belonged to Mary as an inheritance from her mother and had destroyed the documents which would have proved Mary's ownership. Mary asked the king to do justice, not only to preserve the good name and fortune of her family and those of noble families generally, but also to discourage predatory women from preying on infirm old husbands. This document is a striking illustration of the kind of thing that can happen to a child at the hands of a greedy stepmother.[61]

Mary's petition got nowhere; King Charles refused to intervene in what he regarded as a family quarrel.[62] So the Tweeddales went ahead with their plans to take the duchess and the new earl of Lauderdale to court on various grounds, including the duchess's appropriation of the family jewels.[63] They also hoped that, with Monmouth out of favour, they might get some relief from the payment of the debt. Their successes were minimal. Their plan to nullify Mary's renunciations of her inheritance by claiming that Lauderdale had used force and fraud to obtain them went nowhere.[64] The lawsuits against the new earl of Lauderdale and his heirs for, among other things, the

---

60 The terms are for the most part in 'Wrangs'; see also NLS Ms. 14549, fos. 152–3.
61 The petition is in NLS Ms. 14549, fos. 166–7. It will be published, along with 'Wrangs', in the forthcoming volume of SHS *Miscellany*. For Tweeddale's appeals to the duke of York see NLS Mss. 14407, fo. 86, 7026, fo. 5.
62 30 Oct. 1683, Yester to Tweeddale, NLS Ms. 14403, fo. 221.
63 NLS Ms. 14549, fo. 253.
64 *Ibid.*, fos. 170–1. NLS Mss. 14547–50 contain most of the papers dealing with the Tweeddales' relations with Lauderdale and his heirs; as the above footnotes indicate, however, there is much more material contained elsewhere in the huge collection of Yester manuscripts.

teinds of Pinkie, which the Tweeddales eventually recovered, lasted well into the next century.[65] From the duchess they got little enough. Mary did get her £84,000, plus 8% interest, in 1686, but she could not get another £120,000 which her father, in a bond drawn up in 1648, had promised her on his death; the judges ruled that that bond had been superseded by the marriage contract.[66] The rather specious argument that Mary had no right to sign away her jewelry on the ground that she was no more than a trustee for her children got nowhere, but the duchess, as part of a settlement, was prepared to surrender the duke's very valuable library, much of which had belonged to Mary's grandmother. The duchess may have agreed because the Tweeddales were preparing a brief charging her with accepting bribes to influence Lauderdale during his tenure of power. In addition to more mundane political payoffs she was accused of accepting £6,000 for a remission for Lord Banff for having his footman rape a gentleman's pregnant wife, killing her and her unborn child. She was also charged with overweening pride. The city of London made gifts to royal daughters when they married, she allegedly said: why did Edinburgh not do the same for her daughters?[67]

On their other front the Tweeddales had no success at all. There was no mitigation of their debt to the Buccleuch estate, even after Monmouth's treason. Tweeddale appealed at that point to the new king, but James VII and II liked Duchess Anna, and saw no reason to punish her for the crimes and follies of her faithless, feckless husband. In April 1688 Tweeddale finally gave up, sold his ancestral estates in Tweeddale to the duke of Queensberry, and began to settle with Duchess Anna and his other creditors. The final installment of his payments to Anna changed hands in 1690; in the past ten years Tweeddale had paid £71,000 to settle a debt of £40,000 contracted forty years previously.[68] The only relief he received came from King William, who in 1693 renewed his lease of the lordship and regality of Dunfermline, for 57 years. The king stated that he was granting this favour to help recompense Tweeddale for his payments to Duchess Anna, who spitefully protested to the king against it.[69] Her hostility never abated, even after Tweeddale had paid his debt. 'My daughter Dalkeith is very near her time', she wrote to Cromarty

65 The teind settlement is in NLS Ms. 14550, fo. 60.
66 NLS Ms. 14550, fos. 20, 63.
67 The settlement with the duchess is in NLS Ms. 14549, fo. 274, the legal argument respecting the jewelry in fos. 185–6, and the list of charges in fos. 206, 284–5. The library was put up for sale; see 12 Aug. 1689, John Evelyn to Samuel Pepys, *Diary and Correspondence of John Evelyn*, ed. W Bray, 4 vols. (London, 1859), iii, 309. One valuation put its worth at £18,000; NLS Ms. 14548, fos. 192–3.
68 SRO, GD 28, no. 2185, GD 224/924/41. The payment would have been far larger save for the counterclaims, totaling almost £49,500, which the Tweeddales had against the Buccleuch estate; see above, p. 262. Tweeddale's petition to James VII is in SRO, GD 224/924/44.
69 SRO, GD 8, no. 2213, GD 26/5/459. At the time of the gift Tweeddale was lord chancellor; his political career had revived under William II and III. See P. W. J. Riley's book cited above, n. 6.

in October 1694, 'to comfort my friend Tweeddale in his old age'. There would be one more life between Lady Jean's descendants and the Buccleuch estate.[70]

John Hay, second earl and first marquis of Tweeddale – his promotion came from King William in 1694 – was blessed with a happy marriage and a loyal and affectionate, if stupid, son. His father's marriage, to a daughter of Scotland's greatest political figure, Lord Chancellor Dunfermline, his own, to the sister of the richest lord in Scotland, and that of his son, to the only child of the one Scottish politician whom King Charles really trusted, might have helped him build a great career. But that great political career never happened. His genuine political talents and judgement and considerable administrative skills went largely to waste. Those three marriages had led the family to political frustration and financial disaster. The moral of Tweeddale's story is that after 1660 Scottish politics was family politics. They would remain so for the next hundred years at least. Future historians of Britain will ignore this at their peril.

70 Fraser, *Cromartie* ii, 266–7.

Index

Don John of Austria 60
Donaldson, Gordon 25–26, 37, 38, 40, 42, 81, 170
Douglas, house of 66, 76
Douglas, Archibald (1555–1588) *see* Angus, 8th earl of
Douglas, Lord George (1636?–92) *see* Dumbarton
Douglas, James (1516–1581) regent *see* Morton, 4th earl of
Douglas, James (1658–1712) *see* Hamilton, 4th duke of
Douglas, Robert, moderator 206
Douglas, of Whittingham 77
Douglas, William, 6th earl of (1423?–1440) 119
Douglas, William (1635–94) *see* Hamilton, 3rd duke of
Douglas, William (1637–95) *see* Queensberry, 3rd earl and 1st duke of
Douglas, William of Lochleven, earl of Morton (d.1606) 63, 69
Drumelzier, William Hay of 257–258, 263
Drummond, family 246
Drummond, James *see* Perth
Drummond, Lady Jean 138, 149
Drummond, John *see* Melfort
Drummond, Lilias 138
Drumquhassel, laird of 71, 72
Dumbarton, castle 71, 72, 73
Dumbarton, Lord George Douglas, earl of (1636?–1692) 18, 257
Dunbar, battle of (1650) 212
Dunbar, George Home, earl of, of Sprott (d.1611) 4, 5, 16, 101, 109, 124, 134–135, 138, 144, 153, 154–155, 171
Dunbar, William (1460–1530) 25
Dundas, Henry, 1st viscount Melville 13
Dundee, General Assemblies 87, 89, 93
Dunfermline, abbey 239
Dunfermline, Alexander Seton, 1st earl of (1555?–1622) 136–140, 145–157
  agent 157
  and Anne 148–149
  commendator 65, 145
  committee of the articles 147
  convention of the estates 149
  court of session 146, 148, 151
  earldom awarded 151

education 145–146
extraordinary lord of session 146
family 139–140, 145, 146, 155, 248, 250
and General Assembly 152–153
and Huntly 149–150
and James VI 147–157, 171, 248
letters 156–157
Lord Chancellor 3, 4–6, 7, 83–84, 104, 124, 136–140, 144, 151, 152, 171, 222, 248
Lord Fyvie 150
lord of parliament 150
and Mar 150, 151
and Mary 145
negotiator for treaty of union 151
Octavians 149, 150, 157
political skill 147–148, 151, 156–157, 248
privy councillor (1585) 146
provost of Edinburgh 150, 151
religious faith 147–148, 153–155, 157
riot (1596) 150
secretary 69
and Spottiswoode 152, 153, 167
wives 150, 248
Dunfermline, Charles Seton, 2nd earl of (d.1673) 250
Dunnottar castle 175
Dupplin *see* Hay
Durie, John 76–77
Dysart, Elizabeth Murray, countess of 256, 257

Easter Hassenden 252, 255, 260–262
Edinburgh 3, 4, 13
  castle 63, 64, 71, 232
    fall of (1573) 27, 193
  Charles I negotiates with 10
  Charles II visits 211–212
  Cromwell attacks 211
  English agent based in 8, 12, 93, 103, 135, 149, 151, 255
  General Assembly 86
  government from 1603–25 136–139
  government from 1638–51 10
  government from 1660–82 14–17
  Holyrood 17, 263
    James VI at 87, 96
    Mary at 42, 44, 45, 47
  James VI in 17, 113–114
  ministers 95, 97–98, 113
  provosts 43, 150, 151
  riot (1596) 82, 85, 98, 122, 139, 150